ROOSEVELT
AND
HOWE

ROOSEVELT
AND
HOWE

ALFRED·B·ROLLINS, Jr.

Alfred·A·Knopf   NEW YORK

1962

L. C. catalog card number: 62–15578

THIS IS A BORZOI BOOK,
PUBLISHED BY ALFRED A. KNOPF, INC.

FIRST EDITION

FOR

Ernestine

Foreword

WRITING about Louis Howe and Franklin D. Roosevelt has been an exciting adventure in scholarship. The available material, from widely scattered sources, is at some points tantalizingly meager, at others it is enormous in volume, rich in variety. The detective work has been fascinating and the challenge greater because we are, in one sense, too close to the period of their lives, in another sense too far from it—too close to be completely disengaged, too far to be able to talk with the men themselves. But writing a mere twenty-five years after the fact has certain advantages. Many papers have become available which could not have been seen at an earlier date, and yet a host of people are still alive who knew Louis Howe and Franklin Roosevelt and are willing to share their memories and their impressions.

Although no historian can claim to be absolutely objective about events through which he has lived, this book is designed to be *against* no one and *for* no one. In so far as I have been able to do it, I have tried to reconstruct two complex personalities—and their even more complex relationship—as they really were. That the job is impossible is clear. That it must be attempted is the historian's cardinal article of faith.

Writing about Howe and Roosevelt has also been an exciting adventure in friendship. No scholar could possibly wish more genial hospitality, more interested co-operation, more constructive, firm, but gentle criticism than I have had from a vast variety of people: friends, associates, and relatives of Roosevelt and Howe, librarians, historians, editors, and my own professional colleagues.

I am particularly and gratefully indebted to Louis Howe's own family, to Mary Howe Baker and Hartley E. Howe. They have not only allowed me complete access to a wide variety of family papers, but they have also gone to great personal inconvenience to spend many hours talking with me about their father. I deeply appreciate their generous grant of permission to publish excerpts from the family's personal letters. Responsibility for interpretations—and for errors—is, of course, mine. I am especially grateful to Mrs. Baker for the many pleasant days in which I enjoyed the warm hospitality of her home, while we searched together for the family papers and tramped through the sand of Horseneck Beach where Louis's cottage once stood.

I am immensely indebted to Herman Kahn and Elizabeth Drewry and their associates at the Franklin D. Roosevelt Library for their help, their guidance, and their patience during my twelve years of research there. Only those who have worked in the Roosevelt Library can appreciate fully the extent to which its astute and able staff has contributed to the scholarship of modern American history. Over the years I have been especially in the debt of Robert Jacoby, Edgar Nixon, and George Roach.

Many libraries have hospitably entertained this roving scholar. I could not have written this book without the special help of the Adriance Library, Poughkeepsie, N.Y., and the libraries at Bard College, Cornell University, Harvard University, Wesleyan University, Vassar College, and Yale University. The New York State Library, the New York State Legislative Reference Library, and the library of the State University College at New Paltz have been continuingly helpful. And I am especially grateful to the staffs of the Oral History Project at Columbia University, of the Saratoga Springs Public Library, and of the Saratoga County Historical Society, and to Mrs. Edith Fox, the Director of the Regional History Collection at Cornell University.

But no study of Roosevelt and Howe can be done from papers alone. For the help of many of their associates and friends I wish to record my very deep appreciation. Among those who have shared their time and their memories with me have been John W. Davis, William O. Dapping, Charles C. Burlingham, James A. Farley, Morgan D. Hoyt, Constance Parsons Hare, Raymond Moley, Frances Perkins, Charles D. Osborne, Henry Morgenthau, Jr., Eleanor Roosevelt, and John Godfrey Saxe.

Many others have told me what they remember of Louis Howe especially. To Robert H. Baker, Jr., Evelyn Barrett Britten, John Corey, Luther Evans, Elizabeth Gorman, Harriet Allen Kerr, Mrs. Clarence Knapp, Ludger Pacquette, Frank Sullivan, and Monty Woolley I am particularly indebted.

Henry A. Wallace and Sumner Welles answered my questions in writing. Charles Seymour made available the monumental papers of Colonel House and guided me through them and Yale University gave me permission to quote from them. I am indebted to Frederick Osborn for permission to quote the letters of William Church Osborn, and to Lithgow Osborne and Charles D. Osborne for permission to use the rich and extensive correspondence of Thomas Mott Osborne. Fellow Roosevelt scholars have helped in many ways. To Frank Freidel and to Bernard and Jewel Bellush I am deeply in debt for long conversations, continuing encouragement, and special help in a variety of ways. To Samuel Hugh Brockunier, to Arthur M. Schlesinger, Sr., and to Arthur M. Schlesinger, Jr., I am especially grateful. They have taught me much of both scholarship and writing. That I have not always learned as well as they taught is my responsibility.

Daniel E. Button, Murray Silberman, George B. Carson, Jr., Richard Fisher, and Beverly McAnear have been especially helpful at certain stages in this project. Jonathan Daniels, James A. Farley, Mrs. Clarence Knapp, Walter Lippmann, Raymond Moley, and Robert Pendell have generously given permission to publish letters. And I am deeply in the debt of Harold Strauss and his able associates at Alfred A. Knopf, Inc., for a superb quality of editorial comment and a patience and interest that go well beyond the call of duty.

My colleagues in the State University College at New Paltz have helped in many ways over the years, and their continuing encouragement has been deeply appreciated. The Research Foundation of the State University of New York facilitated the work at a crucial point with a Summer Research Fellowship.

This book could never have been written without the immense and sympathetic aid of my wife, Ernestine E. Rollins, who has shared gladly a large measure of the work and the worry, while I have savored the excitement of the task. And to John and Nancy I am also deeply indebted. They have heard about this book endlessly—and all their lives—and their interest is still keen.

ALFRED B. ROLLINS, JR.

State University College
New Paltz, N.Y.

Contents

I · The Winds of Fate

II · A Team in the Making

III · The Time of Testing

IV · Apprenticeship for the White House

V · For the Victors: "Triumph and Tragedy"

Plates

FOLLOWING PAGE 212

All photographs by courtesy of the
FRANKLIN D. ROOSEVELT LIBRARY

Louis McHenry Howe, June 9, 1933
PHOTO BY NATIONAL BROADCASTING CO.
Louis Howe and tennis party, about 1885
Louis Howe, about 1902
Louis Howe in New York, 1932
Louis Howe in Washington, 1920
Democratic Party meeting at Mrs. Roosevelt's, 1924
Roosevelt, Farley, and Howe, 1932
PHOTO BY WIDE WORLD PHOTOS, INC.
Roosevelt en route to Democratic Party Convention, 1932
PHOTO BY UNDERWOOD & UNDERWOOD
The Louis Howes and their son Hartley, 1932
Roosevelt at the C.C.C. Camp at Big Meadows, 1933
Howe and his grandson, Robert H. Baker, Jr., 1934

· I ·

THE WINDS
OF FATE

I

I

⋙-⋙-⋙-⋙-⋙-⋙-⋙-⋙

The Champion and
the Ghost

Dear Old Louis,
Just a line to send my love and tell you,
if it does any good, to take care of your-
self and try not to overdo and worry. All
is really coming out so well and you are
the main spring! (Franklin D. Roosevelt,
May 6, 1931) [1]

"Room 1702 in the Congress Hotel," a newsman wrote. "Keep that number in mind. In all human probability a candidate for President is being nominated in that room this day. And it is by no means improbable that Room 1702 may be the anteroom to the White House. One has that strange feeling in passing its threshold—the feeling that destiny is at work within these walls." [2]

The man in 1702 looked like anything but a kingmaker. Lying

[1] Personal Papers of Louis Howe, hereafter cited as Personal Papers.
[2] Quoted in Lela Stiles: *The Man Behind Roosevelt: the Story of Louis McHenry Howe* (Cleveland: World Publishing Company; 1954), p. 178.

on the floor, propped up on pillows between two electric fans, by an open window, he struggled for breath in a sweltering Chicago heat wave. Sixty-one years old, he seemed aged. Always thin—less than 100 pounds—he had withered away in the ghastly heat until his clothes hung baggy and unkempt from his scrawny frame. His face was pitted and scarred from a childhood accident, his fingers stained from thousands of Sweet Caporal cigarettes, his long neck carefully concealed by a high, stiff collar. This was a peculiar and unimpressive character— until you caught his glance or heard his voice. His deep brown eyes could flash with steely contempt or, quite as often, reflect a soft sympathy which belied his tough, cynical manner; his voice could be cultivated, smooth, and dignified, or it could rasp angrily in a tone that its victim would never forget.

Now, he could hardly whisper. Exhausted from the asthmatic cough which tore at his slight body and the heart ailment which had dogged him for 25 years, he had been there on the floor all night, wheezing and groaning, as the radio beside him blared the raucous confusion from the stadium. Louis McHenry Howe seemed to be fighting death itself.

But, as politicians and reporters knew, this gnarled wisp of a man held power in his faltering hands. His clothes might be baggy. "But there was nothing baggy about his intelligence," one said.[3] His political intuition was sharp and sure. His decisions were forthright and direct. Beside him was the telephone which symbolized a unique political partnership. At the other end of the direct wire was the man who would prove to be the most significant President of the United States since Abraham Lincoln. Howe had been in his suite at the Congress Hotel for a week, ignoring the hullabaloo of convention nonsense, the mobs of delegates who crushed together in the corridors, even the great convention circus itself. But, through that phone, he had controlled absolutely the liaison between Franklin D. Roosevelt and the men who sought to manage his nomination. Big, dynamic, able James A. Farley bore the brunt of the hard work,

[3] Ibid., p. 179.

the incessant talk and maneuver, the desperate rushing about in the convention. Daniel C. Roper, Edward Flynn, and others pitched in to help. But no major decisions were made without the approval of the cultured, genial candidate, who remained carefully remote back in Albany, cut off from everything except his radio and Louis's telephone. No one received orders from F.D.R. otherwise than through Howe.

Now, at 9:15 a.m., July 1, 1932, the Democrats, who had come to Chicago to nominate a sure winner, stumbled exhausted from the stifling, trash-strewn hall where they had spent the night. Three long ballots had led to a crisis for the candidate who had been a front-runner for over a year. Roosevelt had come into the convention with 661½ votes. Throughout the night he had gained only 21½. As he turned wearily to breakfast in the Executive Mansion, Governor Roosevelt knew that Jim Farley had less than 12 hours to raise 100 votes among the fatigued and irritated delegates in the muggy hotels. Sometime during the hectic night, Louisiana's flashy Kingfish, Huey Long, had phoned to tell him: "You're a gone goose." The flamboyant, bitter old party standard-bearer, Al Smith, had gone to Chicago to trounce the man who had nominated him in 1924 and 1928. The coalition of Smith, John Garner, and favorite-son delegations was holding firm. And Roosevelt's own block was in danger, as some of its crucial cornerstones began to crumble. Twenty years of work was about to shatter into sad regrets for Franklin Roosevelt and Louis Howe. One more ballot would make him President or release a flood of desertions that would fatally undermine his cause.

The only hope was Texas. As a dozen members of the Roosevelt team pushed and pulled at John Garner, at his backer William Randolph Hearst, at their Texas and California delegations, Farley plodded wearily to Room 1702. Sprawled out on the floor with the sick little man, he cleared with Louis the all-out maneuver that would stake everything on the Lone-Star State.

Howe seemed almost beyond emotion when Farley returned a few minutes later to tell him that Texas would shift—that the battle was won. He could muster only a hushed whisper: "That is fine." [4] Yet Louis kept at it, by phone, all day: bringing Virginia's Harry Byrd into camp, checking incessantly on what was doing in the Garner delegations. That night, William Gibbs McAdoo turned the tide, by arrangement with Garner and Hearst. "California came here to nominate a President of the United States. She did not come here to deadlock this convention . . . ," announced the man who had been blocked in 1924 by the most magnificently deadlocked convention in American history.[5]

Back East, Franklin Roosevelt leaned happily in his armchair and smiled: "Good old McAdoo!" [6] In Chicago's Congress Hotel, Louis Howe's staff hooted and hollered in hysterical glee. And the little man in 1702, who liked to call himself "Franklin's 'No' man," phoned F.D.R. to receive the dramatic message that Roosevelt would fly to Chicago to address the convention in person. Then Louis turned to his own quiet celebration, with his son and his personal staff. The champagne they drank from paper cups that Friday night had been saved for years for this moment of victory.

Eight and a half months later, Louis was secretary to the President of the United States. He was still largely a mystery to the public, yet no one was so thoroughly identified with Franklin Roosevelt's plans and personality as the man reporters called the "mediaeval gnome," who strolled down the corridor from his second-floor White House bedroom for daily breakfast conferences with his friend of 20 years.

Newsmen had known Louis Howe for years as something more than a keeper of schedules. During the hectic presidential campaign, they had come to sense that the tangled lines of communication and authority in the Democratic camp led inevitably to his obscure and cluttered office. They remembered

[4] James A. Farley: *Behind the Ballots* (New York: Harcourt, Brace and Co.; 1938), p. 145.

[5] Arthur M. Schlesinger, Jr.: *The Age of Roosevelt: The Crisis of the Old Order, 1919–1933* (Boston: Houghton Mifflin Co.; 1957), p. 309.

[6] Grace Tully: *F.D.R., My Boss* (New York: Charles Scribner's Sons; 1949), p. 51.

him as the alter ego who haunted their offices during the long,
dry twenties, demanding headlines for a Democratic Roosevelt,
despite Republican prosperity and power. They had learned to
seek him out at the Roosevelt town house on East 65th Street,
even when the boss himself was out of town, and they had
noticed him cropping up in every enterprise with which F.D.R.
was even sketchily connected. Some remembered him vaguely
as a minute dynamo of activity, scurrying about Madison
Square Garden in 1924 to round up votes for Al Smith. A few
may have noted him in 1924 as a quiet figure in the balcony,
tensely waiting as F.D.R swung himself painfully to the rostrum
for the Happy Warrior speech, which nominated Smith and
served notice that Roosevelt was back in the wars. Here and
there in Washington, a few had known him as the Navy's trouble
shooter during the World War, an ambidextrous genius who
smoothed the Department's labor relations and organized
workers for the Democratic Party at the same time.

Howe was ideal material for the dramatic feature stories
which lent color to the new administration and lightened the
grim news of unemployment, starvation, and disaster. With his
thirst for mystery and his exotic personality, he fulfilled completely the public's demand for an *éminence grise,* a power
behind the throne. The dominant impression which emerged
through the haze of words and pictures was a calculated re-
print of a cliché. There was a patent temptation to compare
Colonel Howe and Colonel House. For a time, Edward M.
House's inflated reputation as a kingmaker and world-shaker
fell on Howe's thin shoulders. Louis was made to seem the real
pilot of the administration—a Machiavellian figure who generously concealed his mastery of the smiling, cultured puppet-
prince. The superficial facts gave color to this mirage. Howe
had been with Roosevelt longer and was closer to him than anyone else. And he did little to dispel the illusions which reinforced this public image. In fact, he helped create them.

But there was another image of Howe. Cynics painted him as a
devoted sheepdog of the administration, barking sometimes,
often trembling with raging frustration, but devotedly bending
to his master's will, keeping his place on the Roosevelt hearth by

his selfless devotion to his prominent friend. The symbols
swallowed up the man they purported to represent. Howe's real
personality and his precise role never broke through. A man of
carefully contrived façade, of disordered habits, of sudden,
brief, and late success, Louis Howe left behind him a record
bedeviled by many a false lead and broken at many a crucial
point. Even close associates confused the trail with an astounding variety of judgments.

The real Howe was neither hearth dog nor Machiavellian
puppeteer. He and Roosevelt had developed a reciprocal relationship firmly based on mutual prospects of gain, cemented by
long and intimate experience. This was no mere Damon and
Pythias story of brotherly love. Modern parallels help even less.
Howe had much too much personal devotion to be a Joe
Tumulty or a Sherman Adams, too little interest in public policy
to be a Colonel House or a Harry Hopkins. His relationship
with F.D.R. came close to being a unique phenomenon of
American politics.

The remarkable partnership began in 1912. But long before
they knew each other, Roosevelt and Howe were being drawn
together slowly by a deep web of circumstance. For Roosevelt,
the path to the White House was first unveiled in 1910, when
Dutchess County Attorney John Mack offered him the apparently hopeless nomination for State Senator. For Louis, the
story had already begun. In 1906, while young F.D.R. was still
struggling with his law courses at Columbia, Howe was traveling the State as a salesman for anti-Tammany politics. Like
Roosevelt, he was a Democrat by inheritance. Like Roosevelt,
he had been brought up under the shadow of Grover Cleveland
and had thrilled to the inspired trumpeting of Theodore Roosevelt. Their mutual heritage was the "good government," sound
money, mildly imperialistic dogma of the anti-Bryan Democrat.

Also like Roosevelt, Howe had burst into politics in an age of
massive dissension, which gave special advantage to the rebel
who dared raise a lance against the Tammany Tiger. Both were
products of the Progressive era. Both were set upon their careers
by the same rebellion of "good government" Democrats against
the machines and the bosses. And both were upstaters, an im-

portant distinction in New York. Since the Civil War, the "City" had been Democratic, the rural areas Republican. Roosevelt and Howe grew up with the peculiar dilemma of the upstate Democrat—they resented the urban bosses, yet they had to live with the fact that it was the urban votes that produced Democratic victories.

There were reformers in both parties, but Republican progressives occupied the stage. Theodore Roosevelt in the White House, Charles Evans Hughes in the Executive Mansion, posed a monstrous problem for Democratic crusaders. Corruption was bipartisan, but the record of their own rapacious Tammany Tiger dominated the headlines. Reform Democrats must either clean up Tammany or take the State organization away from it. The first road was blocked. Charles Francis Murphy had mastered the New York machine completely, rivaling the records of even Tweed and Croker. And Murphy had done it much more politely and carefully than those fabulous pirates. The reformers themselves were split by personal ambitions, and again by ideology. And they were much too closely identified with Wall Street. They lacked both organization and votes. Justice might be on their side, but the balance of power lay with the Wigwam.

Hopeless as reform was, they were driven to undertake it when Murphy attempted to put millionaire-publisher William Randolph Hearst into the Governorship in 1906. Thomas Mott Osborne took the lead. A wealthy, spirited, independent Mayor of Auburn, he called a conference of reform Democrats to stop Hearst at the State convention. The movement failed. But Hearst was swamped by Hughes in the election. Osborne set up a full-time headquarters in Albany to wrest control of the upstate Democrats from Tammany's clutches. He had already begun a search for likely young progressive recruits; one was a Harvard student named Franklin Roosevelt. Now he needed an imaginative and energetic man to build a grass-roots organization. For this job he chose the Saratoga newsman, Louis Howe. Howe could provide the perfect front for their underground maneuvering. In his guise as second-string man for the *New York Herald* in Albany, Louis could retain his listening post. He could also be a personal lobbyist for Osborne, a secret negotiator for the reformers, and a smart manipulator of the press.

Osborne had first come upon Louis when he had "borrowed" four newsmen during the 1906 campaign. Louis had found himself rushing from town to town, filling each day with conferences with party leaders, and working far into the nights to file his stories for the *Herald* and to send his long, confidential reports to his part-time boss in Auburn. He came to know scores of upstate Democrats. By election day, he had established a close relationship with Osborne. He pressed for a place on the payroll and delightedly wrote to his wife: "Isn't it funny Osborne wants me to be practically his private secretary. That is the kind of job you have always been poking me up to getting."[7] But the situation was strangely difficult for Louis. Long embarrassed by insecurity, he was now confused with a wealth of opportunities. He might spend the winter in the West Indies for the *Herald;* he might continue to try for a permanent job on the paper's New York desk. But the future with Osborne looked enticingly expansive. He wrote plaintively home: "I feel the turning point has come in our fortunes dear, and I don't want to make any mistake."[8]

Grace Howe had shared with Louis eight hectic years of insecurity. Irritated with his indecision, she warned him: ". . . don't you come falling back on me to make up your mind for you . . . the child and I can tag along after the band wagon and get on as the chance comes."[9] Louis decided on the big gamble. Throughout November he posted letter after letter to the Auburn Mayor, letters filled with good advice and subtle bids for a salary. He hoped for $50 a week, or "an appointment . . . on one of the State 'snaps' at 2,500 a year."[1] He got $40. He would also have $25 a week from the *Herald* when the legislative session began. But now he was broke, and he begged an advance to buy Christmas presents.

The uneasy sparring went on for six years. Osborne oscillated unhappily between moments of enthusiasm and periods of im-

[7] Howe to Grace Howe, November 19, 1906, Personal Papers.
[8] Howe to Grace Howe [November 13, 1906], Personal Papers.
[9] Grace Howe to Howe [1906], Personal Papers.
[1] Howe to Grace Howe, November 19, 1906, Personal Papers.

patient despair that he would ever be able to free himself of this
pleading little retainer. For Howe, it was a struggle for existence. And it was a struggle for success, after 40 years of failures.
Osborne's political enthusiasms proved episodic and unreliable.
And so did the payroll. In May 1908 Louis was abruptly fired—
one week's notice—and brutally, as it turned out. Unknown to
Osborne, Louis was living at the moment under his doctor's dire
prediction that he would be dead in two months. Louis pleaded
and nobly promised to work without pay. And he found himself
back on salary. Again in 1909 he worked for Osborne spasmodi-
cally. He was on the payroll from time to time as late as 1912.

The job was to build an upstate organization that could
challenge Tammany, that could make the party stand for progressivism. And, incidentally, his job was also to promote Osborne's personal ambitions. As a political strategist, Louis
proved aggressive and imaginative. He would not keep quiet.
His fertile brain produced master plans with frightening pace.
And he was incredibly facile. He proposed a quiet maneuver to
destroy Murphy by capturing the very upstate regulars who
supported the boss. At the same time, he wanted to use William Jennings Bryan to help bring some of the rural organizations into line. Knowing fully that Osborne hated Bryan, he
suggested treachery—"Bryan himself can be taken care of
later." [2]

When no suitable front man could be found among the upstate regulars, Louis swung sharply to the most bitterly anti-
Bryan men in the State. Conservatives like Judge Alton B.
Parker might be brought into line with a bit of subtle planning.
Set up a quiet little dinner, advised Howe, and "spring a set
of 'Fundamental Democratic Principles' . . . on them." Grover
Cleveland, he thought, might be persuaded to draft such a statement in a way to commit the group against Murphy and Hearst,
if the plea could be made that the "true principles of the democratic party were being so twisted by reckless demagogues that
there was a grave danger of their being lost beneath the staggering weight of unwise, foolish and socialistic doctrines." [3]

[2] Howe to Thomas Mott Osborne [1906], Papers of Thomas Mott
Osborne, Auburn, N.Y., hereafter cited as Osborne Papers.
[3] Howe to Osborne, November 24, 1906, Osborne Papers.

The maneuver was never staged. Like many of Howe's plans, it was too cute, devious, and naïve, in a way that betrayed the little manipulator's most serious blind spot. For all his practical turn of mind and cynical outlook, he tended to rely too heavily on mere words, which left much too wide a margin for maneuver. But Louis was not easily stumped. When Murphy appeared to be ready to dump his State Chairman, as well as Hearst, Howe suggested a general drive to elect new, and anti-Tammany, State Committeemen. The letter with which he proposed to initiate this new crusade, in 1907, played up Tammany's opposition to the new Public Utilities Commission. Scarcely a week later he was ready with another scheme, which illustrates the immense elasticity of his political ethics. He would approach Tammany's own financial supporters, August Belmont and Thomas Fortune Ryan, the chief enemies of utilities regulation. They owned the New York machines, he told Osborne, but wanted them only for use in the City. Beyond the Hudson, they were interested mostly in beating Theodore Roosevelt and destroying Bryan-radicalism in the Democratic Party. But they were unpopular upstate, while Osborne could "go out with a brass band." The deal would be simple, ". . . if they are willing to furnish the money for us to secure the state committee and upstate machinery, we in return will see to it that anti-Bryan delegations are secured to the National Convention. . . . The relations between us of course to be never made public. . . ." [4] But Osborne would have none of this dangerous pandering to the men who backed Murphy.

As plan after plan failed, Louis became desperate. He cooked up a scheme to force the State Chairman himself to call a "reform conference." He toyed again with using Bryan, this time to engineer an appropriation from the National Committee for a new "Home Rule Democracy." And he worked more solidly at a plan to commit the county conventions to a reform program.

Behind the wild-eyed scheming lay years of solid work in more practical, if limited, techniques. Already Howe believed

[4] Louis Howe: "Report #5," May 27, 1907, Osborne Papers.

that personal contacts were the taproot of successful organization. Singlehandedly he ran a letter-writing factory from his
office on State Street in Albany or from his front porch at Horseneck Beach in Massachusetts. Scores of notes went out to editors
who published "good editorials." Hundreds of others were
posted to county and town politicians, all over Osborne's signature. A clipping file was started, and Louis spent much time
raising money for the organization. A small-town newsman himself, he had immense respect for the power of the rural press.
He flattered the country editors mercilessly and helped them
with a steady supply of weighted stories to fill their columns.
At one point, he wrote Osborne: "I have started a little anti-
Tammany movement in the Assembly. Some of the other news-
papermen will show it to the upstate people and before long, if
I am not mistaken, you will see them getting their heads together and persuading themselves that they are really being
abused by Murphy." [5]

As secret investigator, he took full advantage of his reporter's
disguise. He spent much time tapping off and filtering the
rampant gossip of the Albany hotels and restaurants. He cultivated Hearst-backed legislators, reporting their confidences to
Osborne. He did what he could to promote trouble among the
regulars like State Comptroller Martin H. Glynn and Lieutenant
Governor Lewis Chanler. At least once, when covering for the
reporters' pool a speech by the Democratic State Chairman, he
carefully phrased his telephoned report to make Murphy's ally
look as bad as possible. Meanwhile, he counseled Osborne to
stay in the background and smother his personal ambitions
until the time was ripe.

At first glance, Louis seemed a failure in these early years.
Most of his ideas were stillborn. Yet the Democratic League,
which Osborne finally launched in January 1910, followed essentially the pattern which Howe had been advocating. Much
of the trouble between 1906 and 1909 lay in Osborne's mercurial
temperament, in the variety of upstate leaders, whose jealousies
made them prey for Murphy, and in the habitual Republican-

[5] Howe to Osborne [1907], Osborne Papers.

ism of the region. Furthermore, from the Civil War to the mid-twentieth century, crusades to free upstate Democrats from Tammany control have invariably ended as ludicrous attempts to make the tail wag the Tiger.

But Howe's apprenticeship was most significant in the patterns he set for his later career with Roosevelt. His ideas and his techniques changed only in minor details through the later years. Already the personal qualities that shaped his success were firmly planted: the tireless work, the unlimited optimism about eventual victory, the endless pessimism about the prospects of the moment, the imaginative planning, and the immense loyalty to the man for whom he worked. His dominating goal was neither reform nor organization. It was simply the personal advancement of his boss. Yet he was no idol worshipper. His reliability was based firmly on his own ambition to rise with his man. And, since he had no particular crusade to push, politics became largely a question of tactics, perhaps of trickery. He could conspire with the machine or damn it, cultivate an enemy or fight him as expediency dictated. The main trick was to create the image which would bring the largest support, without falling so much in love with the pose that it could not be dropped at a moment's notice. Three basic maneuvers became the standard equipment of his craft. First, get control of the press: "If you say a thing is so often enough, it stands a good chance to become a fact." [6] If possible, subtly maneuver your potential enemy to a point where he has to support you or cut his own throat. Finally, cultivate a grass-roots organization which can get out the vote. These techniques had nothing to do with ethics. Howe had no romantic illusions about the roots of politics.

These tactics had their limits and their dangers, some of which Howe himself recognized. He knew they might misfire at any point, and tried always to have an alternate strategy. But the major weakness was Louis's immense confidence in his ability to trick the ordinary man. While he often doubted the press, he assumed that the ordinary voter would believe what

[6] Howe to Osborne [1907], Osborne Papers.

he read. Although he thought that people were selfish, he expected them to accept his own portrait of Osborne as the selfless man of good will. He himself treated political issues with cynicism, yet he assumed that other politicians could be maneuvered into submission by signing a statement of principles.

Only a little less dangerous was his rural cast of mind on some aspects of the political situation. He tended to categorize the world too neatly in a pattern set by his own environment. He had the newsman's overconfidence in what the press could do. He had an upstater's suspicion that anyone connected with the City, and especially Wall Street or Tammany, was bad. He chronically overestimated the potential strength of the upstate Democrats; he shared the Easterner's fears of Bryan, not because of the Commoner's vacuity but because of his "radicalism."

Louis himself spent no time at political inventory. By November 1909 his career as Osborne's strategist seemed finished. He was sunk in despair as he cast aimlessly about for yet another chance.

2

—>>>->>>->>>->>>->>>->>>->>>->>>

Stereotype of a Crusader

*[Theodore] Roosevelt is trying to make
his party radical, which is impossible;
don't let us be forced into the mistake of
trying to make our party conservative,
which is equally impossible.*

(Thomas Mott Osborne,
October 8, 1910) [1]

LATE one October afternoon in 1910, young Franklin Roosevelt
found himself in one of those dozens of Dutchess County hamlets he had never seen before. The streets of London, the Grand
Canal in Venice, were more familiar to him than these dusty,
forgotten little places that lay back in the hills of his own Hudson Valley. Yet for days he had been riding endlessly through
these hills in a gaudy red automobile, soaked by thunderstorms,
covered with dust, bone-tired, a little confused by it all. Suddenly he had become a politician, going to the people he had
never known, to the Republican farmers who had voted their
straight tickets for 60 years in relentless protest against city
Democrats, to the men who were proud that they worked with

[1] Thomas Mott Osborne to John A. Dix, October 8, 1910, Osborne
Papers.

their hands and endlessly hostile to his own friends in the great
houses along the river.

He sat attentively as he listened to the old professional who
traveled with him. A hundred times, perhaps, he had heard
the Congressional candidate, Richard Connell, wring reluctant
cheers from these little crowds of farmers as he whipped a flag
from his Prince Albert coat and shouted: "The same old flag that
waved at Lexington; the same old flag that Sherman carried on
his march to the sea . . ." [2] Now it was his turn, as he carefully
removed the pince-nez glasses which his new friends insisted
made him look haughty and cold. He could never manage the
fervor of the Congressional candidate, but he could tell these
farmers that they were being sold out by their own leaders; he
could promise them that he would be a "real representative." It
was fun, and it was challenging. These shrewd countrymen
were seldom satisfied to listen. And now it came again, heckling
from the audience with the speech hardly begun. Did he stand
for the same policies as Republican Governor Hughes? This was
dynamite, but he was stuck with it. He was quick on the return:
"You bet I do! I think he's one of the best Governors the State
has ever had." [3] There were real cheers as he turned to the well-
remembered phrases he had spoken again and again, on station
platforms, in taverns, to lone farmers harvesting cattle-corn
along the road. It was unusual behavior for a Dutchess County
Democrat; it would take very unusual behavior to impress these
tough, suspicious custodians of his future.

For the young giant running for State Senator, it had all begun just a few months before, when John Mack had sought him
out at the obscure desk in the New York law office where he
clerked. Mack was in trouble. He needed a candidate for State
Senator. F.D.R. seemed to fit the bill—wealthy, young, attractive. To be sure, he was unknown and he might be attacked as
a city boy in disguise. But it didn't really matter much. They
didn't expect to win this post. If he proved inept, there was
little to be lost; if he were decently fit, they might win a few

[2] Morgan Hoyt to Roosevelt, January 27, 1938, President's Secretary's
File (PSF), Franklin D. Roosevelt Library, hereafter cited as FDRL.

[3] *Poughkeepsie News-Press,* October 26, 1910.

more votes and enlist him as a party stalwart. And Roosevelt was eager. Mack did not know that the young fellow was already boasting to friends that he would be President someday. But he did know that the boy wanted a political career. Roosevelt agreed almost at once. Not having to worry about money, completely bored with the law, he was free to explore anything, especially when the fun lay in the same direction as his ambitions.

John Mack was making large-scale plans too. He might throw away the State Senatorship—Democrats had won it only once in the 54 years of the Republican Party's history—but he intended to carry his county and build a solid Democratic organization. He had a good start—a clean sweep of county offices and 20 of the 27 county supervisors in 1909. And there was a larger hope, for in January Thomas Mott Osborne had called together at last the Democratic League which he hoped would "spread the knowledge of liberal principles" and save the State from Tammany. Mack and Poughkeepsie Mayor John Sague fell in with Osborne at once. Roosevelt's nomination for State Senator had been part of the League's mammoth drive to provide full Democratic tickets in all upstate counties and to enlist progressive young candidates.

Mack and Sague had problems with their colleague, State Committeeman Edward Perkins. He preferred the traditional alliance with the Tammany machine. He was suspicious of the reformers; he was contemptuous of the naïve young Senatorial candidate who showed up for his first political conference in riding breeches. But neither Mack nor Sague sensed the deeper problems of the Democratic League on which they pinned their hopes. Louis Howe might have told them. Absent in Europe, he had been warned by an old Albany crony that Osborne would have as much chance managing the tough professionals he was working with as Louis would have trying to stop an Alpine avalanche.[4]

If they had been more careful, Mack and Sague might have seen the lowering clouds themselves. For, when the League had

[4] Frederick W. Crone to Howe, March 6, 1910, Personal Papers.

met, there had been little agreement on "liberal principles" among the bickering, ambitious rebels. They had been reduced to sending out agents to build a machine for unnamed candidates and to supporting undefined principles. They needed a violent Tammany counterattack to weld them together. But Murphy refused to play the ogre. He let them organize the State Committee and elect its Chairman, one of their own men, John A. Dix. He allowed the trial balloons for the Governorship to drift freely in the breeze. And, when the moment came, he quietly punctured them all. The State convention, which Murphy controlled absolutely, nominated Dix himself—exactly the kind of innocuous compromise candidate the Boss needed. The League could hardly object. But Osborne reacted violently to the hoax: "In many respects the choice is absurd, for Dix can't speak, he can't write, and he can't read. . . . On the other hand, he is a clean gentleman of fine presence and would make a good, though not a great Governor." [5]

Yet there was hope. Hughes had retired to a United States Supreme Court appointment, but he had split his Republican Party sharply with his progressive program. His own Legislature had sabotaged the bill he had sold to the voters: clean elections, regulation of insurance and public utilities, pure food laws, conservation of forests, state control of water power, protection of child labor. Theodore Roosevelt had deepened the rift. Charging back into State politics, he had maneuvered a gubernatorial nomination for Henry L. Stimson. He had won the party's label for the progressive program. But the conservative county leaders were angrily preparing to desert him on election day. The Democrats offered the only alternative, even if it seemed a false one. Democrats from Murphy on down to the victory-starved and isolated Committeemen of the upstate counties plunged into their most vigorous campaign in years.

Roosevelt would especially need a vigorous campaign. Republicans tagged him at once as a "rich young man." They told the district that it was only a shabby joke to run this hapless fellow against the stalwart Republican incumbent, John F.

[5] Rudolph Chamberlain: *There Is No Truce: A Life of Thomas Mott Osborne* (New York: The Macmillan Co.; 1935), p. 167.

Schlosser. Then they proceeded to ignore him. Only a frontal attack could meet this treatment. Roosevelt had to reshape a whole set of stereotypes, the disadvantages of his birth and family and what Josephus Daniels later called "the handicaps of the Groton and Harvard brand of education." [6] He had to overcome the lack of an adequate machine in the country areas, and there would be no aid from outside the district. But he was prepared to spend a great deal more time and money than the ordinary candidate in flattering with personal attention the hundreds of people whom no major candidate had ever before reached.

His brilliant, flag-decked Maxwell touring car re-created the atmosphere of circus day and Chautauqua week for the sleepy hamlets in the hills. On the road constantly for four weeks, Roosevelt and Connell traveled over 2,000 rugged miles in their open car. A typical day found them bumping for 30 miles over the rough country roads through the Republican fortress from Millerton to Pawling, with seven scheduled meetings and numbers of unplanned pauses to talk with farmers along the road. When there was no train to be met, no formal rally, they simply set up drinks for all comers in the local saloon or country inn. Connell was the star of the show, manipulating relentlessly the impregnable clichés of patriotism. For F.D.R. himself it was an education, as he learned the techniques from the old professionals who set up his campaign. And it was an education in the rigors of campaigning as well. The arduous month was filled with mishaps. Rutted dirt roads made riding abominably uncomfortable and slow. Rainstorms soaked them and cut their audiences. They hit a farmer's favorite dog. The car broke down frequently, and they had at least one blowout. Connell was hit by a baseball from a sandlot game. Roosevelt himself had to limp through much of the campaign, after having been knocked from the step of a New York trolley by a passing ice wagon.

Roosevelt's own prime asset was his personality. Tall, athletically lean, he had a handsome profile and extremely fine features. He fairly exuded energy, friendliness, and confidence.

[6] Josephus Daniels: *The Wilson Era: Years of Peace—1910–1917* (Chapel Hill: University of North Carolina Press; 1944), p. 131.

Already he had the well-modulated voice which he later perfected into a masterly instrument of persuasion. If his self-
confidence seemed to betray conceit, if his broad enunciation
and his habit of cocking his chin made him seem, on occasion,
haughty and superior, these mannerisms were more than offset
by his genuine interest in the people he met. He might be a
novice at speech-making, but he was a success with small groups.
Already his "plain, straight talks" [7] began with the warm, sincere
greeting he had adopted from Connell: "My Friends!" And he
had an inspired knack for adapting to his audiences. To track
workers on the New York Central he spoke in their native
Italian. He sparred easily with the hecklers in the crowds.

Roosevelt stood as a progressive, but it was a campaign of
symbols, clichés, and glossy superficialities. Anything else would
have been too dangerous when every item in the progressive
creed was explosively controversial. And his own progressivism
was shallow. There had been no time for homework on the
issues. Instead of making promises, he impressed on his listeners
a picture of a boss-ridden Republican Party. He tagged Columbia County leader Lou Payn as "the Sage of Chatham." Republican officeholders were "barnacles." His opponent he could
pillory without mercy, for Schlosser had joined the bipartisan
"Black Horse Cavalry" to vote solidly against Hughes's program.

His own platform was simple and vacuous: "I want to represent you, the people of these counties, and no one else. I am
pledged to no man, to no special interest, to no boss. I want to
stay on the job of representing you twelve months of the year." [8]
Later he could claim all too accurately: "During the campaign
. . . I made no promise in regard to particular legislation. . . ." [9] He ignored such issues as conservation, farm problems, public utilities, the initiative, referendum, and recall, the
direct election of Senators, and labor laws. He came out for
direct primaries only when forced to it, and then vaguely. Instead, he cannily identified himself with the "good"—the good
Republicans as well as Democrats—and tirelessly blasted away

[7] *Poughkeepsie News-Press*, October 27, 1910.
[8] Speech at Hudson, October 27, 1910, Speech File, FDRL.
[9] Roosevelt to John Anthony, June 7, 1911, Group IX, FDRL.

at the "rotten corruption of the New York legislature and the extravagant mismanagement of the State administration." [1]

Republicans were stunned. They tried ridicule—poking fun at his "vaudeville trip for the benefit of the farmers." [2] They tried freezing him out of the press, and he spent $400 on newspaper advertisements featuring the endorsement of Hughes-Republicans. They tried to turn the issue of Bossism against him, and threw him off balance with the charge that Tammany dictated to the Poughkeepsie Democratic machine. He replied plaintively: "You can't tell the people that Murphy controls the Democratic party here. . . ." And he protested that the whole issue of Bossism was "mere dust thrown in the eyes of the people" [3] by the Republican machine. But he soon learned that counterattacks were better ignored. He returned to his familiar promise to be a "positive" representative. A man must stand for something, he said, unless, like the Republicans, he wished to be only "destructive." Precisely what he would stand for he did not say.

The flamboyant, warmhearted, shallow campaign paid off. Roosevelt won an unprecedented majority of 1,140 votes in a total of over 30,000. In Dutchess County he ran far ahead of the State ticket, even though the Democratic sweep was State-wide, with the Republicans losing control of the executive offices and both houses of the Legislature for the first time in 18 years. It was a personal victory for F.D.R. Republican lethargy and squabbling had helped. So had money. He personally spent over $1,700, more than five times as much as any other candidate in the district. But largely it was his own appeal. An unknown in September, he had proved himself in November one of his party's prime assets. And he had played a role that would dictate his future. He owed nothing to Murphy and Tammany. He had made no commitments to the local organization. Independence seemed the keynote to success in Hudson Valley politics.

In the New York State Senate, young F.D.R. would need every special asset he possessed, for he was launching his craft

[1] *Poughkeepsie News-Press*, October 22, 1910.
[2] Ibid., November 1, 1910.   [3] Ibid., October 27, 1910.

in dangerous waters. Knowing Roosevelts too well, one Republican Boss suggested to a Tammany friend: "Take my advice and drown him before he grows old and tough." [4] But young Roosevelt would not be easily drowned. There were now dozens of upstate Democratic legislators without previous records and with uncertain loyalties. Many of them were tied to Osborne's League. But they could not be buried temporarily in unimportant posts while they were being "educated." Fourteen of the Senate committees had brand-new members as chairmen. Roosevelt himself would be head of the Forest, Fish and Game Committee, and would sit on committees on railroads, canals, and agriculture. There might even be a chance for crusading rebels to dislodge Murphy himself, if they could gain the Governor's ear and dominate the caucus. The stakes were high, the possibilities for maneuver many.

The more naïve read Dix's Inaugural Address. It was meaningless on many points, paying only token obeisance to the symbols of reform. His annual message was hardly better. Even conservatives found it "a little narrow in vision. . . ." Young Roosevelt, already aware of the values of ambiguity, commented: "It gives us a good deal to think about." [5] Dix hoped for unity. His appointments smacked of compromise. To the reformers he gave three major positions. Osborne was drafted into the uncongenial job of Forest, Fish and Game Commissioner. But the bulk of the patronage went to the regulars who had produced most of the Governor's votes. And the legislative leaders, young Robert F. Wagner and Alfred E. Smith, had been hand-picked by Murphy himself. These Tammany twins would make it possible for the ubiquitous boss to control the legislature without the inconvenience of endless train and boat rides to Albany and of living out of a suitcase at the Ten Eyck.

The real test would come with the Democratic nomination of a United States Senatorial candidate (until the passage of the Seventeenth Amendment in 1913, Senators were elected by State Legislatures). Immediately after the 1910 election, the League had laid plans to capture this post as a symbol of its

[4] *Boston Herald,* March 11, 1913.
[5] *New York Herald,* January 5, 1911.

new power. Osborne swallowed his own ambitions, fought off Tammany hints of preferment for himself, and agreed on former Brooklyn Mayor Edward M. Shepard as the reform candidate. Elaborate machinery was worked out for co-operation between the city reformers and the upstate League. Montgomery Hare, a friend of Shepard and a director of the League, became the major contact man in Manhattan, where he enlisted the financial support and influence of old Cleveland Democrats like the ex-President's law partner, Francis Lynde Stetson.

It would be a fight to the finish, Osborne proclaimed, against William F. Sheehan, the Tammany candidate. "Blue-eyed Billy's" long career had been strewn with the shadows of scandal and unsavory friendships. A former Speaker of the Assembly and Lieutenant Governor, he had pioneered in building a Buffalo machine to work closely with Croker's Tammany. He had long since earned the hatred of the League's Manhattan leaders by fighting Grover Cleveland and by working for Thomas Fortune Ryan's Brooklyn Transit Company. A close friend and law partner of Alton B. Parker, Sheehan was urbane, wealthy, and regular. To progressives, he was the symbol of corruption while Shepard was the white knight of reform. To older Democrats, this was merely the latest chapter in the ancient Cleveland-David B. Hill schism which had dominated New York politics for 20 years. To many prominent New Yorkers, it seemed also to be an offshoot of the cutthroat competition among the giants of Manhattan finance. Sheehan was the candidate of Ryan and August Belmont; Shepard was the friend of Morgan and William C. Whitney and Morgan's lawyer, Francis Stetson.

For Roosevelt, the choice of candidate posed a stubborn problem. His Putnam County supporter, William Church Osborn, and his friends Thomas Mott Osborne, Sague, and Mack all pressed for Shepard. Republicans in his district added to the anti-Sheehan clamor. To the pressures of personal friendship and campaign promises were added his family's traditions. His father and his older brother had both been prominent Cleveland Democrats, allies of Stetson, Henry Villard, and Shepard against the Croker gang. But his County Chairman, Edward

Perkins, and the Poughkeepsie Democratic newspapers were cautiously regular. He might easily back the wrong team or be caught between them. As early as December 17, however, he had carefully hinted that he might support Shepard. By Inauguration Day he was clear in his own mind that upstaters could not afford the taint of a Tammany Senator.

When the Democratic caucus met on January 16, Murphy's confidence was rudely shattered. Twenty-five legislators were missing, among them Roosevelt. The caucus lacked six votes needed to control the election. The rebels had come from several directions at once—from among Shepard's friends, from the League, from the Brooklyn organization rankling with jealousy of Murphy, from dissident elements in Tammany itself. Outside the Legislature, Hearst ardently joined the attack on Murphy, as did his archenemies, Ralph Pulitzer and Oswald Garrison Villard. Old Stalwarts like George Haven Putnam and Cleveland's former secretary, William Gorham Rice, enlisted again in the fight they had been waging since 1892. What had started as a Shepard movement had rapidly become a rallying cause for anti-Murphy men of every stripe. They were all against Sheehan, but for different reasons. Yet the Insurgents' real problem was organization, not logic. They must keep their group intact and arouse a storm of public opinion that would force Murphy to his knees. After the first callow hope for a quick victory, they lived in constant fear of the handful of desertions, or the Tammany-Republican deal, which could give Murphy control.

F.D.R. became the informal chairman of the Insurgency. He had made the last-minute attempt to swing the Governor to Shepard, and had been the only Senator to sign the initial Insurgent statement of principles. The Insurgents had no boss. Decisions were made by elaborate negotiation. Interminable conferences were carried on by the legislators themselves. Outside the legislature, Osborne, Stetson, Hare, and dozens of others meddled and maneuvered to maintain the deadlock. Roosevelt's job was largely that of spokesman. He made statements to the press almost daily; he was frequently cross-examined by reporters. One hostile paper labeled him "the head

and shoulders of the movement," and another saw him as a
"pliable" young man who had become convinced that "the way
to win imperishable fame was to get out and kill a political boss
ever morning before breakfast." [6] Friendly newsmen soon
began to paint him as the Galahad of the Insurgency. He
blundered occasionally, but he showed a superior talent for
political dramatics. He carried on an eminently successful
propaganda campaign from which Murphy and Sheehan
emerged as unmitigated villains and the Insurgents as selfless
heroes of democracy. Before he had voted on a single bill,
F.D.R. had become one of the most widely known politicians in
the State.

Equally significant was his self-appointed function as guardian of the group. They met daily at 10 and at 5 to shore up
their courage and maintain communications. They knew they
must stand together or be picked off with favors and threats. To
avoid the pressures they would be faced with in hotels and bars,
Roosevelt turned the first floor of his own conveniently located
house into a club for Insurgents. The Roosevelt family quietly
retreated to the upper floors, never quite beyond the range of
the smoke and noise of the constant caucus below. As the fight
dragged on, Roosevelt's responsibilities increased. He became a
bridge between the various groups of supporters and the Insurgents themselves, the chief negotiator with Dix, Murphy,
and Sheehan. Finally, he found himself fighting for his own
political career, as he struggled to hold his allies together in the
last hectic days of the long Insurgency.

In all of this Roosevelt had the help of a new and unexpected
aide, Louis Howe. Howe had come to Albany as usual to take
up his job with the *Herald* and the *Telegram*. He was also working for Osborne again, and throughout the session he played a
dual role. In the columns of his papers he helped to give the
Insurgency one of its best presses in the State. It must have
pleased his editors that he had the most, and the most reliable,
information about what the rebels were doing. He also acted as
an informal advisor to the Insurgents, briefing them on what

[6] *New York Sun,* January 20, 1911; *New York Morning Telegraph,*
January 28, 1911.

was happening among other Legislators and offering suggestions on publicity. He soon came to know Roosevelt well, and
wrote an extravagantly friendly character sketch of him for the
Herald. Louis pointed out the young Senator to his family and
said he was a man to watch. And Eleanor Roosevelt invited
Grace Howe and their young daughter Mary to lunch at the
State Street house.

The Insurgents' tactics changed as the struggle wore on. At
first they hoped for additional defections and a solution within a
week. Within a few days, Tammany was 12 votes short of control. But the desertions tapered off. Anxious to avoid the appearance of forcing their will on the majority, the rebels announced that Murphy must choose the candidate, but that
they would keep veto power. After a week of balloting, they
settled down for a long siege. It lasted two and a half months.
Their most pressing job was to maintain their own block. While
personal relationships remained superficially polite, the regulars
used every conceivable pressure to split off individuals from the
group. Regular Democratic papers castigated them as traitors
and ingrates who had grabbed all the patronage they could and
then deserted to split their party in a senseless struggle for their
own ambitions. Sheehan threatened to go into their own counties and cut the ground from under them. The State Chairman,
Winfield Huppuch, publicly warned them to get back into line.
The National Committeeman ostentatiously spanked them,
and privately tried to wean F.D.R. away. On January 20, the
Sun unleashed the most frightening weapon, the charge that
anti-Catholic prejudice lay hidden beneath their strange rebellion. Roosevelt was privately warned by "some very influential
people" that his anti-Catholicism would be kept in mind in
party decisions about his future. He tried to shrug it off: "I hope
we will be given credit for having more sense. . . ."[7] But he
was soon forced to issue a list of Roman Catholics for whom he
would be happy to vote, and several Insurgents cast votes for
John Kernan to demonstrate their willingness to support anti-
Sheehan Catholics. The religious issue was only one of many

[7] *Albany Times-Union,* January 23, 1911.

weapons. The *Sun* added up the pluralities of the five Insurgent
Senators to imply that they represented only 2,376 voters. The
Morning Telegraph saw the whole movement as a bankers' war
in which the public figures were mere pawns moved by their
own vanity. The *Sun* heaped ridicule on their heads. Among
the new principles, it noted, was the idea that "Minority control
is preferable to any other form of party government, in the
Democratic organization, providing the minority is composed of
the Good, self-certified as such." [8]

Much more effective was Murphy's quiet work with the
county chairmen, State Committeemen, and Democratic editors. There were threats of a mortgage foreclosure in one case,
of the loss of political printing contracts in another, of patronage
losses in others. Delegations came to Albany to persuade their
Insurgent representatives to back Sheehan. Some Senate committee chairmen, like Roosevelt, found their nominations of
clerks for their committees ignored. Some were offered better
jobs; one, a judgeship. Roosevelt himself was alternately
tempted, bulldozed, and ridiculed. He was reported to have
been offered his choice of spots on the next State-wide ticket.
The Democratic newspapers in his district turned against him.
Local Democrats either opposed him or remained quiet. Only
Sague would come to his defense. There was a threat that the
charter for the new city of Beacon, in his district, would be
shelved until he learned to be more helpful. A client approached one of the partners in his law firm to bring pressure
on the young clerk. The only real public support in his district
came from the Republican *Daily Eagle*.

But there was serious weakness in this massive attack. Most
Insurgents were newcomers to politics who owed little to the
organizations and might even gain by fighting them. For most
of them there was no turning back. They were marked men.
And they found heavy rank-and-file support in their mail. Roosevelt was in a particularly strong position. Financial pressure
could not be used against him. And he believed that Independents could hurt him more in his district than Tammany

[8] *New York Sun,* March 29, 1911.

ever could. Principle and ambition happily pointed to the same path.

As the Insurgency moved into its second week, Roosevelt talked with Murphy and with Dix and invited Sheehan to dinner in his home. But the collapse of these personal conferences only hardened the regular organization's bitterness. Encouraged by rumors that the secret field marshals were dissatisfied with Roosevelt and angered by the charge that he was Thomas Fortune Ryan's puppet, Sheehan claimed that Shepard himself had once begged obsequiously for Tammany support. Day after day, the fruitless sessions of the Legislature went on. In ballot after ballot, the Republicans held firmly for Chauncey DePew, the regular Democrats for Sheehan, and the Insurgents carefully scattered their votes. They had long since given up on Shepard; they hoped only to block Sheehan. Early in February, the Insurgency nearly collapsed with the temporary defection of a hard-pressed New York City member.

By the end of the month, both Shepard and Sheehan were discouraged. The Tammany candidate appealed to his native city of Buffalo, but both Erie County Senators remained staunchly Insurgent. The rebels were embarrassed by the public intervention of their most prominent financial supporters, Stetson and George Foster Peabody. Osborne and the New Yorkers were bickering sharply. Shepard finally withdrew on February 26, but the Insurgents held firm. The Governor repudiated Sheehan, and Murphy's own organization was stirring restlessly. Both sides were ready for compromise. Roosevelt made it clear that the Insurgents were "ready to treat with Mr. Murphy . . . and . . . give proper consideration to any suggestion regarding the sort of man to be chosen that Mr. Murphy may care to make." [9] Secretly they were working on a list of candidates to submit to the boss; publicly Roosevelt denied it.

After the first week in March, Roosevelt was involved in complex and secret negotiations, mostly carried on in person or by telephone. The Governor acted as mediator. Hare, representing the Insurgents' New York backers, stubbornly fought against all

[9] *New York World*, March 8, 1911.

compromise. F.D.R. betrayed his own attitude bluntly in a private letter: "Most of us want the kind of man who has the qualifications such as you describe—conservative in regard to business interests and yet a man whose position can never be questioned by the radical element of society. . . . The trouble is going to be that that type of man might not be considered by the organization as a sufficiently good Democrat to work for the benefit of the party along organization lines." [1] Meanwhile, an Albany newspaper noted pointedly: "There seems nothing left for the poor man but to keep on insurging." [2]

With public anger sharply rising over the shoddy spectacle, the rebels played their last card, a deal with the Republicans. Stetson approached the State Republican boss. Minority Leader Edgar Brackett, an old friend of Louis Howe from Saratoga, worked out with Roosevelt a list of four Democrats whom Republicans would support. Howe was their go-between in this sensitive business. But there was trouble on both sides. The outside backers of the Insurgency were badly split, and Brackett could not bring his henchmen into line.

Roosevelt now turned to direct negotiation with Wagner and Smith. But during the night of March 28, the matter was settled by a raging fire in the Capitol building, which Louis Howe happened to be the first to discover. With the building still burning on into the next day, it was essential to complete the farce quickly. After 48 hours of sparring between Murphy and Roosevelt, the majority of the Insurgents agreed reluctantly to enter a caucus. They submitted a list of ten candidates to Murphy—by this time it was a matter of the most flimsy camouflage. Even so, the boss insisted on the addition of Justice James O'Gorman, a Tammany Stalwart. O'Gorman, of course, was his choice. The final decision was made at 2 a.m.; Roosevelt was bypassed. A Tammany leader went directly to Francis Lynde Stetson, and Stetson agreed to O'Gorman's nomination. He and Hare sent word to Albany in the morning that they would use their influence to protect the Insurgents from reprisals.

The rebels were faced with a *coup d'état*. Osborne and Roose-

---

[1] Roosevelt to Walter Taylor, February 17, 1911, Group IX, FDRL.
[2] *Albany Knickerbocker-Press*, March 16, 1911.

velt worked all day to hold them together. But, deserted by
Stetson, promised forgiveness personally by Smith and Wagner,
the bulk of them entered a caucus at 5 that afternoon. Roosevelt
and ten others stayed out. Yet, when he announced his vote in
the election, F.D.R. praised O'Gorman and boasted of victory.
Years later the boast of victory would be recalled again and
again, while the hypocrisy of the moment was easily forgotten.
Edgar Brackett prated in mock sadness: "I would not, if I could,
seek to add to the blunder, I had almost said the humiliation
. . ." of the Insurgents.[3] At their annual dinner, the Legislative
correspondents spoofed F.D.R. unmercifully in a parody of the
popular song:

> *Said Franklin D "There's Got to be*
> *Some new insurgency.*
> *We've got some boys to make a noise*
> *And leader I will be;*
> *For weeks and weeks we fought the fight*
> *Against old Tammany,*
> *But I can't figure out as yet,*
> *Just what was handed me."*

> *Tammany! Tammany!*
> *We've got snugly in our belts,*
> *Scalps of both the Roosevelts,*
> *Tammany . . .*

As the evening wore on, they hit him again and again:

> *What's the matter with Roosevelt and his Plan?*
> *All the other reformers have them on the pan;*
> *Fattened them up with printers' ink,*
> *Then handed them the rinky dink.*
> *What's the matter with Roosevelt? Got the can.*

And they printed tastefully in the evening's program a formal
voucher:

[3] *Saratoga Springs Sun*, April 1, 1911.

The Insurgents, Incorporated.
c/o Senator Franklin D. Roosevelt, Dr.

TO THE STATE OF NEW YORK

Jan. 17—March 31, One Senatorial Deadlock
$347,288.59

PLEASE REMIT PROMPTLY.[4]

In fact, the results were mixed. The Insurgents did beat
Sheehan. They hurt Murphy by their relentless pounding for
two and a half months, but they did not break his power. And
the choice of O'Gorman himself was a clear defeat. The judge
was a Tammany leader. The best that could be said for him was
that nothing could be found against him. But for Roosevelt personally, the Insurgency was of immense significance. It made
him. He had created a political legend upon which he could
build for more than 30 years. He *did* deserve much of the credit.
Neither puppet nor field marshal, he had the much more difficult job of managing the immeasurably intricate relationships
among Insurgents and their backers, who differed on both objectives and tactics. Men like Wagner resented his too effective
play to the galleries. They complained that he was slippery and
hard to deal with, but their anger reflected his evident success.

And for Roosevelt the Insurgency was an accelerated course
in politics. Pushed to the center of a seething mass of intrigue,
he learned the tricks of maneuver and speech by being forced
to use them. He delighted in the roughness of the game, and
gave the impression of a young man thoroughly enjoying himself. Not the least of the lessons he learned was the significance
of "regularity" and the power behind it. He knew by the time he
was through that self-righteousness is not enough in politics. If
he had any doubts, they must have been shattered in the election of 1911. Only 14 of the 24 Insurgent Assemblymen won renomination. Most of his friends were finished in politics within
two years. He was beginning to learn that one had to recognize
power where it lay—that is, if one wanted to be a live politician
who might be partly right, rather than a completely right politician who would most certainly be dead.

[4] April 27, 1911, copy of program in Personal Papers.

3

-》》-》》-》》-》》-》》-》》-》》-》》

A Young Progressive
Finds a Program

Until we get rid of these political man-
chus who now control the party, we might
as well not go to the polls. . . .
(Franklin D. Roosevelt,
March 13, 1912) [1]

AFTER ONE of his many defeats at the hands of his own party,
Roosevelt told the reporters who crowded around him in the
lobby: "This is the last straw on the camel's back . . . we are
going to get a new camel!" [2] This made news; it helped keep the
stereotype brightly burnished. But as the Legislature moved on
into its normal business, Roosevelt's problems multiplied. He
and his friends faced one of the classic dilemmas of modern
politics. They wanted to maintain a progressive bloc, to carry on
guerrilla warfare against the majority on selected issues, but
they wanted to remain Democrats. By 1912 they hoped to capture Murphy's own Manhattan bailiwick.

Yet the Democratic League was weak and riddled with rival-

[1] *Poughkeepsie Daily Eagle*, March 14, 1912.   [2] Ibid.

ries. The Insurgents themselves had little essential unity. Roosevelt personally was being urged to be satisfied with one big victory and co-operate with the machine on small matters.[3] He finally decided to pare the rebel nucleus to the ten or twelve who really agreed on major reform proposals. Even so, there were more defeats than victories. On patronage the machine had its way. Roosevelt stood almost alone in the Senate where the machine's appointments might have been blocked. His attacks on Tammany's special legislation were hardly more successful. He was noisy and brave, but he was also confused and ineffective. He fought against a Tammany amendment to the Highway Commission Bill which preserved the divided responsibility of a three-man commission, and was expelled from the caucus for refusing its discipline. No one followed him out; with two allies, he could have beaten the machine. Forced to vote for a Tammany commission or against an otherwise desirable reorganization, he complained fretfully: "This horrible pudding which everybody has stirred and which has not even been put into the oven, must either be eaten in its indigestible state . . . or must be thrown out the window." [4] Yet when Tammany itself espoused a single commissionership for the Canal System, Roosevelt felt forced to reverse his ground. This time the reform itself would mean complete Tammany control. Sometimes he went along with the organization and sometimes he was outmaneuvered in the elaborate legislative log-rolling.

A case in point was the new "Gaynor Charter" for New York City. Roosevelt was already on record for "home rule," which the Charter generally represented. But "home rule" for Tammany was too much for his reformer friends. Under pressure from Shepard, Hare, and Osborne, he gave his support to the changes they demanded, but carefully avoided committing himself on the Charter as a whole. Then, in the fall of 1911, he was faced with two related and unpleasant facts. The completed Charter he now found impossible; in addition, the regulars had introduced a general reapportionment bill giving all six of the State's new Congressional seats to New York City and making

[3] Price Collier to Roosevelt, January 27, 1911, Group IX, FDRL.
[4] File 31, Group IX, FDRL.

his own district hopelessly Republican. He decided to fight the
Charter openly. He told one reporter that there was "a fine
opening for an energetic trouble-maker." And newsmen predicted: "There is every indication that conditions in the closing
days of the session will make the scrappy times of last winter
look like a press conference." [5] He had three Democratic allies
in the Senate—enough to defeat the Charter, with Republican
help. Mayor Gaynor sent an aide to negotiate, made major con-
cessions, and within a week received Roosevelt's apparent
promise to go along with the revised bill. But the clamor of the
reformers continued. Rabbi Stephen Wise blasted the Charter
as a slovenly piece of legislation in which "every interest has
been consulted except the public interest." [6] Villard's *Post* told
the world it was impossible to make an intelligent decision
within a few days on a 576-page bill which "fairly swarms with
jokers." [7] A small army of hostile lobbyists descended upon the
Legislature. Osborne wired Roosevelt from Boston, begging him
to hold out against it, and F.D.R. flipped again. Gaynor was
exasperated with the upstate meddler he privately called "Mr.
Damn Fool" and "Mr. Know-It-All." [8] But he swallowed his
pride and, with ceremonial humility, sent two last-minute telegrams appealing for Roosevelt's support.

When the showdown finally came, the prior pressures and
decisions were lost in a furious flurry of deals, made and broken.
The Charter and the redistricting bills were scrambled together, with each side fighting for the best combination of the
two. Conferences went on until well after midnight September 29. F.D.R.'s district was restored, and the regulars indiscreetly boasted that he would support the Charter. But three
things upset the deal. The regular Democratic Senator from
Ulster County threatened to vote against the Charter because
his area had been punished to win over Roosevelt. The morning

[5] *New York Press*, September 8, 1911.
[6] Stephen S. Wise: "How Not To Draft a Charter," *North American Review*, CXCIV (1911), p. 369.
[7] *New York Evening Post*, September 22, 1911.
[8] Louis H. Pink: *Gaynor, the Tammany Mayor Who Swallowed the Tiger* (New York: International Press; 1931), p. 173.

papers carried premature news of Roosevelt's desertion. Finally, lobbyists for the reformers caught the late evening train for Albany and, with the help of three anti-Charter city officials, met with Roosevelt at the Ten Eyck for breakfast. They threatened to destroy his reputation. The reaction was instant. One after the other, the rebels reported to the sponsors of the bill that they would not now vote for it. When the Democratic caucus met, Roosevelt and six others stood firm against it. The offending upstaters were well chastised by the reapportionment bill, but the Charter had to be left in committee—dead. Roosevelt indignantly denied that there was any connection between redistricting and his own acrobatics on the Charter. There were few who could believe him.

Roosevelt had almost insuperable problems in tactics. An Insurgent must have a program, and herein lay his chief difficulty. The tremendous activity of campaign and rebellion had left him little time for thought. He had come to public life with only the vaguest notion of the progressivism he espoused. Inspired by Theodore Roosevelt's great example, he subscribed almost instinctively to the general proposition that government must be given back to the people, must be made sensitive to that hazy thing called the "public interest," and must be obdurate against the insidious influence of "special interests." All this, it was fondly thought, could be done by tinkering with the machinery of government so that the voters' wrath could work effectively against offending representatives. But such philosophy as Roosevelt had was etched simply in terms of "good" and "bad." He had little experience with details. He had little concept of the problems and had to build his program as he fought for it.

He adopted at once the whole battery of mechanical reforms long popularized by progressives of both parties. The first step was easy. He sponsored a resolution approving direct election of United States Senators. Tammany was with him on this. Republican Senator Brackett noted wickedly: ". . . he is pleased with a smaller rattle and tickled with a smaller feather than I'd thought."

⁹ *New York Tribune,* April 21, 1911.

The Direct Primary issue was another matter. Direct Primaries had become so popular that few politicians dared to fight the proposed reform openly. Rather, they aimed to manipulate the complicated electoral machinery in such a way as to make the primary impotent. Yet it was on this question that Democrats would have to prove their progressivism. Roosevelt himself was fully committed to an effective system of primaries —one with "office-block" ballots and without party labels. The party's official bill was merely a pious gesture which left the convention system intact where it counted most—in the choice of national convention delegations and nominees for State offices. The Governor temporized until mid-July, when he finally pressed for a complete program of Direct Primaries. Wagner planned to send the Governor's message to the Judiciary Committee without instructions, a sure way to kill it quietly. Then Roosevelt "dropped a bomb in the Senate" when he forced a vote on the proposition to instruct the committee along the lines of the Governor's message.[1] Roundly defeated, he nevertheless aroused three hours of widely reported debate. And he did help to kill the weak official bill. Yet when the party leaders proved adamant in the fall, he voted for this "travesty." Half humorously, he tried to make victory out of defeat: "One of the regular organization men in the Senate told me," he said, ". . . that we had the whole apple and that the strictly organization Senators got the core." [2] Privately, he admitted that it was simply the best bill to be had.

He tried to move on at once from this first step. By mid-January 1912 he had brought together a block of Insurgents and dissidents who succeeded in hammering through an agreement with Wagner in a five-hour fight. The rebels promised to thrash all important matters out in conference, rather than attacking in public. In return, they received substantial agreement to Roosevelt's proposals and some others on Direct Primaries, including the deletion of all party emblems and the reduction in the num-

[1] Elliott Roosevelt (ed.): *F.D.R.: His Personal Letters, 1905–1928* (New York: Duell, Sloan and Pearce; 1948), p. 169; hereafter cited as *Personal Letters, 1905–1928.*

[2] *New York Sun,* October 5, 1911.

ber of names necessary for nominating petitions. Roosevelt was
surprised that they had "stood for so much." [3] But then he was
trapped in a major parliamentary error. The changes were em-
bedded in two bills, a "constructive" one containing the major
reforms and a "corrective" one to clear up minor errors in the
law which must be remedied at once. The "corrective" measure
quickly passed. The "constructive" bill, of course, was soon
bottled up in committee.

On other types of governmental reform, Roosevelt stood with
the progressives when he was pushed to it. He backed away
from personal registration of voters when his farmer-constituents
protested. He favored a short ballot and the office-block ballot,
and he worked hard in committee to simplify the Tammany-
inspired, complicated, and expensive election laws. But he
dodged haplessly on women's suffrage until overwhelming pressure by the lady lobbyists forced him to favor it. He worked for
the new commission form of city government, and he served as
passive sponsor for home-rule legislation sent him by the reform
groups. But there was little spirit in all of this.

For Roosevelt personally, the heart of progressivism lay in
the conservation issue, to which he was directly exposed by his
position as Chairman of the Forest, Fish and Game Committee.
Much of his work was routine, but the problem of the State's
watersheds brought him for the first time to recognize the sharp
conflicts of public interest and private property. Governor
Hughes had set the pattern for water-power policy in 1907 by
advocating State construction of hydroelectric plants, a State
monopoly of all reservoirs and streams in the public parks, care
that power projects would not endanger the forest preserves,
and distribution of State-produced power under "equitable
terms and conditions." The progressives of the Democratic
camp championed the program against Hughes's own Republicans.

A crucial fight in 1911 developed over the proposal to allow
private flooding of State forest lands for reservoirs. Osborne
hurriedly sent the Legislature a substitute measure, which was

[3] Roosevelt to Alonzo McLaughlin, January 18, 1912, Group IX, FDRL.

passed with Tammany and Insurgent backing and became part
of the Constitution in 1913. It provided that only the State
should be allowed to flood its forest lands. Power franchises
might be assigned for 50-year periods, but only with a sliding
scale of compensation for the State and with electric-power
rates to be reviewed by a State agency at ten-year intervals.
Roosevelt had little to do with all of this, but when the emphasis
shifted in 1912 to projects outside the forest preserves, he became active. By now he was willing to commit himself completely to the Hughes-progressive side. He helped pass a bill to
allow State construction and operation of hydroelectric facilities. Two days later he assisted in the defeat by one vote of a
rival measure to authorize extensive private operations in the
area. He tagged it a "vicious bill" and denounced some of his
colleagues, including Al Smith, for supporting a conservation
measure which favored the power interests. The battle won in
the Senate was lost in the Assembly. Progress toward public
power projects was held up for years by split party control of
the State government, and Roosevelt found himself in 1928 making essentially the same fight for public power that he had
made in 1912.

F.D.R.'s most personal concern was in the conservation of
timber, a concern which developed into a lifelong hobby. It was
this problem which inspired him to the clearest philosophical
justification of the public interest. After a two-year fight, he
helped win the battle to promote reforestation by offering tax
exemptions. Then, at the opening of the 1912 session, he proposed a revolutionary approach to the problem—State inspection of denuded private lands on the watersheds and compulsory reforestation under State specifications and at the owner's
expense. State regulation of the time and manner of cutting was
also provided, and the Conservation Commission was to be
aided by a deputy attorney general of its own choosing. Roosevelt complained that the hearings on the proposal were dominated by "scores of people representing the lumber interests." [4]
He tried to build a backfire by bringing Gifford Pinchot to

4 Roosevelt to H. S. Rivenburgh, February 22, 1912, Group IX, FDRL.

Albany. Inspired by the great conservationist, Roosevelt himself went on record dramatically in a speech at Troy. Here he attempted to put into popular language the conservation arguments which had been widely publicized the year before in Charles Van Hise's *The Conservation of Natural Resources in the United States.*

Relying heavily on Pinchot's illustrations, but desperately trying to coin new and unexplosive terminology, he made a fighting plea for the "liberty of the community." His speech turned into a full-scale attack on the theory of unlimited competition and the sanctity of private property. "Community of interests" and "brotherhood of man," he recognized, were unrealistic and utopian phrases. On the other hand, if one spoke of "regulation," the "old fogies" would think it "unAmerican and dangerous." What he wanted, he said, was "co-operation." He was thinking in essentially political rather than revolutionary terms. All it amounted to really, he said, was what the Founding Fathers wanted, "the greatest good for the greatest number." [5] The patriotic appeal in this was less significant than the slogan of the Benthamite Utilitarians. And it was distinctly reminiscent of Theodore Roosevelt's resounding conservation speeches.

Privately F.D.R. soon recognized that the people of New York were not yet ready for the proposition that the State might tell an individual what to do with his own trees. His bill, which also rewrote into the conservation law a large part of the old forest statutes, was passed and approved by the Governor, but only after his replanting provisions had been stricken from it.

While conservation was a personal interest of F.D.R., in Dutchess County farm legislation was a practical political matter. Yet, strangely, it took a good deal of pushing to arouse Roosevelt's interest. For almost two years he fended off decision, while the Grange clamored for an investigation of the commission merchants who handled farm produce. He left to others the sponsorship of the study committee, and bestirred himself only when a political crisis faced him in the fall of 1912. A victim of

[5] File 1, Group IX, FDRL; *Troy Record,* March 4, 1912.

typhoid fever at the height of the campaign, he seemed faced
with almost certain defeat. He could not make the personal
canvass which had won him so many votes two years before. He
had practically no record on the farm issues which interested
his rural constituency so much. Readers of a Dutchess County
paper would have been at a loss to know whether he had represented them at all. Now he had to leave to others the job of
dramatizing "Roosevelt for the farmers." The task fell to Louis
Howe, whom the helpless candidate had chosen to carry on his
campaign. Howe sought the aid of William Church Osborn, the
Chairman of the Legislature's Sub-Committee on Markets.
Osborn obliged handsomely with an advance version of the
statute regulating commission merchants, which he planned to
have introduced in January. It proposed State licensing, bonding, and inspection of the merchants. And it included provisions
to prevent them from selling products at first-class prices while
paying the farmers for damaged goods.

Pushed into it by Howe and Osborn, F.D.R. devoted himself
energetically to agricultural reform as soon as he was able to
leave home. There was a torrent of favorable response. By
early February he had given his support also to bills for facili-
tating co-operatives, agricultural credit banks, and State aid for
the county farm bureaus. He was a little stunned by it all. Late
in December he wrote an old friend: "You will be amused to
hear that I am blossoming out as the particular friend of the
farmer!" [6] He was a little confused also. He had to defend "his"
bill against angry protests before he had had a chance to study
it. He sent Louis to consult with the Commissioner of Agriculture and brought specialists down from Albany to explain it to
his own Grangers. Even his farmers were not completely happy.
They complained of the delays and expense of inspections.
They charged that it was a Tammany trick to create new political jobs. They insisted that merchants be held accountable but
that farmers must not be exposed to the indignity of government meddling. Roosevelt patiently explained at one point:

[6] Roosevelt to Frank Loomis, December 23, 1912, Group IX, FDRL.

". . . I realize that the fault does not lie on one side, for I have heard many tales of methods used by some of our fellow-farmers in packing apple barrels by means of stove pipes, etc. . . ." [7]

Roosevelt's appointment as Chairman of the Senate Committee on Agriculture put him in a position to exploit the advantage Louis Howe had given him. Louis worked for him part time to help build up support: petitions, letters, delegations of Grangers to Albany. But while Roosevelt worked for a joint hearing of the two agricultural committees, pressure groups mobilized on both sides. When the bill was finally introduced, its opponents started an almost hysterical propaganda campaign which lasted for two months. The association of produce merchants sent out bulletins at one- to three-day intervals to legislators and their constituents. "Brother Roosevelt," they complained, would penalize the whole trade because of a few sharks. "We have plenty of law now. . . ." The bill had been written, they said, by a gang of "college professors and statisticians" who had no real understanding of the business. The whole industry would be destroyed! Foreign trade would be driven to other States. The bill would make a $10,000,000-a-year gift to the bonding companies. It would tie up "millions" of dollars in collateral and push "thousands" of small firms over the cliff. Merchants would be ruined by the reckless complaints of irresponsible "carpers." Firms would be "exterminated" for petty errors in judgment. Roosevelt was proposing nothing less than "legalized theft." [8]

The attacks produced results. Roosevelt and Osborn had to weaken the bill seriously. Then, at the crucial moment, when the amended measure was ready to be fought through the Legislature, Roosevelt left for Washington and larger goals. But he knew his reputation rode with this bill, and he fretted endlessly about it. He wanted to leave Louis Howe in a position to work for it aggressively, and he asked one of the friendly pressure groups to turn over $250 to Howe for mailing expenses, as well as a $10-a-week retainer which Roosevelt had promised him for work already done. They balked. He had to pay Howe from his

[7] Roosevelt to C. R. Vandecarr, November 19, 1912, Group IX, FDRL.
[8] Publicity Committee, Fruit and Produce Association: *Bulletin* (February 1913), Group IX, FDRL.

own pocket, while he kept up his own agitation from a distance. A compromise was finally passed, one that he felt was "only a shadow of its former self." [9] The elaborate inspection and publicity provisions had been lost in the struggle, but the young optimist soon rationalized that the bill was a "good start." He could well congratulate himself on the result of this first clash with a well-financed pressure group. But he had no success with his other farm bills.

If Dutchess County made him conscious of the farmer's plight, it left him practically oblivious to the interests of industrial labor. Roosevelt's arrival in politics happened to coincide with a rebirth of the labor issue in New York. Interest in labor legislation suddenly quickened after the murderous Triangle Factory fire in Manhattan on March 25, 1911. The horrible deaths of more than 150 women, caught in the flaming firetrap by locked doors and inadequate fire escapes, shocked the Legislature into action. The urban Democrats took the lead. Roosevelt had nothing to do with the activities of the investigating committee, which, under Frances Perkins's guidance, educated Wagner and Smith to the need for labor legislation. He voted for their safety measures, but on matters not clearly involving health or safety he was hesitant. He opposed labor boycotts, favored the use of convict labor for economic and moral reasons, gave in only reluctantly on the principle of equal pay for men and women, and showed little interest in the problems of pensions and old-age security. Under pressure from the railway unions— the only significant ones in his district—he did, however, fight hard for the controversial full-crew bills.

The most pressing labor issue was the length of the work day and week. In 1911 an attempt was made to limit women and children to nine hours a day and six days a week. This "fifty-four hour" bill became the cornerstone of the program of social legislation which was to make Tammany's Al Smith and Bob Wagner into national figures. But to this crusade the young aristocrat from Hyde Park was at first completely deaf. The bill failed in 1911; its advocates came back with new energy in

[9] Roosevelt to William Church Osborn, May 10, 1913, Group X, FDRL.

1912. Again Roosevelt was bombarded by the manufacturers of his district, but his views were beginning to change and he was now willing to vote against exempting the upstate canneries from the law. The lines in the Legislature were closely drawn on this measure. At the last minute Senate Majority Leader Wagner was able to save the bill by holding the house in session almost forcibly while two absent Senators, Chris and Tim Sullivan, were brought up the hill from the New York night boat. Their votes made possible the bare majority needed to pass the bill, but with the canneries left out. Roosevelt, and Howe for him, later boasted a prominent role in the fight, but he was at best a last-minute helper in what was essentially a victory for party discipline and for the lobbyists of reform groups.

F.D.R. did build something of a reputation as a friend of labor on one bill which was particularly suited to his situation. He joined with an Assemblyman from Buffalo to sponsor a bill for "One Day's Rest in Seven," which had been sent to him by the New York Association for Labor Legislation. This was a piece of legislation he could profitably support, a Janus-faced bill which would appeal to social progressives as a labor measure and to many conservatives for its religious connotation. In fact, its major support came from the churches of his district. Once he had agreed to sponsor the measure, he fought for it tenaciously for two sessions. But he was forced to weaken it seriously, exempting farm and railway workers and finally limiting it merely to factory labor. He kept up the pressure even after his departure from the Legislature, and the bill finally passed. It could not blot out his easy apathy on other labor bills, yet it was striking that a rural representative, with no experience in the labor movement, should be interested at all.

The progressive program grew and he grew with it, although, if anything, he was a shade conservative. There was no synthetic dogma here. He would not accept the tags of *laissez faire*, socialism, or capitalism. In practice he was a pragmatist, not a theorist. Yet he relied on a framework of principle. He insisted at every turn on the "public interest" against private concerns, and saw government as an instrument of social progress. He implicitly rejected the assumptions of Social Darwinism and groped in the direction of John Dewey's evolving Instrumentalism. The art of politics, he thought, lay not in working out vast logical theories of society, but in the practical solution of particular problems. In the fight for timber conservation he could challenge, almost incidentally, the *laissez-faire* assumptions of his fathers. But he did not question systematically the clichés of his era. He merely thought them irrelevant when real problems cried for solution. He was incapable of the hysteria which saw in every snippet of government regulation the threatening hand of conspiracy.

He did not search out his issues. He took what came his way. In 1911 Sheehan drove him to political reform. In 1912 a committee assignment put him in the front ranks of the conservation movement. Howe and Osborn made 1913 his year for agriculture. He took the canned bills, the well-publicized measures the reformers provided for him. And always his gauge was the strength of public opinion. He wasted no lances on futile causes. Sometimes his care for public opinion raised more problems than it solved. He was given to broad, dramatic challenges and threats. He delighted in letting the public know his current ideas, and in so doing, frequently trapped himself. When other politicians would have quietly assessed their forces and completed the maneuver before the public learned of it, Roosevelt, having announced his plans, had often to reverse himself publicly. Beaten often, he never admitted defeat. Even a blunder was cheerily advertised as "a step in the right direction."

If he was sometimes inconsistent, if there was little logic or pattern to his efforts, he was pre-eminently practical. The strong nucleus of Insurgents of which he dreamed could not be assembled, so he maneuvered and schemed for the "regular" support he needed to accomplish anything. Any constant course would have destroyed him in the upwind run he had chosen to make. Instead, he tacked into the wind, now sailing to port and now to starboard, hoping to make haste slowly, which seemed the only way.

4

Vote of Confidence—

1912

Your man Howe is a Corker. . . . He is
the quaintest political promoter in Amer-
ica. (Thomas Pendell,
November 18, 1912) [1]

ROOSEVELT seemed in Albany a somewhat quixotic crusader, but
he played the regular with the boys back home. He was sensitive to their demands. He caused no trouble. While he might
fight the big bosses from New York, Buffalo, and Albany, he was
as anxious as the next legislator to keep the machine sound in
his own district. Yet he was hardly a success. His record on local
legislation was generally satisfactory to his friends, but in lining
up paying jobs he was a failure. The market was crowded with
job-hungry Democrats. F.D.R.'s patronage suffered from the
fact that both the Legislature and the various State departments
were in the hands of the Tammany machine he was fighting so

[1] Group IX, FDRL.

vigorously. And Civil Service had cut down the supply of jobs. Often, as a last resort, he urged his friends to take merit examinations. The protests were raucous. One County Committeeman even threatened to quit politics because the arrival of the fat years had brought him no plums.

The Assembly election of 1911 proved a sobering lesson. Only one of the three Democratic candidates in his district won. And the trend was State-wide. To the regulars it seemed a repudiation of Insurgency. Roosevelt, with a characteristic flourish, called it the Waterloo of the bosses—Murphy had been punished for his treatment of the Insurgents. But there were many elements in the defeat, not the least of which was the fact that the Democratic majority in 1910 had been built of temporary materials: general disgust with Republican control and splits in the dominant party. Democrats could have transformed this into permanent victory only by proving themselves significantly better than the Republican leadership and by establishing a strong organization upstate. In their year of grace they had done neither.

In Roosevelt's own district, the defeats marked a permanent turning point for his prematurely optimistic party, although neither he nor his friends recognized this at the time. Columbia and Putnam counties soon became a lost cause. During 1912, F.D.R. had to face a civil war in his own county, one in which he was the focal issue. His fight against Tammany had alienated an important segment of the Poughkeepsie leadership, including Chairman Ed Perkins. Roosevelt seethed at the "silent treatment" given him by the Perkins-dominated Democratic newspapers. Publicly he forswore all personal ambition and supported Perkins successively for County Chairman and for State Committeeman. Actually, he was desperate. He sent Louis Howe to Mayor Sague for reassurances. And he wrote his wife that Tammany was out to get him. "Of course the trouble," he said, "is that Perkins has no spine but he knows now that if he listens to orders from 14th St. he will have a perfectly delightful little fight on his hands that will not stop easily or quickly." [2]

[2] Roosevelt to Eleanor Roosevelt, July 27, 1912, quoted in *Personal Letters, 1905–1928*, p. 193.

But he had one advantage. He had built a record which clouded with the Tammany taint anyone who dared oppose him.

Meanwhile Roosevelt, like other New York progressives, had been attracted by Woodrow Wilson. For F.D.R. personally, the Wilson movement offered something more challenging than the obscurity and frustrations of the professional Democrat in a Republican county. Wilson's friends had begun to probe the shifting balances of power among the various brands of New York Democrats. Herein lay Roosevelt's opportunity. In a more completely disciplined State, the young State Senator would have climbed the ladder slowly and by the rules. As for the Democratic League, nearly bankrupt financially and politically, a reform President provided its one last hope. During 1911 Wilson began to view the Independents as his best bet in New York, yet the League was not in a position to exploit this interest fully. Its Manhattan members tended to be conservative on both economics and political strategy. They deeply suspected Osborne's plans for a blatant propaganda campaign; they were not at all enthusiastic about the New Jersey Governor.

Nevertheless, George Foster Peabody, Osborne, Mayor Sague, and Franklin Roosevelt all made the pilgrimage to Trenton and Princeton at one time or another in 1911, and Roosevelt made common cause with Osborne in demanding "immediate action of some kind." [3] In December, at Buffalo, he blasted the bosses as "noxious weeds" which must be "plucked out, root and branch." [4] He went on to promise that Insurgents would hold the balance of power in the 1912 Legislature and to predict the ouster of bosses in Queens, Brooklyn, Columbia County, Albany, and Buffalo. Optimism is a small word for what he was selling. In the end it proved as false as prophecy could be. But he captured the imaginations of the anti-Tammany New York papers and he stung the boss of Albany into an hysterical counterattack. "Packy" McCabe told the reporters: "I believe the vigorous men of the party are largely responsible for this embarrassing situation because they have humored and coddled

[3] Thomas Mott Osborne to Roosevelt, November 21, 1911, Group IX, FDRL.

[4] *Poughkeepsie Daily Eagle*, December 26, 1911.

too much the little fellows, fops and cads who come as near
being political leaders as a green pea does a circus tent! Some
leaders may stand for the impudence and arrogance of these
political prudes, but I won't." [5]

After six weeks of the legislative session in which Osborne and
Howe made a last attempt to rejuvenate the Democratic League
and Roosevelt explored the possibility of co-operation with
Wagner, all three began to move steadily toward the Wilson
bandwagon and to abandon all hope of prying New York City
away from Tammany. By late February, F.D.R. was warning
that the State's delegation to the Baltimore convention would be
dominated by Murphy and was demanding a change in the
primary law which would allow district choice of delegates. By
mid-March he was convinced that Wilson was the only candidate who could win the election. Late that month he arranged
a Wilson dinner to precede the State convention at which national delegates were to be chosen. It was a failure. A State
Committee meeting was scheduled simultaneously, and the majority of the upstate leaders either ignored their invitations or
sent their polite regrets. The next day a Tammany-dominated
delegation was smoothly chosen and committed to a unit rule.
The only Wilson man among the delegates at large was Senator
James O'Gorman, whose son-in-law, Dudley Field Malone, was
an intimate advisor to the New Jersey Governor. Roosevelt
pushed Sague to his feet to make a protest and to warn that
there would be demands for polls of the New York delegation
at the Baltimore convention. But Roosevelt himself was frozen
out. Originally scheduled as an alternate from his district, he
found himself scratched from the list when the final decision
was made.

Roosevelt and Osborne immediately planned a "Wilson Conference." F.D.R. would be technically the leader but, away on a
trip to Panama during most of April and May, he would leave
the work for Osborne to do. It was to be an upstaters' group,
filled with rebels. Only George Haven Putnam remained of the
old Cleveland Democrats to grace the Conference with a trace

[5] *The New York Times,* December 25, 1911.

of tradition and Manhattan respectability. Its proceedings reflected the absence of the slow-moving elements in the old
Democratic League. Frozen out of the regular organization,
these Wilson men had discarded strategy for the battering ram.
There seemed no harm in breaking a little crockery when the
customers were unlikely to buy anyway unless a new line of
goods were offered. Reflecting Osborne's views, the resolutions
of the Conference condemned fusion and compromise as un-
thinkable "where principles . . . were involved . . . ," and
damned not only Murphy but the "big business" interests behind him.[6] There was a blunt indictment of one of the party's
senior Congressmen and of many of its heaviest contributors.
Roosevelt himself was only mildly optimistic. They could do no
harm, he felt, and they might even help a little.

The most significant move was to send organizers into every
county north of the Bronx. Three young men were dispatched
immediately after the meeting of May 13, to talk up the Wilson
movement, to sound out the sentiment of county and local organizations, and to scout the prospects for a large-scale protest
meeting. By early June they had made a superficial survey of a
large part of the State. The picture was consistently dark. But
these were merely preliminaries. The three agents had hardly
started before Louis Howe was pleading for a chance to travel
for the Conference. He wrote to Osborne: ". . . my constant
association with matters political has made me, perhaps, better
qualified to report just what can be done in the Wilson matter. . . ." He continued: "I can get an insight into just how bad
a state the League has fallen, and if anything can be done with
it and also I can test out my theory as to how final victory can
be brought about."[7]

Howe was given his chance and justified his boast that he was
"the only one you can entirely trust to handle" the business. His
attitude was flippant, bordering on the cynical, and he was
clearly anxious to impress Osborne, as he always had been. Yet
his detailed and frank reports show a kind of astute manipula-

[6] "Resolutions of the New York State Wilson Conference," Group IX,
FDRL.

[7] Howe to Osborne, May 15, 1912, "Howe Reports," Osborne Papers.

tion of factional schisms which a neophyte could never have managed.

Howe's primary job was to collect a large number of Wilson petitions to present to the Baltimore convention as evidence of the legal delegation's lack of mandate. His tactics were often earthy and devious. Over Roosevelt's signature he wrote urgent letters to his new-found recruits and he argued the value of $10 checks as token payments for workers' expenses. Where Democratic forces were weak, he managed to have the Wilson petitions run as news in Republican papers, trading on his extensive acquaintance with upstate reporters. His comments revealed his hardheaded, spade-calling attitude toward politics. For one district, he recommended the "petition game." He was quick to label a "Murph-heeler" for what he was, and he frankly sketched out the controlling interests in various communities in terms of the specific political debts involved. Where it promised results, he did not hesitate to play both wings of the party against each other.[8]

From Syracuse, Howe wrote to Osborne: "I have framed things up for a very tidy little mess here." The "mess" was a full-scale attack on the local Democratic organization from several directions at once. Howe had been able to find only one man, a new recruit from Republicanism, who was willing to circulate a Wilson petition. Once the petition was well started, however, Louis had persuaded other rebel factions who had no particular love for Wilson to support it on the sly, on the theory that it would earn the boss a "call down from Murphy because he had let his district get away from him." To cap the maneuver, Howe had "framed it up" with reporters on the leading Republican daily to "make believe it represented a demand of the voters for Wilson." They too were willing to "make things unpleasant" for the regular Democratic leadership.[9]

While Howe and other agents were scouting Wilson's upstate strength, Roosevelt was fighting off an inanely premature boom for himself for Governor and making arrangements for direct intervention at the National Convention. He planned a rally at

[8] "Howe Reports—1912," Osborne Papers.
[9] Howe to Osborne [1912], Osborne Papers.

Cooper Union on June 24. After the meeting, members of the Conference would leave for Baltimore on a special train. Barred from the formal delegation, they would act as a pressure group wherever their influence could be felt. Thus the New York Wilson boosters would be represented by two disparate groups, a small phalanx among the elected delegates led by William G. McAdoo and a large body of unofficial visitors under the guidance of Osborne and Roosevelt. This clique of outsiders did not enjoy the confidence of Wilson's managers. In fact, on the eve of their big rally the candidate himself rebuked them for their dramatic and dangerous tactics. And the Wilson Conference proved tremendously unpopular among politicians of real influence. No major speaker would agree to attend the rally. Only 150 petty politicians made the trip to the Convention to live at their own expense in dirty, muggy sleeping cars during the sweltering Baltimore heat wave. Roosevelt made the press on the first day as "the fighting reformer in the New York legislature," [1] but after a small flurry of news stories, the rebels were practically ignored. The headlines went to the regular delegation whose impenetrable discipline was widely advertised. And Murphy fought hard against Wilson to the very end.

The role played by Roosevelt and his friends was peripheral and superficial. F.D.R. attracted people and impressed them. He may have had some personal influence with certain delegates, but there is not a scrap of proof that his group produced a single vote for Wilson. They sent a petition to the Convention demanding Wilson's nomination, with the argument that the marginal State of New York could be carried only by an appeal to the Independents. They added to the noise and the size of the Wilson parade. Under Roosevelt's leadership they crashed the Clark demonstration during the tenth ballot. The sight of a rugged group of Wilsonian New Yorkers fighting it out with mobs of Clark supporters immediately after Murphy's switch to the Missouri Congressman may have had a psychological effect. But while Roosevelt and his friends were contributing to the hullabaloo, others were working frantically on the delegates to

[1] Clipping [June 24, 1912], Scrapbook, Group IX, FDRL.

prevent a landslide for Speaker Champ Clark. Although Osborne and Roosevelt may also have been active in talks with leaders of crucial delegations, such bait as the definite offer of the Vice-Presidency for Thomas R. Marshall of Indiana undoubtedly had more influence than any arguments these New York amateurs might have made.

Yet Roosevelt himself saw the Wilson nomination as a personal victory. In near-hysteria, he wired Mrs. Roosevelt: "Wilson nominated this afternoon all my plans vague splendid triumph." [2] Louis Howe, in Massachusetts with his family, hastily wrote his congratulations along with an invitation to Roosevelt to come up for some swimming. The man who only two months before had been "Mr. Roosevelt" was now "Beloved and Revered Future President." [3]

Osborne and Roosevelt immediately launched a new Wilson organization, the Empire State Democracy. Again Roosevelt became the formal leader and Howe was promised an active role in the machine. They would help Wilson; Wilson could hardly avoid helping them later. Relying on the New Jersey Governor's assurance, now six months old, that he should go on fighting, Osborne planned to "kill off the League gracefully" [4] and unite all anti-Tammany factions beneath the Wilson banner. At the first formal meeting, Roosevelt sounded the keynote with the familiar chant that Murphy had stolen the party from the real Democrats. This frank appeal to Democrats to desert their regular organizations and to present the Wilson managers with a usable anti-Murphy machine had the support of Pulitzer's *World*. But it was doomed from the start. Osborne's Manhattan allies balked at alienating Tammany unnecessarily. Montgomery Hare warned that Murphy could not refuse formal endorsement of the ticket and that nothing could compel the Boss to do more. [5]

[2] Roosevelt to Eleanor Roosevelt [July 1912], quoted in *Personal Letters, 1905–1928*, p. 192.

[3] Howe to Roosevelt [July 1912], Group IX, FDRL.

[4] Thomas Mott Osborne to John Carlisle, July 12, 1912, "Wilson Letters," Osborne Papers.

[5] Montgomery Hare to Roosevelt [July 4, 1912], Group IX, FDRL.

In fact, Murphy had already made his formal commitment. Wilson's prime advisor, Colonel Edward M. House, was counseling a middle-of-the-road strategy which would appeal mildly to Independents without alienating the machine. Worse yet, it had already become apparent that Osborne's shock troops were only a corporal's guard. Five distinct anti-Murphy groups were bidding for Wilson's favor in New York. The candidate faced a confused melee of squabbling rebels instead of the single strong machine he needed.

By mid-August the mercurial Osborne was tired out physically and financially, and ready to quit. Roosevelt himself had developed sharp misgivings. In July he had been desperately fighting for renomination in his district, spending days on the road, talking with "henchmen" in isolated places like Claverack, Copake, Bangall, and Salt Point, and fraternizing in his best election-year manner with the boys at the Hyde Park Fire House. By late August he had won unanimous renomination, despite the fact that other county nominations were sharply contested in the primaries. Suddenly he had to reconcile his independence with the discipline the campaign required. He sounded curiously like his own critics when, in his awkward acceptance speech, he told Dutchess Democrats: "I realize that in places the Democrats are not in accord with one another as they ought to be, and to have success, I believe in unity." [6]

But Roosevelt and Osborne had unleashed a rebellion they could no longer control. On September 19, the reckless Empire State Democracy promised a full anti-Murphy ticket. The next day Roosevelt, Sague, and Osborne resigned. F.D.R. rushed a letter to the local newspapers reaffirming his regularity and promising that he would never bolt the party's State ticket. Piously, he fell in with the new Wilson line. The State convention must be "open" and "fair." Roosevelt perhaps knew that Colonel House was already maneuvering for the nomination of "some unobjectionable Tammany man for Governor . . . who could not bring discredit upon the party." [7]

[6] *The New York Times,* August 25, 1912.
[7] Diary of Edward M. House (September 25, 1912), Vol. I, p. 1, Yale University Library.

Charles Francis Murphy was a master at controlling "open" conventions. In a carefully rigged pageant, his organization nominated Congressman William Sulzer. "Wild Bill" had a record of subservience to Tammany, but he talked progressivism, was dramatic, and had voted "right" when it did not interfere with the machine upon which he depended. He had wide friendships upstate, and he might be expected to win the Jewish vote away from the Progressive Party's Oscar Straus.

Anyone active in politics knew Sulzer's schizoid loyalties and his idiosyncrasies, but Murphy had met Wilson's challenge and outmatched him. Independents left the convention with the empty feeling of having been sold out by their hero. Only Osborne had the courage and the temper to shout defiance. In the convention he had branded the platform a fraud and demanded a showdown between "Woodrow Wilson and the principles of progressive Democracy . . . [and] Charles F. Murphy and the cohesive power of public plunder." When Senator Wagner had branded Osborne a bad loser who merely wanted the Governorship for himself, the angry rebel had jumped to his feet with the cry: "Liar! Liar!" [8]

Like the beaten Empire State Democracy, Roosevelt fell meekly into Sulzer's column. He had been saved by illness from the convention crisis and made his adjustment easily and quietly. But Wilson sickened the beaten rebels with his boast of the "freedom of action and of choice which the convention exercised . . . ," [9] and Osborne retired in disgust, unwilling to support a man he thought ". . . perfectly willing to put the ten commandments to a popular vote and reject them if the vote were adverse. . . ." [1]

Roosevelt meanwhile fought for his political life at home in a three-way battle against Jacob Southard—a "progressive" Republican—and George Vossler, the Bull Moose candidate. F.D.R. knew that his chances were dim, that they depended on the number of regulars who would desert him and the number

[8] Chamberlain: *There Is No Truce*, pp. 182–4.
[9] *New York Evening Post*, October 3, 1912.
[1] Thomas Mott Osborne to Thomas Ewing, Jr., October 7, 1912, "1912 State Convention Letters," Osborne Papers.

of votes the Bull Moose candidate took from him. Despite his reputation, he was in no position to bring in help from the National Committee or to promise extensive patronage, as some of his friends wanted him to do. He planned instead another extensive auto trip. And then, early in September, he came down with typhoid fever at his New York City home. He must accept defeat quietly or hire a full-time man to run the campaign. In desperation, he asked Eleanor to call Louis Howe. Louis knew rural politics, and his sympathies had been generally in the progressive camp. In his paper he had lambasted the "chess men of the great financial interests" [2] who dominated the Legislature, and he had singled out Columbia County's Lou Payn as the tool of the insurance companies. In addition, he was a Democrat who had long since developed a deep contempt for Republican progressivism. Louis had expressed it most bluntly in a skit he had written that spring for the Legislative Correspondents' Dinner in Albany. Its climax had been a purported telegram from Teddy Roosevelt: "If a crazy man hunting for an elephant sees you, throw him out. I was showing Kermit how I shot the pink rhinoceros one day . . . and got so interested I killed the beast by mistake. . . . Tell the keeper I've got a new job for him taking care of new beast I've brought back from Africa. Has ears like a donkey, trunk like the elephant, Whiskers like a Populist. . . ." [3]

Howe could be trusted to fight Bull Moose and Republican elephant alike. More important, he was out of a job. He had quit the *Herald* after Wilson's nomination under the impression that Osborne would keep him on to work for the Empire State Democracy. When Osborne had let him go, he had written to Roosevelt hysterically begging for help in getting a campaign job. He had not even been paid for the work he had already done for Wilson. Now, in response to Mrs. Roosevelt's call, Howe rushed down from Horseneck Beach. He was attracted by something more than an immediate pay envelope, for if he were to continue the career in politics for which he had been serving his seven years' apprenticeship, he must find a new sponsor.

[2] Howe to *Evening Telegram*, May 13, 1907, Personal Papers.
[3] Personal Papers.

Roosevelt offered the only practical hope for Howe's long-range political future. And Louis could never resist a campaign; he loved the excitement, the challenge of politics.

Howe's chain-smoking and generally messy habits annoyed Eleanor Roosevelt. And he showed an appalling lack of concern for clerical routines such as keeping checkbook balances clear. These things proved relatively unimportant. As Mrs. Roosevelt soon recognized, he was an "astute politician" and "a wise reader of newspapers and human beings."[4] And he proved utterly loyal.

Installing Grace, Mary, and his year-old son Hartley in a boardinghouse near Vassar College, Howe made his own head-quarters at the old Morgan House in Poughkeepsie and set to work. He followed the pattern of campaigning laid out by his boss two years before, leaving Poughkeepsie to the organization and concentrating on the rural regions. He never tried the hopeless business of replacing Roosevelt at speech-making, but played on his own strengths. He concentrated on perfecting personal contacts all over the three counties, riding about in an open car with Mrs. Howe, veiled and swathed in a heavy duster. He smoothed out quarrels, reassured the disillusioned, organized forces to bring in the voters, and advertised Roosevelt's virtues wherever he could. He wrote his boss early in the campaign: ". . . keep the temperature down and get on the job. I'm having more fun than a goat and Vote Shaver Southard will know he's been to a horse race before we're done."[5]

Howe brought a touch of inspired glibness and confidence which helped offset the candidate's absence. The full-page newspaper advertisements which he wrote carried the touch of a professional. He concentrated on three issues: agriculture, labor, and bossism. On his own initiative he sought out William Church Osborn to stir up the commission merchant issue. Osborn outlined the program only in general terms and warned him: "I can put these in shape for a Statute if you desire, but it seems to me that it would be a pity to be too specific with the

[4] Eleanor Roosevelt: *This Is My Story* (New York: Harper and Brothers; 1937), p. 192.

[5] Howe to Roosevelt [October 1912], Group IX, FDRL.

class of audience which Roosevelt will address." [6] Howe circulated the candidate's new appeal to the farmers in a letter on October 26, in which he claimed that F.D.R. had personally secured the appointment of Osborn's Commission on Foods the previous winter and that he was now prepared to fight for an agricultural marketing act with real teeth in it. Louis warned his boss: "Here is your first ad. . . . As I have pledged you in it I thought you might like to know casually what kind of a mess I was getting you into. Please *wire* o.k., if it is all right. . . . Your friend the city clerk is going to have a list of every member of the Grange for me tomorrow and we have framed up a great farmer stunt between us which I will talk over with you when I get a chance to run down. . . ." [7] The tactic was superb. A flood of letters revealed that Osborn and Howe had struck gold.

On the labor issue, Howe had less specific ammunition, but he was able to play upon the responsiveness of Roosevelt to the pressures of the railway unions, and he made personal contact with the key labor leaders in the district. He revived the issue of bossism and pressed it much more recklessly than Roosevelt had dared two years earlier. One advertisement in a Columbia County paper smeared Roosevelt's Republican opponent with the reputation of Albany and Putnam County bosses: "WHY SHOULD ANYONE VOTE FOR JOHN SOUTHARD, BOSS BARNES' HENCHMAN AND JACK YALE'S BOSOM FRIEND?" [8]

Howe was alert to every opportunity for a political play. Caught in a campaign in which religion became an issue, he loaned Roosevelt's car and chauffeur to a local cleric "to tote the archbishop up from Fishkill." [9] He played up Southard's lack of campaigning and painted gaudy word-pictures of the suffering Roosevelt dictating statements and advertisements from his sickbed against doctor's orders. He pointed out with deep concern the fact that Southard was a banker and president of a power company, and he made trips to Albany to search out jobs

[6] William Church Osborn to Howe, October 11, 1912, Group IX, FDRL.

[7] Howe to Roosevelt [October 1912], Group IX, FDRL.

[8] *Hudson Register* [October 1912], Scrapbook, Group IX, FDRL.

[9] Howe to Roosevelt [October 1912], Group IX, FDRL.

for demanding supporters. One of Howe's hasty campaign notes indicated the price tags of various important figures on the local scene. One was down for "2500 or more," apparently meaning a job. Another should get a State printing contract, another a job, and a third wanted to be a State Fair Commissioner. One wanted to be in the Labor Department at "1500 or more" and another might be happy as a Coat Room Attendant.[1] Howe and the treasurer of the hastily organized "Franklin D. Roosevelt Club" distributed between them 200 five-dollar checks to workers on or about election day. When rebellion threatened in Hyde Park, Howe scurried about and found the leading offender a job in the State Engineer's Office and then sent him up to Hudson "to work straightening out a few kickers. . . ." He told the culprit that Sague and Roosevelt were responsible for his good fortune. Louis assured his boss: "This pleased Sague very much and everyone is happy and singing the Doxology."[2] Unfortunately, however, the tie did not bind. Three days later the dissenter was asking people to vote against Roosevelt. Hyde Park remained so uncertain that one of Roosevelt's neighbors hired two Burns detectives to watch the voting booths.

Howe was an undoubted success. One enthusiastic friend wrote that he was a live wire who knew how to make the most of every asset.[3] But Louis had a vast amount of aid from Roosevelt's neighbors. F.D.R. himself kept in constant touch with the situation. He mended his fences with letters to Sulzer and to Senator Thomas Gore at National Headquarters. He was constantly informed by Howe, approved most of the advertising in advance, and advised his aide on certain knotty problems. Roosevelt insisted that his name be featured in connection with all meetings, hoping constantly that he would be able to appear at some of them. More important, he was able to call on influential friends from outside the district, Conservation Commissioner George Van Kennan, William Gorham Rice, and even Lieutenant Governor Martin Glynn. Glynn not only spoke for Roose-

[1] Group IX, FDRL.

[2] Howe to Roosevelt, October 31, 1912, Group IX, FDRL.

[3] Thomas J. Comerford to Roosevelt, November 6, 1912, Group IX, FDRL.

velt in Poughkeepsie but also intervened directly with Murphy
to keep hands off.

The expenses were heavy, and F.D.R. had to meet most of
them himself. He reported having spent nearly $1,800, includ-
ing a $50-a-week salary for Howe. The "Roosevelt Committee"
spent over $1,200 more. Relatives and friends gave him per-
sonally $1,400 of this. He was helped by the inactivity of the
Republicans; Southard did no campaigning at all in Dutchess
and Columbia. The Republican newspapers fell back on the
plea that a vote for a Republican was a vote against Murphy
and ignored Roosevelt personally. There were rumors of collusion and corruption in Putnam County. Congressman Connell
died suddenly on October 31.

When the returns rolled in, they showed an astonishing
Democratic victory. Roosevelt had won by 1,631 votes, out-
running every candidate including Wilson. Sulzer carried
F.D.R.'s district, and two new Assembly candidates won. Even
the quickly substituted candidate for Connell's Congressional
seat lost by only 427 votes. The local victory was part of a State-
wide sweep. Wilson carried New York, beating Taft by over
200,000 and Theodore Roosevelt by more than 250,000. The
Democrats rode back into control of the executive offices and
even the Legislature, with 33 of the 51 seats in the Senate and
103 of the 150 in the Assembly.

The basic fact was, of course, T.R.'s powerful third party. In
F.D.R.'s district, the Bull Moose and Republican votes, if combined, would have taken every office including his. But this did
not mean that young Roosevelt's victory was simply the acci-
dental gift of his distant cousin. Many Bull Moose votes might
have gone to the Democrats in a two-party race; many new
votes may have been attracted by the vigorous, three-way
melee. And the Progressive Party had much more appeal on
the State than on the local level. The young Senator may well
have been helped by independents who voted for Colonel Roosevelt and also for his young cousin, yet the election was a personal victory for F.D.R. He saw it as a great vote of confidence
for his Independence. For Louis Howe also it was a moment of
personal triumph. He had earned Roosevelt's deep gratitude.

Even more, he had inspired the candidate's respect, for Howe had proved not only his ability as a politician, but also his willingness to adapt to F.D.R.'s needs and personality.

After 1912 it would be impossible to think of either Roosevelt or Howe without the other. They operated as parts of one political personality. They complemented each other in strengths and weaknesses. With smiles and warmth enough for both of them, the genial Roosevelt specialized in the high-level generalization, in persuasive speeches and personal charm in public contacts, and in the broad questions of public policy. Sardonic, cynical, shrewd, and chronically suspicious and worried, Louis Howe concentrated on the secret maneuver, the manipulation of the press, the organization of personal loyalties and patronage hunger. He was a hugely enthusiastic master of this essential pettiness, for which Roosevelt had neither the patience nor the stamina. Louis proved a shrewd political analyst and, above all, an inescapable and able critic. He might often be wrong, but he was never reticent about his views. This sharp little man could deflate Roosevelt's pride, prod his negligence, and stimulate breadth of thought as no one else could. And he proved a convenient scapegoat for their mutual errors. Howe could arrange, Roosevelt confirm. Roosevelt could absorb the credit, Howe the blame. But, between themselves, they understood that they rose and fell together.

Howe met precisely the hard core of qualifications which Roosevelt demanded in his closest collaborators. He was loyal almost to a fault. He could never be a rival. He was willing to pattern his whole life around the needs of his boss. He could be trusted never to be a yes man at home, but he would seldom be indiscreet and never be treacherous abroad. He was completely devoted to hard work. And he had a keen sense of humor that delighted F.D.R. Something of a court jester, he could lighten the most disturbing crisis with a deft touch of irony or deflate the most pompous official with a poisonous thrust. And, like a court jester, he could absorb unbelievable amounts of half-humorous abuse from Roosevelt himself. Above all, Howe's position with Roosevelt grew from their mutual needs. By 1912, F.D.R. knew he must have a skilled, reliable political amanuensis to help him. And, for Louis, Roosevelt represented his last chance to escape from small-town, small-pay obscurity into the great world of public affairs.

For the first 40 years, life had not been kind to Louis Howe. If he had chosen to look backward in later times, he might have seen a peculiar fate in the defeats and discouragements which had pounded him into the kind of character who so peculiarly fitted Franklin Roosevelt's needs. But Howe was not given to looking backward. He cast into discard the memories of his early failures. The official story of young Louis Howe portrayed him as a successful Albany newsman who had given up success and prominence in his own right to become the shadowy, self-denying but all-powerful President-maker.

The real Louis Howe was something different from this stereotype of glib self-confidence. He had spent his life wandering aimlessly on the borders of New York journalism and politics. He had faced middle-age as a failure. He yearned for power, status, and prominence, but he was debt-ridden and frequently unemployed. He was chronically ill, often unhappy and discouraged. Without Franklin Roosevelt, the future held little for this wise but strange little man, who would never be satisfied with life in small-town Saratoga where the accident of fate had placed him.

5

The Making of a "Mediaeval Gnome"

. . . a young man of rare intellectual and artistic gifts.

(Edward P. Howe, *1893*) [1]

THE LITTLE BOY was five years old in 1876. He was thin, white, frail-looking, already racked with the asthmatic cough that would plague him all his life. Swathed in long underwear despite the April spring weather, he was getting his first look at New York State from the windows of a dusty day coach, speeding along the Central line from Buffalo. Fresh from the prairies of Indiana, he was amazed at the great boulders and stone walls and steep hills of the New York countryside. The older folks with him were distinguished-looking and sad. The father—Captain Edward Porter Howe—was short, portly, already balding at 34. He wore the full, black beard fashionable in the age of

[1] Quoted in Samuel T. Wiley and W. Scott Garner: *History of Saratoga County, New York . . .* (Richmond, Ind.: Greshan Publishing Company; 1893), p. 286.

Hayes and Garfield, and he wore the face of a kindly, sensitive man, although he was driven by an ambition for success that would goad him all his life. The mother was already 45. This was her second marriage, this little boy her only son. Back in Indiana she had left for the moment two older daughters by her first husband. And back in Indiana she had left a world in which Eliza Blake Ray had been a person of distinction. Her father had been the president of the Bank of Indiana and a powerful political figure in the State. Most of her ancestors, like Ed's, had come from the tough Yankee strains which had settled New England in the seventeenth century. She had had money of her own. She had been socially prominent. Nine years before, the future had seemed bright when this pleasant, ambitious, successful young war veteran had offered her the love and security for which she had yearned as a widow with two marriageable daughters. "Lide" Howe had been happy for a time.

Life in Indianapolis had seemed secure for a couple riding high on the upswing of the postwar boom. Ed was Secretary of the Franklin Insurance Company. With her money and with loans, he speculated happily with real estate, and began the construction of a downtown business block to bear their name. Their own home on North Pennsylvania Street was handsome and impressive and in the right neighborhood. They were free to spend comfortable sums on the pleasant things of life—confections, books, horses, and a handsome rig. Ed was able to invest, unproductively, in a race horse which he fondly named for his son, Prince Louis McHenry. The boy himself was carefully protected, riding about in his own pony-drawn phaeton, insulated from the rough neighborhood play, trotted to the doctor for almost daily checkups. In March, a year earlier, they had been gaily planning a European tour. It had been a responsible life too. Ed had joined Lide's Presbyterian church and had become superintendent of the Sunday School. And he had loyally supported their Democratic Party by taking his turn at the hopeless business of running for State Senator from Marion County.

But everything was different now. In less than a year their brave, substantial world had crumbled into dust as Ed found

himself dragged down in the undertow of the panic of 1873. He
had lost everything, his wife's money, his own, and thousands
of dollars borrowed from Wabash College, from banks and insurance companies, and from his church. By February 1876
there were over $16,000 in judgments against him—and no as-
sets. Now their train ride led to Saratoga Springs, where Lide's
half-sister Anna was married to the operator of a sanitarium.
Dr. Sylvester Strong was a kindly man, but for Lide and Ed
Howe it was a shattering experience to plunge, in less than a
year, from affluence to the humiliating role of poor relations in
another man's house.

Saratoga at the height of its vogue was three towns in one.
All the world knew it as a playground for the wealthy. The rich,
the important, the powerful, with their wives and daughters,
strolled along the elm-shaded sidewalks of Broadway, loafed on
the broad verandas of the great hotels or in the shingle "cottages" set in quiet dignity along Union Avenue, which stretched
out to the race track. In July and August the metropolis came
to Saratoga. There were branches of the best New York stores;
Victor Herbert himself led the orchestra at the Grand Union
Hotel. Prominent New York stars graced the summer theater.
At the races, in Richard Canfield's sumptuous casino, or bus-
tling along Broadway, one brushed shoulders with the Vander-
bilts, the Astors, with investment bankers like Spencer Trask or
politicians like young Theodore Roosevelt, but unlike Newport
and Bar Harbor, Saratoga also attracted great crowds of very
ordinary people. It was a magnet for gamblers, racing touts,
horse lovers, and professional breeders from all over the country. The race season brought the Tammany politicians in an annual migration led by Richard Croker and later by Charles
Francis Murphy.

Louis Howe was fated to grow up on the fringes of the environment which produced both Franklin Roosevelt and the
Tammany politicians with whom he tilted. In Saratoga he
would be introduced to many worlds. He would make contact
with the wealthy. He would become knowledgeable in the
ways of Richard Croker's tribe. He would be at home in the
world of reporters, gamblers, and horsemen who invaded the

town every summer. But there would be frustrations in all of this. Saratoga held out to the small-town boy all the attractions of the great cosmopolitan world beyond, with little chance of belonging to it. For Saratoga was also a third town—the sleepy, small upstate village of the permanent residents. And it was here that the Howes would have to make their way.

Their new home was Dr. Strong's Remedial Institute, one of several combined boardinghouses and sanitariums which stood on the edges of the fashionable Broadway district. Ed Howe could be of little help here, and it was many years before he could make a niche of his own in the stuffy, well-established, middle-class environment of the village. He tried free-lance writing without success. His politics did not help. It was a Republican town, and he failed in his try for a political clerkship in Albany. After a year at the boardinghouse, he managed to land a job as reporter on the local Republican newspaper, *The Saratogian*. The pay was small, the reporting petty, but he could rent a small house for his family during the six years of his new apprenticeship.

By December 1882 Ed Howe was ready for a new gamble. He bought the *Saratoga Sun*, a weekly, and turned it into a staunchly Democratic sheet to rival *The Saratogian*. It was a struggle from the start. The *Sun* boasted the "Largest Circulation of Any Paper in Saratoga County," but a weekly could live only with substantial printing business. The competition was ferocious. Often there were four or five print shops in the village alone. Official advertising went to the Republican *Saratogian*, whose editor also held down the postmastership.

The *Sun* was a pioneer in color-printing—black, white, and a rather sad, orange-tinted tomato red. And Captain Howe remained a loyal Democrat, blasting Republicans with unremitting and biased zeal, condemning the corruption in Grant's administration, and promoting religion and patriotism in his columns. During the thin years, the family moved back with the Strongs. Not until 1888, when Louis was 17, could Captain Howe afford to buy a comfortable, Victorian home for them on tree-shaded Regent Street.

While the Captain was establishing himself as spokesman for

Saratoga County Democrats, Louis was growing up in the protected atmosphere of his home and the Presbyterian church. His
half-sister Cora lived with them much of the time. "Code" and
his mother pampered the "delicate" boy incessantly. Plagued
not only by what was thought to be a serious heart condition,
by asthma and severe attacks of bronchitis, Louis also had to
wear a heavy truss from his early teens to the end of his life.
He was forced to spend much time quietly reading. Complimentary copies of new books arrived by the dozens in the Howe
home, as the Captain regularly reviewed them for the *Sun*.
For many years, books were Louis's only escape from the narrow atmosphere of his family life. He was tutored at home and
then sent across the street to attend Temple Grove Seminary
for young ladies. He and Franklin Dowd, the principal's son,
were the only boys in the school. When he did escape from the
house, it was usually under his father's careful guidance. Years
later, men who had been dipper boys at the springs would remember him riding his bicycle down Phila Street to the
print shop in the morning, while the portly, bearded Captain
stumped along behind, leaning heavily on a stout cane.

Louis proved himself a precocious youngster in a bookish
way. Coached by his admiring father, he became a prolific
writer of verse at an age when most children barely grasp the
mechanics of reading. In pallid imitation of Longfellow, Whit-
tier, and Tennyson, he ground out dozens of childishly romantic verses: "The Daisy," "The Dream," "Frost Crystals," "To
My Mother," "How the Lord Comes in Dreams," "The Angel of
Spring." Often they were printed in the *Sun* or *The Saratogian*.
His first publication was "Prayer, the Idea of a Six Year Old
Philosopher." Typical was *Angeli Custodes,* published in Christmas booklet form when he was 14.

> *'Tis midnight. On a barren hill*
> *A humble cottage stands,*
> *And through the cracks with whistle shrill*
> *The wind makes bright the dying brands.*
>
> *A care-worn, weary woman sits within,*
> *Across whose forehead Farmer Care*

Has plowed to drop the seeds of Patience in
And then forgot and left the furrows bare.

"White plumed angels" visit the praying mother and promise
to protect her infant son. After 24 verses in which they see him
safely through the Civil War, the angels finally lose their battle.
In his old age, they lift him to heaven and

. . . *teach the soul with patient care*
The mystic song that's ever sung
By blazing sun and whirling sphere.[2]

There was, perhaps, as much of the old gentleman as of Louis
in all of this. The Captain carefully guided his reading, helping
to shape his fondness for Carlyle and for Robert Louis Stevenson. As he grew into his teens, Louis became the young lion of
Saratoga literary circles. He cultivated the friendship of his father's old crony, poet Joaquin Miller. His impromptu
speeches were much admired. When he was 30, he still received letters from ladies in Nebraska and North Carolina who
fondly remembered his literary talents from their early visits to
Saratoga.

But the elder Howe was not always a successful teacher.
Louis was plagued all his life by nagging problems of grammar
and by highly unconventional spelling. More important, his
docile immersion in his parents' religion failed to grow into active church membership. By his twenties, Louis would have
cultivated an iron reserve about religious matters. Only to his
future wife could he confide that church, for him, was largely
a place of daydreams and relaxation—that religion was a "mysterious feeling" for which he hadn't found a better name.[3]

While the young Louis Howe was something of an introvert,
he was determined to conquer his shyness and physical handicaps. He played golf and tennis, sports he kept up spasmodi-
cally well into the nineteen-twenties. He fished the trout
streams about Saratoga and went with his father for trout
and pike on the lake. At 16, dressed in the brilliant red and

[2] Louis Howe: *Angeli Custodes* (privately printed; 1885). There is a
copy in the Howe Personal Papers.

[3] Howe to Grace Howe, March 6, 1899, Personal Papers.

black uniform of the Saratoga Toboggan Club, he joined the junior races down the steep slide and out over Saratoga Lake. And he bicycled incessantly in an age when the "wheel" was the most popular form of transportation. His cycling proved in the end disastrous, when he caught his toe in the spokes and spilled, face first, onto the gravel roadbed. The painful injuries were probably not half so deeply felt as the permanent, black-pitted scars which disfigured him for the rest of his life and taught him to take refuge in the boast that he was "one of the four ugliest men in the State of New York."[4]

He was always sensitive about his frail appearance and his less than handsome face, in which a rather large nose and ears were strangely married to handsomely prominent deep brown eyes, but he cultivated the active social whirl of his home town. He joined the stag lines at the big hotel dances, where young men were always at a premium, and helped with the entertainment at his uncle's establishment. He led the dances at the annual ball of the local young crowd. He dated visiting ladies, became devoted to whist, the polite card game of the era, and gave lessons in bridge and whist to earn pocket money. Like almost everyone in Saratoga, he was fascinated with racing and soon became familiar with the Casino. There is even a family tradition that he was the real inventor of Canfield, the famous solitaire game developed there. At the opposite pole of Saratoga life, Howe was one of the regulars in the Presbyterian church choir. Often it was merely a trio: soprano, alto, and Louis's tenor.

The family had planned to send Louis to college, hopefully Yale, and his formal education during his late teens was to be continued at the Saratoga Institute, a private day school. He and Frank Dowd moved over together from Temple Grove. But, whether because of his health or finances or inadequate preparation, the plans collapsed. When Louis was 18, Captain Howe, on the brink of a nervous breakdown, took his son on a long cruise to the West Indies. Louis's first experience with the sea was unpleasant. His father, who hoped to pay their ex-

[4] Earle Looker: *The American Way: F.D.R. in Action* (New York: John Day and Co.; 1933), p. 166.

penses with newspaper articles on the cruise, wrote Mrs. Howe gay accounts of the voyage in which he called his boy the "Awful Sailor" and himself the "Ancient Mariner." The old gentleman treated his 18-year-old son like a child, but Louis's enthusiasm for the tropical scenery and for his first chance at horseback riding and sea bathing delighted him. The boy collected coral and snapshots, grew his first mustache, "got the swimming stroke," and generally acted like a teen-ager, despite "Pater's" benevolent guidance. Father wrote proudly: "The Awful Sailor is universally popular and the ladies especially—both old and young—make a good deal of him." Most important, the boy's health seemed to improve. He gained five pounds and the delighted father wrote home that another trip next year would "cure him entirely." [5] Doubtless merely getting out of Saratoga had something to do with this.

Louis fell easily into his father's business. He may have started to work part-time as early as 1888, when he was 17. When he became 21, he was made co-editor and proprietor of the *Sun*. In this partnership Louis gradually took the lead as the older man became ill. Louis spent much of his time riding about the county on a bicycle or behind a horse, rounding up printing business for E. P. Howe and Son. Some of this came from the local tomato canning factories. Other steady income came from printing the advertising slogans widely distributed on buggy whip handles. Gradually Louis also worked into active reporting. Later he would pass on to younger cubs who worked for him his pride in his self-education as a journalist. You didn't have to go to college to become a newsman, he would insist. You simply had to work at it and learn by direct experience. He made a reputation among Saratoga reporters as a thorough digger for the facts. His own boast was that his success lay in knowing his beat, in sensing who would have the facts. In this hard school he developed the breezy style, the lifelong habit of relentless inquiry, and the cynical attitude toward human motivation that marked his later work. He was remembered for his humane generosity to younger reporters and

[5] Edward Porter Howe to Eliza B. Howe, January 13, 1889, Personal Papers.

saved some of them by quietly slipping them the facts they had
neglected to collect. But others recall him sourly as a tough,
nasty, hypercritical competitor. Some remembered chiefly his
"ghoulish chuckle." [6]

Louis's horizons were broadened gradually by the firm's arrangement with the *New York Herald* and the *Evening Telegram*. The Captain had supplemented his income for some
years by serving as local reporter for the *Herald*. Louis succeeded to these responsibilities, and meanwhile, in his early
twenties, he found a new outlet for his overwhelming energy.
He became almost obsessed with dramatics.

Saratoga Springs was a great town for the theater. The summer trade attracted some of the finest performances in the
country. Louis saw such stars as Otis Skinner, DeWolf Hopper,
Ada Rehan, Edwin Booth, and Lawrence Barrett. The professional performances stimulated an unusually active amateur
program. All through Louis's life in Saratoga there was at least
one local theatrical group, and he soon broke into the enchanted
circle. He could lose himself in the fascinating whirlwind of the
production, and here he could gain a special distinction for
which there was no other opportunity in his community. He
took a turn at everything. His love of the dramatic, his pleasure
at working with tools, his tremendous nervous energy, all found
an outlet here. Working long hours constructing and painting
sets, he was also thought by his friends to be something of a
genius at make-up and an innovator at lighting. He was frequently "Programme Publisher," the only man in town who
could deliver a three-color job. And he was a perfectionist,
often insisting that the whole cast travel to New York to see
how the thing was properly done. As a director he was tough,
demanding, exasperated with the clumsiness of his amateur ac-
tors.

His stage debut was in a short piece in an "Art Burlesque
Collection," staged by the Y.M.C.A. when he was 19. Soon he
was deep in the business. In May 1898 he appeared in a play
which Franklin Dowd himself had written. *The Madrigal, a*

[6] W. Axel Warn to Howe, April 17, 1914, Personal Papers.

Society Drama in Four Acts, was staged for the benefit of the local bicycle path. Howe played the low comedy roles for which he would be regularly fated despite his yearning for high drama. Against his friends' leading roles—David Stearin, "versed in oil," and Maurice de Beaufort, "versed in art"—Louis was tagged with the dual roles of Mr. Withers, "versed in horses" and Hiram Potash, "versed in higher culture." [7] Years later, old friends would remember him vividly in another play being drawn across the Town Hall stage as the Prince of Siam in a chariot harnessed to goats. The only remaining photograph of his dramatic career shows Louis and his friend, Elizabeth Gorman, in a sprightly scene beneath a parlor table. By 1900 Howe and his friends, Franklin Dowd and Clare Knapp, were running an active local club which staged regular performances for six years: *Kleptomania, Four-in-Hand, Pink Dominoes,* and *The Magistrate.*

Louis grasped every opportunity. He staged productions to entertain his uncle's guests at the sanitarium, often writing them himself. One, still remembered by a friend of New Deal days, was an operatic farce: *Lonely Lily, the Little Lu Lu of Lost Lake—or the Mutinous Sailor Thrice Thwarted in III Thwarts.*[8] As late as 1909, he directed a high-school class play, prophetically entitled *The Private Secretary.* The students, suffering from his demands for perfection, called him Louis "machinery" Howe.

While Louis was beginning to carve out a life for himself outside his home, the family business prospered. In 1891 he and his father made a long cruise to Europe and the Mediterranean. Louis returned with a trunk of mementos, among them an Arabic sword, a photo of himself on camelback before the pyramids, and an ancient altarpiece from a Spanish chapel. He also brought home the material for long descriptive essays in the *Sun* and dozens of large photographs he planned to use for illustrated lectures. By 1894 the aging Captain seemed to have won his 18-year struggle for a second success. Grover Cleve-

[7] Playbill: "The Madrigal," City Historian's File, Saratoga Public Library.

[8] George B. Hunter to Howe, July 1934, Group XXXVI, FDRL.

land's re-election in 1892 had cleared the way at last for some
Democratic patronage in the town, and Captain Howe became
postmaster. He spent much of his time at the post office now,
and Louis handled the paper and the press.

The idyl lasted only four years. Republican politicians arranged for Captain Howe's forced retirement as soon as they
could after McKinley's victory. But by now the whole cast of
Louis's life was changing as he settled down to steady court-
ship of the girl he was to marry.

6

The Harried Years

Saratoga history ought to be written by
a decade at a time to make a decent letter
full.   (Louis Howe, *May 10, 1900*) [1]

THE NOTE was brief and neatly penned: "Dear Miss Hartley. It
is such a nice day don't you want to take a walk. L. Howe." [2]

Grace Hartley did. She was bored with Strong's sanitarium
and resentful of the dominating mother who had spirited her
away from Fall River and the handsome Irishman there who
had been courting her. She found the slight, glib little reporter
a pleasant companion, though she was "not a bit impressed with
him," [3] she said many years later. But he was fun. And he was
funny. That summer of 1896 proved a gay one—dancing at the
Grand Union, long walks along the shady streets, sharing their
common interest in antiques, stamps, and dramatics. Mother
Hartley was benevolent. Louis was hardly a proper suitor for
the college-trained granddaughter of Cook Borden, one of the

---

[1] Howe to Grace Howe, May 10, 1900, Personal Papers.
[2] Howe to Grace Howe, n.d., Personal Papers.
[3] Quoted in Stiles: *Howe*, p. 15.

founders of Fall River's prosperity, but he was a useful diver-
sion and might help the girl forget her romantic Irishman.

However, Louis's campaign was serious, and it went on
through the summer and fall and winter of 1897 and into 1898.
There were constant letters, occasional trips to Fall River. By
now Mary Hartley objected, and strongly. The Bordens were
a proud family, and Grace was the special pride of a lonely
mother who guarded closely this youngest child and only
daughter. Besides, Grace had recently received a sizable be-
quest in her own name; she must be protected from impecuni-
ous fortune hunters. But Louis was in a hurry—in a hurry to get
married, in a hurry to go overseas as a war correspondent.
They met secretly in Boston that September. Later in the fall,
Grace escaped her guardian for a visit to a girl friend in Saratoga. On November 9, Grace's birthday, Louis took the train to
ride with her part way home. By the time they had reached
North Adams, he had won his battle. They hurried over into
Vermont to be married by a justice of the peace and to share
a hasty candlelit pheasant dinner in a country inn. Grace
went on to Boston the same night; Louis returned to Saratoga.

The brief Spanish war ended without Louis's getting overseas. Throughout the winter he managed occasional visits to the
carefully chaperoned Hartley home in Fall River. Mother Hartley discovered their secret, but she had planned a proper wed-
ding for her daughter and she would not be denied. Pretending
innocence all around, they took part in a formal ceremony on
May 6, 1899, at the Church of the Ascension in Fall River.
Afterward Louis took his now twice-married bride off for a
honeymoon at Virginia Beach.

Mrs. Hartley meant to start them off well despite her misgivings. She made a grand gesture when she purchased the large
house for them at 131 Phila Street. In a shady, pleasant resi-
dential district, just around the block from Captain Howe's
home and only a four-block walk from the *Sun* office, the place
was just the proper kind of base for a rising, respectable young
businessman. It was tailored for a growing family, and the
roomy backyard, with its cool circular summer house, provided
a place for children to play. Both Louis and Grace loved flowers,

and their yard was soon massed with bloom, especially in the iris season.

The house was filled with antiques and decorated with artful touches of Louis's own invention—one, a series of cut-out swallows which flew gracefully around the walls. Later he invented ornaments of real rabbit fur which proved more attractive to the moths than to his family. The house was charming and homey. But their life in Saratoga was uneasy from the start. Grace was frequently ill. Financial difficulties loomed large. Within a year Louis had mortgaged their new home in an attempt to save the family business. Grace loyally defended her husband against her mother's wrath, but she was confused and deeply disturbed by her sudden involvement in the collapse of the Howes' fortunes. Grace Howe never really adopted the Springs. Fall River was her home, and when her first baby was well on the way in 1900, she returned there to await its arrival.

Louis was left behind in Saratoga, desperately trying to earn a living for them. His daily letters recorded the mercurial state of his feelings. Some were corroded with the acid of failures and regrets. He was nearly obsessed with the sadness he had wished on his bride. Many were tender, sensitive love letters. On other days he managed gay reports on the health of the family goldfish and the garden, on the success of his whist party—total cost 25 cents' worth of cheese—or on the vagaries of the choir director or the minister. His best letters were written in church behind the protective choir curtain. Some clergymen, he insisted, "should be barred from the ministry and be compelled to become either undertakers or editors of comic papers." [4] But mostly he was bored, lonely, and worried. Grace, as lonely as he and sadly ill, poured out to her beloved "Bunting" the deep unhappiness she could not share with her family. As the fateful time approached, she sent the detailed instructions he would need if her son should survive her.

The telegram which brought, on June 4, the news of a daughter's birth restored Howe's spirits. He wired: "Don't think Ed-

[4] Howe to Grace Howe, April 15, 1900, Personal Papers.

ward would be a good name after all dear," [5] and set off hastily
to see his child and the bride whom he had all but given up
for lost. Grace and the infant Mary Howe returned briefly to
Saratoga in August. Louis busily paved the way—fixing up a
nursery, getting a gas radiator for the bathroom, checking on
the milk supply—"Jersey, Holstein or plain red cow?" [6] But
early in the fall his family was back in Fall River. Already the
pattern was developing that marked their lives for ten years.
Long vacations with grandmother became the rule, and Saratoga was their base of operations only in the racing season and
the autumn months. There was little to keep Grace there. Louis
went to Bethesda Episcopal church with her, but more often he
was out by himself, at choir practice, at play rehearsals, or drinking ale with the informal group which met weekly in the old
Worden Inn for gossip and relaxation. There was little room
for Grace in all of this. They played whist together, but Louis
was a sharp cardplayer who represented the local club at State
meetings, while Grace was always an unlucky amateur. There
were occasional picnics, fishing excursions, or trips to the races.
Eventually Louis invested in a car, and they bumped around
the country over the dusty roads. They were great auction fans.

When they were all home together, life centered around
"Kiddens," as her doting father called the baby Mary. "Pop"
proudly started a baby book, entirely of his own making. In
addition to the essential facts of his child's progress, Louis decorated it with verses for Mary:

> *The elephant scratches his painted hide*
> *And says I'm nothing but wood inside,*
> *Which really is lucky as lucky can be,*
> *For when Mistress Mary gets hold of me,*
> *If I had things inside to break,*
> *I'm afraid I'd have a stomach ache.* [7]

An amateur photographer, Louis made the "Kid" his major
subject. He took scores of pictures: jolly grandfather Howe,

[5] Howe to Grace Howe, June 4, 1900, Personal Papers.
[6] Grace Howe to Howe, July 14, 1900, Personal Papers.
[7] Howe Family Baby Book, Personal Papers.

with his white beard, bouncing the smiling baby on his knee; Mistress Mary, presiding imperiously over a small mountain of toys on her third Christmas; an infant Kiddens, smiling gaily from her wheeled highchair. And when they were separated there were fantastic letters to Mary, relaying the doings of their favorite mouse with "Impy," the monstrous black master of the Howe's feline ménage.

Louis was a fond father but often a lonely one as his family's visits to Grandma became longer and longer. There was little choice. He could hardly feed them, for he and his father were already facing disaster at the turn of the century. The Republican stranglehold on the county and the changing economics of the newspaper business were slowly pushing them into bankruptcy. They fought hard, making a last plunge with a new color press in 1899, but late that year they lost their business to creditors. Louis tried to buy a half interest for Grace and himself, but already deep in debt, he could not raise the necessary $4,000. Grace was appalled at the business of "throwing money into a bottomless pit." [8] Although Louis and his father continued to manage the newspaper briefly, Grace forecast their fate accurately when she protested about the old Captain's ways: ". . . there seems to be no hurry in him . . . I think I shall go insane with . . . lack of common sense where least expected." [9] By February 1900 they had lost the paper itself. The old Captain's career was finished. A constantly hopeful but helpless old gentleman, always expecting one more great chance, he was soon bedeviled by a variety of illnesses. The elder Howes moved in with Louis, and Louis's half-sister "Code" came with them. Grace found it impossible to accept a home with three mistresses. She was glad to flee to Fall River whenever possible. Even Louis was distressed at his parents' kindly, relentless domination of his home. At 30 years of age he found himself paying a 25-cent fine whenever he was late for dinner.

Louis fished haphazardly for a career. For a time he managed to hold on as reporter and salesman at the *Sun* for the pittance

of $10 a week, but he was fired in September 1901. He smarted
under his mother-in-law's contempt and his wife's well-meant
rebukes: "I married you for better, for worse. . . . I couldn't
go through another entire winter like last Winter. . . ." [1] Grace
was proud, and when Louis gratefully accepted an extra
week's work from the man who had just fired him, she blew up:
". . . wild horses wouldn't have forced me into it—go out on
the road and run up trade for a man who had just discharged
me! Not much!" [2] But Louis's pride was swallowed up in desperation. He was glad to take occasional assignments from his
old enemy at the *Sun* for the next six years. He saved money
from expense allowances by living in 50-cent rooms and going
without breakfast, to scrape together the train fare for an occasional trip to see Grace at Fall River. He gambled carefully
for income, and reported delightedly to his wife when he had
won $2.58 at faro, with a 15-cent limit, or had picked up two
dollars on a race. In his desperation he even practiced "doping"
the horses, hoping to try a career of bookmaking at the California tracks. But this mirage dissolved like so many others.

His mainstay and great hope was his work for the *New York
Herald*. This was part-time and petty, but it gave him a tiny
retainer throughout the year and steady work during the race
season. He picked up an occasional five-dollar bill for covering
conventions. Much of the work was dull routine, providing pictures, checking stories involving Saratoga visitors, and excavat-
ing facts for the New York staff writers. He had to be available
24 hours a day. He might be asked to check whether W. C.
Whitney had mortgaged his home to Hetty Green, whether
Canfield was forbidding women to play at the Casino, whether
a lynching had actually taken place in Washington County, or
whether Lillian Russell was really suing her ex-manager. He
wrote a weekly 600-word society letter during the season. He
spent one night driving around in the rain for hours checking
information on a New York embezzler. Another evening saw

[1] Grace Howe to Howe, September 28, 1901, and October 9, 1901,
Personal Papers.
[2] Grace Howe to Howe, October 5, 1901, Personal Papers.

him riding the trolley lines in a neighboring county from 7 p.m. until 2 a.m., and resorting to petty bribery to dig out the story on a vote-buying charge.

At the track he acted as assistant to a regular racing reporter, and he picked up extra change by doing an occasional special for other papers. Once in a great while there was a chance to write a big story. He spent much time following the leads provided by his old friend, Edgar Brackett, who was rapidly becoming an important cog in the State Republican machinery. In 1899 he went to Montreal to interview an Aguinaldo agent, who had just fled Washington. His most dramatic piece was the story of Theodore Roosevelt's harried buckboard ride down the mountains to North Creek on the night of President McKinley's death. He turned in a notable hard-hitting and thorough analysis of the "powers" behind Governor Hughes's enemies. And Hughes made more good copy for him when the Governor's anti-gambling drive closed down the Casino and the track at Saratoga.

Louis often dreamed of earning a living as a free-lance. He was delighted to sell a piece to *Town and Country* for $15, and won a $20 book-review prize from the *New York Journal*. But the first real opportunity appeared when he landed *Herald* sponsorship for a West Indian trip during the 1901-2 season. It was to be a carefree business holiday, with Grace and with her young, fun-loving cousin, Asenath Borden. Grace proved a poor sailor, but 'Senath was an ideal companion. Together she and Louis rode horseback far into the interior of Dominica searching for the Caribs, swam in the surf each day at Barbados, competed in pistol shooting at a bottle from the rail of the ship. And together they ate hearty dinners while Grace fought back seasickness in her cabin. Between November and late January they had visited most of the West Indies, ranging all the way from the Danish Islands to a river trip into the interior of British Guiana. Asenath noted in her diary the dirt, poverty, and insects of the tropical ports, but Louis spun out lurid feature stories: "The Strangest Shipyard in the World—How the Dutch Colonists of Saba built boats in a crater of a volcano and lowered them three hundred feet to the sea"; "Pirates of the Spanish

Main"; "An Interview with the High Priestess of the Voodoo
Worshippers"; "The Last of the Cannibal Caribs." He had the
good luck to have been at St. Pierre, Martinique, a few days
before it was devastated by a volcanic eruption, and his feature story on the town was a masterpiece of the passionate,
tear-jerking journalism of his day. He recalled the "rollicking,
naked diving boy . . . chanting a saucy poem," but mostly he
recalled the market, with its colorful fruit and flowers—and its
girls:

> From between the pages of my notebook as I write falls a
> bright flower, roughly pressed, its petals not yet faded, its
> leaves still green. Daphne gave me that—bronze-limbed,
> black-eyed Daphne of the market place.
>
> Perfect in form and color as were the fruits of the wicker
> tray before her, so was Daphne. La Belle Negresse of the
> market place. Around the brown gold sapodillas, Daphne
> had thrown with careless grace a tangle of brilliant tropic
> flowers. Over her own brown-gold skin, the same artist had
> draped wondrous-hued Madras, its dazzling colors rivalling
> the blossoms themselves.
>
> "Would Monsieur buy the fruits of the pauvre petite
> Daphne?" Most assuredly Monsieur would . . . and when
> Monsieur declined the change, she picked, with dainty fin-
> gers, the rarest flower on the tray and fastened it to the
> lapel of his coat.
>
> That was scarcely three weeks ago. The flower has not
> yet faded—but "pauvre petite Daphne"—I wonder where
> under the mass of molten lava "with flames everywhere,"
> lies her charred form? [3]

Louis sold his articles to McClure's syndicate for only $25 to
$30 apiece, but he managed to cover the expenses of his trip.
And in September 1902, through an appointment to the New
York editorial staff of the *Herald,* he finally managed to break
away from the limited opportunities of Saratoga. Leaving Grace
and Mary to visit in Fall River and return to Saratoga by them-

[3] *Boston Herald,* May 18, 1902.

selves, he settled briefly into boardinghouse life in Manhattan.
But his health gave out, despite "abundant cautions" from Pater
and dire warnings from Grandmother Hartley that ". . . he
does not take care of himself and needs looking after, and cannot expect to kick around like a strong man." [4] He had to return
home at the first of the year. Louis had also made enemies in
New York. When he tried to go back again, the managing editor
of the *Sun* refused to have him, and an opening on the *World*
failed to come his way. In the fall of 1904 he took a petty job
as secretary for a new Business Men's Association in Saratoga
at $15 a week. He began to feel positively "perky" about money,
promised his absent wife that he would board the old folks out
for the winter, and boasted that $60 a month was more than
they had been spending. This steady salary would keep them
while he tried his hand at short stories. In July Grace had been
begging her mother to advance the Christmas present money,
but in October Louis was happily investing $100 in an ancient
Oldsmobile.

By the fall of 1906 Howe had pleased the *Herald* editors
enough to land a more lucrative post as assistant to the staff man
in Albany during the legislative sessions. This paid $40 a week,
but only for the season, which might be as short as two months.
It fated Louis and his family to a peripatetic existence which
was to last much of their lives. Young Mary was never able to
finish out an academic year in any one school. Starting at Saratoga in the fall, she would move with her family to Albany in
January and attend St. Agnes's school briefly. The spring term
would be completed in Fall River. For Grace, the lonely life in
a furnished apartment was a dismal prospect each winter.

Louis could punch hard as a news writer, but his greatest
strength was his thorough research. In Albany he was scarcely
ever home, haunting the Press Club, the Capitol, and the hotel
hangouts of the politicians, spending hours searching old news
files and records for background material. He was not always
successful. He was sometimes reprimanded sharply by the New
York office for missing a beat, but he was adept at spotting fea-

---

[4] Edward Porter Howe to Howe, November 19, 1902, and Mary J.
Hartley to Grace Howe, January 31, 1903, Personal Papers.

tures, and he developed something of a specialty in political analysis. In a prestatistical age, he won a considerable reputation in newspaper circles with his painstaking surveys of public opinion and his predictions of election results. By the campaign of 1906 he was able to command $75 a week while he traveled upstate to analyze the trends. In 1908 he was assigned to the *Herald*'s city headquarters to help write the New York State and New York County stories for the election extras.

Despite the excitement of his unusual career, Howe faced a serious crisis by the winter of 1908. Financially broke, he was frustrated sharply by the great gap between his own achievements and the goals set by his family and environment. He did have marketable talents. Keen perception and wide interests were coupled with an energy and enthusiasm which drove him to phenomenal work loads. But he had learned to recognize his own limitations. After years of fighting a sense of inadequacy about his personal appearance, he had come to make the most of his wrinkled, prematurely old face, his thinning hair. He cast aside challenges which demanded a dynamic first impression he could never muster. He seemed sometimes to cultivate as a virtue the general impression of careless nonchalance which hung about him. He had a profound contempt for the superficial world of fashion and for neatness. Chain-smoking his inevitable Sweet Caporals, he allowed the ashes to drift day after day over his coat and trousers. He seems to have known clearly that he could sell himself only on the basis of his quick mind and nimble talent for analysis and maneuver, and he certainly knew that he must hitch his future to someone else's star. His arrangement with Thomas Mott Osborne had saved him for a moment, but by May, 1908, he was deep in gloom again.

His father's death left a vacuum he could never quite fill. Fired by Osborne, he faced actual poverty. Worse yet, heart trouble had finally driven him to see an Albany doctor who had given him two months to live. After four months in hopeless retirement at Horseneck Beach, Louis returned to Albany with complete contempt for doctors. Yet for the rest of his life the old symptoms would recur after a few months' hard work. And for four more long years, he and his family would exist on odds and ends of jobs, never certain of the future except for the brief affluence of the legislative season. There were occasional assignments from Osborne and always the dim hope of a future with him. Louis's many contacts paid off briefly for them in 1909 and 1910, when he worked for the Saratoga Springs Commission.

This new State Commission was headed by Spencer Trask, a wealthy Saratogan whom Louis had known for years. With Trask's support and Osborne's, Louis was chosen to study the European watering places in the spring of 1910. He ghost-wrote reports for Trask. He and Grace traveled gaily for months in Europe. Louis's own report gave the Commission the evidence it needed to prove that public operation could be profitable, and it helped win the appropriations which made possible, within three years, the State's control of all the 163 springs in the resort town. But there were elements of tragedy here, as in almost everything Louis had touched. Trask was killed in a railway accident, traveling on a ticket Louis had bought for himself. And Louis and Grace returned from Europe, both desperately ill. Louis's mother had died while they were away, a sad and aged invalid, yearning for her absent son and dead husband. Louis's heart condition was critical again. Grace herself was nauseously ill, discouraged and worried.

The future took on new proportions when their son was born in November 1910. And then there came a shock so rude and deeply felt that neither Grace nor Louis Howe could bring themselves to talk about it later. Within a week the child was dead of meningitis. Louis tempered the bitterness of those sad weeks when he wrote years later the lonely page in the "Baby Book" for Edward Hartley Howe:

. . . There are no records of the little brother's life set down within this book because they are written in our hearts and nothing can ever wipe them out.[5]

[5] Personal Papers.

· I I ·

A TEAM
IN THE MAKING

7

>>->>->>->>->>->>->>->>

Fighting Tammany
with Its Own Weapons

Of course, I know you will appreciate
that I must consider myself free at any
time to express my own views. . . .
(Franklin D. Roosevelt, *June 15, 1914*) [1]

BOTH Roosevelt and Howe looked forward sadly to the 1913 Legislature. Franklin wrote an old friend: "We are going to have a very interesting, though somewhat difficult session . . . and I fear it will take a good deal of tact and tenacity to come out of it with a whole skin." [2] Independence might be good politics in the Hudson Valley, but it was of little value to him in a Legislature filled with enemies.

Louis's situation was even more uneasy. For two years he and his family had scraped along on odds and ends of income. There had been good pay during the legislative sessions and occasional unexpected bonuses like the Roosevelt campaign the

---

[1] Roosevelt to William Church Osborn, June 15, 1914, Group X, FDRL.
[2] Roosevelt to Henry deForest Baldwin, November 19, 1912, Group IX, FDRL.

previous fall. Yet there had been much work without pay—for Wilson and for Roosevelt's marketing bill—long periods when only Mother Hartley's cool hospitality had saved them. There had been one bright moment—the birth in November 1911 of the son they had so much wanted. Young Hartley Edward brought gaiety to Louis's household. Now there was all the more reason to search desperately for security. But neither of his patrons seemed to offer much future. Osborne was finished in politics, and Roosevelt seemed caught in a blind alley.

Neither Franklin nor Louis had much enthusiasm for the new Democratic Governor. "Wild Bill" Sulzer was good at the gestures of popular Democracy. He renamed the Executive Mansion "Peoples' House"; he ostentatiously refused a carriage and walked to his inauguration through the crowded streets. But his judgment proved poor as he recklessly insisted on an investigation of Tammany corruption. It was a job that had discouraged Hughes and broken Dix. It would destroy Sulzer, for he came with dirty hands to the task of exposing the machine that had made him. Roosevelt agreed with Sulzer on legislation more frequently than not, although he was never forced to take sides. During January and February he spent much of his time trying to build his influence with the new national administration. While Louis rode herd on the Commission Merchant Bill, Franklin joined other pilgrims on the road to Trenton to press the claims of the New York Independents. He managed on his first trip to miss his return train, and ended up riding back to Princeton with Wilson himself. He may even have had a chance to hint at his own hopes for a Washington job.

On Inauguration Day the clouds broke for the uncertain young rebel when Josephus Daniels offered him the post of Assistant Secretary of the Navy. Roosevelt was being considered in other quarters too; McAdoo had sounded him out on a Treasury Department post during the train ride to Washington. But there was no hesitation when Daniels accosted him that morning in the Willard Hotel. This was a lifetime's chance to escape from the frustrations of local politics. He was like a romantic boy in his love for the Navy, and he was deeply conscious of the unfolding parallel between his career and that of the redoubtable Teddy, who had once sat at this Navy desk. To be a junior cabinet member after only three years in politics was practically unprecedented. For the administration, the matter was not so easily settled. Independents welcomed the appointment of this young "boss-eater," but Senator O'Gorman was unenthusiastic. He had to be assured first that he would control the New York patronage. Wilson was still straddling the warring factions, and the Republican press sourly predicted that Tammany would get the appointments while Roosevelt's nomination would camouflage the deal.

O'Gorman had good reason to be worried, for Roosevelt set out at once to mobilize Federal patronage for the upstate anti-Tammany Democrats. Recognizing that his own stature and the whole upstate movement would be assessed by the extent to which Wilson helped his "friends" and punished the "machines," F.D.R. intended to make himself the Federal spokesman for New York and see to it that the right friends were helped.

His first move was to send for Louis Howe: "Dear Ludwig, . . . Here is the dope. Secretary—$2,000—Expect you April 1, with a new uniform." [3] The clever little reporter was superbly fitted to handle the political side of Roosevelt's office. The job of private secretary suited precisely Howe's love of conspiracy and his particular talents, and it offered him the kind of security in his chosen profession of which he could hardly have dreamed. He would have a larger steady income than he had ever had before. He protested—half jokingly—"It will break me." [4] But he was delighted and so was his family. Meanwhile, Roosevelt kept in his office his predecessor's secretary, Charles H. McCarthy, who could steer them through the first difficult months. Always jealous of each other, the two secretaries nevertheless served Roosevelt well. Eventually McCarthy would succeed to Howe's position when Louis moved up to become Special Assistant at $3,000 a year, and would come to handle many political matters with a finesse which smacked of Howe's teaching.

[3] Roosevelt to Howe, March 19, 1913, Personal Papers.
[4] Howe to Roosevelt, March 23, 1913, Group XXXVI, FDRL.

The relationship between Roosevelt and Howe was an easy one from the start. Louis later confessed that on his arrival in Washington he knew so little that he was reduced to "blotting Franklin's signature." [5] Within a few weeks, however, they had established the intimate collaboration which was to characterize the rest of their lives together. Howe was the doorkeeper, adept in excuses and explanations that kept his boss's office free of nuisance callers. But he was never really a secretary or clerk. Fellow planner and conspirator, he was close to all of Roosevelt's decisions on policy and managed large areas of their work specifically delegated to him. In fact, there were two Assistant Secretaries as long as this team occupied the office.

Theirs was the close rapport of men who understood each other, who shared a bumptious zest for the humor of life. Howe could absorb almost unbelievable amounts of good-natured badgering from Roosevelt. And he could give as well as take. When the careless Howe was tardy in forwarding some important construction plans, Roosevelt wired him: "Plans have come. Please have your arm cauterized at once." [6] Later F.D.R. would write to his wife about Louis: "I shall try to clean up his back work for him! He is so wonderful on the big things that he lets the routine slide." [7] Roosevelt's personal letters to Louis suggested the relaxed familiarity of intimate friendship. "*Lieber Ludwig*," he would write, "*Hier bin ich, mit grosse gesundheit und vergnügen*—which being translated means, I feel like a whole flock of fighting cocks," and he would happily close, "our best to youse all, F.D.R." [8]

Their first job was to fight clear of Sulzer. When the Legislature staged a Tammany-inspired impeachment proceeding, Roosevelt carefully remained aloof. He did nothing to help the man who in March he had hoped would "prove . . . to have a spine and also a brain to make it move in the right direc-

[5] Quoted in Stiles: *Howe*, p. 42.

[6] [Roosevelt] to Howe, September 23, 1913, Personal Papers.

[7] Roosevelt to Eleanor Roosevelt [September 14, 1916], quoted in *Personal Letters, 1905–1928*, p. 329.

[8] Roosevelt to Howe, n.d., Personal Papers.

tion." [9] Louis betrayed their joint contempt for the hapless blunderer: "I see where he says the truth will prevail. Such being the case, where would he get off?" [1]

Keeping out of the Albany mess proved easy. But getting control of the Federal patronage was a monumental task. Roosevelt was not nearly so prominent as were a number of other New York Democrats. Senator O'Gorman spoke for Tammany, but he also occupied a key legislative position, as did the New York Congressional delegation which was largely sensitive to regular leadership back home. Representative John Fitzgerald as Chairman of the Ways and Means Committee was not only a leading agent for the New York machine, but also a major potential stumbling block for the administration's program. In naval matters Roosevelt would be especially aware of the situation that made Wilson often choose to give in on appointments rather than jeopardize important legislation. There was also rivalry among the squabbling, back-biting progressive groups. McAdoo clearly led the parade of influence here. Edward M. House played a decisive, although hidden, role in many decisions. Dudley Field Malone exploited to the hilt his sponsorship by his father-in-law, Senator O'Gorman, and by Colonel House. George Foster Peabody, Lewis Antisdale of Rochester, Bernard Baruch, Governor Martin Glynn, and John Purroy Mitchel, Mayor of New York with Wilson's aid in 1913, all maneuvered uneasily to control appointments. Joseph Tumulty, close to the President at all times, kept a wary eye on New York and worked tirelessly to maintain the regulars' support of the administration. Wilson's position was unenviable. He could not rely safely on any single rebel group, nor could he conscientiously turn to Tammany. He avoided any clear policy. The several government departments were turned into competing factions, compounding the mess with their frequently conflicting judgments on the political balances involved.

This confusion worked in Roosevelt's favor. He had a fighting chance to become the official representative for large numbers of anti-boss Democrats with whom he had worked in State

[9] Roosevelt to Frederick Northrup, March 28, 1913, Group IX, FDRL.
[1] Howe to Roosevelt, June 30, 1913, Group X, FDRL.

politics. Roosevelt and Howe soon found themselves in agreement on basic strategy. Every plea for influence was to be
treated seriously. No letter went unanswered unless it demanded Roosevelt's public commitment to some hopeless splin-
ter cause. He and Howe would spend months maneuvering in
Washington to fill a small country postmastership for a friend,
all the time keeping up a barrage of correspondence to assure
the people involved of their interest and activity. Where the
desired position was unavailable, painstaking diplomatic negotiations would be undertaken to find a substitute job and to
sell the applicant on the outcome. In areas where the Independents were weak, Louis went out of his way to spot available jobs and round up suitable candidates. Gradually he and
Roosevelt built up the impression that the Office of the Assistant
Secretary of the Navy was the place for an Independent to
write for help in Washington. Even appeals from political enemies were received politely and handled smoothly. In such
cases they generally replied with lugubrious letters about the
extent to which rascally Republicans had tied up patronage
with Civil Service regulations. In emergencies Howe could always explain in some detail how "wicked" it would be for Roosevelt to use his official position to do purely political favors.
No enemy received a line from Roosevelt's office that could be
used to pin political favoritism on him or give an excuse for
umbrage.

This tough, clever aide and his smooth, sometimes devious,
boss worked together so closely that it is difficult to distinguish
where Howe's role ended and Roosevelt's began. Yet the basic
outlines of their division of labor are clear. Roosevelt handled
directly the occasional approaches to persons of cabinet status
or to Wilson himself. Meanwhile, and more effectively, Louis
developed a network of personal contacts with secretaries and
junior officials which made it possible for him to operate in
patronage matters before they reached crisis proportions. At
first he was Roosevelt's leg man. Within a year, however, he
was virtually in command of the routine political maneuvering.
Most of the letters which went out to their New York constituents were drafted by Howe for Roosevelt's signature. People

back home soon recognized that the best way to enlist Roosevelt's influence was to talk with Louis. Though much of the work was done by personal calls and telephone, 43 boxes of patronage papers remain as mute testimony to Howe's hard work in implementing the political tactics upon which he and Roosevelt had agreed.

Louis had a particular advantage in the Post Office Department, where there were no New Yorkers of considerable rank. He won the confidence of Daniel C. Roper, the Assistant Postmaster General, who faced the staggering job of processing candidates for 60,000 offices. The glib New Yorker impressed Roper with his intimate knowledge of State politics and his apparent sincerity about raising the quality of the postmasters. As Louis built his network of upstate advisors, his hold on the postmasterships tightened gradually. He was able from the first to hold up "unfit" candidates. By April 1914 Roper was positively "chummy," and Louis was receiving lists of openings and candidates in advance. While he pigeonholed the unacceptable ones, he rounded up suitable candidates for Roosevelt to sponsor. Often he knew more about the Congressionally sponsored candidates than the Congressmen themselves did. When the Civil Service was involved, Howe was given lists of the first three men on the examinations. If the first name was not acceptable to them, he and Roosevelt contacted their local leaders to build up a dossier against the unlucky person. In time the Post Office Department even furnished information on the types of reasons they would accept for refusing appointments to the top men on the lists. Thus armed, Louis could often place his own cohorts in jobs, even if they had come out third in the competition. Such difficulties as arose were innate in the very lack of organization which F.D.R. was trying to remedy. All too often they found they had backed the wrong man or that they could not decide between two equally attractive but mutually incompatible leaders. The delicate problem of bucking Tammany Congressmen without bringing on open warfare also impeded their plans. In addition, all of this maneuvering was done in open defiance of both Postmaster General Albert Burleson and Senator O'Gorman. These old warhorses had little sympathy with attempts to double-cross the regulars in Congress.

Typical of the tedious negotiations was the case in July 1914 of the Postmasterships at New Rochelle and Ossining. Here Roosevelt hoped to break the power of the Westchester County Chairman. Howe first arranged to have local supporters force Congressman Taylor to submit a compromise candidate, and suggested to the Department that the nomination be approved, although the Congressman obviously hoped that it would be turned down. This move backfired when the Independents themselves objected. The Congressman was resentful, and Roosevelt was reduced for the rest of the year to merely blocking the organization at every turn. He even wrote to Burleson that nomination of the official candidate ". . . would seriously hurt the chances of Congressman Taylor for reelection, even though Taylor himself may believe otherwise." [2] In June 1914 he shifted tactics, recklessly warning Taylor that his man could not be nominated and holding up two other appointments to convince him. The deadlock continued, and in January 1915 Roosevelt was still trying to arrange adequate backing for Independent candidates.

This was as good an example as any of the single-minded tenacity with which Roosevelt and Howe pursued their objectives and of their audacious and versatile tactics. Sincere in their aim to provide high-quality appointments, they were, nevertheless, realistic and uninhibited in their use of the machine's own methods to beat the bosses. By midsummer of 1914 the results were mixed. Several of the lesser appointments were so weakly contested that Roper simply inquired whom they wanted. But in some cities, Binghamton for example, politics were so complex that F.D.R. had to negotiate for over a year before it was safe to act. He lost some battles when Burleson ruled that no appointment would be held up if a Congressman certified that it was essential to his re-election. There were occasional complaints about "mutton-headed" moves by his own friends. But Roosevelt's position was being recognized; some of

[2] Roosevelt to Albert C. Burleson, May 24, 1914, Group X, "Patronage," FDRL.

his agents were basking in his reflected power. The recognition was sometimes embarrassing, and Roosevelt wrote one frustrated politician: "I supposed you had more common sense than to believe in the silly newspaper stories that I am the official patronage dispenser for the State of New York. . . ." [3]

They soon learned the serious limits of their influence. One was their lack of a machine back home. After an early failure, Howe wrote his boss: "If his friends had spent a little more money on carfare and a little less on postage stamps . . . he might have gotten along better." [4] Another was their lack of friends in crucial posts. The Post Office Department might be helpful, but they soon learned not to tangle with William Jennings Bryan's State Department. Attorney General James McReynolds proved a tough and hostile roadblock to their influence in the Justice Department. But their chief problem was Colonel Edward M. House, whose influence was immense and who played a devious, erratic, an often unpredictable game. They lost a crucial test in the Collectorship of the Port of New York because of House's maneuvering. This was the key patronage post, and they thought they had House's agreement that it would go to Sague. But quietly, and with no warning to F.D.R., House dumped Mayor Sague on what was little more than a whim.

The most nagging problem was the complicated situation in New York City which had plagued Osborne's Democratic League throughout its entire life. In the municipal campaign of 1913 House pushed Wilson into guarded support of an anti-Tammany fusion ticket. The administration's position pleased no one. Tammany was incensed and its Congressmen reacted sharply against the President. Senator O'Gorman was temporarily appeased with an important appointment for his son-in-law, but his bitterness deepened into open warfare by the spring of 1914. The progressives were no happier. The fusion ticket had won, under the leadership of dynamic young John Purroy Mitchel. But Wilson's support had been so guarded that pro-

---

[3] Roosevelt to William H. Martin, July 23, 1914, Group X, "Patronage," FDRL.

[4] Howe to Roosevelt, June 30, 1913, Group X, FDRL.

gressives felt they had been left on a limb by the administration. Worse yet, New York appointments were being held up generally in the confusion. Faithful Democrats of all stripes were being penalized while their neighbors in more disciplined States received speedy consideration. National officials were swamped with irate letters of protest from the New York progressives. Some of this could be put down to personal pique. Louis Howe became so disgusted with one malcontent that he sent his letters to Roosevelt labeled "another attack of hysterics." [5] But the administration had reasons to worry. The elections of 1914 would be an important test of strength. Without some degree of unity, Democrats could hardly carry New York.

Roosevelt himself was worried, for his own Dutchess County was more tangled than most in the web of indecision. The bitter subsurface struggle which his own independence had complicated now broke into an open rift over the Poughkeepsie postmastership. He had to block the candidate of the county organization and support John Townsend, upon whom his own friends had finally agreed. He was ranged squarely against both O'Gorman and the regulars in his own district. A showdown was essential. If Roosevelt could not bring national aid to his own beleaguered friends, his fight for an upstate machine was lost. He finally went to the President personally and arranged an interim appointment for Townsend, despite the sharp opposition of the Senator, who had pigeonholed the nomination in committee.

But the victory was hollow for both Roosevelt and the party. O'Gorman took personal offense; it was nearly two years before the recess appointment could be confirmed. Worse yet, Roosevelt felt constrained to allow other organization candidates in the county to go unopposed and thus alienated close friends. Probably the most unfortunate result was the construction put upon the business by *The New York Times,* which implied that Poughkeepsie had been the major test case and that all New York appointments would require Roosevelt's approval in the future. An explosion was inevitable. Dutchess County

[5] Howe to Roosevelt, June 30, 1913, Group X, FDRL.

leader Edward Perkins resigned from the State Committee in protest against Roosevelt's "high-handed" methods. Perkins's Poughkeepsie newspaper burst out with a vicious charge that Roosevelt was really moved by hatred of the Irish and of Catholics in general. And the New York *Telegraph* advised Wilson to drop the reformers and depend upon his faithful Congressmen. Roosevelt yearned for an open fight, but his advisors calmed him down. He explained politely to all who would listen that the President made appointments and that he was personally much too busy with the Navy to interfere.

The fight in Dutchess County, like that all over the State, had been successful enough to split the party, but not enough to heal it again under progressive leadership. And that leadership itself was badly divided. Early in the fall of 1913 Colonel House had launched his own fuzzy plan to build a completely new upstate organization around the new Governor, Martin H. Glynn. House's agents bungled badly; by pandering to an old regular like Glynn, they drove away many of the rebellious Independents of the upstate counties. And Roosevelt bristled over this challenge to his own plan. He had been working quietly; now he proposed a conference in Washington between the President and the upstate leaders, and he vigorously collected ammunition to prove to Wilson that the President had had strong support among the Independents before Baltimore. House ignored the young conspirator. On the first of the year Roosevelt carried his fight to the press in a symposium on Democratic organization published in the *Evening Post* and carefully staged by Louis Howe. Here Roosevelt proclaimed that the only way to victory was to regain the confidence of the Independents "above the Bronx," who had backed the Democracy in 1912 and deserted it in 1913. All good Democrats, he said, must use the primary to sweep their own districts clean of Tammany's "upstate satellites and stop worrying about the other fellow's area." [6]

The real situation belied this bit of verbal bravado. Wilson still favored compromise to buy legislative co-operation. House

[6] *New York Evening Post*, January 15, 1914.

had failed to convert Glynn to progressivism; Roosevelt had failed to cut the Governor out. Early in February Glynn himself took the initiative in a much-publicized conference with the President, National Chairman McCombs, and Roosevelt. The published accounts smacked of a deal. The Tammany issue was avoided; the task of electing pro-Wilson Committeemen would be left to the rank and file in the primaries—a devious way of keeping the organizations intact. There was also a hint that Roosevelt and Glynn would support McCombs for the Senate. Roosevelt was outraged. That night he sent a telegram to the Tilden Memorial Dinner in New York: "The democratic leaders of our State can find no better example to follow today than that of Samuel J. Tilden, a man who was big enough to realize that there can be no compromise with criminals, no alliances with grafters. . . ." [7] It was an attack on Glynn. For Roosevelt, there would be no pacification of the bosses. But he could go no farther. He pleaded with McAdoo, who could or would do nothing. He asked, and was refused, Wilson's permission to write an article for the *World* on the New York situation. And the irate protests of the upstaters continued. Even Frank Polk, who in January had been privy to Colonel House's plans, now wrote to Roosevelt: "We are completely at sea as to what the national administration have in their minds. . . ." [8]

Meanwhile, the problem of upstate patronage was embarrassing Roosevelt seriously. He lost the fight to control the appointment of the Federal Attorney for the northern district, although he jumped on the bandwagon at the right moment to garner what credit he could. In the difficult Buffalo area, his enemies landed the postmastership. His own agents were squabbling badly, and the press played up his spotty record.

While F.D.R. hesitated in confusion, Colonel House tried to pick up the pieces of his broken strategy. Thinking it was necessary at last for Wilson to strike out at Tammany, House advised one of his aides to repudiate Glynn and his cohorts in a public statement. The President snapped back angrily at House's breach of discipline. Two weeks later House undertook to bring

[7] *New York Herald,* February 10, 1914.
[8] Frank Polk to Roosevelt, March 16, 1914, Group X, FDRL.

all New York patronage under his own control, with the advice
of McAdoo, McReynolds, and Burleson. He thought he had the
President's approval, but when they submitted certain anti-
Tammany appointments, Wilson refused to send them to the
Senate. O'Gorman's suggestions were also being shelved. The
disgusted Senator threatened to issue a public statement early
in June disclaiming all responsibility for New York appointments.

Now Roosevelt threw off, at last, the restraints under which
he had struggled. He wrote recklessly to even casual acquaintances in opposition to Glynn. He collected material to be used
against the Governor. He predicted defeat in November and
snapped that the party's promises would not matter if it ran unfit candidates. He insisted only that the platform be brief, with
all "the usual flub-dub and empty phrases cut out entirely." [9]
His petulant pessimism was well founded. A rival "Anti-Boss
Democratic League" had suddenly appeared. Colonel House
had departed for Europe on more urgent Presidential business,
leaving the New York Democrats to stew without his stirring.
McAdoo was appalled at the confusion, and House's old friend,
Thomas Gregory, complained: ". . . that n.g. bunch of progressives is hard to regulate." [1] The party faced the 1914 election in
New York hopelessly and bitterly divided.

[9] Roosevelt to H. V. Bruce, July 17, 1914, Group X, FDRL.
[1] Thomas W. Gregory to [Edward M. House], June 15, 1914, Papers of
Edward M. House, Yale University Library.

8

Collapse of the

Progressive Dream

*I cannot bear the thought of the election
of a reactionary Republican to the Senate,
and . . . I have decided to get into the
race, and hope it will help the Democracy
of the State to get on its feet again and in
line with the best thought of the Democracy of the Nation.*

(Franklin D. Roosevelt
to Randall Saunders, *August 14, 1914*) [1]

As ROOSEVELT rushed back and forth from Washington to New
York that humid summer of 1914, he faced a crisis which could
grind his hopes to dust. If he and his friends sat quietly, the
regular organizations would sweep the primaries and kill their
rebellion in its cradle. If they challenged the machines in the
primaries, they might be crushed. Roosevelt and Howe knew
better than most that the anti-boss machinery they had been

[1] Group X, FDRL.

drafting was hardly off the drawing boards. Some finished sections of it were grinding with friction. Yet McAdoo in Washington and many of their agents upstate clamored for action. The President stayed ominously aloof. Roosevelt was the most hesitant of the conspirators, but he was tempted. A rebel victory in the primaries might give Wilson the necessary assurance to put him on their side. There were times when nothing seemed worse than the muddled ambiguity of the moment.

It was a summer of hysteria, of mad maneuver in many directions. Roosevelt tagged along in July with a plot to field a combined Independent-Democrat and Bull Moose ticket. He joined with McAdoo and others in the bitter subterranean fight for Wilson's support; they were blocked by Tumulty and John Fitzgerald. They approached Theodore Roosevelt, but he would have none of their ambitious plans. Finally in despair they challenged Tammany to a duel in the Democratic primaries. The gubernatorial candidate would be John Hennessy, Sulzer's flashy investigator of State corruption. Roosevelt would run for the Senate. He thought he had Wilson's approval, but if he did, it was of little help. The President was carefully guarded, to allow him to leave the ship whenever it should start to sink.

F.D.R. had to make this decision alone. McAdoo pushed in one direction; Josephus Daniels hauled in the other. He had the counsel of neither Louis Howe nor his wife. They were both on vacation, and he had time merely to warn them by telegram before the word of his candidacy was formally released. He did not expect to win. To one close friend he frankly confessed: "I protested, but finally agreed to be the goat . . . at least this ticket will cause a pretty distinct line-up and will give the voters their first opportunity to express themselves." [2] He was caught in the web of his own commitments. Having talked rebellion, he could hardly refuse to lead the march on the barricades. Having fought for the direct primary as a tool for ousting Murphy, he could hardly allow the machinery to rust. His public announcement asked the voters to make a clear choice between "reactionary politics and politicians" and "intelligent progress

[2] Roosevelt to Montgomery Hare, August 31, 1914, Group X, "Senatorial Primary," FDRL.

and honest administration in Government." But he hedged a bit: "I have always fought within party lines and I seek the regular and legal means of giving these voters a chance." [3] Privately, he apologized to his friends: "I'm doing this, old top, only thro' a stern sense of duty!" [4] To Louis he protested feebly: ". . . my senses have not yet left me." [5]

He departed at once to join his family at Campobello, where they awaited the birth of Franklin, Jr. Howe rushed back to Washington to keep the desk clear and get the campaign rolling. The headquarters in Manhattan was put in charge of Stuart Gibboney, McAdoo's chief political aide. Louis himself was busy with the "campaign of publicity" [6] they had planned. He "nosed around" New York to renew old contacts with the press and discovered that John P. Gavit of the *Post* was ready to forgive Roosevelt his youth and fall into line. He had long known Gavit and throughout the spring had been feeding him material on the progressives' plans in New York. Howe warmed the friendship of another editor by promising to make "a personal matter" out of a postal appointment in which the man was interested. He merrily wrote his boss: ". . . the office will not be vacant until July 23, 1915, so we get the moral effect of helping him without complicating matters." [7]

Louis had a great respect for the power of the rural press, but he thought its co-operation could be enlisted cheaply. He wrote Roosevelt: "You see I was a country newspaperman myself and I know how pleased your rural editor is when he gets a personal, friendly letter from a high official in Washington subscribing to his paper." Roosevelt did not agree to the expensive proposal to subscribe to all upstate journals, but Louis went ahead with letters to all Democratic and Independent editors upstate, requesting their advertising rates: ". . . some of them

[3] Press Release, Group X, "Senatorial Primary," FDRL.

[4] Roosevelt to Dudley [Field Malone], n.d., Group X, "Senatorial Primary," FDRL.

[5] Roosevelt to Howe, August 13, 1914, Group X, FDRL.

[6] Roosevelt to Gustavus Rogers, August 24, 1914, Group X, "Senatorial Primary," FDRL.

[7] Howe to Roosevelt, August 18, 1914, Group XXXVI, FDRL.

will surely fall for it, and others will print your letter because it
booms newspaper advertising. . . . Do you get me Steve?" [8]
Later he captured free space with a boiler-plate item distributed to the upstate press, featuring in reckless headlines the
claim that the national administration supported Roosevelt.
Playing on his close friendships with labor leaders, Louis wan-
gled endorsements from union locals in the Navy Yards and persuaded the International union presidents with whom he had
worked to send copies out to locals all over the State. He himself mailed out thousands of handbills containing the resolutions
of endorsement, to be distributed at factory gates. He blundered badly, however, when he allowed unfriendly New York
newspapers to catch him in the act of distributing printed materials without the union label.

Meanwhile, Louis worked closely with Gibboney in using
patronage to buttress their campaign, and Burleson seemed co-
operative. But the Postmaster General was soon under attack
from Congressmen and finally laid down the law to the conspirators. As Howe described it to Roosevelt: "Burleson . . .
told him that he would appoint a Digger Indian to any post
office that Gibboney recommended where there was no Democratic Congressman, but that he would be blankety-blanked if
he would go over the Congressmen's heads at this time." [9]

Roosevelt's biggest worry, as he awaited the birth of his son
at Campobello, was the character of his opponent in the primaries. He and his friends had purposely stolen the march to
throw "the burden of proof on the other attorney." [1] They may
have hoped that Murphy would let them have the nomination by default. When a New York paper announced that
Glynn had come out for F.D.R., Louis wrote his boss: "This
would be funny and a bit awkward, but I can see the politics
of it— The truth is that they haven't a thing to say against you
and no one is anxious to bell the cat—particularly when they

[8] Howe to Roosevelt, n.d., Group XXXVI, FDRL.
[9] Howe to Roosevelt, August 28, 1914, Group X, "Senatorial Primary,"
FDRL.
[1] Roosevelt to Dudley Field Malone, August 14, 1914, Group X, "Senatorial Primary," FDRL.

have an idea that the President occasionally pats him on the back, calls him 'pretty pussy' and gives him a nice saucer of warm patronage milk to drink!" [2]

Barring the miracle of an unopposed race, Roosevelt hoped fervently that the boss would nominate Hearst. When the pre-primary conference met at Saratoga, however, Murphy tried to make it as innocuous as possible. Taking the high ground that the conference could not agree on nominations in violation of the spirit of the direct primary, the boss left the road clear for quiet agreement later among the leaders and hinted that there would be no strong endorsement of Wilson in the platform. Howe was immediately alarmed and ghosted a tart, incisive telegram to State Chairman William Church Osborn. Approved by McAdoo and Gibboney, and authorized finally by Roosevelt, this wire was released: "Every man at conference should be made to stand squarely for or against support of administration's policies in order that Democratic voters may endorse or repudiate their leadership at the primaries. Please make this public." [3] Osborn tried to bury it, but it had already been released to the press by Gibboney. Roosevelt, who complained of Osborn, "He's getting quite canny in his old age," [4] was pleased with the maneuver. Howe went farther with an "under the ribs dig" at Osborn by releasing the wire to the papers a second time with a covering letter to put the State Chairman in the worst possible light. [5]

During the rest of August the situation deteriorated rapidly. Petitions for the insurgent ticket came in slowly. Money troubles loomed large, and Howe warned his boss that he'd better start building a personal campaign chest. F.D.R.'s long vacation did not help; his busy little aide begged him to "shoot a few holes"

[2] Howe to Roosevelt, August 24, 1914, Group XXXVI, FDRL.

[3] Howe to Roosevelt, August 25, 1914, Group X, "Senatorial Primary," FDRL.

[4] Roosevelt to Stuart Gibboney, August 28, 1914, Group X, "Senatorial Primary," FDRL.

[5] Howe to Roosevelt, August 29, 1914, Group X, "Senatorial Primary," FDRL.

in the Republican platform to keep himself in the newspapers. Louis pleaded desperately for administration support, but Wilson, House, and McAdoo all played it safe with silence. Worse yet, Tumulty was busily building a patronage backfire, and two prominent Tammany appointments were announced. Despite Roosevelt's personal pleas to them, some of his own officeholders upstate remained quiet. One postmaster wrote that he was following the sentiment of his district and would oppose Hennessy. Howe demanded "sudden and swift reprisal" for a "traitor" like this.[6] There were limits to insurgency; even Independents had a place for discipline.

F.D.R. further complicated the confusion by failing to appear at the formal opening of the campaign at Cooper Union on September 2. Irritated beyond control, Louis demanded a "ringing message"[7] of explanation with some good excuse for his absence, like a Red Cross fund-raising meeting. The press immediately assumed that Roosevelt was beginning to pull away from the encumbrance of the blundering Hennessy and would run as an Independent. As late as September 8, no definite plans had been made for Roosevelt's personal campaign, except for the scheduling of an initial rally in Buffalo. Worse yet, Murphy had finally picked just the kind of unobjectionable candidate F.D.R. most feared. The choice of James W. Gerard, a wealthy Tammany stalwart who happened also to be Wilson's Ambassador to Berlin, was a stroke of the kind of genius that had made the boss's reputation.

Roosevelt's situation was all but hopeless. He gradually developed the thesis that Gerard's nomination was merely a Murphy trick to take advantage of the Wilson administration's record. He professed shock at the thought that Murphy would "drag an Ambassador away from his duties in order to have him serve as a respectable head for a bad ticket."[8] The slogan, re-

[6] [Howe] to Stuart Gibboney, August 28, 1914, Group X, "Senatorial Primary," FDRL.

[7] Howe to Roosevelt, September 2, 1914, Group X, "Senatorial Primary," FDRL.

[8] *Utica Press*, September 8, 1914.

peated over and over again, claimed of Gerard: "If he is a fit man for Senator . . . he will decline to run."[9] While Roosevelt challenged him publicly, Bryan and McAdoo mustered all their influence to persuade Gerard to withdraw. Caught behind the British blockade with inadequate information, the Ambassador oscillated between the pressures from Washington and those from New York, fruitlessly sought direction from the President through Colonel House, and finally announced his acceptance. He then proceeded to put himself in the strongest possible position by ignoring the whole campaign and elaborately tending to his nation's business in Berlin.

On September 11 Roosevelt opened his crusade against the Tammany boss who "regards a platform as a green-goods circular to delude honest voters" into approving his choice of racketeers.[1] The tour of upstate counties went on for 17 vigorous days, but inefficient planning sent him the length of the State four times. The campaign was spotty, with vast areas left untouched. Even in the counties he reached, Roosevelt was handicapped by lack of preparation and by youth and inexperience. He impressed many as a friendly, rather vague, but scarcely great, young man. The campaigners ran out of money and had to resort to personal loans, which were not finally paid until lawsuits had begun to accumulate against the candidates in 1916.

The core of the campaign was Roosevelt's attempt to convince voters that Gerard would be Murphy's tool, but his voice re-echoed in an empty room. Despite the ardent attempts to make Gerard seem unpatriotic if he campaigned, a silent tool of Murphy if he didn't, the Ambassador remained remotely mute. Roosevelt soon began to appear as a frantic and unstable terrier, nipping at the heels of a dignified administration workhorse. He finally lost control and blurted to reporters that it was "difficult to campaign against moles."[2] And there was constant peril that his attacks would backfire. F.D.R. might be so effective in

[9] Roosevelt to A. C. Dwyer, September 16, 1914, Group X, "Senatorial Primary," FDRL.

[1] *The New York Times*, September 11, 1914.

[2] *Rome Sentinel*, September 25, 1914.

his attacks on his own party that he would be disowned as
a traitor by the rank and file. It was hard to believe that he
would repudiate Tammany's support if he won the primary.
He finally resorted to the uneasy rationalization that he wanted
"revolution" to get rid of the "tyrants" and then harmony, once
the Democrats had been "set free." [3] The fundamentally good
Tammany he did not oppose. The completely evil Murphy
he would fight to the end.

Preoccupied with this fight against the personal Devil of the
New York Democracy, Roosevelt did little with the issues. Hennessy stumped the State with violent charges of corruption
against Governor Glynn and every boss from Buffalo to Manhattan, but he soon became a liability upstate, where his broad
brogue and flashy manner made his rural audiences think him
a clown. Wilson's neutrality merely added to the confusion. The
President hurt the jerry-built rebel campaign when he publicly
repudiated the statements of Dudley Malone and privately ordered this last national administration spokesman off the stump.
On the other hand, the appointment of a pro-Roosevelt man
to the Collectorship at Syracuse was widely resented by the
regulars. As the tempo of F.D.R.'s campaign increased, his cautious patronage beneficiaries read the signs from Washington
and moved quietly away from him. When the primaries were
held on September 28, both Hennessy and Roosevelt were
buried in an avalanche.

Roosevelt made the most of it with the claim that upstate
"autonomy" had been achieved. But his claims could withstand
little study. Although he carried a bare majority of the upstate
counties, many of them were politically insignificant, with
total Democratic votes of only 200 or 300. The only urban area
which went for Roosevelt was Rochester, long dominated by
the effective Wilsonian machine of Lewis Antisdale. Except in
Buffalo, where the vote was reasonably competitive, no upstate
boss had suffered even a shallow dent in his armor. Even in
the counties which he won, F.D.R.'s margin was slim, and
Gerard had carried a number of distinctly rural regions. The

[3] *Olean Herald,* September 12, 1914.

simple fact was that Roosevelt and McAdoo had attempted a premature test of a rickety organization.

For the national administration, the situation was only mildly difficult. Colonel House, active again now that the war was over, began to play the peacemaker, treating McAdoo and Roosevelt with benevolent tolerance. Like other rebels, Roosevelt had no choice except to endorse Gerard. While Hennessy finished his career with a straightforward bolt from the party and many of the Independents assuaged their feelings by spiking Glynn and running a separate "Anti-Murphy Democrats for Gerard" slate, Roosevelt dove frantically into the last week of the campaign with eight speeches supporting all the regular candidates.

The thumping Republican victory in New York forced administration leaders to a reappraisal. McAdoo, Malone, and House retreated precipitously. Burleson demanded an end to amateurs, but Roosevelt rebounded with a ringing charge that the Democrats had been repudiated because of their subservience to Murphy. The day after the primary, Howe had planned an elaborate campaign of letter writing to reassure the upstate supporters and to outline a new method of financing with emphasis on local spending in the counties. Roosevelt didn't have the money to manage this, but he and Howe did begin to renew their contacts and especially to develop more reliable information on the loyalties of their supposed friends. Incorrigibly optimistic, F.D.R. insisted that the sound tactic was to force the administration off the fence, and he renewed at once his attempts to swing patronage in his direction. But now he was almost alone in Washington.

His only effective channel of influence remained the Post Office Department, where Roper gave him practically full sway in the innumerable fourth-class appointments. He was aided by Burleson's anxiety to clean up these petty matters; many of the offices had remained for two full years in Republican hands after the Wilson sweep of 1912. Roper agreed to a system in which F.D.R. was given priority over even Congressmen, if he could demonstrate the support of a single county Committeeman. Meanwhile, Howe worked out with O'Gorman's secretary an agreement to accept county committee endorsement of the appointments, unless special circumstances arose. Louis was swamped throughout the winter with a mass of maneuvering on these petty positions, yet they provided little real strength. In the process, Roosevelt became deeply involved in violating the spirit of the Civil Service, though he had been for years an ardent public defender of the idea. To disappointed applicants, he emphasized his strict adherence to the system. Nevertheless, to a close friend Howe confided: ". . . the Post Office Department has made it very clear to us that if we want some other man they will take a pretty thin excuse provided it comes from us for the appointment." [4] The fact that Roosevelt crossed out "pretty thin" and substituted "good" when he signed the letter scarcely veiled his feelings on the matter. Where they lost a battle, Roosevelt was anxious to have successful candidates informed that they had really had his endorsement all along.

Howe knew this was a "delicate game." He carefully briefed his friends that ". . . all conversations should be merely along the lines that you are anxious to make recommendations as to who is best fitted for the office *in the hope that* the Post Office Department will be favorably impressed . . . it will be perfectly obvious who has the ear of the Department without playing our own trumpet about it. . . ." [5] Publicly Roosevelt insisted that he was merely trying to straighten out the tangled mess into which the post offices had fallen. Privately, however, Howe protested: "I am having all kinds of trouble keeping the brakes on. . . . The Postmaster General has a mad desire to get everything cleaned up. . . ." [6] The criteria Roosevelt set for appointees were simply friendliness to Wilson and to the Independents. From the outside, the fight looked suspiciously like a struggle to replace Murphy with F.D.R. When candidates had taken the anti-Murphy oath and had been instructed to work with certain key upstate leaders, Roosevelt felt compelled to

[4] Roosevelt to Louis M. Antisdale, December 7, 1914, Group X, FDRL.
[5] Ibid.
[6] Roosevelt to Louis M. Antisdale, April 1, 1915, Group X, FDRL.

explain in elaborate detail that he wanted them "to come to a friendly understanding" and not to think of it as "boss rule." [7]

By midwinter, appointments to the smaller offices were moving through in large numbers with Roosevelt's endorsements, and F.D.R. was impressed by the number of upstate politicians who were making pilgrimages to the Navy Department with "olive branches." [8] But optimism was premature. The rewards were not enough to weld the upstaters together, and grumbling continued. Indiscretions and betrayal of confidence got F.D.R. in trouble with Burleson. Sometimes their local contacts misled Howe and Roosevelt. Once they found themselves supporting a county chairman who was illegally holding down a Civil Service job, and in another situation, they were tricked into taking sides in a nasty religious vendetta. Howe sometimes found his devious tactics resented on the local scene; he often misjudged and got involved in a fight they could not win.

By the summer of 1915 it was all over. The jobs had been largely filled. The collapse of Roosevelt's dream of an independent organization followed inexorably. Even Louis could not ignore their failure. He had known all along that ". . . two thirds of them would slide back at the prospect of any loaves and fishes from the other side." [9] Now, he saw their hard-won allies slip from their control. During the summer, Roosevelt's personal concern with Congressional support for naval legislation made him see at last the need for discipline as the 1916 election approached. His anti-Murphy tirades died away to mild reminders that Independents, as well as regulars, must be appeased if real unity were to be gained. He suddenly discovered that the Tammany issue was simply a ghost, kept alive by Republican propagandists. His capitulation came too late, however, and his influence in New York decreased rapidly. By the spring of 1916 he was powerless to prevent the election of a State Chairman he bitterly opposed. Because of Glynn's intervention, he lost the Hudson postmastership in his own district to a personal enemy. Only in Dutchess did his influence remain

[7] Roosevelt to Antisdale, January 23, 1914, Group X, FDRL.
[8] Roosevelt to Antisdale, December 15, 1914, Group X, FDRL.
[9] Roosevelt to Antisdale, February 2, 1915, Group X, FDRL.

uncontested, but his home territory was rapidly slipping into its old Republican ways.

Convinced at last, Roosevelt retreated into naval business and kept scrupulously free of all political maneuvers in the spring and summer of 1916. He spiked all attempts to boom him as a State candidate or to revive the rebellion. Wilson's choice of Governor Glynn as keynoter for the National Convention sealed the marriage of the national administration and the regulars in New York. At the St. Louis convention, Roosevelt played the colorless role of administration supporter in the ranks. Colonel House planned for New York a machine campaign, relying heavily on the ward workers to bring out the votes. Roosevelt would have preferred a strong stand on the domestic legislative program rather than the emphasis on foreign policy Wilson dictated. He was sad over the vacuous platitudes of the State platform. He was also powerless. Harmony was carried so far that McAdoo and Roosevelt were kept out of New York at the direct request of the regular organization. Roosevelt and Howe kept up a stream of letters to the old Wilson leaders upstate. Some of these must have been surprised to hear that the things they had fought for had "in large measure, been adopted as the general policies of the Democratic Party in this State." [1]

The policy of harmony failed in New York. The party ran poorly in the city; Wilson lost the State by nearly 110,000 votes. It became popular to blame Murphy for knifing the ticket, but equally important had been Governor Hughes's popularity, controversies over the Federal Reserve and the Adamson Eight-Hour Day laws, and the general disgust with Wilson's lack of policy on political matters. Roosevelt was incorrigible. He professed to see in Wilson's narrow victory the "debacle of plutocracy"; [2] he boasted inordinately of the mild increase in the Democratic vote in his own upstate region.

Between the campaigns of 1916 and 1918 Roosevelt practi-

[1] N. G. Schlamm to Chester Platt, October 19, 1916, Papers of Chester C. Platt, 1915–17, Regional History Collection, Cornell University, Ithaca, N.Y.

[2] Roosevelt to David Gray, November 24, 1916, Group X, FDRL.

cally ignored New York politics. The increasing naval work pre-occupied him, while political starvation and personal disillusionment were forcing his old allies into private life. Roosevelt could hardly avoid the same fate himself when it came time to leave Washington unless he could work out a future with the Tammany machine he had fought so long. Once the United States entered the war, the press of official business gave him an excuse for avoiding the fruitless vendettas he had helped create upstate. The last gasp of independence came not from F.D.R.'s farmer-Democrats, but from the New York City reformers who had left him hanging in 1914.

The repudiation of the youthful progressives was nowhere better symbolized than in the diverse fates of Dudley Field Malone and Franklin D. Roosevelt. Malone's disgust was boundless. He supported the Socialist ticket and ended his career. Roosevelt, similarly frustrated, set about to join the enemy. After several months of political retirement, during which he patched up his relationship with Glynn, he dramatically signaled the new era by appearing in 1917 as the featured speaker at the Wigwam's most sacred ceremonial, the Fourth of July celebration. Many a rural rebel must have squirmed at the pictures of Murphy and Roosevelt celebrating the peace.

Roosevelt's new role as a regular almost immediately proved embarrassing. Early in 1918 elaborate plans were laid by some of his erstwhile enemies to run him for Governor. The plot thickened as it became apparent that Murphy might co-operate. Roosevelt recognized that the timing was wrong, that he was too young, that the party was unlikely to win anyway, and he worked as hard as he ever had in politics to avoid this nomination. Instructing his friends to make sure that this boom was squelched, he declared publicly for William Church Osborn and toyed privately with the nomination of Al Smith. Then, at the height of the crisis, he left on a two months' inspection tour of naval facilities in war-torn Europe. Before sailing, he appealed personally to the President to prevent a political draft. Knowing that Wilson had expressed some interest in young Roosevelt's candidacy, F.D.R. warned him that he would leave his war job only for active duty at the front.

By July 17, a week before the party conference, all upstate candidates had been eliminated and the county leaders had agreed on Al Smith, despite Murphy's reluctance to lose the advantage of having an upstate candidate. Now the much-sought party unity was strangely shattered by Church Osborn. A moderate peacemaker during the active struggles, Osborn decided to make a primary fight for the Governorship long after all hope of insurgency had been killed. Roosevelt faced exactly the same dilemma he had put to Osborn in 1914, but the situation was doubly embarrassing because of F.D.R.'s public commitment to him. Louis Howe, as caretaker of Roosevelt's fortunes, was distraught at the possibility that his boss might have to choose between two old associates, when he had already put into writing his support of the evident loser. Consulting both Wilson and Daniels, Louis relayed his warning to F.D.R. through Mrs. Roosevelt: ". . . it seems wise to maintain a masterly absence until after the primaries. After they have had a few days to cool down, Mr. Roosevelt can unequivocally come out for the man selected by the voters of the primaries, and no one will feel hurt." [3] Roosevelt, as it turned out, kept free of entanglements almost too effectively. Returning on September 19, a bed-ridden victim of the flu, he issued his "unequivocal statement" for Smith as soon as the polls had closed.

With women voting for the first time, with Tammany trying its first gubernatorial candidate from its own stables, with the incumbent Governor Whitman displaying a creditable record, Smith's chances seemed slim. Wilson muddied the situation with his ill-advised appeal for a Democratic Congress to support him at the peace conference. Nevertheless, Smith won by a narrow margin, a token of the party's reunion and a sign that the anti-boss issue was dead.

For the remainder of the Wilson administration, Roosevelt and Howe played dispiritedly at the complex game of patronage. Howe made a bid through Smith's secretary for an alliance between Roosevelt and the Governor to control appointments in the State, but he was ignored. The one project that interested

[3] Howe to Eleanor Roosevelt, August 17, 1918, Group XXXVI, FDRL.

them greatly was an abortive attempt to finance a new Democratic newspaper in Poughkeepsie. As the administration drew to a close, the young crusader, who had come to Washington to build a progressive machine, faced political extinction. His own plans smashed, he was not yet securely accepted by the regulars. If he had a future, it would depend on his national reputation and not on his actual power in his home State.

9

In the Navy

I get my fingers into about everything,
and there's no law against it. . . .
(Franklin D. Roosevelt [*1913*]) [1]

POLITICS might be intriguing and critically important, but for
Roosevelt the Navy itself was sheer joy. Amateur sailor, student
of naval lore, he had astounding self-confidence and a deep
admiration for naval personnel. He bounded into the work in
March 1913 with unparalleled enthusiasm. Within days he
wrote to Louis: "This is real work down here, but I love it." [2]
After signing a pile of papers which he could not possibly
understand, he boasted: "I am baptized, confirmed, sworn in,
vaccinated—and somewhat at sea! . . . but I hope luck will
keep me out of jail." And to his mother: "I will have to work like
a new turbine to master this job—but it will be done if it takes
all summer." [3] He had no real doubts. Within two days he was

---

[1] Quoted in Josephus Daniels: *The Wilson Era: Years of War and After,
1917–1923* (Chapel Hill: University of North Carolina Press; 1946), p.
253.

[2] Roosevelt to Howe, March 19, 1913, Personal Papers.

[3] Roosevelt to Sara Delano Roosevelt, March 17, 1913, quoted in
Personal Letters, 1905–1928, p. 199.

"beginning to catch on." [4] By July he was singeing the admirals' beards with an insolent note from his clerk: "The Assistant Secretary desires that the first paragraph of the attached letter to Congressman O'Brien be rewritten in such a way that he will be able to understand what is meant." [5]

Unhappily the specific responsibilities of the Assistant Secretary were not those which fitted his particular interests. He would have been happiest to concern himself with the great matters of strategy and command, but his chief responsibilities, as the department's business officer, were procurement, supply, civilian personnel, and the management of the sprawling shore installations. Roosevelt came to it innocent of management experience of any kind. Fortunately he did not have to set up new procedures. The Navy had developed its own tradition-bound processes for managing the 65,000 men of its establishment and the $140,000,000 of its annual appropriations. Roosevelt would have to rely heavily on the Bureau of Yards and Docks, the Bureau of Naval Personnel, and the Bureau of Supply and Accounts, each with an admiral or captain in command and each with its regular staff of civilians and yeomen to process the interminable paper work. His major task would be to breathe new life into the ancient establishment.

Both he and Howe had brought from the outside a mild impatience with the seniority-dominated system of preferment, a civilian's disgust with elaborate red tape, and a positive anger at inefficiency and "nice-lady" admirals. Howe would save as a permanent memento the file copy of an order F.D.R. had to sign to approve the expenditure of $3.50 for the burial of a dead cow at Mare Island. Roosevelt expressed his pent-up fury at the constrictions of tradition with his brief note to Daniels: "I beg to report that I have just signed a requisition (with 4 copies attached) calling for the purchase of 8 carpet tacks." Daniels's mild rejoinder—"Why this wanton extravagance? I am sure that

[4] Roosevelt to Eleanor Roosevelt, March 19, 1913, quoted in *Personal Letters, 1905–1928*, p. 200.

[5] Roosevelt: "Memorandum to Bureau of Supply and Accounts," July 14, 1913, Group X, FDRL.

two would suffice" [6]—hinted at the paternal tolerance with which the Secretary treated his ebullient young assistant.

In fact, the relationship between Daniels and Roosevelt remained difficult throughout the whole eight years of the Wilson era. Roosevelt was often impatient, frequently angry, sometimes insubordinate. Daniels seemed to him a misfit in the job; it was no secret that F.D.R. had fond private hopes that his mentor would someday resign and leave the leadership to him. Daniels was unfamiliar with the naval customs in which Roosevelt took so much pride. He hardly knew a jib from a mainsail, a barnacle from a binnacle. A prohibitionist, he seemed for a time more interested in drying up the Navy than in building it. And personally, the two men were worlds apart. F.D.R. found Washington doors open to him at once, his passport the Roosevelt and Delano names, his Harvard and Groton friendships. He never met Daniels in the whirl of this social life. The temperate, deeply religious North Carolina editor was the product of an environment Roosevelt never quite learned to understand. He was a rural, middle-class outlander, a representative of the vast common heart of America which the eastern aristocracy had not yet recognized. Daniels and his charming wife could entertain with grace, when they must. But they conscientiously avoided the distractions of social Washington.

Daniels had invaluable qualities which Roosevelt came only slowly to appreciate. He knew a good deal more about politics and government than did his young assistant. He was completely at home with the southern and western rural leaders who dominated the Congressional committees. He even looked like them, with his black felt hat, his black suit and shoestring tie, his mussed hair and general air of small-town nonchalance. And he had humility, something Roosevelt was never to display conspicuously. He was a bit dowdy beside the smooth, athletic giant who towered over him in the office. But he knew how to handle Roosevelt effectively. He made it clear that authority lay at his desk, while he gave his brash assistant much leeway,

[6] Roosevelt to Josephus Daniels, n.d., quoted in *Personal Letters, 1905–1928*, p. 299.

overlooked even conspiracy against himself, and refused to crush the impertinent eagerness which made Roosevelt a useful prod to his own caution. He kept his temper when Franklin played the dirtiest trick in the bureaucrat's book—a demanding letter to Daniels, with a carbon copy to the President himself. Daniels had been warned by Elihu Root: "Whenever a Roosevelt rides, he wishes to ride in front." [7] But he managed to make effective use of this driver, without ever letting him have the reins for long.

Roosevelt made things as difficult as possible. His best opportunities came when Daniels was out of town and, as Acting Secretary, he could wield power. He reminded the newsmen that, when Teddy had been in command, things had happened. He allowed the impression to build up that he was more friendly to the staff than was Daniels, that things could be done when F.D.R. was "Acting" that would never be managed otherwise. But Roosevelt was more careful with realities than he was with impressions. The things he expedited on his days of power were likely to be matters which Daniels would eventually have supported.

Neither Roosevelt nor Daniels stuck to the official division of labor. The Secretary intervened constantly in controversial matters within Franklin's bailiwick. F.D.R. himself boasted: "I get my fingers into about everything, and there's no law against it." Nevertheless, he was careful to dissociate himself from Daniels's less popular policies. He was glad to avoid involvement in his superior's drying up of the officers' wine mess, although he privately confided to Howe: "That wine order is . . . on the whole absolutely right. It took nerve to do it, but tho the Secy will be unpopular in a small circle for a while, it will pay in the end." [8]

There was considerably more than personality conflict and ambition in their differences. Roosevelt was instinctively a Big Navy man. Daniels kept a firm weather eye on the civilian con-

[7] Quoted in Josephus Daniels: The Wilson Era: Years of Peace—1910–1917 (Chapel Hill: University of North Carolina Press; 1944), p. 127.

[8] Roosevelt to Howe, April 9 [?], Personal Papers.

cerns of peace and budget. He soon alienated the powerful
Navy League and betrayed, on occasion, a Jeffersonian suspicion of naval growth. Daniels wanted a Navy to fit the President's neutralism and anti-imperialism. F.D.R. wanted a Navy
ready for action in a world of power politics, and he thought his
role was to educate Daniels, Wilson, and the public on the
realities of power. He had romantic attachments to the Big
Navy; he could become nearly lyric over battleship reviews:
"The big gray fellows were magnificent as they went past, with
all hands at the rail, and I only wish a hundred thousand people
could have seen them." [9] He was never so happy as when he
boarded a flagship and received the booming salute due his
official position. He had also been schooled in the writings of
Admiral Alfred T. Mahan and the actions of Theodore Roosevelt. He had no doubts.

As soon as he reached Washington, Roosevelt was adopted by
the Big Navy crowd. Before he had come to know Daniels at
all well, he was chummy with Colonel Charles McCawley,
whom the Secretary would shortly try to oust from his apparently permanent Washington post, and with Henry Cabot
Lodge and his son-in-law, Augustus Gardiner, Republican sales-
men for naval power, and with news-baron and Chicago-
imperialist Robert McCormick. Within the department Roosevelt found kindred spirits in Admirals Bradley Fiske and William
Fullam, both of whom would be moved out by Daniels as soon
as he could manage it. Roosevelt was torn constantly between
cautious administration policy and his own drive for naval expansion. He supported the admirals' position in the Japanese scare
of 1913 and was overruled by the President himself. When
Wilson's Mexican policy of "watchful waiting" reached the crisis
stage, he let himself go with bombastic promises of action which
neither Daniels nor Wilson appreciated.

Absent in California, F.D.R. heard of the incident at Vera
Cruz from the newspapers and from Howe's letters and wires.
Admiral Henry T. Mayo had pitched the country close to war
with his ultimatum demanding a Mexican salute to the Ameri-

[9] Roosevelt to Eleanor Roosevelt, October 26, 1913, quoted in *Personal
Letters, 1905–1928*, p. 211.

can flag in apology for the arrest of a naval shore party. Howe wrote Roosevelt dryly: "I'm afraid Mayo is not a good watchful waiter!" [1] F.D.R. almost seemed to welcome the break. He was a dynamo of frenzied activity as he doubled the working force at a new radio station in San Diego, warned naval officers to be ready for action, issued orders for the reception of Marines from the East Coast, and suggested to reporters: "We're not looking for trouble, but we're ready for anything." [2] California newspapers announced that F.D.R. was personally directing the mobilization on the West Coast. When news came that Congress had approved the use of force, Roosevelt cheered the decision and singled out for scorn the handful who had voted against Wilson in the House: "Just thirty-seven by their vote put themselves in their true character. . . . These men cannot see above party affairs." [3]

But Daniels had no intention of leaving the Pacific to his bellicose assistant. He had given Roosevelt no special authority, had merely asked him for "suggestions." Now he called him home. The order was flattering, kindly, and relayed as a suggestion through Howe. But it was firm: "Secretary says that as most of the vessels on the west coast will be down in Mexico and in view of the great help you can be to him in Washington, he thinks the wise course is for you to return as originally planned." [4] During the long train trip home, Roosevelt issued statements to the press which left the general impression that full-scale war was imminent. Meanwhile the President had accepted the mediation of Argentina, Brazil, and Chile, and the lid was clamped abruptly on F.D.R.'s impetuous outbursts.

Nevertheless, Roosevelt had made Navy capital of the trip. He was worried that the fleet might be split between the two oceans once the Panama Canal was finished. On the West Coast

[1] Howe to Roosevelt, April 11, 1914, quoted in Frank Freidel: *Franklin D. Roosevelt: the Apprenticeship* (Boston: Little, Brown and Co., 1952), p. 229.

[2] *Portland Oregonian,* April 20, 1914.

[3] *Seattle Post-Intelligencer,* April 21, 1914.

[4] Howe to Roosevelt, April 22, 1914, Group X, FDRL.

he had blasted the idea again and again. And now, in the early summer of 1914, he quietly maneuvered within the department for a completely new cruiser force to alternate with the main fleet from the Atlantic to the Pacific as strategy demanded. He quietly bypassed Daniels in the process, and arranged public support for his position by both Admiral Mahan and Theodore Roosevelt.

He pushed for action in the Caribbean when crises in Haiti and Santo Domingo brought threats of European intervention. As Acting Secretary, he conferred with Wilson and Secretary of State Bryan and sent a force of Marines for more "watchful waiting" at Guantanamo Bay. Unlike Daniels, F.D.R. had no misgivings about his nation's role in the area. With uncritical enthusiasm he supported the activities of his Marines in Haiti, which they finally occupied in July 1915. As late as 1919 he would urge that the Navy quietly take title to one of the few remaining unused islands of the Caribbean and then slip the matter over on Congress later with a casual reference to it in an appropriation bill.

The outbreak of the war in Europe on July 28, 1914, polarized the conflict between Roosevelt and his boss. During the growing crisis, the exasperated F.D.R. had exploded to his wife that there had been much work but "without resulting . . . in any *definite* policy of construction." [5] Now he betrayed in his letters both a sheer hopelessness about Daniels and a callow preoccupation with his own importance. He complained of the "idealistic nonsense" of "dear good people like W.J.B. and J.D.," who had "as much conception of what a general European war means as Elliott has of higher mathematics." Daniels refused his and the admirals' pleas to move the battleship fleet up from the Caribbean. "Some fine day the State Department will want the *moral* backing of a 'fleet in being'!" protested Roosevelt, "and it *won't* be there." [6] He confided to Eleanor in a hectic note: "I am *run-*

[5] Roosevelt to Eleanor Roosevelt, July 19, 1914, quoted in *Personal Letters, 1905–1928*, p. 229.

[6] Roosevelt to Eleanor Roosevelt, August 2, 1914, quoted in *Personal Letters, 1905–1928*, pp. 238–9.

ning the real work, although Josephus is here! He is bewildered by it all, very sweet but very sad!" [7] He worked well after midnight, evening after evening. Charles McCarthy confided to Howe, who was on vacation: "The Boss has been the whole cheese in this European business and is going along great." [8]

Wilson's decision to maintain neutrality found strong support from Daniels. He blocked the demands of Roosevelt and the General Board for a strong building program, but F.D.R. soon cast off these restraints. In October 1914 he gave an interview to the press in which he warned that, to keep its fleet in readiness, the Navy needed 18,000 more men than the legal limits allowed. This was public support for Daniels's most bitter Congressional enemy, "Gussie" Gardiner. Roosevelt knew what he was doing; he had warned Eleanor that this might mean trouble for him but that the country must know the "truth." When he was compelled to appear reluctantly before Gardiner's House committee, he avoided contradicting his boss outright, but his testimony left no doubt of his contempt for Daniels's assurances that the fleet was ready for action in its present state. Provided by the Department staff with extensive figures, he argued that 30,000 to 50,000 more men were needed to man the Navy for war. And he continued to conspire with the crusading Congressman, providing him secretly with naval information which Daniels had refused. At the same time he worked on the Secretary to make maneuvers in 1915 more realistic in a way which would demonstrate the Navy's inadequacy.

He knew war was inevitable; he had no sympathy for Germany. He wrote to Eleanor: "I just know I shall do some awful unneutral thing before I get through." [9] He hardly tried to do otherwise. He maintained his close personal contacts with the British Ambassador, cultivated other Allied representatives, and tried to go to England to observe the British naval staff work.

[7] Roosevelt to Eleanor Roosevelt, n.d. [August 5, 1914], quoted in *Personal Letters, 1905–1928*, p. 243.

[8] Charles H. McCarthy to Howe, August 8, 1914, quoted in Freidel: *The Apprenticeship*, p. 239.

[9] Roosevelt to Eleanor Roosevelt, n.d., quoted in *Personal Letters, 1905–1928*, p. 267.

Everywhere he went he talked up the Navy, and at the Panama-Pacific Exposition he dramatized the service with a trip below by submarine. By May 1915, with the successive sinkings of the *Gulflight* and the *Lusitania* and the consequent loss of American lives, young F.D.R. found public opinion oscillating more and more to his side of the argument. In early June the President finally had to make his decision. Secretary Bryan resigned because of his unwillingness to sign a sharp note to Germany on the sinking of the *Lusitania*. Roosevelt wrote in disgust: "J.D. will *not* resign!" [1] He promised to make things "hum" when Daniels went away on his vacation and worried fretfully over Wilson's refusal to "rattle the sword." But the President pushed aside his arguments for a Council of National Defense, and the most he could do while Daniels was away was to "spring" his proposal that an extensive Naval Reserve of both men and privately owned power boats be organized.

He and Daniels worked more amicably now that the President had finally approved the development of a naval expansion program, but F.D.R. would continue to insist on running while Daniels would prefer to make haste, with certainty, more slowly. It was six months before Daniels would finally approve Roosevelt's plans for private power-boat squadrons and for a summer civilian training cruise. Roosevelt bounced about the country in the spring of 1916, whipping up enthusiasm, but recruits came in slowly, and many were turned down in the rigorous Navy physical examinations. Operational personnel shuddered at the thought of four weeks at sea aboard ancient battleships with hundreds of landlubbers; some of the civilians protested that the ships would be dirty, that land camps would be better. Roosevelt was impatient with little problems: "Why all this pessimism?" he wrote. "When we come right down to it, we shall never get preparedness without universal training of some kind and I believe that every individual effort . . . is a step toward united action in a bigger way." [2] He was exasperated when Daniels dubbed the affair "The John Paul Jones Cruise."

[1] Roosevelt to Eleanor Roosevelt [June 10, 1915], quoted in *Personal Letters, 1905–1928*, p. 270.

[2] Roosevelt to R. E. Cropley, June 20, 1916, Group X, FDRL.

He complained to Howe: "It is an awful mistake to leave the Department for more than five and a half minutes at a time!" [3] Nevertheless, the end result pleased him immensely. The press was good; the recruits enthusiastic. He returned from the maneuvers with more eager demands for a regular reserve, and he managed to get approval for a limited program. It was hardly under way before the war outmoded it.

Meanwhile, F.D.R. talked preparedness and barely tolerated the President's moderate foreign policy. "Either we want adequate preparedness or we want none. Half a navy is worthless," [4] he charged. In Cincinnati he warned that, without a big battleship Navy, the nation would have to reconcile itself to a millionman standing Army and to the loss of influence in South America, of world commerce everywhere, and of the Panama Canal itself. He argued with Daniels incessantly over the building program. Like the admirals who advised him, he demanded a larger battleship and cruiser force, and everywhere he promoted his personal hobby, small boats for harbor and coastal patrol. Privately he cursed: "J.D. is too damn slow for words." [5] Publicly he became so sharply identified with the activists that he was often mentioned as a possible successor to Daniels. A less patient chief might have ousted him on the spot.

In February 1917 Roosevelt tried to force the issue. In Daniels's absence he took to the President himself a part of the Navy's elaborate mobilization plan, an order to bring the Atlantic Fleet back from Cuba for cleaning and refitting. Wilson refused. Like Daniels, he still dreamed that war might somehow be avoided. Nothing must be done to put the United States in the role of the aggressor. Meanwhile, Roosevelt sought, and found, a legal technicality which would allow the Navy to loan six-inch guns to private shipping firms for protection against submarines. Wilson balked again, preferring a request for special legislation, which promptly foundered on a filibuster. While the President temporized, Roosevelt fumed. He sought out Colonel House

[3] Roosevelt to Howe [August 8, 1916], quoted in *Personal Letters, 1905–1928*, p. 317.

[4] *Binghamton Press*, January 24, 1916.

[5] Quoted in *Personal Letters, 1905–1928*, p. 339.

to complain about Daniels and to warn against dividing the fleet. On March 11 he dined with his cousin Theodore and other leading Republicans: J. P. Morgan, Leonard Wood, Elihu Root. Here he committed himself to an active conspiracy to bring bipartisan pressure on Wilson, but was saved from his own indiscretion by the President's announcement the next day of a firmer policy, providing for the arming of merchant ships.

The declaration of war on April 2 only stepped up the friction between Daniels and Roosevelt. Neither personality would change overnight. Daniels insisted on deliberation. Roosevelt wanted action: ". . . the weeks, and the months, are piling up and I should very much like to see some definite action taken." [6] And, in September: "I am sorry to say that conditions are to all intents and purposes no better. . . ." [7] As late as January 1918 Roosevelt would send his boss a long, impertinent memo, entitled: "We have left undone these things which we ought to have done." [8] In his own bailiwick he tried to set the pace. In fact, his staff had made such thoroughgoing arrangements for supplies that the President had to intervene on behalf of the beleaguered and belated Army.

Gambler and activist that he was, F.D.R. never fully appreciated Daniels's problems. No one really knew, at first, what the Allies needed. There were sharp conflicts within the staff and with the British. Should the American fleet remain intact or should the destroyers be sent to Europe? Should transports be convoyed? Roosevelt almost instinctively pressed for both the convoys and the dispatch of destroyers. The formal visit of the British and French missions to the United States late in April gave him his best chance. He had a full day with them on the Potomac before they had met anyone else in Washington, and encouraged them to request heavy American action and commitment. At the British Embassy he publicly criticized his own government's laggardly pace. His published plea, in *Scribner's*, for universal military service enforced the impression that he was *the* man of action in Washington.

[6] Roosevelt to Josephus Daniels, June 26, 1917, Group X, FDRL.
[7] Roosevelt to Josephus Daniels, September 7, 1917, Group X, FDRL.
[8] Roosevelt to Josephus Daniels, January 7, 1918, Group X, FDRL.

Roosevelt was genuinely worried about the danger facing the Allies and the administration's slow reaction to it. He took seriously the disaster reports sent back to the department by Admiral William S. Sims, the Navy's observer in England. He wrote Eleanor in Campobello that she must take the "chicks" and run for the woods if a sub should appear in the bay. His speeches warned that the nation must settle down to real war. When the first American troops reached France in June, he said publicly that it was "mere luck" that they had arrived.

Privately he and Louis Howe had been deeply concerned about this. Louis confided to his wife: "There may be a submarine or two over here pretty soon, as we have reports of them in mid-Atlantic and headed this way. Thank God the troops that were sent over on my plan for fooling the Germans got over all right without accident. There are some more due in a few days that are going on a plan of the War Department. I hope they will get over all right too, but if they don't I will at least not feel the personal responsibility I did about this lot. . . ." [9]

Early in the summer Roosevelt found a willing ally in Winston Churchill, the American novelist who happened to be both a friend of the President and a graduate of Annapolis. Churchill offered his services as a writer, and Roosevelt determined to use him for conspiracy as well as propaganda. F.D.R. turned him loose in the department, and Churchill soon came to share his view of the lethargy and delay. He complained that the operation had "hookworm." F.D.R. was delighted when the novelist finally decided in midsummer to take a lengthy memorandum of the difficulties to Wilson himself. It brought results. Wilson wrote to the Secretary recommending that younger men be given more of the leadership and that the Navy be vigorous in its anti-submarine program. Although the Secretary left the staff generally intact, including Admiral William S. Benson, the Chief of Operations, whom F.D.R. had been mercilessly criticizing, the machinery of the department as a whole did speed up. By the fall of 1918 Roosevelt was busy and satisfied enough to abate his carping criticism. Yet he would still note, on occasion,

[9] Howe to Grace Howe, June 20, 1917, Personal Papers.

that it would take "lots more of the Churchill type of attack" to put things in the proper order.[1]

While Roosevelt was concerned with the submarine problem as a whole, he could do little more than snipe and fret at the general strategy being employed. The major movements of the Atlantic Fleet and of Allied strategy were well outside his bailiwick. He did pursue with dogged insistence two proposals which especially captured his imagination. One was his demand for a fleet of small boats to patrol American harbors and participate in sub patrols overseas. The other was a tradition-shattering plan for a gigantic anti-submarine net across the North Sea.

The small-boat fleet was closest to his heart. It grew naturally from his own yachting experience. He took seriously the scared estimates of the Division of Operations that the Navy must have over 4,000 such small craft for harbor protection, scouting, and mining operations. The Bureau of Construction and Repair finally hit upon a 110-foot wooden submarine chaser as the standard craft, and Roosevelt eagerly followed the records of its production throughout the spring of 1917, chafing as usual at delays. Meanwhile, he fought for a program of smaller, 50-foot boats, displaying in the process the immense self-confidence and steely determination which annoyed many of his subordinates. Failing to convince the Secretary and the General Board, he used every tactic in the book to have his way. His imagination spun out a score of special jobs which such boats could perform in the protected waters to which their size would confine them. He sent Howe to threaten a strategically placed captain who had opposed the plans. He wore Daniels down until, tired of it all, the Secretary asked in his diary: "How much of this junk shall we buy?"[2] Finally Roosevelt went ahead on his own, using his wartime right to approve matters as Acting Secretary, even when Daniels was in town. A small number of the small

[1] Roosevelt to Eleanor Roosevelt [August 17, 1917], quoted in *Personal Letters, 1905–1928*, p. 357.

[2] Quoted in Jonathan Daniels: *The End of Innocence* (Philadelphia: J. B. Lippincott Co.; 1954), p. 217.

boats were built, but even Roosevelt came to recognize the maneuver as a failure.

This incident illustrated also another aspect of Roosevelt's immature impulsiveness, his occasional naïve reliance on an impressive idea man. In pressing for the 50-foot craft, he was almost certainly following the advice of a genial, big-talking promoter named Arthur Patch Homer. Homer had helped round up private yachts and had been sent by Roosevelt on various special missions to Europe. Both Louis Howe and F.D.R. had come to admire this affable businessman as a go-getter with ideas. Pat Homer had a flair for dramatizing his role in everything he touched. When he sent cablegrams, they were invariably the superconfidential kind which he would request in advance be exempt from the eyes of naval censors. Homer was also, as it happened, using the stationery of a motor company which might expect to get contracts if the program of 50-foot boats could be sold to the Navy. Homer's operations, under the friendly guidance of Howe and Roosevelt, were to give F.D.R.'s enemies their most convincing evidence that Roosevelt was influenced by his friends in awarding Navy contracts.

Meanwhile Roosevelt fought even more doggedly for his North Sea anti-submarine net. He had aroused the President's interest as early as 1916, but both British and American naval staffs insisted the idea was impractical, requiring as it did a half million mines. Roosevelt pressed the matter with the British, but Lord Balfour felt the North Sea could hardly be closed to neutrals. Daniels supported the British position.

Here the matter should have ended, had it not been for F.D.R.'s impatient confidence and the help of Lester Jones, head of the Coast and Geodetic Survey. Jones arranged for a special committee to investigate the idea and reported that it was practical. Roosevelt undertook to rebut the British objections. Five hundred million dollars was a small price to pay for bottling up the German subs, he said. Further, if Norway did not fulfill her neutral obligations by keeping her coastal waters free from belligerents, it was only fair to "carry out this duty for her." [3]

[3] Roosevelt: "Memorandum on the submarine situation," May 24, 1917, quoted in Freidel: *Apprenticeship*, p. 314.

Then Roosevelt went to the President himself. Wilson was in-
clined to be sympathetic to any proposal for trapping the
"hornets" in their nests. Meanwhile, F.D.R. received a windfall
in the form of inventor Ralph G. Browne's plan for electrically
triggered mines. This suggested a combination of the net and
mine ideas which had been rivaling each other in the planning,
and it helped tip the balance among the senior officers to Roosevelt's side. Finally, late in October, F.D.R. wrote a sharp letter
to Daniels. The thing must be done, he demanded, as nothing
else had been done, with quick decision all down the line. It
must be taken out of regular channels and put firmly in the
hands of two men, one American, one British. He sent the
President a copy of the memo.

Without upsetting regular channels, Daniels authorized the
project the next day. He continued to doubt, yet had little
choice, with his staff and the President both in Roosevelt's camp.
By the time of the Armistice, 70,000 mines had been laid in the
North Sea barrage at a cost of $80,000,000; the net was never
completed. Roosevelt claimed for it a major share of the credit
for the crucial collapse of German fleet morale, but there could
be no real proof of this; air and subchaser and destroyer attacks undoubtedly contributed to the outcome. Yet for Roosevelt himself it was a great personal victory. He had taken on the
entire naval world with the same adolescent zeal with which he
had once fought New York bosses. And he had won. Years later,
in the White House, he would quietly dictate a file memo to
make certain that history would deal rightly with his major
contribution to Allied victory.

10

>>>->>>->>>->>>->>>->>>->>>->>>

Business Politicians
for the Navy

*. . . no other Assistant Secretary of the
Navy ever gained as great a measure of
respect from the workers and their representatives as has Mr. Roosevelt. . . .*
(The Federal Machinist, *July 1920*) [1]

THE BULK of Roosevelt's work was the less dramatic, but more
important, management of the Navy's shore business. Here
Louis Howe played a significant role. The only person whom
Roosevelt could trust completely, he became the Assistant Secretary's eyes and ears and his secret agent in many a sensitive
business. Howe had even less experience than Roosevelt for
this role. Yet his long career had given him a deep contempt for
stuffy authority, a shrewd judgment of human motivation, and
an expertness in subtle arrangements that would prove invaluable. His responsibilities were what F.D.R. gave him. Before he was through, he had found himself dealing with an im-

[1] Vol. I, p. 1.

mense range of problems, from the procurement of labor to expediting the delivery of key items for ship construction, from working out agreements with trolley companies for adequate service to naval installations to investigating prostitution and gambling in Navy towns. His varied talents made him a useful pinch hitter and trouble shooter. He brought material together for both Daniels's and Roosevelt's speeches and wrote some of them. He wrote large sections of the Secretary's annual reports. He was sent to inspect the Guantanamo Naval Base and to negotiate the sale of a wrecked Navy tug in Newfoundland.

Ordinarily the Navy's business matters were handled routinely in the various bureaus. But an interested civilian official would find more than enough to do. Customarily, Roosevelt and Howe concerned themselves with items which came to their attention in one of three ways. They might notice inconsistencies or in-efficiencies reflected in the documents which came across their desks; they might investigate complaints which came to them from naval personnel, politicians, or the community; or they might intervene widely as they followed up some generalized objective of their own design.

Gradually they worked out procedures for handling the mat-ters in which they were interested. Documents in question and complaints from the mail would be referred to the proper office for the preparation of a letter for Roosevelt's signature. The re-ply or comment, if unsatisfactory, would lead to personal in-vestigation within the department, often by Howe. If the matter proved particularly troublesome, Louis would head out to the installation involved to interview personally the people con-cerned and to take a direct look at the problem.

The professional Navy men could take Roosevelt in their stride, but Howe was more difficult for them to accommodate. His personal messiness disturbed their instincts for spit and polish. Howe rebelled at having to step aside for admirals and showed everywhere his contempt for rank. His tie might always be Navy blue, but he was no sailor. He cut recklessly through channels and seemed to be spying on everyone. With it all, he seemed to have no outward qualifications for naval manage-ment. As Louis became increasingly identified as Roosevelt's personal trouble shooter, commanding officers learned to expect their orderly procedures to be sharply upset whenever he appeared. As late as the summer of 1917 Howe could complain to Roosevelt about the habitual failure of the Bureau of Navigation to keep up with his inquiries for interested Congressmen, and McCarthy could write bitterly: ". . . the Division of Aviation should be informed that when I go to that office for information, I am not going for myself, or for my health, but for the Assistant Secretary of the Navy." [2] But most officers went out of their way to satisfy this annoyingly curious little agent, who so evidently shared in Roosevelt's power. In fact, by 1916 Louis had built his own direct lines of communication with labor leaders, naval constructors at the various yards, and agents within the naval contracting firms. This complex of contacts proved time-consuming in the extreme, but it provided him with a constant check against the official reports which filtered up through channels.

Howe and Roosevelt were fortunate in the Paymaster's team which Daniels had given them in the general reorganization of 1914. The Paymaster General, Samuel McGowan, proved to be not only a master manager and a stickler for economies, but also a wise staff man. He could co-operate with Roosevelt and Howe in the most important things, while subtly blocking some of their wilder notions. When he detected a tendency in Roosevelt to be swayed by the latest caller, McGowan quietly took to awarding contracts in a hurry and mailing them out once the final decision had been made, to avoid the confusion that sometimes came with F.D.R.'s afterthoughts. Howe's information was not always as accurate as that of the bureaus, and McGowan's staff was not above holding up his recommendations for checking. McGowan and his inseparable assistant, Christian J. Peoples, were soon tagged by Daniels the "Gold Dust Twins." Roosevelt, who called them "My Heavenly Twins," was deeply grateful for their loyal efficiency. He and Howe were able to work intimately with the Twins when their relations with others in the department were often strained.

[2] [Charles H. McCarthy] to Roosevelt, July 11, 1917, Group X, FDRL

In the matter of contracts and costs, Daniels, Roosevelt, and Howe found themselves on common ground from the start. They were all anxious to save money, Daniels in order to lower the cost of government, Roosevelt to make more money available for construction, and all three for political purposes. They bent much of their energy in 1913 and 1914 to revamping the Navy's contract system. In this they were further inspired by the administration's general anti-trust policy. But long before the President sent to Congress the message which eventually inspired the Clayton Act, Daniels, Roosevelt, and Howe had turned the Navy Department upside down with their own private war against monopolies. Roosevelt himself may not at first have been so concerned as his junior and senior colleagues. Daniels and Howe shared an emotional hatred of big business, which, as Democratic editors, they had been feeding their rural constituencies for years. But F.D.R. soon fell into line as he sniffed the possibilities of significant savings.

Daniels took the lead in the spring of 1913 when he noticed the department's habit of giving occasional large contracts without competitive bids, of accepting, without objection, identical "competitive" bids, and of dividing contracts among the bidders. When three major steel companies submitted identical bids twice in a row for the *Arizona's* armor plate the Secretary lost his temper. Howe and Roosevelt were assigned to investigate this evident collusion as well as rumors that the same companies were making identical steel for foreign nations at lower prices. Their report relayed the department staff's defense that it was necessary to divide the work among the three mills at the lowest bid offered in order to maintain all in a state of readiness. Roosevelt then passed the buck. Congress must decide whether to build a Navy plant, encourage real competition, or, if current practices seemed wise, provide direct and open legislative subsidy rather than the hidden cushion of collusive bidding. At the same time Daniels requested a Congressional investigation of the steel companies, including their financial reports, and the help of an expert not connected with either the private companies or the Navy. Congress was no more eager to tangle with the great steel companies than was the department, although after four years Daniels finally obtained an appropriation for a Navy owned and operated armor-plate factory. F.D.R. was something less than enthusiastic about this particular operation; he claimed privately that he had tried to cut the appropriation to provide merely a small pilot plant, for the purposes of experimentation, of establishing actual costs, and of providing a nucleus for emergency expansion.

Roosevelt was intrigued, however, by the method Daniels chose for immediate action. Sent to New York to negotiate with the agents of an English company, F.D.R. came back with a distinctly lower bid than domestic mills had made. The American firms were forced, in turn, to reduce their prices momentarily, and the Secretary could announce proudly to the press that the scramble had saved the country $111,875 on the building of this battleship.

The armor-plate situation had hardly cooled before Roosevelt and Howe attacked the coal industry. Here a tight monopoly had been built up with the aid of the department's insistence on careful quality control. An "accepted" list of mine owners whose pits had been carefully inspected received notification of the fleet's needs, and no really competitive bidding was promoted. Howe himself led the way in challenging this practice. In the spring of 1914 he found the whole complex business on his desk, when Daniels transferred the responsibility for coal contracts from the Paymaster General to the Assistant Secretary.

Here Louis tackled more than he could handle. Falling in with the suggestions of a coal broker who had been barred from the accepted list because he could not meet the standard requirements, he set up new specifications which threw the contract open for public competition. The results were book savings of many thousands of dollars but also a tornado of reaction. Louis worked out a letter to an irate West Virginia Congressman in which he blandly pointed out that the mines in his State could, after all, not actually be in bad shape: ". . . if they really needed the Navy business, they could get it by sharpening their lead pencils and bidding, and if they do not need the Navy business there will be no particular hardship." [3] But a storm of

[3] Roosevelt to William E. Chilton, July 13, 1914, Group X, FDRL.

complaints from ship's engineers about excessive ash and clinkers and excessive volatility put Howe on the spot. When the House Naval Affairs Committee interested itself in the problem in the fall of 1915, Louis tried to defend his policy with an elaborate statement for Roosevelt and Daniels attacking the coal trust. F.D.R., caught off base by Howe's careless figures, squirmed unhappily through a cross-examination in which he satisfied no one.

Although Howe had blundered badly in detail, he had made a major contribution by setting a new direction for the department. Under McGowan, who now reasserted his bureau's responsibility, a practical system of wide competition was developed which saved approximately $200,000 on coal in 1915. This experience undoubtedly taught both Roosevelt and Howe a considerable respect for McGowan and a little humility in the complex business of procurement. Louis did not attempt again to go out for domestic bids directly, but he did attack what he thought to be a vicious system of block bidding for commissary supplies, a system under which firms could place a winning total bid by quoting low on items they did not expect to provide and high on those which they would sell to the Navy in large quantities. In the process, he also made available a wider selection of brands for the sailors aboard ship, reaping for himself the anger of the *Army and Navy Register,* which claimed that he was forcing seamen to buy obscure products. As he often did, he arranged things so that the blame for "the wicked performances" would fall on "my wicked self." [4]

Sometimes the department had to reverse its policy of fighting the trusts, as, for example, in December 1916 when Howe was sent to beg the co-operation of the Guggenheim brothers in arranging a pool for immediate supply of scarce copper to the Navy at cost. The greatest successes, however, came with their continued search overseas. Roosevelt discovered tremendous savings in carrying fuel to the Caribbean and Pacific by Navy colliers. These ships could be used as freighters on their return trips. He was able to buy tin in Singapore, shellac in Calcutta, nitrates in Chile, at substantially lower prices than the American

[4] Howe to Roosevelt, April 4, 1914, Group X, FDRL.

market offered, at the same time making available materials which would soon be in short supply. This kind of thing was risky. Howe, who had particular responsibility for the Chilean gambit, had to short-circuit the State Department and waive certain naval specifications as well. He was a very nervous assistant until the tests at Norfolk Navy Yard proved the materials of superior quality.

The efforts of Daniels, Howe, and McGowan produced a record of which they could justly boast in the 1916 campaign. McGowan furnished his superiors with a statement of savings which added up to $1,300,000. Howe particularly boasted of their drive to standardize specifications and to increase the efficiency of the department's accounting system. There were new competitive examinations for paymasters. In addition, the Navy was better prepared for crises than it had ever been before, with its new program of stockpiling standard supply items for ships and stations to replace the antiquated "order as needed" procedures which had long been used.

After May 1917 Howe's role changed. As Special Assistant to the Assistant Secretary, at $400 a month, he was appointed "expert in the Bureau of Supplies and Accounts . . . on reduction in prices and in securing competition on general miscellaneous purchasing." Some department wags called him "Daniels' spy." But "Bo," as one admiral tagged him, worked closely and smoothly with McGowan and his able assistant, John M. Hancock. And he worked in increasing independence of Roosevelt. He sat as a member of the Munitions Board, several labor boards, and other committees. His authority as virtual assistant secretary in charge of trouble ran increasingly to construction problems.

He liked to tell many years later the story of his having held up the opening of the Hotel Pennsylvania in New York by commandeering its turbine for a Navy ship. Actually, this and a handful of other incidents have tended to obscure the interminable stream of special cases which constituted much of his work. Roosevelt's friendliness to officers in the field encouraged special appeals, as did the experience which Howe had gained with Emory S. Land in trying to get the *New Mexico* launched

before the 1916 election. Howe might be annoying. Land nick-
named him the "chief squid," and later joked that Louis had
driven him back to sea duty, but he got things done. If a truck
were needed at Philadelphia, machinists at Portsmouth, or special castings at New York, Howe was soon on the telephone
about it or en route for a personal investigation.

Much of the work involved the Navy Yards. Their chief problem was the friction between commanding officers and naval industrial managers. F.D.R. soon became identified with the latter
in their constant sniping at the military officers who got in their
way. Roosevelt sought to strengthen the authority of the Assistant Chiefs of the Bureaus of Construction and Repairs, Yards
and Docks, by appointing officers to these positions in place of
the chief clerks. Howe became personally friendly with the industrial managers of all East Coast installations and was frequently used by them to bypass channels and take their complaints directly to the Assistant Secretary. To the manager at
Portsmouth he could write: "All kinds of heavy artillery shells
are bursting around my head over this matter. . . . Please forward, at once, an immediate alibi of some kind that I can get
by with, as the Council of National Defense, the Priorities Board,
the Secretary of War, the Industrial Service Section of the Production Division, Ordnance Department, Army, the Labor Department and one or two others that I think I have forgotten
about have called my attention to it most forcefully." [5] And he
could temper their impatience with humor. To the commandant
of the Washington Yard he could write: "The little boat you sent
floating in the ocean . . . has wandered slowly through the
War Department, with frequent visits to the Navy Department,
and has now reached somewhere along the line its nineteenth
endorsement. The net result is that the Army admits that it did
wrong, but asks to keep the men as they probably are too old by
this time to do effective work. I would suggest we let it go at
that, but before so notifying the Army, I am sending all the
papers down to you for endorsement number twenty." [6]

When necessary, Howe could reprimand these special friends

[5] Howe to L. S. Adams, September 10, 1918, Group XXXVI, FDRL.
[6] Howe to Arthur Willard, August 19, 1918, Group XXXVI, FDRL.

with suave finesse. To the manager of a steel plant at the Boston Yard he could suggest that the factory needed reorganization, and could hint mildly that the plant could be moved to another location if necessary. Louis would note with delight that a special representative of the department had kept things humming at Portsmouth until he had "the Admiral scared pink." [7]

Early in 1913 F.D.R.'s penchant for efficiency led him into troubled waters at the Boston Yard, where the first steps of the Taylor system of production efficiency were being introduced by some young engineers. The Taylor system was variously viewed as a relentless exploitation of labor or as a "scientific" system of improving production. Roosevelt was taken with the idea, but the forceful opposition of both the older naval officers and the labor unions scared him away from it. Howe remained much preoccupied with the need for professional assistance in production techniques. He recommended one volunteer to his boss late in 1917: "If this man knows the right kind of efficiency and is not one of those Taylor system cranks, it might be worth considering. . . ." [8] A few months later, he persuaded Roosevelt to give up the idea of having the Office of Naval Intelligence investigate what was wrong with the Portsmouth Yard and send "an honest to goodness production man without prejudice" instead. [9] In the long run, however, the fantastically complicated administrative system of the yards proved too much for them. As late as January 1920 Louis was still searching for an effective principle of reorganization, still unable to give Roosevelt definitive advice on whether it would be better to employ "brute force" or to "try to handle it by a conciliatory conference." [1]

In addition, there were marginal problems as varied as a rainbow in their busy lives. Howe spent much time during the war on transportation tangles and on emergency housing for the civilian personnel of the yards. He and Roosevelt even dabbled

[7] Howe to L. S. Adams, September 10, 1918, Group XXXVI, FDRL.
[8] Howe to Roosevelt, November 28, 1917, Group XXXVI, FDRL.
[9] Howe to Roosevelt, January 22, 1918, Group XXXVI, FDRL.
[1] Howe to Roosevelt, January 30, 1920, Group XXXVI, FDRL.

in diplomacy when they intervened to settle a row between a private shipyard and the Argentine government over payment for a battleship. The Portsmouth Naval Prison was a special challenge. Daniels was determined to turn it from a penitentiary into a rehabilitation center. The natural choice for commander was Thomas Mott Osborne, who had retired from politics into criminology. As warden of Sing Sing, he had practiced such progressive notions as prisoner self-government and prisoner-run canteens. He was fond of inspecting institutions by serving a voluntary term as an anonymous prisoner inside. Regular naval officers were appalled at the thought of having "criminals" graduated back to the fleet, and Osborne worried Roosevelt with fretful complaints about naval red tape. Roosevelt was patient. Consider his note to a general about an Army draftee whom Osborne wanted for his staff: "Here is a man whom you will probably shoot if he doesn't turn up at Yaphank this afternoon. On the other hand, as he is in the Navy, we will shoot him, if he does turn up at Yaphank. Please prevent this by leaving him in the Navy. He is web footed." [2] It was all very wearing.

And there were problems of spies, subversion, and hysteria. Neither Louis nor his boss was in a mood to tolerate dissension. Howe took a hand in organizing naval censorship. He rounded up confidential information on "sedition" from friends in the newspaper world. He could pointedly inquire: "Since when have my good friends in the machinists' union joined hands with that gang? I remember distinctly a little conversation with you, within the last forty-eight hours on the I.W.W. and bolshevik situation, which does not gee with this report at all. . . . I am really somewhat disturbed and I wish you would let me know frankly just how badly the situation is getting out of hand. . . ." [3] Roosevelt and Howe recognized that the Office of Naval Intelligence frequently confused union activity with disloyalty. When this happened, they quietly filed the reports. But Roosevelt could be sharply intolerant. He sent a copy of an obscure upstate New York publication to the Attorney General with the wish that the department could "send the writer and his whole

[2] Roosevelt to General McLain, n.d., Group X, FDRL.
[3] Howe to J. J. McEntee, January 31, 1919, Group XXXVI, FDRL.

plant to Atlanta for the rest of their natural lives." [4] When a firm with a Navy trucking contract allowed its vehicles to be used after hours to distribute Socialist propaganda against the Liberty Loan, F.D.R. demanded "action." [5] He was delighted with the Espionage and Sedition Laws.

Their most significant challenge lay in labor relations. Here Louis proved more useful than in any other pursuit, aside from politics. He had no more early interest in organized labor than had F.D.R., but he had come to appreciate its political significance. More important, he could move on an intimate basis with the labor leaders in a way Roosevelt never could. He became immediately identified as a friend of the unions and helped Roosevelt develop a rapport with labor which was to prove useful both in politics and in the burgeoning problem of keeping up naval production.

Roosevelt's genial approach made it natural for him to turn his frequent Navy Yard inspection tours into political occasions. He made a habit of cheery speeches to the labor forces in which he stressed their common cause and the opportunities which he expected would come to their yards as the building programs advanced. His view of labor relations was still naïve; he tended to stress the line that they were all members of the same club. Howe, with McCarthy's advice, went much farther. Using his position as keeper of F.D.R.'s door, he arranged regular entree for labor leaders and conspired to make Roosevelt's office the customary place for their complaints. Albert J. Berres, the president of the International Machinists Union, and N. P. Alifas, the president of the Metal Trades Council, soon became intimates of Howe and regular callers on his boss. By early in 1915 they had learned to trust Louis's discretion and brought directly to him innumerable complaints against general policies and particular decisions of the various naval constructors.

Howe showed distinct skill in handling these sticky problems. Many he was able to solve by mild "suggestions" to the

[4] [Roosevelt] to Samuel J. Graham, April 14, 1917, Group X, FDRL.
[5] Roosevelt to Office of Naval Intelligence, November 21, 1917, Group X, FDRL.

responsible officers, written on Roosevelt's stationery and with his signature. But soon Louis's own scrawl proved sufficient. A note to the commandant of the Philadelphia Yard relaying one of Berres's complaints was typical: "This seems like a very reasonable suggestion, and I would be much obliged if you would take the matter up and let me know what you think about it." [6] Within days, Berres was writing him gratefully that the "suggestion" was now in effect. When the labor leaders followed up with a request for a general policy affecting all yards, Howe laid bare the dynamics of his approach. He suggested that comprehensive changes in policy were sometimes "misunderstood," while much could be done with individual cases as they arose.[7] Louis often noted, as he did to the manager at Norfolk, that there was something to be said for both sides of the case under discussion, but that it wouldn't hurt to give in a little to labor in the interests of better feeling.

Often Howe personally investigated cases of alleged discrimination. On rare occasions this resulted in direct orders from Roosevelt overruling the officer involved, after Howe had built up a sufficient dossier of evidence. More often, however, there was a quiet local solution. Howe was successful enough with this kind of maneuvering so that he could occasionally call off the union wolves when they were on weak ground or when their demands were particularly embarrassing. Thus, to soothe resentment aroused by a mismanaged incident, he could write confidentially to Alifas: "I beg you to be merciful and let the . . . case stand. . . . The necessity of getting out airplanes is so great that I for one do not honestly feel like impairing our war work by starting a young riot over a case like this which has such uncertain foundations. If you will be content to let this lie, I will try to be extra generous on the next case. . . ." [8] When some of his friends got out of line, he could cut them down quickly: "I am not going to bring this letter to Mr. Roosevelt's

[6] Howe to Commander, Philadelphia Navy Yard, May 15, 1917, Group XXXVI, FDRL.

[7] Howe to A. J. Berres, June 25, 1917, Group XXXVI, FDRL.

[8] Howe to N. P. Alifas, n.d., Group XXXVI, FDRL.

attention . . . the use of the word 'insists' to the Government, is not a diplomatic way to get things done. . . ." [9] Sometimes Louis shelved the complaints quietly: ". . . the best thing to do with this is to forget that they ever complained until they complain again. . . ." [1]

But personal diplomacy with labor could backfire. When he bungled, Louis was not above throwing the whole problem back to the yard itself, with a cheery bit of advice that direct complaints by the men should be encouraged: "A constantly open crater is less dangerous than a volcano which gets stopped up and is likely to blow its own head off." [2] Sometimes his patience wore thin: "Just to look at this makes my head ache. . . . I don't know anything about and don't want to know anything about it." [3] Occasionally he drew Roosevelt into an untenable position. In one such case, F.D.R. wrote tartly to a union leader: "I have gone absolutely the limit. . . . As we have recognized your patriotic work, we may ask in return that you recognize the extremely unpatriotic actions of ————." [4]

Daniels was finally persuaded in 1918 to centralize all labor matters in Roosevelt's office, where they inevitably landed on Howe's desk. Louis decided what to handle himself, what to forget, and what to send to Roosevelt. He sat as the Navy member of Felix Frankfurter's War Labor Board and substituted regularly for Roosevelt on the Shipbuilding Labor Board. But there were areas of labor relations which Howe was never able to master. Jurisdictional disputes were always dangerous, and the American Federation of Labor politely refused to help. Louis wrote plaintively at one point: "Can't we bury this troublesome matter until the morning after the entry of American troops into Berlin . . . ?" [5] He had to help with the Liberty Bond drives, but he complained bitterly of some of the "vicious practices . . . nearly approaching coercion" which were used in the

[9] Howe to James O'Connell, September 3, 1918, Group XXXVI, FDRL.
[1] Howe to Roosevelt, March 10, 1919, Group XXXVI, FDRL.
[2] Howe to Watt, October 20, 1915, Group X, FDRL.
[3] "Memorandum for Mr. Curtis," July 16, 1917, Group XXXVI, FDRL.
[4] Roosevelt to Valentine, July 8, 1918, Group XXXVI, FDRL.
[5] Howe to John Alpine, August 9, 1918, Group XXXVI, FDRL.

Navy Yards.[6] The question of using Negro labor in the Yards was particularly explosive. Hoping the ghost would go away, he hastily filed the first requests for policy statements on the question. Pushed hard, he had to write finally: "I have talked over the colored brothers' privilege with Mr. Daniels, and I have only cold comfort to give you. Mr. Daniels' view is that the best thing to do is to do nothing. . . . I would suggest that you do the best you can, and not refer the matter to us. . . ."[7] Later, he would get his union friends to settle a strike at Key West which had grown out of the use of Negro labor, but he quietly hinted to the local commander that perhaps "their services will eventually be dispensed with without any official action on our part."[8]

In general, Roosevelt and Howe were successful in personnel relations. Their common-sense approach of "a friendly little talk" paid large dividends. Even during the first seven months of 1916, when there were 2,000 strikes and lockouts throughout the country, the unions remained friendly with the Navy. Howe's immense skill in the day-to-day juggling of personalities had much to do with this. But much of the reason for their success lay in their constructive approach to wage negotiations. Louis insisted that Roosevelt attend to these personally, so that adjustments could be made before the figures went to Daniels. This enhanced their bargaining power with the leaders, and Roosevelt identified himself with several union demands, including the reduction in the number of separate pay ranks and the inclusion of cost-of-living rises in the wage formula.

But in wage matters, no Navy administrator could consider merely labor's demands. With fixed appropriations, higher wages often meant fewer workers. The Navy's standards affected the work of other agencies and of private industry. The Navy and its private contractors were caught in cutthroat competition for skilled men. Roosevelt and Howe agitated for a national labor administrator to standardize wages and conditions of labor, but the Labor Department balked. The final solution was a series of

[6] Howe to Roosevelt, March 10, 1919, Group XXXVI, FDRL.
[7] Howe to Fred G. Coburn [1918], Group XXXVI, FDRL.
[8] Howe to Benton Decker, June 19, 1919, Group XXXVI, FDRL.

committees. While these groups gave the Navy something to lean upon, they were negotiating rather than directing groups. Roosevelt and Howe often found themselves at odds with the other services over marginal matters of interpretation. As late as 1919 Howe would be seeking a "soothing statement" to "keep the record clean," in a case where the Army was "tearing off hunks of atmosphere because we are paying nine dollars a minute, or something like that. . . ." [9] Yet the official rates set by the various committees were especially useful with the private naval contractors. A potentially disastrous strike at Fore River was settled promptly when Roosevelt pressed the company to adopt the rates current at the nearby Boston Navy Yard. On the other hand, the department aided the contractors by refusing to hire men who had declined work at the private establishments.

The problems of competitive procurement went well beyond wages, and Howe inherited most of them. He advertised for help widely; his union friends provided lists of available men; he negotiated constantly over transfers of skilled men from one town to another. All the services were plagued by mechanics who jumped about from job to job, in search of better conditions and wages. Howe's tactics were vigorous. As late as mid-1918 he would tell the Assistant Secretary of War that he would stop advertising for men when the Army did. But the competitive techniques could backfire. His union friends had to be warned sharply not to recruit men away from the Navy, and Howe had to write many a "scamping" letter to private contractors threatening an appeal to the War Industries Board if they did not stop raiding his yards.

As the war drew to a close, Howe fought for a general policy of an eight-hour day, a 48-hour week, and equal pay for men and women. He and Roosevelt were increasingly disturbed over work stoppages. Roosevelt himself yearned for a Universal Military Service Law under which labor as well as troops might be drafted. He told a Syracuse audience: "We wish to give labor a

[9] Howe to Charles W. Parkes, January 7, 1919, Group XXXVI, FDRL.

large share, but we can't stand for any small group in a community holding up the whole community." [1] When the various
labor boards were dissolved abruptly after the Armistice,
Roosevelt and Howe were desperate. They tried to emphasize
compulsory arbitration, and Howe took the initiative in a labor-
management conference in June 1920, to work out a plan. But
management balked, and labor no longer completely trusted the
Roosevelt-Howe team, for in the strike-torn year after the Armistice Roosevelt had become increasingly testy about the unions. During the New York tugboat strike in March, which Louis
had been working for months to prevent, Roosevelt almost
destroyed their liaison with labor by hastily agreeing to send
Navy tugs to provide fuel for the city. He reversed himself at
once, but was soon lashing out more generally at the fact that
"half a million men . . . [could] tie up the whole country." [2]
Their demands for compulsory arbitration were premature, at
least, and neither Roosevelt nor Howe seems to have appreciated the extent to which the authority of the government and
the discipline of war had eased their own path to labor peace.

Closely akin to the labor problem was the task of handling
political influence in the department. An astounding amount of
their time was taken up by favor-seekers. Most of the interminable investigation and correspondence fell to Louis, and he handled it with monumental attention to detail. But few favors
were done. Howe generally sent the letters to the pertinent
bureaus. Well-schooled in this essential pettiness, officers down
the line prepared replies for the Assistant Secretary's signature,
quoting the pertinent regulations or circumstances which made
the requests impossible to meet. This was frequently enough
even for Congressional inquiries. Often the legislator merely
wanted the matter off his desk without creating an enemy. Only
occasionally did Louis let his guard down, as he did with Franklin's old Harvard roommate, Congressman Lathrop Brown: "My
honored and revered boss says he will stow a slice of onion in

[1] Clipping, December 26, 1919, Scrapbook No. 9, FDRL.
[2] Frank Freidel: *Franklin D. Roosevelt: the Ordeal* (Boston: Little,
Brown and Co.; 1954), p. 24.

his handkerchief so that he will be able to shed real tears in pleading the case. . . ." [3]

Sometimes favors were done for Roosevelt's old political and personal friends, but never for Howe's. Weight regulations were occasionally waived for enlisted men. When a clear case of personal hardship could be documented by an important political friend, a discharge might be arranged. Often Roosevelt would indulge in the innocent yet productive business of sending through channels an application for a commission. He sometimes arranged a transfer which did not appear unsuitable. He was glad to provide friendly politicians with souvenir relics of the *Maine* for some public park. But the lines had to be drawn between "legitimate" and "unfair" influence, and Roosevelt developed a number of smooth formulae for handling denials which he personally had to explain. Most useful was the guileless suggestion that the quickest way to join the Navy was to visit the local recruiting office. Sometimes he would explain how the special favor requested would do injustice to another serviceman, or he would take refuge in dolorous descriptions of how "our Republican friends tied up the navy yards under civil service regulations, so that it is practically impossible to make any appointments whatever by favor. . . ." [4] On occasion, ambiguities would serve. Thus a leading Democrat in Dutchess County, who wanted to serve as an advisor on Russian affairs, was told that Roosevelt would be delighted "to see that the State Department clearly understands your peculiar qualifications for giving sound advice on the matter. . . ." [5]

There were some types of intervention which could not be handled routinely. The President's Secretary, Joseph Tumulty, referred a flood of indiscriminate items to Roosevelt for personal attention. The whole department knew that Tumulty must be handled with care. They could say "no," but only with good reason. Howe would write one of the admirals: "This man was sent over to us by Mr. Tumulty with . . . one of the 999,000 anti-scale compositions for boilers. . . . If you have a donkey

[3] Howe to Lathrop Brown, October 2, 1915, Group X, FDRL.
[4] Roosevelt to Edward J. Dugan, February 2, 1915, Group X, FDRL.
[5] Roosevelt to Samuel Beskin, n.d., Group X, FDRL.

engine at some convenient place where you can pour some of
the stuff in and go through the form at least of a report on it,
it would relieve the situation considerably." [6] But Louis could
use Tumulty in return: "Here is a little buck of mine I am
passing. . . . If you could just send me a little note saying that
you would take pleasure in doing what you could for him . . .
it would be the saving of my young life." [7]

More weighty than even Tumulty's influence was that of a
few Congressmen who could embarrass naval appropriations.
Some of them viewed the Navy Yards as their private patronage
preserves. The situation was particularly sticky in Brooklyn, because of Representative John Fitzgerald. He was a regular
whom Roosevelt had fought; he had been in politics when
Roosevelt was in his cradle; he was Chairman of the House
Ways and Means Committee. F.D.R. was forced to treat Fitzgerald with the greatest care, patiently receiving his endless
visits to the department and working to satisfy the interminable
complaints he relayed from his henchmen in the yard.

Roosevelt's life teemed with responsibility and action, but he
was increasingly restless. Able-bodied and fit, he felt uneasy
about sitting in Washington while others fought. "Uncle Ted"
prodded him. He was also conscious that an active war record
could be useful in politics. But his Big Navy friends discouraged
him from enlisting. They were appalled at losing his influence
within the department. Even the President objected. The best
Roosevelt could do was wrangle from Daniels permission to
make an inspection of the Navy in Europe during the summer
of 1918. He was as eager as a boy for the excitement, the danger, and the glamor of war. As usual, his enthusiasm carried
him well beyond his limited authority to make recommendations. He dabbled in diplomacy, talked with King Albert, Marshal Joffre, and King George, and he pummeled Daniels with
cable after cable complaining of red tape, defective airplane
parts, and poor organization of the naval air arm. In September
he returned, exhausted, desperately ill with the flu, more anxious than ever to get overseas, perhaps as an officer with the

[6] Howe to R. S. Griffin, May 14, 1918, Group XXXVI, FDRL.

[7] Howe to Joseph Tumulty, January 15, 1918, Group XXXVI, FDRL.

heavy artillery on railroad mounts in action along the German front. He had written his wife: "The more I think of it, the more I feel that being only 36 my place is not at a Washington desk, even a Navy desk. I know you will understand." [8] To friends, he implied: "I have a sneaking suspicion that you will see me over here soon in a different kind of a job." [9]

Louis Howe, who had been watching New York politics and Navy business for his junketing boss, wrote wryly to Mrs. Roosevelt: "I wonder if he knows that it has been practically decided to accept no volunteers whatever under the new draft, and also that married men with children are not going to be called. I fear that he will have a somewhat strenuous time getting the President to waive regulations particularly as I feel the President has sufficient judgment to know that things would go very badly here if he should leave." [1]

Roosevelt pressed his claims for active duty, but Wilson handled him smoothly. It was too late, the President said. Peace was already on the way. While Daniels campaigned for Democratic Congressmen, Roosevelt stayed on in the department. But now he was bored, and he was worried over demobilization. There would be criticism in the new Republican Congress. He wanted to supervise the dispersal of U. S. Navy property in Europe. Daniels hesitated, but Roosevelt brashly threatened to disclaim publicly all responsibility if he was not given the assignment. On New Year's Day, 1919, he was aboard ship, en route to England and France.

[8] Roosevelt to Eleanor Roosevelt, August 20, 1918, quoted in *Personal Letters, 1905–1928*, p. 440.
[9] Roosevelt to Frederick Huidekoper, September 5, 1918, Group X, FDRL.
[1] Howe to Eleanor Roosevelt, August 23, 1918, Group XXXVI, FDRL.

· III ·

THE TIME OF TESTING

11

$$\ggg\text{-}\ggg\text{-}\ggg\text{-}\ggg\text{-}\ggg\text{-}\ggg\text{-}\ggg\text{-}\ggg$$

The Hopeless Crusade—

1920

There was, of course, no upsetting the set-
tled, unreasoning desire for a change. . . .
(Franklin D. Roosevelt,
November 9, 1920) [1]

"I can tell you . . . perfectly frankly that I do not propose to
make an early Christian martyr of myself this year if the Democratic Party does make some fool mistake at San Francisco," [2]
Roosevelt wrote to an old friend in February 1920. This was his
mood. The party's future seemed dim, his own future outside of
politics uncertain. It had been a grim year, aside from the
pleasant interlude in Europe with Mrs. Roosevelt and a staff of
close friends. Most of the work had been done by devoted and
efficient aides, like John M. Hancock, and Roosevelt had
boasted of large savings and improved relations with the Allies
as a result of his trip. There had been even deeper profit in his

[1] Roosevelt to Langdon P. Marvin, November 9, 1920, Group XV, FDRL.
[2] Roosevelt to Nelson Drummond, February 14, 1920, Group X, FDRL.

conversion to Wilson's foreign policy. Watching the Peace Conference from its fringes, talking at length with the President while they returned together aboard the *George Washington,* the young imperialist had become a vigorous advocate of the League of Nations.

But at home in March there was only strained uncertainty. Troubles lay in the offing from every quarter. He spoke out frequently and strongly, but there was little chance for achievement with a Republican Congress and with a nation letting down after the war crisis. He still believed in power. He spoke for the League, but he worked for a Big Navy and Universal Military Service to strengthen his nation's influence. In France he had caught the vision of air power. He supported vigorously the Navy's pioneer transatlantic flight by a squadron of four seaplanes. He fought for expansion of American radio development to prevent its domination by European interests. And he flailed out against ". . . anarchy, and Bolshevism, against class hatred, against snobbery. . . ." [3] He refused to join the witch hunts of that violent year, but he left no room to doubt that he believed in capitalism and in moderation.

Roosevelt's real problems would come from a Congress hot for scandals to exploit in an election year. He sought to steal a march on them with his own broad, sharp criticisms of wartime administration. He blasted away at low salaries, rigid Civil Service procedures, and red tape, and he advocated a budget system with long-range planning and a personal inspection force at the disposition of the Secretary of the Navy. He found his demands for "business re-organization" popular, and he hewed away at this line again and again, in testimony before Congress, in speeches and articles. The *Literary Digest* pleasantly summed up his statements under the heading: "Another Roosevelt Headed for the White House." [4]

But his attack was insufficient to keep the Congressional sleuths away from his door. In March and April 1920, with the help of Admiral William S. Sims, the Senate Naval Affairs Committee probed and publicized the Navy's wartime problems.

[3] Quoted in Frank Freidel: *The Ordeal,* p. 19.
[4] *Literary Digest,* LXVI (June 19, 1920), p. 42.

Roosevelt was tempted at first to support Sims—many of the charges were the same ones he had been making before 1917. But there were personal dangers he could not wish away. In a speech at Brooklyn on February 1, 1920, he tried to escape the dilemma by boasting recklessly of the personal risks he had taken to prepare the Navy for war. The implication was clear that the rest of the administration had been negligent. Both Daniels and Wilson were incensed. Roosevelt tried to "explain" his remarks the next day. He had learned his lesson and he happily escaped being called by the committee to testify. But he was plagued by other charges which questioned his own personal integrity. One such incident grew out of a prominent officer's public complaints that Osborne was sending homosexuals back to the fleet from Portsmouth Prison. Roosevelt himself answered so hotly that the officer thought his career had been blighted and demanded an inquiry to clear his name. Roosevelt quashed the case, but the inconclusive charges and countercharges left an unhappy public record. This fracas was hardly quieted before a Providence newspaper publisher was charging that anti-vice squads under Roosevelt's authority at the Newport naval base had themselves resorted to perversion to obtain evidence. Roosevelt and Howe had once co-operated with this newsman in attempts to clean up Newport. "It will make rich reading if he tells half of what I know to be true . . . ," [5] Louis had written his wife. Now the editor was after Roosevelt's scalp, and the charges would be aired again and again during the Presidential election year.

F.D.R.'s chief problem was his increasingly dim future, and his chief danger, a premature draft for some hopeless race. When clumsy king-makers approached them, Howe promptly cooled them off: "We thought you had been in the political game long enough to have learned by this time to keep both your feet on the ground." [6] And Roosevelt awkwardly proclaimed: "I sometimes think we consider too much the good luck of the early bird and not the bad luck of the early worm." [7] Although

[5] Howe to Grace Howe, June 20, 1917, Personal Papers.
[6] [Howe] to Thomas Lynch, May 26, 1919, Group X, FDRL.
[7] Roosevelt to Henry Heymann, December 2, 1919, Group X, FDRL.

prospects for a nomination for President seemed ridiculous,
F.D.R. might have had the Senatorial nomination in New York,
but he avoided it. He thought being in the Senate "stupid," [8]
he told a friend. Besides he had to make some money. Mostly
he wanted to avoid being caught on a weak or conservative
ticket. He did what he could to keep "old line worn out Reactionaries" [9] to the State ticket, and he pushed for Al Smith for
the Governorship, but his influence was weak. He had to put
up with the indignity of a primary fight for convention delegates in his own district. "It is certainly an awful commentary
on our ability to handle the practical end of things . . . ," he
wrote Sague. "It merely gives courage to disturbers of the peace
like Eddie Perkins. . . ." [1] He wanted to keep the State's delegation to the San Francisco convention from being saddled with
a unit rule under which Murphy could control them. He wrote:
"It should be buried like the dodo and other prehistoric ani-
mals." [2] But, distrusting the dodo's other enemies, he left them
to be crushed in the State convention.

Roosevelt entrained for San Francisco to the music of another
newspaper boom for him as a Presidential candidate. He was
wise to scoff at it, but anything could happen in the undisciplined open convention which gathered there. The party
lacked a compelling issue, except for the League, and it was
afraid of that. And it lacked leadership. The remnants of the
old Wilsonian liberals were scattered by personal rivalries and
spiritual disillusionment. The prophets of internationalism who
spoke for Wilson's second administration were split by party
lines and dominated neither camp. Wilson himself was ill, in-
accessible, and, incredibly, nourishing third-term ambitions.
There seemed little hope for anything better than a dull compromise ticket, forged by the trading of the "practical" bosses.

Roosevelt was strangely quiet. He did grab headlines by
wresting New York's banner from its guardians and joining in

[8] Mrs. Charles Hamlin: "Some Memories of Franklin D. Roosevelt,"
FDRL.
[9] Roosevelt to Winfield Huppuch, February 13, 1920, Group X, FDRL.
[1] Roosevelt to John Sague, March 15, 1920, Group X, FDRL.
[2] *Albany Knickerbocker-Press*, May 6, 1920.

the wild demonstrations for President Wilson, but he left the fight against the unit rule to others. He sided with Tammany against a "dry" plank and supported Al Smith as a favorite son. Later he deserted both his McAdoo friends upstate and his Cox friends in Tammany to scatter his votes among other contenders. He carefully stayed out of the attempt to force a poll of the New York delegation. He was in no man's camp. When the time came, he joined the winner's parade for Governor James M. Cox, the candidate of the urban bosses.

Then suddenly Roosevelt found himself being nominated for the Vice-Presidency—so suddenly that he had to hurry out of the hall when he heard his name being presented. The vote rolled in with organized precision, and he was chosen by acclamation. A close friend wrote home that no one had to push hard for Roosevelt; the enthusiasm for him was irresistible.[3]

The smooth little play had been carefully arranged by three different groups. Franklin's own friends, John Mack, Tom Lynch, and Lathrop Brown, had been at work. More important, Judge Timothy Ansberry, a friend of Cox, had sounded out both the Governor and Charles F. Murphy. Finally, Edmond Moore, Cox's manager, had checked with the boss again. Murphy reluctantly agreed. If Cox wanted him, Roosevelt would have Tammany's support. For Moore it was a matter of balancing the ticket; F.D.R. was an Easterner, a Wilsonian, and a progressive who might sweeten the taint of machine support that soured Cox's nomination. For Murphy, it was simple expediency. If he wanted a New Yorker on the ticket, he had to take Roosevelt. F.D.R. was expendable in a lost cause; Al Smith was not. For Roosevelt there was no choice at all, although either victory or defeat might end his career.

Roosevelt set out at once to make the most of his role. He promised a "speaking campaign," not a "front porch affair."[4] The platform gave him scope for the kind of campaign he wanted. Its endorsement of the League, its promises of a budget system and of new Senate rules to expedite business, fell neatly

[3] Grenville T. Emmett to Langdon P. Marvin, July 8, 1920, Group XV, FDRL.

[4] *Salt Lake City Tribune*, July 10, 1920.

into the line he had been taking throughout the spring. Louis Howe advised him to get Cox to announce that Roosevelt would be assigned "the details of the work putting government departments upon a business basis, as well as eliminating the more archaic senatorial rules. . . ." [5] Roosevelt went him one better and asked Cox to proclaim that the Vice-President would sit with the cabinet. But his hopes were dashed. The Governor would do nothing to alarm Congressmen that a "White House snoop" [6] was in their midst. There were no announcements. Roosevelt had to follow his leader in making the League of Nations the key issue.

Back home on July 13, Roosevelt found a carefully arranged welcome for him at Poughkeepsie and Hyde Park, where his speeches called for a clean campaign, free of mud-slinging. But within 24 hours the mud was deep. When Harding charged that the League issue had been forced on them by the discredited Wilson, Roosevelt lashed back at "a certain type of senatorial mind which cares more about squaring an ancient grudge against an individual than it does to consider the true welfare of the nation." [7] As he journeyed to Washington to see the President, and to Columbus for a National Committee meeting, F.D.R. began his heavy barrage in a series of press conferences. The League would save the United States from the frightening necessity of massive defense; it would adjust the trade rivalries and uneven concentrations of population which caused modern war. On immigration, he assayed a positive approach— planned language education and financial inducements to draw the aliens from the slums.

On August 9 he was home for his official notification ceremony. The grounds of his mother's home were crowded with local admirers and national dignitaries as he arose to make his first formal address of the campaign. The long speech allowed him to bring many facets of policy into an organized framework. It was a well-finished talk. He had learned much of campaign

[5] Howe to Roosevelt, July 7, 1920, Group X, FDRL.

[6] James M. Cox: *Journey through My Years* (New York: Simon and Schuster; 1946), p. 238.

[7] *Washington Post,* July 15, 1920.

techniques in ten years. It was frank and aggressive. He laid down his commitments squarely. The two major issues were American participation in the League and businesslike reorganization of government.

He argued that the League was a "practical solution of a practical situation," but he bowed to the reservationists. The Constitution would remain supreme. His real appeal was to the emotions. "There must be no equivocation, no vagueness, no double dealing with the people on this issue. The League will not die. An idea does not die which meets the call of the hearts of our mothers." And, while he slyly challenged Republicans to take arms against the motherhood of the nation, he fended off criticism of Wilson's war record: "We have seen things on too large a scale to listen in this day to trifles, or to believe in the adequacy of trifles."

For the problem of governmental inefficiency he prescribed major surgery. The much-needed budget system would treat only marginal symptoms. Cumbersome Congressional procedures must be simplified. The departments must redistribute duties and standardize processes with "common sense." The Civil Service must be given an adequate salary scale to keep it from being the dumping ground for the inefficient. And businesslike reorganization involved something more—intelligent and continuous planning, especially in utilizing the nation's resources. Resources included population. Education must be extended to the 5,000,000 illiterates. Immigration laws must be refined to exclude physical and moral incompetents. Working conditions and urban living standards, the protection of women and children, the communications of the rural areas, must all be improved. "Our efforts in the past have been scattered. It is now time to undertake a well-considered, co-ordinated plan of development, so that each year will see progress along definite lines."

On Harding's "normalcy"? "We must see that it is impossible to avoid, except by monastic seclusion, those honorable and intimate foreign relations which the fearful-hearted miscall by the Devil's catchword 'international complications.'" Again: "We cannot anchor our ship of state in this world tempest, nor can

we return to the placid harbor of long ago. We must go forward
or flounder." This was a testament to Wilsonian liberalism, and
it was a summary of Roosevelt's own political faith, welded out
of ten years' experience.[8]

As the representative of the liberals, Roosevelt was to spend
most of his time west of Chicago and in his own State. Stephen
Early, whom F.D.R. had especially requested for the job, had
already gone ahead to obtain publicity, check the local arrangements, and sound out public opinion for the nation-wide swing.
Early was a prominent Washington newsman and a close friend
of Louis Howe. Roosevelt himself traveled with a small staff in
a private car attached to scheduled trains. His old secretary,
Charles McCarthy, remained at National Headquarters to make
upstate New York his special interest, and Louis Howe stayed
in Washington to help Daniels with wage negotiations. It was
important to maintain F.D.R.'s good relations with labor. Besides, Howe needed the money his steady job brought in. More
important, he had his cap set for Roosevelt's old position. He
was Acting Assistant Secretary briefly. During late July and
early August the newspapers buzzed with rumors that F.D.R.
had recommended him, and it was even reported that his
nomination had been sent to the President. But Howe's ambitions were larger than his bargaining power. This was too significant a post to be wasted on a political unknown. And Louis had
his enemies. The editor of the *Providence Journal,* who had led
the attacks in the Newport and Portsmouth issues, now turned
his guns on Howe. Louis's old union friend, Alifas, came to his
rescue with the public charge that Howe was being attacked
because of his pro-labor record. Nonetheless, Daniels himself
was cool. When Roosevelt tried to help his friend by telling the
Secretary that Howe had been offered a $20,000-a-year job in
private life, Daniels wrote in his diary: "He believes it. I have
a great big swallow, but I cannot swallow that." [9] The President
himself resented Roosevelt's acrobatics on the Sims charges. By

[8] Quoted in *Personal Letters, 1905–1928,* pp. 500–8; see also Group XV,
FDRL.

[9] Quoted in Jonathan Daniels: *End of Innocence,* p. 314.

the end of the summer Louis's hopes were dashed, and on September 30 he resigned as technical assistant.

Howe had chafed constantly at his isolation from all the political fun, and McCarthy pleaded with Roosevelt to bring the little manipulator up from Washington to run their personal headquarters. At the end of September Louis rushed to join Roosevelt on the second tour of the West. He helped with speeches and press releases, carefully cultivated the Associated Press men on the train, and took advantage of his free time to begin a conscious program of educating Eleanor Roosevelt in the wiles and wonders of politics. And he lightened the trip with betting pools on the size of the crowds—the loser to wear a huge, comic tie for the day.

The first trip, which lasted from August 11 to the end of the month, took Roosevelt to California and back, with speeches at 20 major cities. Scores of brief track-side talks kept him busy between principal stops. He covered 8,000 miles in 20 states, averaging six speeches a day and making as many as 26 in two days in the State of Washington. He spoke most frequently on the League, hammering away at Harding's evasive handling of the issue. He varied the diet with appeals for progressive attacks on the nation's problems. He assaulted the reported $30,-000,000 Republican campaign fund and Harding's "front-porch" campaign. Everywhere he appealed for the support of independents, and he tailored specific pleas for certain areas: in Minneapolis, the high cost of living; in Yakima, land reclamation; in Fargo, the machinations of the meat packers and the eastern bankers. At Missoula, he promised greater naval development on the Pacific Coast. In California, he praised Cox as the "Hiram Johnson of the East." [1] Harding's promise that he would be sensitive to the wisdom of Congress gave Roosevelt a chance to wind up his trip at Indianapolis with a blast at the "reactionary" Senators: the people wanted, he said, "a leader, not a syndicate presidency." [2]

F.D.R.'s appeals were soon answered. Theodore Roosevelt, Jr.,

[1] *The New York Times*, August 25, 1920.
[2] Ibid., August 31, 1920.

followed him around the circuit, explaining of Franklin: "He is a maverick—he does not have the brand of the family." [3] The *Outlook* saw nothing original in his acceptance speech and said that he made a better argument for Harding than for Cox. *The Times* found his castigation of Republican Senators a joke: "You who have been bludgeoned on the head by Theodore ought not to wince when tapped on the wrist by Franklin." [4] At the other extreme, the *New Republic* accused him of talking about an "Imaginary League," [5] when he insisted that American participation would have settled the current Russo-Polish border clashes. The most violent criticism centered on an offhand statement made at Butte, Montana. In an attempt to answer the complaint that the British Empire had six votes in the League Assembly to the United States' one, Roosevelt had emphasized the unity of policy of the American Republics. The Associated Press quoted him as boasting: "Well, I will say that the United States has at least twelve votes in the Assembly of the League. . . . I have something to do with the running of a couple of little Republics. Until last week, I had two of these votes in my pocket. Now Secretary Daniels has them. One of them was Haiti. I know, for I wrote Haiti's Constitution myself, and if I do say it, I think it was a pretty good little Constitution." [6]

Roosevelt's denial on August 22 was not well publicized. Harding picked him up on the indiscretion in a speech several days later. F.D.R. then complained that he had made no such "deliberately false" statement about controlling Latin American votes. He had merely said that the interests of the American Republics were "broadly identical." [7] He did not deny specifically the comment on the Haitian Constitution. The story did not die easily. Several members of the audience at Butte corroborated the newsman's report. F.D.R. was able to force the

[3] *New York World*, September 18, 1920.

[4] *The New York Times*, August 19, 1920.

[5] "Mr. Roosevelt's Imaginary League," *New Republic*, XXIII (August 25, 1920), pp. 348–9.

[6] *The New York Times*, August 9, 1920. For other versions see Scrapbooks, FDRL.

[7] "Statement for the Associated Press by Hon. Franklin D. Roosevelt, September 2, 1920," Group XV, FDRL.

Outlook to apologize for a critical editorial on the matter, and Harding publicly accepted his explanation, but Roosevelt had to deny the story again as late as 1928.

While Roosevelt's ideas were fairly conventional and his attacks occasionally marred by indiscretion, his personality was wondrously effective. Cox came to appreciate his talent for making friends in small groups and for charming audiences *en masse.* One friendly reporter wrote: "He gets . . . the last ounce of appeal-power out of each sentence. . . . The physical impression leaves nothing to be asked—the figure of an idealized college football player, almost the poster type in public life; . . . making clean, direct and few gestures; always with a smile ready to share, sincerely, one is sure, in the audience's humor. He speaks with a strong, clear voice, with a tenor note in it which rings—sings, one is tempted to say—in key with . . . that intangible, utterly charming and surely vote-winning quality. . . ." [8] Even Henry F. Pringle, involved 12 years later in sharp criticism of Roosevelt's political morals, would admit: ". . . he had a pleasing personality . . . a magnificently strong physique. He seemed to be an excellent type for a Vice-Presidential candidate; he had no discernible enemies and was perfectly contented in his obscure role." [9]

Roosevelt knew from the start that his was a hopeless cause. He recognized that the League issue would require "an educational campaign to clear up many of the misunderstandings. . . ." [1] But after his western trip he adopted a pose of renewed confidence, while McCarthy pointed hopefully to scattered omens of support from the faithful of the old Bull Moose Party. Privately, however, Roosevelt, Cox, and McCarthy all complained of inept management, poor public relations, and inadequate financing. Roosevelt was particularly incensed: "Make Republican campaign ridiculous," he insisted. "Use T.R. Jr's full statement about the Republican Party winning the war. Use the Republican gumshoe campaign in Maine that Canadian

[8] *New York Evening Post,* August 10, 1920.
[9] Henry F. Pringle: "Franklin D. Roosevelt—Perched on a Bandwagon," *The Nation,* CXXXIV (April 27, 1932), pp. 487–9.
[1] Roosevelt to W. R. Campbell, July 26, 1920, Group XV, FDRL.

troops are being sent to Poland by the League of Nations. Use, in the proper way, Republican whispering campaign in the backwoods section of Maine that the democrats have 60,000 *useless* clerks in the departments in Washington, and that on March 4th Harding, if elected, will *replace* them with 60,000 tried and true Republicans." [2]

Although he criticized large Republican funds, Roosevelt would have been glad to have been able to match them. He himself contributed $5,000, his mother $3,000 more. He also bore a large amount of his personal campaign expenses and worked to raise money from his friends upstate to help liquidate the National Committee's debt. McCarthy complained that blunderers at National Headquarters had failed to recognize big contributors when they came to call, but this was the beginning of a general apathy among wealthy Democrats which was to haunt the party for years. The campaign finished deep in debt, which hung over the heads of the candidates and Committeemen for years.

Roosevelt opened his eastern campaign with a two weeks' tour of New England early in September. By now all thoughts of an impersonal campaign were gone. He claimed Coolidge wanted the President to be merely a clerk. He inveighed against the Republican platform as a "hymn of hate." [3] He pounced upon Harding's remark that too much had been made of independence in politics.

The real problem was that the upstate New York vote might determine who carried the key state. Roosevelt's deeply disenchanted allies wrote him long tirades against McAdoo's ambitious maneuverings, against Wilson, Tammany, and the patronage mess—and they threatened an Independent ticket. T. M. Osborne raised the familiar complaint: "It's the same old story—throwing away our opportunities because of our rotten apology for a Democratic organization." [4] The Republican opposition raked up the ancient stories of anti-Catholic prejudice,

[2] "Memorandum for Mr. White," September 6, 1920, Group XV, FDRL.
[3] *The New York Times*, September 16, 1920.
[4] Thomas Mott Osborne to Roosevelt, August 4, 1920, Group XV, FDRL.

and the explosive prohibition issue cut deeply into the party. Roosevelt ignored any rehearsal of past embarrassments, and Howe urged him to use the same tactics on prohibition and Tammany. But he could not remain quiet. Although Al Smith headed the State ticket, Roosevelt courted the rebels by ambiguously approving an independent campaign organization, so long as it did not assume the character of a "political machine." [5] He kept quiet on prohibition—in New York—but to Southerners he wrote uncomfortable letters which explained that Cox would enforce the law—Congress and the courts were not likely to approve changes anyway—and that he was much impressed with the "splendid results" of prohibition.[6] On September 20 he started a six-day canvass of the central and northern counties. A second tour at the end of the campaign would cover the southern tier and the west.

The upstate campaign featured none of the old anti-bossism. There were promises to bring down the high cost of living, to increase food production, to improve transportation and markets for farmers, and to police the market profiteers. There were promises to regulate essential industries like coal, to guarantee reasonable prices. But it was all very vague. Mostly he damned Republicans on the League issue. He said they were gambling for the "hyphenated vote"—that "small but very dangerous element which was not loyal during the war." [7] They had conspired at a secret meeting "to kill the League of Nations for the sake of partisan advantage," [8] even before they had read the draft.

At the end of this quick tour, Roosevelt was considerably sobered. To a friendly reporter, he would say only: ". . . if we had sufficient time to present our arguments before the people, I have not the slightest doubt as to the choice they would make. . . ." [9] There were good reasons for his caution. Little real work was being done upstate. Refusing to dignify his campaign with

[5] Roosevelt to George Foster Peabody, July 24, 1920, Group XV, FDRL.

[6] Roosevelt to Russell Bowie, July 30, 1920, Group XV, FDRL.

[7] Press Release, Syracuse, September 22, 1920, Group XV, FDRL.

[8] Roosevelt to R. S. Baker, February 20, 1922, Group XIV, FDRL.

[9] *New York World,* September 27, 1920.

rational replies, Republicans were plastering the rural weeklies with boiler-plate articles questioning his intelligence. "Ridicule is the most severe weapon that can be aimed at any man," they proclaimed. "Nevertheless, Franklin D. Roosevelt, by his actions and his utterances, makes it impossible for the people to treat him seriously. As it is, however, he is young, very young." [1] In the midst of F.D.R.'s upstate tour, Howe wrote desperately to Sague: "For Heaven's sake, give me some information about what is being done in New York State. . . . I can't make head or tail of this madhouse of a campaign. . . ." [2] The reply was dismal, but accurate: "In my judgment New York is lost to the National ticket and irretrievably so." [3]

Roosevelt left almost immediately on a second tour of the West to face a national situation hardly better than that in New York. Swinging through the central states, he went as far as Colorado and then returned through Illinois, Indiana, Michigan, and Ohio. He spent less time on defense and concentrated on Harding personally. The Senator had a weakling's voting record, he said. No one knew where Harding stood. The Republican candidate advocated tariffs for privileged groups rather than scientific protection such as Cox would promote. Harding was the tool of "Wall Street gamblers and money trust interest." [4] Roosevelt sought to answer Republican charges of corruption by playing up the bipartisan nature of the war effort and by pointing to Republican inefficiency in the war with Spain. Republicans were divided sharply on the League question; F.D.R. labeled them with relish—"League Liars." [5] When Harding tried to recoup by announcing that a French spokesman had approached him about a new kind of League, Roosevelt gleefully pounced on him and, with Cox and the State Department, forced him to a retraction.

A last broad swing through West Virginia, Maryland, New Jersey, Connecticut, and Westchester County brought F.D.R.

[1] New Rochelle Pioneer, September 25, 1920.

[2] Howe to John Sague, September 20, 1920, Group XV, FDRL.

[3] Sague to Howe, September 22, 1920, Group XV, FDRL.

[4] Roosevelt to C. H. McCarthy, October 9, 1920, Group XV, FDRL.

[5] The New York Times, October 12, 1920.

finally to the traditional mammoth rally at Madison Square
Garden and to his own personal election-eve climax at Hudson.
During the last week he played the League issue for all that
was in it. In the City he advocated Ireland's membership in
the League. Everywhere he railed against the "hard-boiled"
Republicans who would close their eyes and vote for Harding
even though they favored the League. And he associated the
Republican candidate with a sacrilegious cartoon in which the
League appeared as Wilson's "Immaculate Conception." [6]

But this energetic, three months' campaign of over a thousand
speeches in 32 states could do little except prove Roosevelt's
fighting spirit. He feigned optimism until the end, even assuring
Cox during the last week that the "so called silent vote" would
carry New York for them,[7] but he had long since lost hope. To
clinch the approaching disaster, the Republican National Committee embarked on a smear campaign against F.D.R. just eight
days before election. It released a letter from John Rathom, the
Providence publisher, accusing Roosevelt of lying when early
in the summer he had denied removing from the Navy files the
records of a man convicted on a morals charge. This was dynamite. At any moment the odorous charges that he and Osborne
had condoned moral turpitude might be raked into the open
again. In his own paper Rathom wrote: "If there are two characteristics in which Mr. Roosevelt is utterly lacking, they are
the qualities of frankness and manliness." [8] Roosevelt issued an
angry denial which Arthur Krock helped him work out, and he
sued for libel. But the damage was done.

The disaster on election day was more shocking than even
Roosevelt could have expected. The New York Democratic
Party was nothing more than a ruined shell. Harding polled
more than twice as many votes as Cox in the State. Democrats
carried not one State office, not one county. Worse yet, Republicans had captured most of the new voters. This was a
sample of the national trend.

Roosevelt saw it as a "tidal flow of discontent and destructive

[6] Ibid., October 25, 1920.
[7] Roosevelt to James M. Cox, October 23, 1920, Group XV, FDRL.
[8] *Providence Journal,* August 12, 1920.

criticism," [9] the inevitable backwash of the war. To his law partner he wrote: "I can only hope that the Republican administration will be able to satisfy these people, but the probability is that they will kick just as hard against the next administration as they did against this one. . . ." [1] To another friend he genially confided: ". . . the victory of Harding has brought under one tent everybody with a grouch in the whole United States. The result will be one of the finest little cat-fights you ever saw. . . ." [2] But to leaders like Al Smith he prescribed the medicine he had been selling since 1911: rebuild the upstate Democratic organization.[3]

Roosevelt did not foresee the 12 years of national Republican monopoly, and he was not ready to accept the slow political atrophy which was the ordinary fate of defeated vice-presidential candidates. He now had a reputation of his own, distinct from that of the Wilson administration. He expected to lead.

[9] Roosevelt to Anna K. Henderson, November 9, 1920, Group XV, FDRL.

[1] Roosevelt to Langdon P. Marvin, November 9, 1920, Group XV, FDRL.

[2] Roosevelt to George Marvin, November 15, 1920, Group XV, FDRL.

[3] Roosevelt to Alfred E. Smith, November 9, 1920, Group XIV, "Smith File," FDRL.

12

──────────────────────
->>>->>>->>>->>>->>>->>>->>>->>>
──────────────────────

Life in Suspense

. . . the doctors assure me that I am recovering very rapidly and there is no reason to fear any permanent effects from my illness.   (Franklin D. Roosevelt, *September 22, 1921*) [1]

FOR THE Roosevelt and Howe families, the disillusioning 1920 campaign had been merely an interlude in the more pressing business of finding a future. Life had been good to them all during the eight Navy years. It would be all the more difficult to readjust. For Grace, "Kiddens," and "Bubkins," as young Hartley was soon called, Washington had meant their first opportunity for an uninterrupted family life. Mary, who had missed much of the seventh and all of the eighth grade in the family's perambulations, was rushed into private school to prepare for college. And Louis was home with them throughout the year. Eleanor Roosevelt, now mistress of a busy household of growing children, found Washington life intriguing but demanding. An incessant round of ceremonial calls soon merged into the enervating whirl of dinner parties and teas. Sometimes Mrs. Roosevelt and Mrs. Howe drove about town together in the

[1] Roosevelt to Robert Goldsmith, September 22, 1921, Group XI, FDRL.

afternoons, with Grace minding the children in the car while
Eleanor made her official visits. Both found their husbands im-
mersed in work. In the Navy Department the hours were late
and uncertain, especially as the war approached. Evening engagements abounded, and trips to the far-flung yards were frequent. Both families took to long summer retreats from the
Washington humidity, the Roosevelts at Campobello, the
Howes at Horseneck Beach. The men shifted for themselves,
with brief vacations to break the routine.

For Eleanor Roosevelt, as for Grace Howe, there were compensations. For the first time she was free to run her family and
household without the dominating omnipresence of her husband's formidable mother. The Roosevelts' entertaining often
included congenial friends from the New York and Boston society within which they had moved. Blessed with adequate
domestic help, Eleanor could go along on some of the longer
visits to enjoy the fun of traveling as a V.I.P.

The Howes' social life was drastically limited. They could
not afford servants, and Grace's day was filled with cleaning
and cooking, grocery-shopping and long walks in Washington
parks with young Hartley. They made some close friendships
with the younger Navy couples, among them the Richard E.
Byrds, who lived in the next apartment, but there were few
parties. It became a family custom for Grace and Mary to take
turns staying with Hartley while the other went down to the
old Navy Building next to the White House to tear Louis away
from his work between 6 and 7. Then there would be a hasty
supper in a nearby lunchroom and often a breakneck dash
across town to make an early movie. On other evenings Louis
would come home late from the office to roughhouse with
Hartley or to read him adventure stories before bed. It seemed
to Grace that this upset the boy's nerves and disturbed his
sleep, and she wheedled from a Navy doctor the written prescription: "Your boy must be put to bed immediately after
dinner and must not be played with or read to thereafter. . . ." [2]
Family dinner at home was an unusual occasion.

[2] Personal Papers.

At first they had no auto, but in 1918 Louis bought a new
Overland touring car, and they spent Sundays picnicking in the
Virginia or Maryland countryside and exploring the muddy
back roads. Louis's Overland was his prized possession for ten
years, although his colleagues did not always appreciate it.
They were appalled when Louis ordered one of them to chauffeur William Howard Taft to a Navy Department conference
in it, and were greatly relieved that the portly ex-President
preferred to walk.

Hartley, like the Roosevelt boys, enjoyed his visits to the
Navy Department and the excitement of Washington parades.
Mary was much absorbed in the drastic challenge of making
up for the haphazard nature of her elementary-school days. As
the two families became closer, there would be long evenings
in which stamp-enthusiasts Uncle Franklin, Grace, and Louis
sat around the dining-room table with their collectors' gear,
while Aunt Eleanor knitted and joined in the conversation.

But Louis's main recreations remained the hobbies of his
earlier days. He and Grace often played whist, and he sang
regularly in the choir of the nearby St. Thomas church which
both the Roosevelts and the Howes attended. He remained an
avid little-theater buff, a leader in the Drama League Players.
Still given to comedy, he directed *The March of the Tortoise*
at the Belasco, in which Postmaster General Burleson's wife
played a leading role. This history of womankind in three
acts generally went to prove that, while her progress was slow,
she eventually made it. Howe also played in a farce called *The
Movie Finger Writes*. He collaborated in writing and producing
a pantomime, *Fe, Fi, Fo, Fum*, which a dramatic critic called
"funny, every minute of it." [3] His most notable role was as
Beamish, the complaining clerk, in George Bernard Shaw's
wartime comedy, *Augustus Does His Bit*. Louis was also stage
manager for this production at Poli's Theater in 1917.

Louis and Franklin could usually salvage two to four weeks
each for vacations with their families by the sea. They often
arranged official trips to Newport, Boston, or Portsmouth, with

[3] Clipping, Personal Papers.

quick excursions to the beach on the side. Roosevelt frequently arranged to be dropped off at Eastport, Maine, by a naval vessel. Even Howe created something of a stir by arriving once off Westport Point aboard a destroyer. Under the influence of sailor-Roosevelt, Louis became interested in model boats. For the real things, he was something less than enthusiastic. Never much of a sailor, he was useful chiefly at the oars, when the family was stranded offshore by calm or tide. But when Hartley reached the proper age, Louis bought a small catboat for the boy and a motorboat for Mary.

In the cottage at Horseneck Beach, which the Howes had rented first in 1908, Louis had found his real home. The salt air and sunshine and the soothing roll of the breakers, the quiet neighborhood—only two cottages nearby, and these deserted in the autumn months—all conspired to heal, relax, and comfort. It was as secluded a spot as one could find along the southern New England shore. Their cottage was a square, two-storied structure, with a broad porch running all around. Set in front of the dunes, it commanded a sweeping view of the broad Atlantic. Almost at the front step, the rolling surf provided relaxing bathing for children and adults alike. Around the point to the north lay the quiet anchorage of the Westport River. With no telephone and no road, it was a peaceful retreat from the world. Only the most determined visitor would take the electric cars down from Providence to Fall River, and the stage to Westport Point, and then tramp the long mile and a half through the dunes and along the beach. Telegraph messages were left at Lulu Hammond's general store in the village, to be picked up when the Howes came in. The grocery and milk wagons were the only vehicles to reach their cottage. It was not until 1933 that Louis would break this pleasant isolation by building a packed-sand road to reach the barn and by putting in electricity.

Here Louis could fish the river, splash about in the surf with his antique breast stroke, and develop his latent talent for drawing and painting. Self-taught as an artist, he nevertheless evolved a fine command of perspective and line and a clear sense of the principles of design. Working almost always with watercolors, he learned to handle his brush with fine, precise strokes and his use of color was particularly successful in his studies of the dunes and sandgrass, sea and skyscape about the cottage. He experimented with portraits and had a fair amateur's success with sketches of Grace and his children. But he never became a finished painter. It was only a pastime, and he never worked at it steadily enough.

This was also true of his other hobbies. Possessed of vast interests and widely ranging native talents, he played at this and that constantly throughout his life, but sought mastery in none of his artistic hobbies except, perhaps, the drama. A precocious poet, he had settled down by his late thirties to satisfy himself with a constant stream of doggerel to amuse his family and friends. Occasionally he wrote a piece of serious verse for close friends. An ardent home carpenter, he eventually installed a lathe in the barn, but he was never a craftsman. He had too little patience to finish the rough furniture he made, although an occasional piece, like his subtly shaped whale's-head lamp, betrayed the loving care of an artist. One of his favorite activities for many years was producing a series of elaborately contrived fireworks displays for the Fourth of July, complete with intricately decorated programs for his family and guests.

Despite his tough exterior, Louis was an artist at heart. His deep sensitivity showed nowhere more clearly than in his horror at the war he helped to run but never saw, except from afar. In June 1917, for example, when French officers had briefed the Munitions Board on gas warfare, he wrote his wife: "For the most part they were little, thin-faced, thin-whiskered, soft-voiced men and to hear them quietly stand up and describe how they found one trench that was very deep with 2300 men in it and fired gas shells into it until every man was killed and like tales seemed like a dream of some kind and as if one was listening to some kind of play. . . ."[4]

Life was difficult in some ways for the Howes during Navy years. Despite steady increases in Louis's salary, they were hounded by debt. They managed to buy their beloved cottage

[4] Howe to Grace Howe, June 20, 1917, Personal Papers.

at the beach, but they had to scramble in 1914 to save the
Phila Street house from a foreclosure. Louis's chronic heart
trouble and asthma continued, although his family never knew
of his most serious crisis. In New York on business for Roosevelt
in September 1913, he collapsed in a hotel room and was revived only after several hours of work by the house physician.
Later he wrote Roosevelt: "I took a chance that what was the
matter was the same old thing and followed the course that
pulled me through before, filled up with strychnine and beat
it for the beach. For a week I was in bad shape but the pain in
my heart left me suddenly just as it did before, and today I can
run up the sand pile in front of my house without seeing black,
which is my old test for cured. I may have to be a little careful
for a week or two after I come back, but I am honestly o.k. and
fit for work. . . ." [5] Roosevelt helped keep the bad news from
Howe's family and extended his leave. Apparently there were
no more attacks like this. But his health remained naggingly
poor, and in the winter of 1917–18, he was very ill with the flu.
He worked constantly under a cloud of apprehension. "I have
taken it for granted," he warned F.D.R., "that sooner or later
I would ignore the danger signals too long and drop out like a
snuffed candle." [6]

Howe never learned to relax completely with family and
friends as Roosevelt did. He carried his work with him constantly. Trips to Massachusetts and back were often hedged
about with conferences or business chores en route. Many a day
at Horseneck Beach was spent on the porch in furious letter
writing or work on draft documents. When he was in Washington without his family, he became lost in his work. Never a
reliable correspondent, he oscillated between long periods in
which he wrote no letters to them and flurries of remorseful
notes in which he tried to convince them that they were always
in his thoughts. Often there were little peace gifts, as to Mary:
"Dear Enfant . . . Here is some real paints. . . . See if you
can be a real painter when you use them." [7] And sometimes

[5] Howe to Roosevelt, October 10 [1913], Group XII, FDRL.

[6] Howe to Roosevelt, n.d., Group XII, FDRL.

[7] Howe to Mary Howe, n.d., Personal Papers.

there were really big gestures of his affection, for example, the months of maneuvering that climaxed in Mary's being chosen to christen a submarine at Portsmouth Yard.

Throughout the last year in Washington, life became more expensive and more uncertain for the Howes. While Louis worried about his salary in a Republican retrenchment, expenses increased. Mary was now a junior at Vassar and planning a trip to Italy the following summer. Eleven-year-old Hartley was in private school, and in December 1920 they moved to a new, more expensive apartment. Louis had always been plagued by black moods. Late in 1919 he wrote: ". . . everyone . . . is indifferent, or hates me, or is afraid of me, or uses me to get what they want. . . ." [8]

Roosevelt never fell into such deep self-doubt, but even he was worried about money. "I am honestly a fit candidate for a receiver . . . ," he wrote to one old friend. [9] His family was hardly underprivileged, but his salaries in ten years of public life had never come near his living and campaigning expenses. Indeed, his ambitions had been a drain on both his mother's and his wife's pocketbooks. And he began to realize his immense obligations to his growing family. Both Louis and his boss had begun to cast about for new opportunities as early as January 1919. They wanted to get rich—and quickly. Howe hit upon a wealthy young naval lieutenant who "thinks you are about the finest thing that ever happened." This attractive admirer had come to Louis with hazy plans for an export business and with assurances of a million dollars in capital. Louis confided to Roosevelt: "He has no more idea than a cat as to how to go about it. . . . If you are still fond of your Haiti project, this looks like easy money. . . ." [1]

The Haitian project never developed, but both Roosevelt and Howe became involved in an elaborate oil scheme which might have destroyed their political futures. This involved an oil refinery to be built in Grace Howe's home town of Fall River

[8] Howe to Grace Howe, October 9, 1919, Personal Papers.

[9] Roosevelt to Wendell P. Blagdon, December 17, 1919, Group X, FDRL.

[1] Howe to Roosevelt, January 16, 1919, Group X, FDRL.

with money largely borrowed from the Navy. Navy tankers
would supply it, and in return, the government hoped to obtain
a steady fuel supply on the eastern seaboard and help break
the rising price curve. It seemed a pleasant solution for both
the Navy's problems and Fall River's lagging economy. Roosevelt fought the project through, past the stolid resistance of
Daniels and some of his admirals. He and Howe had no financial interest in it, but their friend Pat Homer did. They were
involved in a related scheme to prospect for oil. Roosevelt had
a $5,000 investment in Homer's Washington Oil Syndicate.
Louis somehow came to own 500 shares in the same scheme
and sent them to Grace with the warning that they should be
turned over to Roosevelt if anything happened to him. F.D.R.
would sell them for at least $5,000, he said, and if the wells
came in, the income would be about $7.25 a day. Louis was
cultivating his friend Pat, and he hoped for a job with the firm
when he had to leave Washington.

Roosevelt boasted about the refinery as a great personal
achievement, but it turned out sadly. Oil prices dropped; the
Navy branded the whole thing an error. Roosevelt sold out
his shares early in 1920. Both he and Howe soon came to wish
the whole thing forgotten.

Roosevelt had other and firmer resources. In March 1920,
months before he had left the Navy, he arranged to accept a
law partnership with two friends of roughly his own age. Since
he was still obviously bored with the law, the firm of Emmet,
Marvin, and Roosevelt was little more than job insurance for
him. His quest for broader horizons led to a $25,000-a-year
vice-presidency with the Fidelity and Deposit Company of
Maryland, a large surety bonding house. Politics had something
to do with this. Like Roosevelt, Van Lear Black, the Fidelity's
President, was a Democrat, an adventuresome go-getter, and a
yachtsman. At the same time, Roosevelt could offer wide con-
nections in business, labor, and politics, and a salesman's personality. In addition, he might be useful in the sticky business
of getting along with the New York State Banking Department.
For Roosevelt, it was ideal. He could spend half his day at the

law firm, and Black proved immensely tolerant when he spent
much of the other half at personal politics.

F.D.R. bid strongly for acceptance in the conservative business world. His frequent interviews and articles stressed the
need for natural readjustment from wartime conditions. He
advocated "saving and investing," and he glamorized the surety
business as the "balance wheel" of the industrial world.[2] But his
own investments were gloriously and recklessly imaginative.
He plunged into an ill-fated venture to sell small bond certifi-
cates through the banks, on the pattern of the government's
Liberty Loan. He frankly admired Louisiana sugar land specu-
lators who had made 100 per cent profits during the war, and
he inquired into chances for quick wealth in cotton lands and
radio. He even played fitfully with the vast dream of interesting
the electrical industry in harnessing the tidal energy of Pas-
samaquoddy Bay.

His enthusiasm was endless. With business prospects enough
for two or three men, he bounded restlessly into fund campaigns for a Woodrow Wilson Memorial, for the Lighthouse for
the Blind, the Boy Scouts, and Near East Relief. He kept in the
news with dozens of speeches for the Navy, and he played
politics as if the rest of his interests were merely temporary
hobbies. He pressed on the Democratic National Committee his
demands for reorganization, for a positive program, for relentless attacks on Harding. In his interminable correspondence
with old political friends, he kept up this attack. And he piped
a similar tune to the State organization. But he had learned the
lessons of rebellion. Everything must be done through the regular machines, so that there would be no taint of insurgency,
no resentment at "a fool attempt by high brows to do the impossible."[3] Much time and work went into the failing fortunes
of the Dutchess County Democracy. He might be living in the
great double house on East 65th Street, which his mother had
bought for them, but he had no intention of abandoning the
base of his upstate reputation.

[2] Quoted in Freidel: *The Ordeal*, p. 93.
[3] Roosevelt to Adelbert Scriber, May 20, 1921, Group XI, FDRL.

Despite all the busyness of his four-sided career, Roosevelt settled back into the pleasures of upper-middle-class life which he had largely pushed aside for ten years. The five-day week in the city for business and the children's schooling were relieved by the habitual country week ends. Anna was now 15. The boys ranged from five to 14, a time for romping and games and rough outdoor sport. At the great estate at Hyde Park, Saturdays and Sundays would be "very quiet but plenty to eat and wash it down." [4] There would be riding and golf, sailing on the river, and perhaps even the old ice yacht could be unlimbered on occasion. Already a member of the Harvard Club and of Racquet and Tennis, F.D.R. now sought nomination to the Century Club, distinguished for its progressive and literary traditions. Above all, there would be the long summers at Campo, which he had missed so much during the war. He eagerly negotiated early in May 1921 for the services of a local captain to prepare his two sailboats and motor launch for the summer's fun.

Meanwhile, Howe was working out his own personal fortune in Washington. His problems were more complex. Older by ten years than Roosevelt, he found himself again at a crossroads with few signposts. He had been swept from obscurity and he had innumerable business acquaintances and a creditable management record, but he had worked in Roosevelt's shadow. And he had no Hyde Park base or Harvard security to which to return. Most important, he had to decide whether to fight for a place on Roosevelt's payroll or to strike out recklessly, and for the first time in his life, on his own.

After the campaign, he had eight months more in the Navy Department in which to think and plan. Daniels had invited him back with a warm note of appreciation for ". . . your ability and resourcefulness and the excellent service you have rendered and will continue to render, I trust, as long as I am in office." [5] Louis joked that they wanted him around just to have a scapegoat for Republican criticism. But he proved immensely

[4] Roosevelt to Stephen Early, December 21, 1920, quoted in *Personal Letters, 1905–1928*, p. 514.

[5] Josephus Daniels to Howe, August 27, 1920, Personal Papers.

useful, and he stayed on to help Harding's appointee over the transition. He toyed throughout the winter with a range of tantalizing offers: the city editorship of a New York paper, an executive position with Homer's New England Oil Company, among others. But by March 1921 his decision had been made. He would join the Fidelity and Deposit as Roosevelt's assistant.

Throughout the year, the Roosevelts and Howes remained friends. Grace and Eleanor exchanged warm and gossipy letters and favors. Eleanor was glad to run down to Vassar to check on Mary when she was ill, to help her choose a Junior Prom dress, to offer the use of their furniture stored in Washington when the Howes moved into a larger apartment. She sent along good woolen socks for Hartley that Elliott had outgrown, asked Grace for 20 pounds of brown sugar from the Navy Commissary —they couldn't get in New York the kind Franklin liked—and asked for the return of a rug the Howes had been using, since it would help to brighten Franklin's somewhat cramped and colorless Wall Street office.[6] In return, Grace and Louis could do innumerable errands for the Roosevelts in Washington, and Eleanor would appreciate their help greatly.[7] They were close enough so that Eleanor could confide some of her frustrations to Grace. Finding that Franklin had dinner engagements for Tuesday, Wednesday, and Thursday, after he had complained that he would have to work every night to learn the surety business, she confessed that the prospects for the peaceful life she cherished seemed daily more dim. Franklin might protest that it was only for this week, but she already sensed that private life would be just as hectic as Washington life.[8]

Early in the summer, Franklin and Louis were driven even more closely together as they played out one final bit of Navy drama which held danger for both of them. In the Newport investigations of the old charges of immorality and incompetence the Republicans had found something to criticize. Roose-

[6] Eleanor Roosevelt to Grace Howe, January 20, 1921, Personal Papers.
[7] Eleanor Roosevelt to Grace Howe, February 22, 1921, Personal Papers.
[8] Eleanor Roosevelt to Grace Howe, December 27, 1920, Personal Papers.

velt had been worried about this for a year. He had pressed Daniels to close the official investigation before he left office, and he had sent letters to the department to clear himself of personal responsibility for the vice squad which had been technically under his office. But the matter did not die easily. With a new administration, a Senate subcommittee launched a major investigation which ran eventually to over 6,000 pages of testimony. Dominated by the Republican majority of 2 to 1, it soon began to look like a lynching party. Roosevelt thought he had an invitation to testify before the committee, but was eventually refused the courtesy, although extensive time was given to the statements of the Providence publisher who had so assiduously bedeviled him for over a year, and of a Navy doctor who was fighting to defend his own reputation and professional status.

Early in July Roosevelt finally went off to Campobello and Howe to Horseneck Beach for the long vacations they had promised their families. Grace and Louis planned to go up to Campobello in mid-July to join the Roosevelts for several weeks, but on Wednesday, July 13, Howe received a hectic telegram from friends in Washington warning that the Senate subcommitte's report would be a severe censure of both Daniels and Roosevelt. Could he reach Roosevelt in time to do any good? Louis walked across the dunes to Westport Point to wire F.D.R. that he would go to Washington at once. Roosevelt decided at first not to return, and Howe went on alone to find that there was little to be done. Howe returned on the week end to discover that Roosevelt had squeezed from the committee their reluctant agreement to let him study the monumental testimony for a few hours and make a formal rebuttal on Monday. They finally decided to compare notes in Boston on Sunday. F.D.R. would go on to the hearing alone. Louis, Grace, and Hartley would head north for Campobello.

When Roosevelt reached Washington, he was completely dismayed. The committee insisted that it was not necessary for him to speak. After much argument they agreed to hear him at 8 in the evening, but by 4 in the afternoon the newsmen had been given the unamended report of the two Republican

Senators, complete with a mass of detail which the papers found "unprintable." Roosevelt worked all day and far into the night with Steve Early on a lengthy press release to establish his innocence, but the dissenting report of the single Democratic committee member and Roosevelt's own rebuttal were overshadowed. He sadly concluded that the only thing to do was to file an official statement with the committee and wait. In fact, the furor died quickly, but F.D.R.'s rankling resentment remained.

He headed back to New York for an intensive and exhausting two weeks of work. Then he ran up to Bear Mountain for an outdoor conference of the Boy Scout Council on July 27. He rushed over to Hyde Park for a hasty week end, and then headed north on Van Lear Black's yacht. In Campobello he kept up the intense schedule. He arrived tired out from hours at the wheel of the yacht, as he piloted it into the tricky harbor in rough weather. But there were guests to be entertained and five young boys to prod him on to the rough fun they all enjoyed. He fished for hours the day after they arrived, baiting hooks for his guests from New York, falling overboard into the icy water, and spending hours in dripping wet clothes. There was no thought of impending disaster. They gaily planned a three-day camping trip up the St. Croix River for everyone except the two smallest boys, Franklin and John. Grace Howe, writing to Mary, could find nothing more disturbing to report than the fact that life had proved too vigorous for some of the guests, who received "most opportune telegrams . . . which made it imperative that they should start back for N.Y. . . . ," and that "Dad has slipped on the tennis court and is going through a great performance of having everybody wait on him. . . ." [9]

The crisis broke upon them on Wednesday, August 10. F.D.R. had spent an unusually strenuous day. Sailing, fighting a forest fire for hours, he joined the boys in a two-mile trot across the island, a frigid swim in the Bay of Fundy, and then the long run home. Back in the living room of the old frame house, he

[9] Grace Howe to Mary Howe, August 7, 1921, Personal Papers.

sat down to read the mail and the papers and gradually found himself overcome with a heavy fatigue and depression he had never known before. Suspecting lumbago, he climbed upstairs soon after dinner. He would never walk unaided again, but it would be weeks before the full awareness of his illness would reach his family and himself. After a feverish, chill-ridden night, Roosevelt was able to move about only slowly in the morning with his left leg dragging. By afternoon he couldn't stand on his right leg; by Friday morning the muscles in both had refused to work. His temperature stood at 102. He ached all over. By Saturday all the muscles below his chest were involved as well as those of his thumbs, and his legs were numb and helpless. The Roosevelts' old family physician at first thought it merely a cold or the grippe, but by Saturday Eleanor and Louis knew that Franklin was in desperate condition. The children were sent off on the camping trip they had planned. Grace Howe went along with them. Louis stayed to help Eleanor with the 24-hour challenge of nursing Franklin and with the innumerable details of business and household arrangements. A visiting physician at Bar Harbor diagnosed the trouble as a blood clot on the spinal column. He prescribed massage. Louis and Eleanor took turns for hours on end rubbing F.D.R.'s feet and legs—a painful and tragically mistaken treatment which increased the damage to the muscle tissue. The fever continued for a week. Eleanor and Louis did not discuss with Franklin the possibilities of a long convalescence and Eleanor dreaded the day when they must. Franklin himself, dismally depressed, maintained his cultivated façade of gaiety, managed even to joke a little.

While they marked time at Campo, Louis was busily seeking help from the outside. He wrote long, highly descriptive letters to Franklin's uncle, Frederick Delano, who consulted New York specialists. They noted the possibility of infantile paralysis, and their diagnosis was finally confirmed by a Boston specialist who came up on August 25. Howe also acted as a shield for Roosevelt against the outside world. He and Delano carefully conspired to keep Franklin's mother from being alarmed. Delano met her when she docked in New York from her European vacation and broke the news personally. Howe handled the business and political correspondence which Roosevelt could not even sign, managing many routine things without giving a hint of the crisis and confiding only to trusted associates that Roosevelt was seriously ill. No one outside the family was allowed to know that F.D.R. had polio.

During the mounting crisis at Campobello, Eleanor Roosevelt and Louis Howe became closer than they had ever been before, as they worked together in their common endeavor. There was little time for questioning or long-range plans. Aided by the optimistic forecasts of the doctors, they simply reacted to the challenge with the constantly underlying assumption that everything would return to normal. Louis may have had in mind the need to handle matters in such a way as to protect his boss's political future. He could hardly have avoided it. There had long since grown between them a warm intimacy that made the problem for Louis much more than one of political expediency. He and Eleanor were both concerned over the dismal depression which at times broke through Franklin's contrived façade. They both were anxious to insulate him from the publicity which would exacerbate his growing feeling of helplessness. Both were concerned to protect the children and his mother from the full enormity of the crisis. Together as a team they planned the careful tactics of dissimulation and studied optimism which every motive dictated. Eleanor wrote gratefully of Louis Howe: ". . . thank heavens he is here, as he has been the greatest help." [1] And Franklin's uncle wrote glowingly of Howe's performance.[2]

They were aided by Roosevelt's own formidable drive. He worked for hours to move his foot muscles, despite the intense sensitivity which for nearly six months made every movement and every touch a source of sharp pain. He fought back constantly against the threatening gloom. With Howe's help he accepted membership on a Vassar Endowment Drive committee and on the Executive Committee of the New York State Demo-

[1] Eleanor Roosevelt to James R. Roosevelt, August 14, 1921, quoted in *Personal Letters, 1905–1928*, p. 524.

[2] Frederick Delano to Roosevelt, September 4, 1921, Group XIV, FDRL.

cratic Party, even before his disease had been properly diagnosed. He managed to joke with the children, and when his mother rushed up from New York, he staged a major act of cheery nonchalance for her benefit. Shocked by the damage to his legs, she nevertheless wrote her brother: "He . . . seems very bright and *keen*. . . . He and Eleanor decided at once to be cheerful and the atmosphere of the house is all happiness, so I have fallen in and follow their glorious example. . . ." [3]

The game was played out with perfection. Eleanor and Louis firmly agreed that Roosevelt must return to the city, so that he could move back into a normal life as directly as possible, and Uncle Frederick Delano sympathetically handled the New York arrangements. When the doctors finally allowed the move on September 13, Louis arranged to have his friend carried secretly to the train. While the crowd gathered at another dock, carefully misled by a Howe-inspired rumor, Franklin made the painful transfer on his stretcher from boat to jolting baggage cart and then through a window of the private car his uncle had sent him from New York. When reporters finally caught up with them, he managed to give an impression of gay self-assurance for the New York papers.

Roosevelt was safely bedded down at Presbyterian Hospital in New York under the care of an old school friend, Dr. George Draper. Only then did Eleanor and Louis release the front-page news that he was a victim of poliomyelitis. But now they could also promise a quick and complete recovery, on the basis of preliminary examinations. The papers carried the flat statement: "He will not be crippled." [4] Actually Roosevelt was to remain in great pain and with increasingly dim prospects for over a month. For weeks his fever would mount on occasion to 102. The specialists began to feel that he might never be able to sit up, and even suspected that his arm muscles might be involved. But F.D.R. himself remained incorrigibly optimistic, or at least maintained the pose. He took great pride in the strength of his arms, pulled himself about by a strap over his

[3] Sara Delano Roosevelt to Frederick Delano, September 2 [1921], quoted in Freidel: *The Ordeal*, p. 100.

[4] Quoted in *Personal Letters, 1905–1928*, p. 532.

bed, and threw punches at visitors to prove that he wasn't done yet. He insisted that he would leave the hospital on crutches. Actually, by October 28, when he was moved to his New York house, he was able to swing himself with only a little help into the wheel chair, and in December he was predicting that he would walk without a limp by spring. This was the beginning of a studied pose of determined optimism which he would feature for eight long years. No matter how slow the progress, he would always hold out in front of himself the firm hope of complete recovery. At first he may have been the victim of his family's and his doctor's will to encourage him, but he soon came to thrive on his own deep reserves of moral power.

For Roosevelt there was probably never any question about the future, except perhaps in private moments of abject despair when all seemed lost. If there was to be a future, it would be the kind he had planned all along. He set himself single-mindedly to the task of getting back to it. But for everyone else around him the fall of 1921 was a period of sharp adjustment. The children would have him home with them more than they ever could have hoped under normal conditions, but the vigorous outdoor week ends at Hyde Park and the rough physical fun at Campobello were gone forever. Their father could never lead the way again on hikes, cross-country rides, on the tennis court and golf course and skating pond. Only at swimming or in the roughhouse sessions before dinner on the library floor could he recapture his masculine camaraderie with the boys. And for the children, as well as the adults, there was the nervous tension of a crowded household, a life centered on Father. With the stream of secretaries, visitors, and business associates, their home became an office and a political clubhouse.

For Eleanor Roosevelt it was a moment of tragedy and triumph. Always a shy person, ridden with feelings of inadequacy, she had long played the role of quiet supporter to her husband's ambitions. Preoccupied with her growing family, longing for a nice and quiet life, she might have been expected to counsel retirement. But Eleanor had shown in the crisis a steely loyalty and power of decision which even her

husband had probably not recognized. She insisted at once that
everything be arranged to push Franklin back to his normal
career. With Louis Howe's aggressive, sometimes hard-boiled
support, she began to develop a career in social work and
politics, perhaps as much designed to create a productive life
for herself as to aid her husband's plans and to keep his interest
in life. At home she found herself doing numerous things for
the household which her husband might ordinarily have handled, dealing often alone with the complex problems of five
young children, and at every point having to cope with the
jealously kindly dominance of her dynamic mother-in-law, who
hovered over the family with an air of mission and command
which kept the household on constant defense. Only once did
Eleanor's children see the tears that betrayed her deep tension,
as she struggled to hold her own ground between two strong-
minded personalities.

Sara Roosevelt had her own difficult adjustment to make.
She had always been immensely proud of Franklin, but she
had accepted only reluctantly the unorthodox political career
to which he had devoted himself. Furthermore, she had never
been challenged in her domination of their family life when
they were at Hyde Park or New York. Now it seemed only
natural for her to continue to lead, as she viewed the future of
her crippled son, his malleable and quiet wife, his brood of
young children. She wanted to take them under her protective
wing. It made no sense to her for her son to struggle hopelessly
against odds in politics and business when there was money
enough and the great house at Hyde Park and the infinite harmless pleasures of the country gentleman's life. All through the
fall and winter she kept at her crusade to take her children
home to the atrophying leisure of the country, to the enervating
life of permanent guests in Grandmama's ménage.

But Sara Roosevelt was pitting wits and weapons against
adversaries she could not match. Although there was probably
little danger that Roosevelt would succumb to her chiding invitation to retirement, the constant pressure must have been a
wearing obstruction to the more serious business of life. Much
as she loved him, Sara Roosevelt seems never to have under-

stood her son's drive for independence, which was as deep and strong as her own. And Roosevelt had help, from his doctors, from Eleanor, and from Louis Howe, all of whom saw clearly that his recovery depended upon his incentive to fight. It was not the noise and confusion and challenge of the 65th Street house that might kill him, as his mother feared, but the useless boredom of life on the porch in the country. As she began to lose the battle, Sara Roosevelt's carping insistence assumed a pettiness unworthy of her. Often she added to the very confusion she deplored by setting the family against itself over insignificant things.

There was nothing that Sara Roosevelt resented more than the constant presence of Louis Howe, who had moved into the large third-floor room with private bath. Although she was most gracious to Mrs. Howe, as her social code required, she found nothing of merit in Louis. It seemed an unnecessary nuisance and expense to have this disreputable outlander underfoot all the time, taking up good space, intimate to the family's most personal problems, and shaping the household's routines to his own needs. His personal sloppiness, his hacking cough and undisciplined smoking habits, the nauseating incense he burned in his room, his acid tongue and careless manners— all this repelled her. But there was more. Louis Howe stood as an omnipresent symbol of everything she wanted Franklin to renounce. It was Howe who kept the politics boiling, who helped push Eleanor out into active life, who brought a constant flow of strange and vulgar characters to the house.

Nonetheless, Howe was in the family to stay. The Roosevelts would never again be able to plan without him. When polio struck, the future had been dictated for him. There could be no question of his leaving Campobello until his friend was back in New York. No one knows precisely what was said between them during these weeks, but by the time they had arrived in the city, Louis had decided to stay on as Franklin's personal aide. The decision must have been a difficult one. He was marrying himself irrevocably to his crippled friend's fortunes. Almost 50, with his wartime contacts and prestige rapidly receding, he was pushing aside whatever hopes he may have had for economic and personal independence. And he was committing himself to a life in which his own family must bend its future to Roosevelt's needs. He must ask Grace to give up the hard-won security and independence of their Washington years and 11-year-old Hartley to share his father with the Roosevelt family. But he was deeply indebted to Roosevelt. F.D.R. was his warm and close friend. Howe had his negative characteristics, but lack of loyalty to those he loved was not one of them. He may still have had Presidential hopes for his boss. He may even have felt incapable of striking out on his own. But even had the situation been hopeless, Louis Howe could never have deserted his only close friends after they had plumbed the depths of tragedy together at Campobello.

13

—»»-»»-»»-»»-»»-»»-»»-»»

Rebuilding

*I am still on crutches and cannot possibly
play golf myself for a year or two.*
(Franklin D. Roosevelt,
December 15, 1923) [1]

HOWE'S new job was as varied as Roosevelt's interests. He became, quite literally, F.D.R. with legs, doing all the innumerable things the boss would have done could he have walked.
He stood in for Roosevelt at business, political, and philanthropic meetings, bought prints and antiques for him at auc-
tions, ran family errands, even tried to be substitute-father for
the Roosevelt boys on occasion. Louis was immensely secure.
He was needed as he had never been before. But there were
limits: "Lord knows, I have acted as your alter-ego in many
weird commissions," he once wrote Franklin, "but I must positively and firmly refuse to risk my judgment on neckties,
watches or pajamas. . . ." [2] Yet Howe took the initiative in
Roosevelt's life in a way which could never have been tolerated
in a lesser friend. Not the least of the tasks he assigned himself

[1] Roosevelt to John Adriance, December 15, 1923, Group XIV, FDRL.
[2] Howe to Roosevelt, September 1 [1921], Group XXXVI, FDRL.

was that of keeping up the boss's morale. For seven long years he managed an atmosphere of gay activity in the 65th Street house, his tactics ranging from elaborately staged parties and a sardonic running commentary on life, to the more profound gambit of playing politics with deadly earnest, as if disaster had never struck.

Roosevelt's annual birthday parties with the Cuff-links Club gave him his best opportunities. Here, once a year, F.D.R. could relax with the close friends to whom he had given gold cuff links as mementos of their arduous 1920 campaign. And here Louis could pamper his own thirst for drama. Louis wrote the scripts, manufactured the props, and carefully coached his old gang in the skits designed to needle and delight their beloved one-man audience. One year he exploited some of the juicier items of their Navy career. "Apropos of Hayti, he should present Franklin with a couple of skulls of Haytians which he dug up in the local graveyard for amusement," he wrote McCarthy who was to represent the Marines in the tableau. "You will probably remember the unfortunate incident." [3] Another year it was a radio program from station B.U.N.K., featuring Professor Irving Fishcake of Yale—Irving Fisher had been a distinguished Roosevelt advisor on the League of Nations. Fishcake answered political questions:

Q. What has the income tax done for the U.S.A.?
A. It has made us a nation of liars.
Q. What are the duties of the Vice-President?
A. To attend formal dinner parties and run the largest hot air plant in the United States.
Q. What is the salary of a Cabinet Officer?
A. $12,000 and leasing privileges. [4]

He was fond of making Al Smith the butt of their fun. The dinners were invariably masculine in tone, a trifle bawdy, and, despite prohibition, mildly alcoholic, as were Louis's frequent reunions with the old gang in Washington: ". . . my brand has no wood alcohol in it, and I have my doubts of the batch you

[3] Howe to C. H. McCarthy, January 7, 1924, Group XXXVI, FDRL.
[4] Personal Papers.

furnished last year. . . . Get the gang together and let me know the date for the big drunk!"[5] Actually Louis was cautious about liquor; he had seen too many good reporters ruined by it.

But Louis's organized fun went well beyond these formal occasions. He was anxious for something to replace Roosevelt's much-regretted golf, sailing, hunting, and fishing. One happy possibility was model building. Franklin, Louis, and Elliott took to building working models to be sailed annually on the Hudson for a challenge cup which Mrs. Roosevelt donated. And Louis regaled his boss with "Very Limited Editions" of his own spicily humored and water-colored cartoon booklets. The most famous of these was "The Log of the Houseboat Larooco, Being a More or Less Truthful Account of What Happened, Expurgated for the Very Young."[6] This humorous memento, dedicated to Ananias and Sapphira, the patron saints of all lying fishermen, was only one of many. A striking example of the brand of humor Louis and Franklin loved so bumptiously was Louis's "Pathetic Ballade of Mr. Dives, with a brief mention of Mr. Lazarus, Intended to show the W.C.T.U. that there is one Place Where you Can Not Get a Drink." Dives, the wicked, broils through three cantos in a steam bath lined with posters: "Join the Don't Worry Club"; "Please Report Any Dissatisfaction: It amuses us to hear complaints"; "Guests who have Summered in Fall River Can Obtain Blankets of the Janitor." Louis's definitive moral: "Never cultivate a thirst where it is inconvenient to satisfy it."[7]

When they were separated, Louis's letters kept up the light-hearted mood: "I took breakfast with 'Uncle Fred' before your Mama arrived, and filled him full of cheery thoughts and fried eggs."[8] Or again: "I have just finished carving two pumpkins for Hartley. . . . The Tragedy pumpkin was a lean, long dyspeptic looking vegetable and I have managed to achieve a remarkable resemblance to Mr. Hearst! . . . later according to ancient custom they will be carried in solemn procession down

[5] Howe to C. H. McCarthy, January 7, 1924, Group XXXVI, FDRL.
[6] FDRL.   [7] Personal Papers.
[8] Howe to Roosevelt, September 1 [1921], Group XXXVI, FDRL.

the beach—to the great wonderment of such dissipated sea
gulls as have not yet retired—Probably striking much terror
into the hearts of such hardened old night wandering clams as
have not closed their shells. . . . Save a cocktail for the wan-
derer's return." [9]

Roosevelt, for his part, badgered Louis incessantly. He never
allowed Howe to forget Grace's garbled telegram with its comment on Fall River weather: "Love growing colder." Later
Louis could retaliate when, during Missy LeHand's illness,
Eleanor received from Franklin the telegraphic pronouncement: "Messy better live." [1] Even when Franklin gave his friend
a handsome new Bible, he felt impelled to write in the flyleaf:

> For Louis McH. Howe's
> Soul and Delectation and English
> From one who has Read it. [2]

This job demanded everything of Howe. He had hopefully
proposed to Grace that they rent a place in the city, but she
knew if he was that near the Roosevelts he would never be
home, and besides, they couldn't afford city rents. She suggested
instead that she live in Poughkeepsie, close to Mary at Vassar
College, but far enough away from 65th Street so that Louis
could really relax on week ends. He became a regular Friday-
night commuter. He was often exhausted by the excitement
and challenge of his job and slept 12 to 15 hours of a Saturday
or Sunday. In one of his familiar black moods, he wrote: "It
will not be such a very long time. . . . All the doctors have
told me that my terrible struggle had burned up my life and
that between fifty and sixty some little thing—a cold or something like that would take me away. . . ." [3] He worried that he
would lose contact with his growing son, and knew Grace was
upset over his long absences. He was constantly torn by conflicting loyalties.

After Mary had graduated from Vassar, Grace returned to

[9] Howe to Roosevelt, n.d., Group XXXVI, FDRL.
[1] Howe to Roosevelt, April 26, 1927, Group XXXVI, FDRL.
[2] Owned by the Howe family.
[3] Howe to Grace Howe, July 10, 1922, Personal Papers.

Fall River to carve out a secure life for herself and Hartley
and a home for Louis when he could come. Grace lost herself in
Hartley's interests and in an immense range of philanthropic,
social, and political matters. With Louis's world so hectic and so
alien, she had put down roots firmly in the familiar atmosphere
of Fall River, among the old friends of the Borden family. She
and Hartley traveled widely, to California and to Europe, and
in 1924 she dived into the Al Smith campaign with a zeal that
created a permanent role for her in Massachusetts politics.

Louis came home regularly, spending every week end he
could with Hartley and his friends in Fall River or at the beach.
He followed eagerly his son's budding interest in journalism,
his career at high school and at Harvard. In Louis's new Stude-
baker they toured the New England countryside for antiques,
arrowheads, and mineral specimens. Louis watched with studied respect his daughter's work in astronomy at the Lick Ob-
servatory and, as a graduate student, at Radcliffe. When Mary
came to New York, she got the red-carpet treatment, swank
restaurants, theater, church at the Cathedral of St. John the
Divine. Grace's momentary dismay at the family's awkward
new living arrangements never broke through the surface. She
visited often at the New York house and at Hyde Park. Roosevelt spent two long vacations at the cottage next to Howe's on
Horseneck Beach, and Elliott, who was Hartley's age, made
visits which Grace welcomed keenly for the fun the boys had
together. When Mary was married in June 1926, Eleanor was
delighted to be asked to help the bride choose her gown.[4] There
continued between Eleanor Roosevelt and Grace Howe until
her death a warm exchange of letters reflecting their mutual
understanding and respect.

Louis's prime interest was Franklin's political career, but the
entire Roosevelt household was preoccupied at first with the
heartbreaking struggle to put the boss back on his feet. By
March 1922 he was wearing the heavy steel braces which would
curse him the rest of his life. He was determined to be rid of
them. Throughout the summer at Hyde Park he drove himself

---

[4] Eleanor Roosevelt to Mary Howe, May 5, 1926, Personal Papers.

relentlessly, swimming three times a week at Vincent Astor's pool in Rhinebeck, practicing in the humid Hudson Valley heat to walk with crutches. He fell frequently, sometimes dangerously. The results were disheartening. That winter he could get down to his office occasionally. Around the house, he shocked his friends by dragging himself—crablike—across the floor, but this helped him push aside his dreadful fears of being caught in a fire. And he was inordinately proud of his strong shoulders and arms that made it possible for him to wrestle with his boys on the floor, two at a time. By the summer of 1923 he was using a child's double swing, parallel bars, even a tricycle to exercise his wasted muscles, although primarily he felt that swimming would accomplish the miracle on which his hopes were staked. "The water put me where I am," he would sing out to his friends, "and water has to bring me back." [5] He was optimistic beyond all sense. In December 1923 he fondly expected to be playing golf again within "a year or two." [6] By 1924 he could demonstrate to friends around the little pool Mrs. Roosevelt had built some distance from the Hyde Park house that he could stand with water only to his armpits. And he had learned to swallow the indignities of his desperate circumstance. He could joke about his "dropping overboard gracefully by means of davits . . ." [7] from his houseboat to his fishing skiff.

Throughout the twenties, they searched constantly for a substitute for Campobello. The houseboat *Larooco* served him well in Florida waters for four years, but it was expensive and too limited an environment. During the summer of 1924 he spent several weeks with Louis at Horseneck Beach. Here there was privacy. He could scoot up and down the sand from the house to the surf without being watched by strangers. There was the completely relaxed atmosphere of Howe's rough board cottage and the salt air and surf. He boasted that he was roughing it, although his idea of the simple life was a little different from

[5] Interview with Louis Depew by George Palmer, January 5, 1948, Transcript in FDRL.

[6] Roosevelt to John Adriance, December 15, 1923, Group XIV, FDRL.

[7] Log of *Weona II*, FDRL.

Louis's. He wrote an old friend: "As you know Louis' cottage is wee and there is really no room and we live in a distinctly informal way with only two of our colored servants to do everything." [8] He came back the next summer to rent the adjoining house for three weeks, but then he moved over to nearby Marion, to try the experimental treatments of Dr. William McDonald. He was deeply elated, for by December he could walk a short distance with only one brace, but by 1927 he was staking his hopes on the mineral baths at Warm Springs, Georgia, to which their old friend George Foster Peabody had introduced him two years earlier.

Under ordinary circumstances Roosevelt might have been barred from a further business career. Fortunately he had a reasonable amount of money to invest, as well as the firm friendship of his boss, Van Lear Black. Black insisted that he remain on the Fidelity payroll. He could not really manage the New York office, as he had intended. Away from the city for many months each year, he left it in the hands of the able professionals of the regular staff. But he tried to keep control of major policy decisions, and he resented the inevitable tendencies of the staff to bypass him. He was almost peevish in his rivalry with the able executive who did his work and often complained that he was not being kept informed, that the company was not using his potential for introducing "really big men" to their business.[9] Some of his more imaginative ideas were vetoed by Black himself. F.D.R. was brought up short in February 1928 when two of his key men went over to a rival firm. He dived into the reorganization of his office, hit the newspapers with an advertising campaign, and hastened to assure Black: "We have our fighting clothes on and it will work out all right." [1] By August his old friend, with whom he had long been on a "Van" and "Frank" basis, would cable his delight at the way Roosevelt

[8] Roosevelt to Livingston Davis, September 3, 1924, Group XIV, Roosevelt Papers.

[9] Roosevelt to E. A. Hamilton, March 17, 1924, Group XIV, FDRL.

[1] Roosevelt to Van Lear Black, February 25, 1928, Group XIV, Black File, FDRL.

was handling both business and politics. Black's chief concern
was that F.D.R. might work too hard.[2]

What Black mainly expected from Roosevelt was the new
business his name and friendships might bring. Howe had
started working at this as soon as Roosevelt had returned from
the hospital in 1921. His best contacts were with labor. Louis
renewed their old friendships, and by January Roosevelt could
boast: "Some of my good friends at the head of the Federation of
Labor have been kind enough to pass the word along the line
generally that the Federation considered me as an old friend,
and suggesting that whenever possible bonds should be placed
with the company. . . ."[3] Louis was resourceful. He had an
easy rapport with these old labor cronies and could joke with
them about organizing an expedition to rescue from the Holly-
wood "vamps"[4] one of their brethren, absent too long in California. But he could also persuade Roosevelt to invest in the
A.F. of L. Bank, to intervene on labor matters with Mayor John
Hylan, and even to send a "cunning little pardon case"[5] to Governor Smith in a fruitless appeal for special handling. When the
bidding on bond prices got rough, Louis would take a train to
Washington to see William Green himself, and Franklin would
invite the labor leaders for a visit to his houseboat retreat. Not
even good friends, as it turned out, would let their firm handle
large issues when their bids were high, but Louis brought in
much small business.

They also brought in some business through political contacts. Howe's old friendship with the State Treasurer may have
helped increase their percentage of the State business. Roosevelt gave jobs to sons of Tammany and Brooklyn politicians, and
Louis fondly reminded old naval contractors that F.D.R. was in
a new business now. Their office volume doubled in five years,

[2] Black to Roosevelt, August 3, 1928, Group XIV, FDRL.

[3] Roosevelt to William E. Barton, January 18, 1922, Group XIV, Fidelity
and Deposit File, FDRL.

[4] Howe to James O'Connell, March 17, 1927, Group XIV, Fidelity and
Deposit File, FDRL.

[5] Howe to Mr. Graves, July 30, 1924, Group XVI, FDRL.

and Roosevelt proudly announced that it was the result of a "high standard of business ethics, courteous treatment, prompt service and sound business judgment." [6]

Roosevelt remained vice-president on leave at the Fidelity even after he became Governor, but his law practice was another matter. He chafed at having his name "at the tail end" [7] of the firm and complained that his partners' business was dull; they were annoyed that he did little. He soon made a new arrangement with Basil O'Connor, which gave him a steady income of at least $10,000 a year and offered more exciting prospects. O'Connor was immensely patient with this non-practicing partner, who was seldom in the office, refused to argue cases against the government he had recently left, and apparently handled only one matter throughout the whole decade.

Roosevelt's real ambition was to make quick profits in the apparently booming economy. But the buoyant optimism that served him so well in his physical recovery and in politics played him false in his speculations. He was generally a poor judge of both men and propositions. He was reckless in investment, although he worried genuinely about his income and pinched relentlessly on clothes and other petty expenses. He could never risk quite enough to control a proposition—$5,000 was his conventional limit. He was seldom home to manage his affairs. For months at a time Howe had to carry his responsibilities without the power of decision. Louis made no big blunders, but he lacked both the experience and the power to make fortunes for his absent boss.

The Compo Bond proposition, which they had helped to launch before the polio attack, was typical. This was a plan to raise capital for investment by selling through the banks small denomination bonds especially issued by Compo for the purpose. By November Howe was writing disgustedly to Pat Homer: "What do you mean 'what is Compo doing besides catch-

[6] Roosevelt Press Statement, February 23, 1928, quoted in Freidel: *The Ordeal*, p. 14.

[7] Roosevelt to Black, September 24, 1924, Group XIV, Black File, FDRL.

ing suckers?' You've got it all wrong. . . . Compo is doing everything in the world except catching suckers. They have built enough castles to fill all Spain, and have considered 97 varieties of bond—any one of which will bring in a net income of not less than $10,000,000. . . ." [8] But, he went on to complain, they had not yet moved to destroy the legal barriers. Howe was especially angry because, he said, he had personally argued that the Fidelity should set up a special department to guarantee the Compo bonds. By the summer of 1922 the corporation had finally won a favorable decision from a widely respected judge, who ruled that the Compo certificates were just another way of receipting bank deposits and that the conspicuous use of the words "United States of America" at the top of the certificates did not really confuse the purchaser. Howe tried to persuade Homer to take the franchise for Massachusetts, and Roosevelt may have played a role in getting Al Smith to open the sale of Compos at a prominent New York bank in December 1922.

Within a year, however, Roosevelt was worried. He wrote, but did not send in, his resignation from the Compo Board of Directors in 1923, when he felt that its tentative plan to issue surety bonds would conflict with his obligation to Fidelity. He repeated the procedure a year later, when he feared that a proposed national advertising campaign would damage his reputation. The company finally went into gradual liquidation in 1925. Roosevelt's investment had been only $2,500, but the entire affair had involved an immense amount of time and considerable risk to his personal reputation.

F.D.R. took fliers in nearly a dozen speculative ventures during the 1920's. Often he loaned his name as well as his money, but left the management to others. Two of these ventures speculated in European securities and in devalued German marks. Two others dabbled in automatic vending machines and portrait camera booths. One planned to sell advertising space in taxis, another to market Maté in the United States. He took a plunge in oil. When his wildcatters struck sulfur, Howe needled him without mercy: "Why not go into the sulphur bath industry—

---

[8] [Howe] to A. P. Homer, November 4, 1921, Group XIV, FDRL.

look at Hot Springs!" [9] But Louis himself lost a chunk of his small capital in another oil scheme. All of this cost them money, and it was dangerous politically. Later Roosevelt would be attacked as a reckless plunger who was willing to speculate on German misery, displace labor with vending machines, and lend his name to the most questionable propositions. They did, in fact, blunder into one dubious real estate deal which brought Roosevelt a tart reprimand from the Society for Promoting Financial Knowledge.

They were taken in most magnificently in the lobster fattening operation to which Pat Homer attracted them early in 1922. Howe was hopelessly sold on the genial promoter. He could kid Homer about his interest in Ziegfeld girls: ". . . if I were your Missus, I would keep you tied up around the house for a week or two"; [1] but he was careful enough to demand majority control for Franklin. They got it, and it turned out to be a majority responsibility for the debts—$26,000 dollars' worth.

Sometimes they consciously exploited their government contacts. Louis got old friends in Washington to probe the government's attitude toward a potential Panamanian mining venture; Franklin threw his prestige into the balance to argue publicly against the creation of a moth-ball fleet—one of the companies in which he was interested hoped to buy some of the surplus merchant ships. Louis maneuvered endlessly to set up a profitable venture for them in getting hold of certain German properties held by the Alien Property Custodian. And they sought government aid at every turn for an ambitious project to finance and build an airship service linking major American cities. They hoped to take the lead through the control of certain German patents in the United States. They then planned to lease a naval air base and hire personnel temporarily on leave from the naval airship projects, and they tried to get officers of the department to let them in on the Navy's plans and to check their cost figures for them. Louis spent much of his time for two years on the complicated problems of this corporation, but they were stumped by

[9] Howe note on letter: V. B. Baker to Gentlemen, February 23, 1924, Group XIV, FDRL.

[1] [Howe] to Homer, February 23, 1922, Group XIV, FDRL.

the bickering among the engineers and owners, and they failed in attempts to enlist millionaire backers. The grim fact was that Roosevelt had bet on the wrong kind of aircraft.

Yet they were neither blind nor immoral; they were simply naïvely optimistic, and most of their sins were those of omission rather than commission. Roosevelt spurned a number of questionable but interesting propositions and resigned quickly from others which smacked of double-dealing. Howe sometimes caught on swiftly enough to save them from losses: "This Company *seems* to be going very well. *But* my advice is to let the other fellow buy the stock." [2] Often they invested not for money but for an idea: in Democratic newspapers like the *Evening Post;* in the model tree farm at Hyde Park; in Warm Springs.

As if all this were not enough, Roosevelt tried his hand at writing, which intrigued him almost as much as politics. He talked much about it: two books on the Navy, perhaps a history of the United States, a life of John Paul Jones. But he produced little: several political articles, largely ghost-written by Howe; some editorial work on local history documents. The fact was that he had neither the temperament nor the training for serious writing. The man who boasted about his abbreviated education —"I chucked the M.A. and got a trip instead which in many ways was more valuable" [3]—and who explained that he had always liked travel and adventure books best, could muster neither the patience nor the discipline for sustained research and writing. "I am always in the delightful frame of mind of wanting to say 'yes' to anything in the way of writing," he confessed, ". . . always providing that the writing is to be done next week, or the week after. . . ." [4]

It was much the same with philanthropy. He could seldom say no to the causes in which he believed, but he did little about them himself. The hard work was necessarily left to Howe. Louis was delighted, for heading fund-raising committees kept the boss's name in the papers and helped to build a public image

    [2] Howe note on letter: Clarence Sherwood to Howe, October 5, 1922, Group XIV, FDRL.
    [3] Roosevelt to Burke Royce, September 25, 1922, Group XIV, FDRL.
    [4] Roosevelt to George Marvin, September 12, 1922, Group XIV, FDRL.

for him, despite the Republican monopoly of politics. But before the twenties were done Louis would be swamped. He found himself fighting a rear-guard action, from item to item, as Roosevelt sentimentally refused to cut down his growing list of directorships, memberships, and chairmanships. F.D.R. was an overseer at Harvard, a trustee of Vassar and of the Flower-Fifth Avenue Hospital, president of the Navy Club, on committees for Near East Relief, for the Woodrow Wilson Foundation, and for the Boy Scout Foundation of New York. He was chairman of drives for St. John's Cathedral and the American Legion. And both he and Louis worked endlessly to search out financial support for the expeditions of their old friend "Dick" Byrd.

For both of them much was learned through all of this. Louis's later interest in the C.C.C. stemmed directly from the Scouting work he had done for his handicapped boss. Roosevelt himself received an education in business self-regulation that would profoundly affect his attitude toward the N.R.A. a decade later. As president of the American Construction Council, he sought to bring stability to the building trades and rescue them from their scandal-ridden reputation. The job paid nothing and it promised many headaches, but Roosevelt was intrigued with the pattern being set by the "czars" of moviedom and baseball, Will Hays and Judge Kenesaw Landis. The job offered publicity and a dignified challenge to build upon his wartime experience with management. Howe himself had explored something very close to this idea with his 1920 proposals for labor-management boards to stabilize employment and working conditions.

Although the whole concept of industrial self-regulation skittered along the edges of the anti-trust laws, the American Construction Council and several other such associations were being launched with the active support and benevolent guidance of Secretary of Commerce Herbert Hoover. The first meeting set the objectives: the smoothing out of the seasonal cycles, the gathering of information to facilitate broad planning, the development of a code of ethics. Roosevelt knew precisely what he wanted for the industry: thorough research; regular conferences to allocate construction dates, material, and labor; the rebirth of the "guild" spirit to improve both the quality and the supply of labor; and a vigorous public relations program. He hit the newspapers again and again with bold statements to arouse confidence in the industry. But in the real job of building an effective trade association he failed. It never became the regulatory force of which he dreamed. He had been asked to organize anarchy, and he did not personally work very hard at it. Without pay, he was neither willing nor able to exercise the kind of leadership Hays and Landis were doing. In fact, no one did. Roosevelt read the riot act to his directors in a hectic meeting at his home in May 1923: the Council had "not done one darned thing . . . except collect dues from some 115 different organizations. . . ." [5] He jammed through resolutions requesting the banks to curtail credit for speculative building during the summer, the Federal and State governments to slow their construction programs until October, and the Department of Commerce to set up an agency to collect statistics on the costs of construction. But his belated gestures did nothing to scale down the desperate summer competition for materials and labor, and Hoover took a dim view of doing the Council's research work at government expense. They finally hired a staff member for research and fund raising. By February 1924 Louis was spending two mornings a week on Council business, but Roosevelt had soon lost interest and virtually ignored "our poor little organization." [6] Louis was able to raise enough money to boast: "We . . . can look the Sheriff in the face." [7] Yet by 1928 Roosevelt bluntly predicted: ". . . the only practical results will be obtained by a good far reaching period of depression throughout the construction industry. That will automatically eliminate the unnecessary organizations. . . ." [8]

The significance of all of this lay not in what was done, but in its impact on F.D.R.'s thinking. He had gone into the American Construction Council with a firm belief in industrial planning

[5] Governing Board, American Construction Council: "Minutes—May 16, 1923," Group XIV, A.C.C. File, FDRL.

[6] Roosevelt to Grosvenor Clarkson, June 5, 1924, Group XVI, FDRL.

[7] Howe to Roosevelt, February 14, 1924, Group XXXVI, FDRL.

[8] Roosevelt to Dwight Hoopingarner, March 26, 1928, Group XIV, FDRL.

and a complete scorn of government regulation: "[It] is not feasible. It is unwieldy; it is expensive . . . it means higher taxes. The public doesn't want it. . . ."[9] He came out with the most practical reasons for believing that the job could not be done without governmental sanctions.

After 1924 their real enthusiasm went into the National Crime Commission. A private organization to investigate the roots of the current crime wave and to work for solutions of the problem, the Commission offered a variety of opportunities. It could keep Roosevelt in the public eye; it could give Louis a part-time but steady job, so that he could handle Roosevelt's interests but not be completely dependent upon Franklin's pocketbook. F.D.R. had already tried to place Louis on the Taconic Park Commission payroll and had aroused Park-Czar Robert Moses's righteous wrath. Howe became Assistant to the Chairman of the Crime Commission and held the job until 1933. He apparently drew $400 a month from the Commission, and Roosevelt pieced out his salary with additional payments.

Neither Howe nor Roosevelt had shown any marked interest in the crime problem, but now they began to act as if it were a deep and abiding passion. Howe took the responsibility seriously and soon developed a deep interest in the problems on which he was being paid to work. He spent much time raising money for the Commission, issued a steady barrage of propaganda, and made himself a serious student of the crime wave. Some of their old friends could hardly believe the news. T. M. Osborne, bitter and cynical after seeing his reputation destroyed in the prison reform wars, warned them not to get mixed up in "the circus," loaded with great national figures whose interest was superficial—". . . nothing can come of such a body . . . but more 'bunk,'"[1] he protested. A year later he was needling Howe: "How does the Crime Commission go? Apparently crime still flourishes."[2] Louis could humor his old boss: "I grieve at your light and flippant view of the Crime Commission. . . . Like all critics, I observe that your theory of keeping an unpreju-

[9] *The New York Times,* June 4, 1922.
[1] Thomas Mott Osborne to Roosevelt, August 10, 1925, Osborne Papers.
[2] Osborne to Howe, June 29, 1926, Osborne Papers.

diced and unbiassed mind consists in adopting the tactics of the
noble ostrich and absolutely refusing to come anywhere near
any place where you might get a few facts on the subject." [3]
F.D.R. protested gently: "I am not certain that it is all the
bunk!" [4]

In the Crime Commission Louis had found at last a place
where he could operate freely, without feeling himself always a
part of Roosevelt's team. He made a personal crusade against
the "fences" who dealt in stolen goods, blasting out against the
"modern Fagins" who paid youngsters to "shark them in the
swag." [5] He fought to make the possession of small arms illegal,
trotting out research reports to fight off the claims of the arms
manufacturers that it would be dangerous to deprive citizens
of their right to protect themselves with a pistol. He worked
for modern criminological laboratories and for police training
schools. He gloried in his personal appearances before various
legislative groups and boasted of one radio program for the
Commission: "Did you hear the [broadcast]? The voice was
F.D.R.'s but the words were all *mine!*" [6]

But the Commission's impact was weak. It was always near
bankruptcy. Near the end of his service Louis would confess
that the only real achievement for which they could take credit
was the setting up of several official crime commissions in the
various States, including New York. However, there were long-
range personal benefits for both of them. Louis credited to Roosevelt much of his own work and gave his boss a reputation as a
crime-buster which F.D.R. hardly deserved. In 1932 and 1933
Howe would advertise Roosevelt as the first President with a
working knowledge of the crime problem, and credit his boss
with the first proposals for an "American Scotland Yard." [7] In
addition, in the work of the Crime Commission Howe came to
know and admire Professor Raymond Moley of Columbia. When

[3] Howe to Osborne August 6, 1926, Osborne Papers.
[4] Roosevelt to Osborne, September 5, 1925, Osborne Papers.
[5] Clipping, Personal Papers.   [6] Fragment of letter, Personal Papers.
[7] William Seagle: "The American National Police: the Dangers of Federal Crime Control," *Harper's Monthly*, CLXIX (November 1934), p. 754.

the time arrived to collect a brain trust, Louis would play a decisive role in making Moley its leader.

Most of Roosevelt's scattered interests diminished in significance after 1926, as he became almost completely preoccupied with Warm Springs, Georgia. The buoyant, hot mineral waters, the mild winter climate, the remnants of a decayed and disheveled winter resort here, all intrigued him. He noted distinct improvement in his leg muscles after a brief series of self-designed exercises in the water. When stories in an Atlanta newspaper brought an unexpected flow of health seekers, he became a *de facto* physiotherapist and general counselor for the guests. In April 1926 he purchased the 1,200 acres and the building, planning to use them as an experimental center for the treatment of polio victims. This was a crusade with him, but he also expected to make money.

Eleanor Roosevelt took a dim view of this $250,000 risk. And well she might, with his erratic business record. But Howe's enthusiasm was unbounded. He scurried around New York, enlisting the help of Roosevelt's various staffs in raising money, lining up F.D.R.'s personal friends and associates in good causes. He was full of publicity ideas, and his associate at the Construction Council, Dwight Hoopingarner, came up with an attractive commercial possibility. "Hoopy" suggested a chain of resorts from Lake Placid to Warm Springs, with major financial backing and with the therapeutic project merged into it at first, to provide a good start. Roosevelt encouraged him mildly but insisted on leaving "Hoopy" on his own to work at the problem for over six months without any commitment from his boss. Howe had warned him: "My idea would be to talk only about the therapeutic project and carefully conceal the fact that you are going to run a competitive social resort on the side." [8] He pressed Roosevelt to come home to help with the money raising: ". . . a little concentrated work when we can lead our victims up to your desk for lunch is a far safer way of handling the important people." [9] Furthermore, he demanded some concrete evidence to

[8] Howe to Roosevelt, March 14, 1927, Group XXXVI, FDRL.
[9] Howe to Roosevelt, March 9, 1927, Group XXXVI, FDRL.

present to the "malefactors of great wealth," and wrote Roosevelt: "As every patent medicine faker has discovered, nothing lures the 'come on' like a before and after photograph. Why, God only knows!" It would be difficult but he reassured Franklin: ". . . you're an ingenious cuss and might think of some way in which this could be done. Perhaps just one photograph showing them doing a hundred yard dash or shovelling coal or something another after treatment, together with the statement that, when they arrived, it required two stretchers and an ambulance to get them down to the pool, might do the trick." He begged Franklin for photos for the rotogravure sections, "particularly if any part of the golf links can be dressed up to look like golf links." [1]

Roosevelt, as usual, was gaily optimistic. He plunged more deeply, buying an additional 1,750 acres for farm experiments, chiefly cattle, and built a scenic drive along nearby Pine Mountain, all at his own expense. To an aunt he boasted: "My one fear is that this gentle charm will appeal to some of our rich friends who are suffering from nervous prosperity and that they will come down here and ruin the atmosphere." [2] But he was soon forced down to earth. Louis had failed in his attempts to reach John D. Rockefeller, Jr., and Roosevelt's own letters to millionaire acquaintances brought nothing except good wishes. In the spring of 1927 he finally worked out with Louis a professional fund-raising operation which proved adequately productive. An old friend, Major Redfield Proctor, managed the drive, but they all pitched in. Louis and Hoopingarner scurried about New York. Sara Roosevelt gave a select party for her friends at Tuxedo to enlist their aid. Franklin himself entertained a string of wealthy prospects at Warm Springs. By the end of the year, the Georgia Warm Springs Foundation had been organized with the full panel of distinguished backers for which Louis had been agitating: George Foster Peabody, Herbert Straus, William H. Woodin, New York bankers Harvey Gibson and Russell Leffingwell, Henry Morgenthau, Basil O'Connor, and John Raskob of

[1] Howe to Roosevelt, April 1, 1927, Group XXXVI, FDRL.
[2] Roosevelt to Mrs. W. Sheffield Cowles, June 29, 1927, quoted in *Personal Letters, 1905–1928*, p. 624.

General Motors. A unique symbol of the future was the $25,000 check Edsel Ford sent to provide a glass enclosure for the swimming pool.

By the spring of 1928 F.D.R. had charted out a new life, varied and extensive enough for three ordinary people. He could not walk alone, but he was sure he would in time. And as a gentleman dilettante, he was having a wonderful time: collecting—stamps, prints, historical manuscripts; fishing, swimming, and engaging in interminable conversation. One measure of his new career was the wide range of clubs and societies to which he belonged—45 of them. Another was his phenomenal success at capturing newspaper notice despite his physical handicap and political retirement. From 1921 through 1927 he had been noticed in one way or another on nearly 200 occasions by *The New York Times* alone. But his real goal remained a political career. While he played at finance and hobbies and worked at the deadly serious business of learning to walk, he judged every move with an eye on Albany and Washington.

14

$\ggg\text{-}\ggg\text{-}\ggg\text{-}\ggg\text{-}\ggg\text{-}\ggg\text{-}\ggg\text{-}\ggg$

Fight for a
New Democratic Party

*The Democratic Party is the Progressive
Party of the country, but it is not and I
hope never will be the radical party of
the country which is a very different thing.*
(Franklin D. Roosevelt,
December 12, 1924) [1]

Roosevelt and Howe had not waited for political opportunities.
They made their own. From their point of view, Franklin's disability was merely another fact to be managed. He could not
rush about appearing at conferences and meetings, as he once
had. But there were profound advantages. The fact that he was
chair-bound contributed to his efficiency and gave him a physical remoteness which could be useful. He was forcibly kept from
too close an identification with the party's failures until the
proper moment came for the recovery of his lost ambitions. Now
that Howe had to make all the contacts, it was easier for him to

[1] To James Edgerton, December 12, 1924, Group XVI, FDRL.

shoulder the blame and keep Roosevelt disengaged. Polio had a
monumental influence on the timing of F.D.R.'s career, but it
had little effect, if any, on his ideas. They grew from threads
spun long before his illness.

One of these was the demand for reorganization of his party,
which he sprung on the National Committee in October 1921
and which he pressed for vigorously in the hundreds of letters
he and Howe sent out to remind political friends that F.D.R.
was still active. There were three goals: a vigorous, full-time national machine; a regular conference to make the party fully
representative of the rank and file; a conscious drive to make it a
vehicle of liberalism against Harding and Coolidge reaction. His
would be a moderate and pragmatic liberalism, shying away
from "the more radical views, such as those of the non-partisan
league. . . ." [2] He seldom dealt with specifics, yet there was an
occasional prophetic gesture. He favored changing the Presidential Inauguration to January 1: "I can see no possible objection to it, except by those people who cannot understand that
our Constitution was written nearly a century and a half ago." [3]
He supported laws to protect investors by making available to
them information on companies issuing stocks. On foreign policy, he sought a more specific balance between reality and his
ideals. Late in 1922 he wrote Governor Cox: ". . . the country
[is] beginning to recognize that national isolation on our part
. . . from our own purely selfish point of view will bring hard
times . . . cut off exports, etc. etc. . . . I am not wholly convinced that the country is quite ready for a definite stand on our
part in favor of immediate entry into the League of Nations . . .
but I am convinced we should stand firmly against the isolation
policy of Harding's Administration." [4] He stood for realistic mod-
ification of the League. But the World Court was different: "It is
perfectly ridiculous for us to remain out. . . . Joining . . . can-

    [2] Roosevelt to Stephen Van Tassell, November 13, 1922, Group XI,
FDRL.
    [3] Roosevelt to the *New York World,* February 15, 1923, Group XI,
FDRL.
    [4] Roosevelt to James M. Cox, December 8, 1922, Group XIV, Cox File,
FDRL.

not possibly entangle us." [5] He toyed with a referendum on the League. It would probably be considered "radical, bolshevik, etc., etc.," [6] but the idea was good for headlines, and it was on the side of the angels. He drafted his own Peace Plan for a new association of nations, "saving face, honor, and all the other fool things they may think have to be saved. . . ." And he warned against mere gadgets which might distract "hopeful but unworldly people" from the "preliminary complications out of which grow the causes of war. . . ." [7] Yet he had real hopes. "We are beginning to get rid of the Chinese Wall philosophy . . . ," he wrote Edward Bok. [8]

Eleanor and Louis helped. Mrs. Roosevelt became chairman of the Women's Division of the Democratic State Committee and worked with the Women's Trade Union League. Her new friends helped to educate Franklin on current issues, and, with Louis's aid, she edited the *Women's Democratic News*. Eleanor hewed to a slightly more dogmatic line than did her husband. She supported the Democracy, she said, because it had "been more concerned with the welfare of the people at large, and less with the growth of the big business interests." [9] Louis worked pitilessly to help her master the craft of politics. He upbraided her for the nervous giggle which punctuated her speeches in the wrong places; at least once he made her memorize to perfection the talk he had written for her. Thirty years later she recalled his advice vividly: "Have something to say, say it, and then sit down." [1] He taught her how to make up a dummy, to proofread, to read newspapers. He wasn't happy until she could master *The Times* in half an hour.

On his own, Louis agitated for a more dynamic national organization. "I'm afraid we are too apt to file away our light ammunition until the campaign is actually started . . . ," he wrote.

[5] Roosevelt to S. C. G. Watkins, May 21, 1923, Group XI, FDRL.

[6] Roosevelt to William E. Verplanck, April 12, 1923, Group XI, FDRL.

[7] Roosevelt to George Marvin, January 29, 1924, Group XIV, FDRL.

[8] *Poughkeepsie Star,* July 30, 1923.

[9] Ruby Black: *Eleanor Roosevelt* (New York: Duell, Sloan and Pearce; 1940), p. 54.

[1] Eleanor Roosevelt: *This Is My Life* (New York: Harper and Brothers; 1937), p. 352.

And he suggested that they pounce upon Coolidge's appointment of patronage-monger Bascomb Slemp as his secretary.
This would have to be done by the women, he said: ". . . we
are all tarred with the same brush." [2] Roosevelt himself helped
short-circuit a plan to make Henry Ford the financial angel of
the Democracy: ". . . if we go after Henry's money, we must
swallow Henry. . . ." [3]

In State politics, where William Randolph Hearst was trying
to reassert his ambitions, there was more fruitful work to be
done. Roosevelt worked hard to persuade Al Smith to come out
of his business-retirement and save the party from a Murphy-
Hearst partnership. Smith needed little urging. He had his own
deep dislike of the publisher. The "Dear Al"-"Dear Frank" exchange of letters, in which he announced that he would accept
the nomination for Governor in response to Roosevelt's public
inquiry, was probably a carefully arranged maneuver. Roosevelt
claimed the credit for Smith's change of heart, but left it to Al
himself to fight off Murphy's insistence that Hearst be allowed
to run for Senator. Accepting a compromise Senatorial nominee,
Dr. Royal S. Copeland, Al swept the convention like a storm.
Louis wired his boss triumphantly: "Al nominated with great
enthusiasm, Morgenthau and your Missus led the Dutchess delegation with the banner three times around the hall," then confided that the good doctor had been nominated "in the hope
that he could keep the cooties out of Congress." [4] When both
Smith and Copeland carried the State by narrow margins, Roosevelt wrote the new Governor in sheer elation that it was the
"first incentive to effective organization" in twelve years.[5]

This was a different Roosevelt from the one who had fought
Tammany many years before. In seeking the tempo of the new
era he had come to appreciate the social welfare program which
Smith had espoused so effectively. And he had learned to make
the best of the materials at hand. He could joke now about ". . .

[2] Howe to Cordell Hull, August 15, 1923, Group XI, FDRL.
[3] Roosevelt to Byron Newton, December 20, 1922, Group XI, FDRL.
[4] Howe to Roosevelt, September 29, 1922, Group XXXVI, FDRL.
[5] Roosevelt to Alfred E. Smith, November 9, 1922, Group XIV, Smith
File, FDRL.

the Republican clamor about Tammany Hall domination of the State. . . . Democrats from above the Bronx are perfectly able to take care of themselves." [6] He still remembered how the bosses had "worked the game" [7] against him in 1916, yet could write blandly: "Of course, most of the objections to Tammany Hall date back to the Days of Boss Tweed. . . ." [8]

Now Roosevelt and Howe pinned their hopes on a Presidential nomination for Smith. The Governor carefully denied his candidacy until February 1924, and for a time they could only help set the stage. Roosevelt's chief worry was the explosive liquor issue, which Smith's enemies rapidly exploited. Privately, F.D.R. wished the whole dangerous mess could be taken out of party politics with a national referendum: "The Wets are feeling so cocky that they believe they could carry it—the Drys are so sanctimoniously satisfied that they ought not to be afraid of the issue being put to a popular vote." [9] But Smith could not escape so neatly. In the summer of 1923 he faced an act of the Legislature repealing the State's prohibition enforcement law. Roosevelt rushed to console him: "I am mighty sorry for the extremely difficult position in which you have been placed over this darned old liquor question. . . ." He advised a veto "on the big, broad ground" that the State was morally obligated to support Federal enforcement. Then there could be a special session to amend the "unworkable, costly" enforcement law with a pallid and general directive to local officials to support the Federal government, without placing "people twice in jeopardy for the same offense." [1] But Smith had other advice from Charles Francis Murphy. He signed the repeal act and compounded his problems by forthrightly insisting that beer and wine should be legalized at once.

Roosevelt was shaken, but he stood firm against the blandish-

[6] Roosevelt to Edward J. MacGregor, November 2, 1923, Group XI, FDRL.

[7] Roosevelt to George Henry Payne, February 3, 1923, Group XI, FDRL.

[8] Roosevelt to W. J. Meininger, August 6, 1928, Group XVII, FDRL.

[9] Roosevelt to C. H. McCarthy, July 24, 1923, Group XIV, FDRL.

[1] Roosevelt to Alfred E. Smith, May 21, 1923, Group XIV, Smith File, FDRL.

ments of friends who had other candidates. Howe took some
courage when Smith called a law enforcement conference and
"talked so seriously and solemnly to them about enforcing prohibition laws as to really create a doubt" that he was a wet.[2] But
Louis deeply suspected that the 1924 convention would deadlock on the liquor issue. The candidate of the rural Protestant
prohibitionists would be William Gibbs McAdoo, President Wilson's Secretary of the Treasury and son-in-law.

Their own role in the convention would be peripheral. Roosevelt busily spiked all attempts to divide the Smith camp by cultivating a boom for him, while Louis played endlessly at the
business of arranging a few complimentary votes for his boss. He
used old friends in Massachusetts and Indiana, labor leaders in
the District of Columbia, and even F.D.R.'s old secretary, who
now worked for a Colorado Senator. He begged Franklin to invite Boss Jim Curley of Boston for a cruise on the houseboat. It
all failed. When the convention finally met, there was only one
vote for F.D.R. But there were other rewards. Boss Murphy
himself had called quietly at the 65th Street house to ask their
aid in lining up delegates. Then, only weeks before the Madison
Square Garden convention, the Smith camp was demoralized
by Murphy's sudden death. The machine was left without its
chief strategist; there was no substitute in sight. For Roosevelt
it was a fortunate if melancholy accident. He issued a suitable
statement: ". . . New York has lost its most powerful and wisest
leader."[3] Five days later Smith announced that F.D.R. would
head the New York "Citizen's Committee" to promote his candidacy. There was no real manager except Smith himself; Roosevelt became the spokesman and the symbol. But although it
may not have been intended, he refused to remain merely respectable window-dressing.

Roosevelt and Howe organized the Smith headquarters as en-
thusiastically as if it had been their own. Louis set up a mass-
production factory for handling prodigious amounts of correspondence. A gigantic list of Committee "members" was drawn
up to demonstrate Smith's broad support in his own State. Form

[2] Howe to Roosevelt, February 25, 1924, Group XIV, FDRL.
[3] Typewritten copy of statement, FDRL.

letters, over Roosevelt's signature, were sent out in reply to the 400 or 500 letters received each day. And there were daily news releases. Eleanor headed the Women's Division. Louis and Franklin drafted the statements which they hoped would create for Smith an aggressive public support. Yet in all this they were handicapped by the Governor's own careful silence and were sometimes checked by his friends at headquarters, particularly Belle Moskowitz, the one-woman Smith brain trust. They could be repudiated at any moment. However, they had the field to themselves, and for a time could hope to push the Governor in their own direction by the line they stressed.

They praised his "business-like record," his "progressivism," and his "common sense," his "tremendous grasp of fundamentals," and his belief in government "representative of no class or narrow interest." And they underlined Smith's ability to rescue the government from Harding's "system of checks without any balances." [4] "We have had two Presidents recently," Roosevelt wrote, "President Harding, who talked platitudes and relied on Daugherty and McLean, and President Coolidge, who thought platitudes and relied on C. Bascomb Slemp. . . ." [5] But they had to be careful. When there were requests for specifics, Roosevelt could glibly reply: "I have talked with Governor Smith about the problem in a big national way. . . . I found he had such familiarity with the underlying principles upon which . . . reforms must be established as to convince me that . . . we would make more progress toward really efficient government than we had ever done in the past history of the country." [6]

To the discouraged professionals they argued that Smith was the only candidate who could win, since he could carry the three essential New England States, New York, New Jersey, and Delaware, plus Illinois. The South would stay in line, despite his wetness and his religion. "There will be an awful howl from the Ku Klux Klan, but . . . Georgia and Texas, the hot bed of the Klan, will not go Republican in any event. . . ." [7]

[4] Form letter and Press Statement, Group XVI, FDRL.

[5] Roosevelt to Camden Taney, May 14, 1924, Group XVI, FDRL.

[6] Roosevelt to Henry R. Micks, May 9, 1924, Group XVI, FDRL.

[7] Roosevelt to Robert Murchie, June 6, 1924, Group XVI, FDRL.

Louis McHenry Howe, June 9, 1933.

*Louis McHenry Howe
and a tennis party
at Saratoga Springs, New Yor[k]
About 1885.*

*Louis McHenry Howe.
About 1902.*

uis McHenry Howe in New York, 1932, at campaign headquarters.

Louis McHenry Howe in the office of the Assistant Secretary of the Navy. About 1920.

*Mrs. F. D. Roosevelt has a Democratic Party meeting at her home,
49 East 65th Street, New York, 1924.*

left foreground: *right foreground:*
Eleanor Roosevelt   *Louis Howe*
                              Grace Howe

bearded man, center across table:
Henry Morgenthau, Sr.

Governor Franklin D. Roosevelt with James Farley and Louis Howe, looking over congratulatory messages after the election, November 9, 1932.

Governor Franklin D. Roosevelt in Chicago, en route to the Democratic National Convention, July 4, 1932. Howe holds draft of the acceptance speech which he wished Roosevelt to use.

James A. Farley
    Louis Howe
        Franklin Delano Roosevelt

*Mr. and Mrs. Louis McHenry Howe and
their son Hartley at campaign headquarters
in New York on election night, 1932.*

President Roosevelt visits the C.C.C. camp at Big Meadows in the Shenandoah Valley, Virginia, August 12, 1933. (Second from left) Louis Howe, Harold Ickes, Robert W. Fechner, F.D.R., Henry A. Wallace, Rexford G. Tugwell

Louis McHenry Howe and his grandson, Robert H. Baker, Jr., at Westport, Massachusetts, 1934.

And the eastern "progressive" could carry the West if he campaigned there. Actually they were running scared. Howe complained that convention arrangements were in McAdoo's hands. They desperately fought a claim that the two-thirds rule had lapsed, and Roosevelt joked sadly with Josephus Daniels: "There is still, of course, a chance . . . you and I can end the deadlock dramatically and effectively by putting your candidate and mine into a room together armed with a complete Navy outfit ranging from bean soup to 16" guns with orders that only one man can come out alive. Probably neither will come out alive and a grateful convention will give us the nomination by acclamation. . . ."[8]

Giving Smith a record which would appeal to both West and South proved all but impossible. He had said virtually nothing on the significant national issues, and they had to retreat to inane ambiguities: ". . . I am strongly in favor of the League of Nations, am perfectly willing to take my chance with Governor Smith . . .";[9] "As for Foreign Relations, Governor Smith cannot possibly misunderstand them as Coolidge is. . . ."[1] Smith would "accomplish reform of the tariff" and "meet the difficulties of [the] present [tax] law."[2] The farm problem was particularly difficult; the best they could do was to force Senator Copeland into a public statement which might lead the West to believe that Smith understood and favored farm relief, and to have pro-Smith editorials in rural eastern newspapers mailed to southern and western delegates. Privately, Roosevelt contented himself with advising Al to read up on agricultural problems: ". . . all these relief plans are unsound and create only temporary relief . . . only two things will do the *average* American farmer permanent good—one, tariff reduction on everything he uses on the farm—two, helping restore the buying power of Europe."[3]

Most of their time had to be spent fending off religious preju-

[8] Roosevelt to Josephus Daniels, May 26, 1924, Group XIV, Daniels File, FDRL.

[9] Roosevelt to Marjorie MacCracken, May 13, 1924, Group XVI, FDRL.

[1] Roosevelt to Henry R. Micks, May 9, 1924, Group XVI, FDRL.

[2] Form letter, Group XVI, FDRL.

[3] Roosevelt to George VanNamee, n.d., Group XVI, FDRL.

dice and the prohibitionists. Roosevelt received his share of
KKK letters: "Thousands see you are a black mark on the name
you bear. . . . Keep the Pope out of the U.S. He is bad enough
where he is." [4] He ignored these, but he answered angrily some
of the more responsible McAdoo supporters: "Honestly, any talk
of injecting religion into the campaign is coming from the states
in which the Klan is notoriously strong, and you and I as good
Americans cannot afford to stand for anything which would destroy the fundamentals of our government. . . ." [5]

The cry that Smith would scuttle prohibition could not be
passed off so easily as the creature of un-American trouble-
makers. The Governor was on record against the Eighteenth
Amendment. Roosevelt was forced to the weak position that
Smith "would enforce without fear and favor" [6] whatever might
be the law of the land. He pleaded for concern with more important issues, while he sketched a pathetic picture of a Governor
maligned by gossip: "I can only tell you that he used to drink
beer in the old days, that after 'prohibition' came in, he tried
drinking whiskey and found it was poison to his system. Since
last Autumn, it happens to be a fact, that he has been entirely on
the water wagon. . . ." [7] And again: "I knew T.R. and Harding
intimately and never quite understood where these nasty lies
originated any more than I understand them now in connection
with Governor Smith." [8] Roosevelt hoped to climax the defense
with a letter he had drafted, branding the issue a "red herring"
dragged out by an "impotent and rudderless Republican administration. . . . With the present policy of non-enforcement
of the unenforceable . . . I have no sympathy. . . . A temperate people are a happy and contented people, and to that
end all my acts and words will bend." [9] But Smith would have
none of this mealymouthed double-talk. He blew up much of

[4] "Fours, KKK" to Roosevelt, May 26, 1924, Group XVI, FDRL.

[5] Roosevelt to S. B. Amidon, June 6, 1924, Group XVI, FDRL.

[6] Roosevelt to A. B. Geary, May 12, 1924, Group XVI, FDRL.

[7] Roosevelt to Marjorie MacCracken, May 13, 1924, Group XVI,
FDRL.

[8] Roosevelt to E. J. Woodhouse, June 5, 1924, Group XVI, FDRL.

[9] Group XVI, FDRL.

Roosevelt's careful work with his own fiery letter to a pressure group, in which he stood firm for beer and wine, despite the Eighteenth Amendment: "There is no committee or any other power . . . that will . . . prevent me from giving full expression to just what I think about any public question."[1] Even Roosevelt's friends at the *Post* lampooned his artful dodging: "Franklin D. Roosevelt at the Manager's desk looks like a magnificent St. George who is just throwing off his mail coat after side-stepping the distilled dragon. Why fight dragons when they can be side-stepped?"[2]

The Tammany Tiger had to be side-stepped too. Eleanor stressed her hatred for Tammany, her admiration for Smith. Franklin and Louis turned their major disadvantage into a virtue. There would be no "deals," they said. Smith did not need to sell ambassadorships, cabinet posts, or "licenses to pilfer the nation's treasury or natural resources. . . ."[3] And they begged their enemies to conduct a pure campaign, free of personal vilification. This was all to the good. Smith was the most vulnerable of candidates, his machine the most disorganized, but, in fact, Smith's friends were doing the best they could at the traditional game. Howe could threaten a back-sliding delegate with pressure from the unions. When the District of Columbia delegation threatened to desert, he saw its leader and "practically told him if he knew which side his bread was buttered on he would vote for Smith."[4] Tammany was carefully planning to load the galleries with a claque of noisemakers. As the convention drew near, Smith took over personally, with Murphy's old friend George Brennan of Illinois to handle the "practical" negotiations. Roosevelt was pushed aside as the Governor stressed states' rights, ignored the issues of Wilsonian liberalism, and got set for his first test of strength in the attempt to introduce a condemnation of the Ku Klux Klan into the party platform.

Yet the Roosevelt luck held. The death of Bourke Cockran, Tammany's silver-tongued orator, had left Smith without a suit-

[1] *The New York Times,* June 9, 1924.
[2] *New York Evening Post,* June 18, 1924.
[3] Press Release, n.d., Group XVI, FDRL.
[4] Roosevelt to C. H. McCarthy, July 30, 1924, Group XVI, FDRL.

able man to nominate him. The choice fell on F.D.R. Smith had
to gamble that Roosevelt could still make a speech, balanced
precariously on his steel braces. The Protestant upstate progressive "gentleman" might help offset the image of the cigar-
smoking, brown-derbied machine politician, so deeply distrusted in the West and South. The speech was written by
committee. Roosevelt himself fretted endlessly over the too
"poetic" Happy Warrior [5] phrase that would help make his reputation. But it was a wild success. The convention's reaction for
Al was spontaneous, despite the claque of fire sirens and noisemakers Tammany had arranged to support it. And for Roosevelt
himself there was liberal, slightly astonished praise. No one who
watched him make his painful way on crutches to the rostrum,
then dominate the whole arena with his presence, could ever
again imagine that he would be contented with retirement. Walter Lippmann wrote him the next day: "Your speech . . . was a
moving and distinguished thing. I am utterly hard-boiled about
speeches, but yours seemed to me perfect in temper and manner and most eloquent in effect. We are all proud of you. . . ." [6]

No speech could clinch this nomination. The party settled
down to the most vindictive deadlock in its history. Along the
margins of the McAdoo camp, the struggle became a self-
righteous crusade against rum, Romanism, and Tammany. To
the Governor's supporters, McAdoo soon became a synonym for
hate, prejudice, and the Klan. Roosevelt's counsels of moderation were pressed aside. McAdoo came into the convention with
431½ votes, Smith with 241. Both blocks had been hardened by
a vicious fight over the anti-Klan resolution. After 64 bitter ballots, even Roosevelt had lost his temper, demanding in an insolent letter to McAdoo: "It is incredible that you would be willing
to ruin your party by . . . dog-in-the-manger tactics. . . ." [7]
After 103 enervating ballots, the sweltering, exhausted, bank-

[5] Joseph D. Proskauer: A Segment of My Times (New York: Farrar,
Strauss; 1950), pp. 50–1.
[6] Walter Lippmann to Roosevelt, June 27, 1924, Group XVI, FDRL.
[7] Draft of letter: Roosevelt to William G. McAdoo, July 4, 1924, Group
XVI, FDRL.

rupt convention chose a hopeless compromise ticket and adjourned.

The party dispersed from Madison Square Garden to inevitable defeat. Tagged with the Wall Street label, undramatic, conservative John W. Davis was bound to alienate much of the West and South; his running mate, Charles W. Bryan, the vacuous, dull brother of the "great commoner," would drive away much of the East. But for Roosevelt personally, the sad convention was a towering landmark. Throughout the bitter maneuvering, he had retained intact the wide respect his nominating speech had earned him. The convention had made him a defender of religious liberty, and it had made him a candidate to be reckoned with in the future. Even the tough boss of Kansas City, Tom Pendergast, thought F.D.R. might be the man for 1928. And privately Franklin warned: "It will not be very long, according to the doctors, before I shall be really back in the game, legs and all. . . ." [8] Yet there was little he could do at the moment for the Davis ticket. They didn't want him, or Howe. But Eleanor was active in the women's work, and Louis managed to find his way into a minor niche in the State campaign machine. Together they rigged up a motorcade in which Eleanor and her ladies followed Republican Teddy Roosevelt, Jr., about the State, driving a car adorned with a gigantic teakettle —a steaming reminder of the Teapot Dome scandals.

Davis's disaster was no worse than Roosevelt had expected. He candidly admitted: "In 1920 . . . I remarked . . . that I did not think the nation would elect a Democrat again until the Republicans had led us into a serious period of depression and unemployment. I still think that forecast holds true. . . . Every war brings after it a period of materialism and conservatism. . . ." But he moved at once to claim the leadership when the moment came. He had the same old prescription: Democrats must "get rid of their factionalism and localism, get a better hearing from the press and put their national organization on a sound financial basis. If we can do that and stop talking about

[8] Roosevelt to Irving Washburn, July 24, 1924, Group XVI, FDRL.

candidates for three years, we may win in 1928!" [9] By late November he and Howe had worked out a plan to poll the entire membership of the 1924 convention on the reasons for the disaster. The form letter requesting this information was carefully designed to plant Roosevelt's own views firmly around the country—the familiar demands for a full-time organization, better communication with the rank and file, and more publicity. The letter also echoed their dream of a national conference of party leaders and their own firm commitment to the progressive line: "The Republican leadership has stood and still stands for conservatism, for the control of the social and economic structure of the nation by a small minority of hand-picked associates . . . we are unequivocally the party of progress and liberal thought." [1]

The reaction was tremendous, and it brought to the surface all the diverse complaints that had bedeviled the party for years. Southerners thought they had been ignored in the North. Westerners complained that the South and North ran the party. Scapegoats abounded: Bryan, the Socialists, the urban bosses, the radicals, the self-seekers, the middle-of-the-road politicians, the reactionaries, Wall Street, the Negroes. The whole maneuver contained enough dynamite to blow up whatever little party unity existed. Roosevelt had bypassed the bosses and had proposed a national discipline these petty barons could only dread. Yet his bid for unity seemed a fake, coming as it did from an ambitious Smith-man, loaded as it was with his own dogma. His stress on not talking about candidates was hardly more than a blind. He wrote to Smith: ". . . it is better to encourage local candidates who would have delegates not unfriendly to you as a second choice than to build up a strong anti-Smith feeling at this time." [2] And he gleefully promised: "If McAdoo's fool friends will only continue their idiotic policy of perpetually pressing his claims . . . he will be entirely and automatically eliminated

[9] Roosevelt to Willard Saulsbury, December 9, 1924, Group XVI, FDRL.

[1] Roosevelt to Charles F. Murphy, Group XVI, FDRL.

[2] Roosevelt to Alfred E. Smith, September 17, 1926, Group XIV, Smith File, FDRL.

very soon." [3] For himself, he was uncertain. To a close friend he confided that he did not expect another Democratic year until 1932. But to the world at large he insisted that the candidate would be "the man who during the next four years has most unselfishly and with least thought of personal advantage devoted himself to the task of bringing the party back to . . . the real things that make it better to be a Democrat." [4]

As Roosevelt and Howe knew, the Circular Letter could do little more than arouse interest. They proposed to follow it up with a national conference aimed at establishing a permanent full-time organization to carry on a continuing fight on national issues. Louis worked out the dimensions of a vast program almost identical with the one he had sketched for Osborne 20 years before. The conference would lead to a relentless attack on Republicanism—designed to catch headlines—to a massive correspondence factory, and to an intricate network to tie national headquarters to the local workers.

Roosevelt discussed the conference with Senator Thomas J. Walsh on his way to Warm Springs. While Roosevelt wintered in the South, Louis scurried about trying to round up support. He got Colonel House to introduce the plan to a secret dinner of distinguished Democrats: Davis, Cox, Bernard Baruch, Henry Morgenthau, Sr., and others. He talked with Davis, whom he thought "thoroughly sold," [5] and with Davis's hand-picked National Chairman, Clem Shaver. He maneuvered to get *The New York Times'* support. But then, exhausted from overwork, he had to "beat it to the beach" [6] to avoid the hospital rest his doctors advised. He half apologized after a meeting with Walsh and others: "The Washington Conference was a huge success but it almost killed father." [7] But he was not worried; everything was set except the date of the big convention.

Louis provided his boss with painstaking summaries and analyses of the replies to the Circular Letter. As a result, Roosevelt

[3] Roosevelt to Smith, April 7, 1925, Group XIV, Smith File, FDRL.
[4] Roosevelt to P. A. Reeves, December 11, 1924, Group XI, FDRL.
[5] Howe to Roosevelt, February 27, 1925, Group XIV, FDRL.
[6] Howe to Roosevelt, n.d., Group XXXVI, FDRL.
[7] Roosevelt to Thomas J. Walsh, February 28, 1925, Group XI, FDRL.

was able to claim that his correspondents were "overwhelmingly agreed" on the program he and Howe had, in fact, been planning from the start. The party must be one of "progress and liberal thought." [8] The machinery must be large and permanent; the publicity constant and sharp. Howe had carefully briefed him to stress the difference between "national party" issues, on which all were agreed, and merely "national issues," like prohibition, which could be conveniently "left as our forefathers intended, for each state to pass upon. . . ." [9]

On March 8, 1925, they played out their little plot with a public letter to Senator Walsh, carefully arranged in advance. They had done everything they could to make Roosevelt a selfless leader above partisan rivalries, and it was only in private that he indicated his desire to "speak a few words as 'temporary chairman' " [1] of this novel convention, and only to Shaver directly that he dictated the precise arrangements. He wanted to tap the grass roots, to keep most Congressmen, as well as National Committeemen, out of it. It did not take much prescience to see that Louis's plan implied a Roosevelt-dominated machine.

But Louis's self-confidence proved as misplaced as it often had in his years with Osborne. The reactions were ominous. Southerners, Westerners, McAdoo men, most Congressmen, were deeply suspicious. Daniel Roper warned that the party had already gained enough headlines from its fights.[2] A more rabid partisan wrote that he was sick of the New York crowd trying to play the tail that wagged the dog.[3] Shaver balked at once. Louis threatened to go over his head if he did not call the conference, and fretted that the Republicans were trying to persuade Democrats that they couldn't even get together ". . . to discuss better organization without meeting the fate of the famous 'Kilkenny cats.' " [4] Roosevelt bombarded Congressmen

[8] Roosevelt to Young Men's Democratic Club, Kansas City, quoted in Donald Scott Carmichael: *F.D.R., Columnist: the Uncollected Columns of Franklin D. Roosevelt* (Chicago: Pellegrini and Cudahy; 1947), p. 21.

[9] Howe to Roosevelt, February 20, 1925, Group XXXVI, FDRL.

[1] Roosevelt to Thomas J. Walsh, n.d., Group XI, FDRL.

[2] Daniel C. Roper to Roosevelt, March 18, 1925, Group XI, FDRL.

[3] G. W. Williams to Roosevelt, April 2, 1925, Group XI, FDRL.

[4] Howe to John W. Davis, April 8, 1925, Group XI, FDRL.

with appeals to avoid an "inferiority complex." [5] But Louis was getting little help. He protested to Roosevelt: "I find it hard to put complicated situations clearly on paper and, to be brutally frank, even harder to get a reply from you in time to count much." [6] There was small comfort for him. The next letter from Roosevelt airily announced: ". . . prepare as many letters for my signature as possible. You know perfectly well that I will answer none of them in long hand. . . ." [7]

Louis soon realized that he had been outgunned again. As the reaction strengthened, Shaver announced that he would cut the organization to the bone and pay off the party's debts. Roosevelt made a last desperate bid to rouse the Congressmen to action by relaying reports that eastern newspapers opposed the conference out of fear of a Democratic Congress in 1926. By late April he was quietly retreating, covering his confusion with a new project for ". . . a smaller conference—not more than six or eight people. . . ." [8] The small conference, in January 1926, proved little more than an informal talk between Roosevelt and leading southern and western Congressmen. It had no effect on the party at the moment, but it was the beginning of Roosevelt's own liaison with men like Cordell Hull, Joseph T. Robinson, and Thomas J. Walsh, a liaison renewed regularly, when he passed through Washington on his way to and from the South each year until 1932.

Roosevelt did not give up easily. He pressed Shaver constantly for more effective campaign machinery, trying to make places in the organization for friends like Hull and Walsh, Claude Bowers and Louis Howe. But he tended to get cool, blunt replies, like the one from Jesse Jones which insisted that the National Committee was already doing what Roosevelt was demanding. [9] And Howe sourly warned him from time to time: ". . . everything is just as it was—a mess." [1]

[5] Roosevelt to William A. Oldfield, April 8, 1925, Group XI, FDRL.
[6] Howe to Roosevelt, February 20, 1925, Group XXXVI, FDRL.
[7] Roosevelt to Howe, March 11, 1925, Group XXXVI, FDRL.
[8] Roosevelt to Oldfield, April 21, 1925, Group XI, FDRL.
[9] Jesse Jones to Roosevelt, March 26, 1928, Group XVII, FDRL.
[1] Howe to Roosevelt, n.d., Group XXXVI, FDRL.

Their grand optimistic gesture had failed—partly because Roosevelt himself was suspect, partly because it was too grand for the tradition-bound professionals, but largely because there were, in fact, few "fundamental principles" on which Democrats could agree. Roper had been right. Roosevelt helped little to clarify a national Democratic position, for he dealt in slogans and easy compromises. He himself could not define the limits of his liberalism, although he could write glibly: "We cannot surely progress unless each advancing footstep is placed on firm and tried ground. . . . I believe the victory will not go to the swift, and I believe that it will certainly not go to those who hold the Republican theory of standing still." [2] Elsewhere he protested that the Democracy was not "conservatism with a move on," but "Progressivism with a brake on." [3] He was much impressed with Claude Bowers's analysis of *Jefferson and Hamilton*. Hamilton, Roosevelt said, was "a fundamental believer in an autocracy. . . . Jefferson brought the government back to the hands of the average voter. . . . Perhaps we shall find another Jefferson." [4]

But he shunned specifics that might have given meaning to his liberalism—and might have destroyed both party unity and Franklin Roosevelt. He sought a tax program "which would be fundamentally sound and at the same time make a constructive appeal." [5] He protested: "Republican newspapers are still trying to tell people that the Democratic Party stands for free trade. . . . Make it clear that this is rot, that we seek to maintain legitimate American industries, but believe that no tariff should give them exclusive right to overcharge the American public. . . ." [6] He proclaimed happily: "Farm conditions must be improved and can be without paternalism." [7] He said virtually nothing about the League of Nations these days. Sometimes he was pressed hard for specifics, as he was by *The New York Times* on

[2] Roosevelt to James Edgerton, December 12, 1924, Group XVI, FDRL.

[3] Roosevelt to DeCourcey W. Thom, July 20, 1925, Group XVI, FDRL.

[4] *New York Evening World*, December 3, 1925.

[5] Roosevelt to Alfred E. Smith, April 8, 1925, Group XIV, Smith File, FDRL.

[6] Roosevelt to Holston Bartleson, May 21, 1925, Group XI, FDRL.

[7] Roosevelt to J. W. Reed, April 25, 1925, Group XI, FDRL.

the war debt settlement with Fascist Italy. Louis protected him with the short statement: "Mr. Roosevelt never takes a stand on any important question without trying to get all sides of it."[8] Then Howe set about quizzing important political and financial leaders: Owen D. Young, Newton Baker, Walter Lippmann, Baruch, and others. He warned Roosevelt to dodge the hot question in which the alternatives seemed to be a deal with Mussolini or no deal at all. Roosevelt quietly warned Senator Walsh not to "oppose without clear or sound reasons. . . . We cannot, for instance contend against the settlement on the mere ground that we do not like Mussolini or that the proposed Morgan loan may be used by the Dictator to finance another war. . . ."[9]

Yet away from Howe's cautions and criticisms, Roosevelt could assert himself in revealing ways, as he often did in his columns for a Georgia newspaper during the winter. Sometimes his views looked backward into his own narrow environment. He could propose a more liberal immigration policy for Europeans, for example, but he assumed that Asians must be barred—for the "real" reason, the "undesirability of mixing the blood of the two peoples."[1] He could propose a national plan for placing newly arrived immigrants throughout the country, but he could also claim: "For fifty years the United States ate a meal altogether too large . . . some of it . . . almost poisonous. The United States must, for a short time, stop eating, and when it resumes should confine itself to the most readily assimilable foodstuffs."[2] Louis would have agreed, but he would probably not have said so in public.

And Louis might not have been so frank as was Roosevelt with his offhand statements which looked into the future. Of the timber business, for example: "I prophesy that it will become a government enterprise in the next generation. . . . It is fine talk and very soothing to think of the individual as complete

[8] Howe to Roosevelt, n.d., Group XXXVI, FDRL.

[9] Howe to Thomas J. Walsh, February 22, 1926, Group XI, FDRL.

[1] *Macon Daily Telegraph*, April 30, 1925, quoted in Carmichael: *FDR: Columnist*, p. 58.

[2] *Macon Daily Telegraph*, April 21, 1925, quoted in ibid., p. 39.

master in his own home. . . . A man has the legal right to go to his bank, draw out his balance in paper money, go home and put it in the stove. If he does it, however, he is apt to land in the lunatic asylum. We have not yet reached the common-sense age which will, in like manner, send the farmer who burns off his wood lot to the home for incurables!" [3] And he groped slowly in his letters toward the compromise between states' rights and nationalism which he unveiled dramatically in the New York State Democratic Convention of 1926: "If we accept the phrase 'the best government is the least government' we must understand that it applies to the simplification of governmental machinery, and to the prevention of improper interference with the legitimate private acts of citizens, but a nation or State which is unwilling to tackle new problems, caused by the immense increase of population and by the astounding strides of modern science, is headed for decline and ultimate death from inaction. . . ." [4]

Roosevelt's own ambitions required a waiting game. If national politics proved frustrating for the moment, there was productive work to be done in New York. He and Howe maneuvered carefully to avoid a premature blight. Fearing a draft for the Senatorial nomination, Louis warned him before the State convention: ". . . I hope your spine is still sufficiently strong to assure them that you are still nigh death's door for the next two years. Please try and look pallid, and worn and weary. . . ." [5] But Roosevelt was delighted to be keynoter, to blast "Republican prosperity" as the "most dishonest drivel that has ever been used as an excuse to change the subject." [6] He avoided Louis's phrase "Jackals of Corruption" as well as Howe's advice to concentrate on the industrial recession in Maine—"Here is the Republican party's favorite child, look at the darned old thing!" [7]— and he recklessly raised the prohibition issue, because the Re-

[3] *Macon Daily Telegraph*, April 18, 1925, quoted in ibid., p. 34.
[4] Draft, Group XI, and Press Release, September 27, 1926, FDRL.
[5] Howe to Roosevelt, n.d., Group XXXVI, FDRL.
[6] Press Release, September 27, 1926, FDRL.
[7] Howe to Roosevelt, September 9, 1926, and n.d., Group XXXVI, FDRL.

publican Senatorial candidate was a wet, too vulnerable a target
to resist. His dry friend, Josephus Daniels, consoled him:
". . . you took only a light bath and came out in fine shape.
. . . Nobody could call you an emersionist [*sic*] like Al Smith;
they would rather think you took yours by sprinkling or pour-
ing. . . ."[8]

Smith rode easily back to the Executive Mansion, and Robert F. Wagner went on to a lifelong career in the Senate.
Roosevelt looked forward to 1928. Smith would move, either up
—or out. And his own road ahead would at last be clear. He
did everything he could to help Smith move, picking timely
issues to publicize and seeking to push Al in the right direction.
In 1927, a year of disaster in the Mississippi Valley, it was flood
control. Throughout the summer, Roosevelt flailed away at
Coolidge's inaction and at the ineffectiveness of Secretary of
Commerce Hoover's program. Howe advised him to issue a
"ringing demand in the name of humanity" for Federal action.
"In other words," Louis said, "raise hell generally." [9] Roosevelt
did, with press releases, with a proposal for a centrally managed
plan for inland waterways and flood control, with a proposal
for a nonpartisan committee to force Federal action. When
Hoover proposed a similar plan, Roosevelt shifted tactically to
protest "the dissipation of energy and loss of valuable time
through too broad a consideration" of the problem.[1] But his
trend was clear. Early in 1928, appearing before a Senate committee, he forecast the point of view which would flower five
years later in T.V.A.: ". . . the problem of the Mississippi wa-
tershed would have been considered a federal matter by the
framers of the Constitution. . . . Furthermore, it is physically
impossible . . . to arrive at any fair division of costs and responsibilities. . . . As a practical business matter, the construction and maintenance of whatever is decided on should be carried through by a centralized organization which, in the nature
of things, should be under Federal control. This responsibility

[8] Josephus Daniels to Roosevelt, October 1, 1926, Group XIV, Daniels
File, FDRL.

[9] Howe to Roosevelt, n.d., Group XIV, FDRL.

[1] Georges St. Jean to Roosevelt, August 31, 1927, Group XI, FDRL.

carries with it the responsibility for financing—all of it. . . ." [2]
Privately he prodded Al Smith: ". . . eventually we as a nation
will undertake the storing of waters on the higher reaches of
the tributary rivers and in conjunction with those, will develop
hydro-electric power for the benefit of the whole people of the
United States. This is sound doctrine and it is time it was said
by somebody in authority." [3]

Early in 1928 he turned to foreign affairs again. He was moving rapidly toward the Good Neighbor policy. He counseled a
bold attack on Republican imperialism in Nicaragua. In a memo
to Smith's advisors, he insisted: "Only in rare cases . . . can
there be any possible justifications for intervention. . . . When
such a rare case happens, it seems to me that the civilized world
now demands that action should not be taken by one outside
nation alone without consultation with its neighbors." [4] And, old
Navy man though he was, he was now opposed to new construction: ". . . it . . . is merely handing a cudgel to the State
Department to use over the heads of other nations. . . ." [5]

On Europe he was more cautious, contenting himself with
caustic cracks in private at "pin headed local politicians," [6] and
with supporting harmless resolutions that could not pass: "The
Republicans are running around in circles. . . . Go ahead and
stick another pin in them." [7] He dodged comment on the Kel-
logg-Briand Pact to outlaw war, following Louis's sharp advice:
". . . The reputation you have . . . should not be jeopardized
by backing up every day dream of the impractical theorist." [8]
Now he told his wife's close friends in the World Court crusade
it was "far more important to elect friends of the World Court
than . . . to make platform declarations." [9] He himself stuck a
few pins into Republican policies in an article in *Foreign Af-*

[2] Roosevelt to H. D. Stephens, January 27, 1928, Group XVII, FDRL.
[3] Roosevelt to Alfred E. Smith, May 20, 1927, Group XIV, Smith File,
FDRL.
[4] "Memorandum for Colonel Greene," Group XVII, FDRL.
[5] Roosevelt to Meyer Jacobstein, March 5, 1928, Group XVII, FDRL.
[6] Roosevelt to Esther Lape, October 17, 1927, Group XI, FDRL.
[7] Roosevelt to Claude Swanson, March 31, 1928, Group XVII, FDRL.
[8] Howe to Roosevelt, May 24, 1927, Group XIV, FDRL.
[9] Roosevelt to Esther Lape, June 14, 1928, Group XVII, FDRL.

fairs, wherein he noted their fizzling naval disarmament conferences, their "backward steps" in Latin America, their abdica-
tion of the nation's "moral leadership." It was a performance
that could only benefit him if Smith should need him as Secretary of State, but there was one sentence in the article which
would haunt him years later: "Only the most excited of the
admirals will seriously consider the possibility of invasion either
of the United States or of Japan by sea." [1]

As the 1928 convention approached, Roosevelt found himself
on the margins of a Smith campaign managed by the Governor's
own personal staff. He worked on his dissident southern friends,
did what he could in his letters to build a backfire to religious
prejudice, and spent ten days in May traveling for Al in the
Midwest. Neither he nor Howe had much hope. Louis was appalled at the early blunders made by Tammany. Both thought
Smith would be nominated, then defeated. Franklin claimed
Southerners would let Smith have the nomination and "get it
off . . . [their] chests." [2] Louis said more bluntly that Al's enemies would nominate him, then knife him at the polls. And
Franklin betrayed their mutual doubts to Daniels: ". . . I am
doubtful whether any Democrat can win in 1928. It will depend
somewhat on whether the present undoubted general prosperity
of the country continues. . . ." [3] His mood was mild: ". . . the
present gray period may last for another ten years. But there is
just the possibility that if Smith is elected, he will prove equal
to the task of new leadership. In my judgment, it is at least a
gamble worth taking!" [4]

Louis was much more concerned with keeping Roosevelt in
Smith's good graces and momentarily out of the running for any
office. When the Southern drys tried to adopt him in place of
Al, Louis "threw enough cold water on the idea to extinguish
the Woolworth building." [5] He squelched a Hearst rumor by

[1] Roosevelt: "Our Foreign Policy: A Democratic View," *Foreign Affairs*, VI (July 1928), pp. 573–86.
[2] Roosevelt to Will R. King, March 10, 1927, Group XI, FDRL.
[3] Roosevelt to Josephus Daniels, June 23, 1927, Group XI, FDRL.
[4] Roosevelt to J. W. Atwood, June 6, 1928, Group XVII, FDRL.
[5] Howe to Roosevelt, April 26, 1927, Group XIV, FDRL.

planting a newspaper quotation from "one of Mr. Roosevelt's
closest friends: 'Frank is not and will not be under any circumstances a candidate for the Presidency.'"[6] And Roosevelt merrily told a newsman he had seen so many Presidents that he
would "rather do my bit as a private in the ranks."[7] Yet there
were opposite dangers, and Louis constantly warned his boss to
keep Smith well informed of his friendship.

The convention at Houston was dull. Roosevelt was prominent—he was floor leader for Smith, and he made the nominating speech. But there was little to arrange; there was little
room for his influence. Quiet preconvention work with the
bosses and the favorite sons, and a deep compulsion to avoid a
deadlock, gave Smith the nomination on the first ballot. Roosevelt had failed to get the Vice-Presidency for Cordell Hull, but
he could hardly object to Arkansas's Joseph T. Robinson, who
was also among his southern cronies. There was little to which
he could take exception in the pallid platform. The ambiguous
statements on foreign policy and liquor might have been taken
from his own careful letters. But he was a little embarrassed.
To Newton Baker, tireless advocate of the League of Nations, he
confessed: "You are not alone in having unhappy sessions with
yourself over the platform. If you or I had been the candidate,
we would have ordered it otherwise—and thereby insured our
defeat. . . ."[8] He blamed Smith's "advisors" for the "glittering
generalities."[9]

He was soon disillusioned with the campaign, and disgusted
when Smith underlined the liquor issue in his acceptance speech
and made himself more vulnerable still in his choice of John
Raskob as National Chairman—a wet, an Easterner, a General
Motors millionaire. "Things depend so much on the way they
are put . . . ,"[1] he protested. In addition, his pride was hurt.
He might boast to his mother that he had turned down the National Chairmanship, but to Van Lear Black, he angrily con-

[6] Howe to Roosevelt, n.d., Group XXXVI, FDRL.
[7] Roosevelt to Stanley Prenosil, May 24, 1927, Group XIV, FDRL.
[8] Roosevelt to Newton Baker, July 12, 1928, Group XVII, FDRL.
[9] Roosevelt to Clark Eichelberger, July 20, 1928, Group XVII, FDRL.
[1] Roosevelt to Harry Byrd, August 20, 1928, Group XVII, FDRL.

fided: "I had especially hoped that the publicity end of things would have been put under some really big men with imagination and organizing ability, but . . . it is a situation in which I can find little room for active work. . . ." [2] He and Louis found refuge in the Division of Commerce, Industry and Professional Activities, and Mrs. Roosevelt headed the women's work. But Roosevelt was soon bored. He retired to Warm Springs late in September, leaving his share of headquarters work in Louis's capable hands. There was little to interest a Roosevelt in a campaign run by Belle Moskowitz "with the aid of the General Motors publicity and advertising section." [3]

[2] Roosevelt to Van Lear Black, July 25, 1928, Group XIV, Black File, FDRL.
[3] Ibid.

· I V ·

APPRENTICESHIP
FOR THE
WHITE HOUSE

15

Drafted for Governor

If they are looking for a goat, why doesn't Wagner sacrifice himself?
(Louis Howe *to* Franklin D. Roosevelt,
September 26, 1928) [1]

ROOSEVELT had hardly reached Warm Springs before Smith was planning a new and critical job for him—the fight for the Governorship of New York. Al may not have been sold on him personally, but there was no other acceptable candidate in sight. Upstate politicians wanted Roosevelt because he might win and thus assure them State patronage, Louis Howe warned his boss. Furthermore, it was necessary to have a "protestant with an unsullied record and unblemished character. . . ." [2] Both Roosevelt and Howe were upset. Franklin wanted to continue his treatments and see the Warm Springs Foundation firmly established. Worse yet, the timing was wrong for his career. They would probably lose. Louis expected Hoover to get two terms in the White House. Roosevelt should run for Governor in 1932, and be ripe for the White House in 1936.

[1] Group XIV, FDRL.
[2] Proskauer: *Segment of My Times*, p. 63.

Roosevelt ignored all messages from New York, leaving Louis to face the artillery back in the city, where he persuaded Senator Wagner that it would be unfair personally to F.D.R. to make him run. At the same time he warned Franklin that health would be the only acceptable excuse and insisted on a categorical statement that would end the draft forever. The New York leaders spoiled this move at once. Herbert Lehman could be nominated for Lieutenant Governor, they said, and could act for Roosevelt during legislative sessions. Louis retorted that his boss would never run for a job and then leave it to an understudy. Privately he was worried that Franklin might weaken. He cautioned his boss that his absence would be headlined by newsmen as a maneuver for a draft, and demanded a specific statement for the press. And he argued hotly; "I do not believe your running will really induce anyone to vote for Al, but on the contrary some of your friends now voting for Al for your sake will vote for you and not for Al if you run. . . ."[3] The pressure mounted. Smith called from Milwaukee to urge the case in person. Roosevelt refused in a public telegram as blunt as courtesy permitted. He went on to argue that two more years would see him "rid of leg braces. . . . As I am only forty-six," he wrote, ". . . I owe it to my family and myself to give the present constant improvement a chance to continue."[4] But he warned his mother: "I have had a difficult time turning down the Governorship. . . . I only hope they don't try to stampede the Convention tomorrow and nominate me and then adjourn!"[5]

While Smith frantically sought to solve his problem through interminable conferences in his Rochester hotel room, Roosevelt made himself unavailable. Unable to reach him, the politicians descended on Louis and threatened to send a personal agent to Warm Springs if Roosevelt refused to talk with them by phone. In near panic, Louis wired his boss for an outright refusal, while Smith's aides tried to keep Eleanor Roosevelt with them to help

[3] Howe to Roosevelt, September 26, 1928, Group XIV, FDRL.

[4] Roosevelt to Alfred E. Smith, September 30, 1928, Group XIV, Smith File, FDRL.

[5] Roosevelt to Sara Delano Roosevelt, September 30, 1928, quoted in *Personal Letters, 1905–1928*, p. 645.

when they finally got through to her husband. It was long after midnight when they argued it out with the reluctant draftee by phone. Smith, Raskob, Wagner, and several others took turns in the conversation. One after another Roosevelt's objections were turned aside. The Governor insisted that F.D.R. was needed; Lehman's full-time help was promised; Raskob personally undertook to arrange financing for Warm Springs. And dozens of telegrams from friends piled up through the night to support their demands. When Smith asked him pointedly whether he would refuse the nomination if it were actually made, Roosevelt could offer nothing but silence. His refusal to say "no" was enough. Two days later, he was nominated by acclamation. Roosevelt had little choice. He made a serious personal sacrifice, which he could conscientiously have refused, but for one fact— his presidential ambitions. Smith had pressed the demand until it represented Roosevelt's last chance for political advancement. If he refused to serve after every possible concession had been made to his personal commitments, he could scarcely expect the party's help when his own moment came. When he sought to explain his decision, he was fond of quoting a friend: "You got caught off third base in a squeeze play, and were run down and tagged just as you were sliding for home plate. . . ." [6]

His close friends were sad. Missy LeHand, his loyal secretary, hoped that he would lose the election and resume his struggle to walk. Eleanor telegraphed: "Regret that you had to accept. . . ." [7] Louis was incensed at the argument that they must accept the inevitable. The job was to control situations, not to bow to them. He wryly wired: "By way of congratulations dig up telegram I sent you when you ran in senatorial primaries." [8] To his wife, Louis sadly wrote: "We are much upset and are praying that we get licked, but it looks bad." [9]

If the Smith forces had bargained for a name and a reputation, they got a candidate and a leader. Roosevelt bounded into

[6] Roosevelt to Frederick A. Delano, October 8, 1928, Group XVII, FDRL.

[7] Eleanor Roosevelt to Roosevelt, October 2, 1928, Group XVII, FDRL.

[8] Howe to Roosevelt, October 2, 1928, Group XVII, FDRL.

[9] Howe to Grace Howe, October 3, 1928, Personal Papers.

activity as if he had never entertained a doubt. He could hardly allow himself to be a mere shadow, relying on Lehman and Smith. And he had to fight off the burgeoning propaganda that he was an unfortunate, physically incompetent victim of political exploitation. It would be all too easy for the public to believe his own frequently asserted claims that he was not ready for office yet. He issued a sharp, angry statement: "I am amazed to hear that efforts are being made to make it appear that I have been 'sacrificed' by Governor Smith. . . . I was drafted because all of the party leaders . . . insisted that my often expressed belief in the policies of Governor Smith made my nomination the best assurance to the voters that these policies would be continued. . . . That is something too important to let any personal consideration weigh in the slightest." [1] Smith himself had a better reply: "A Governor does not have to be an acrobat. We do not elect him for his ability to do a double back-flip or a handspring." [2]

The best answer would be Roosevelt's own dynamic campaign. He made three major speeches for Smith in Georgia, and punctuated his trip home with two more, in Cleveland and Boston. But it promised to be the most difficult campaign he had ever undertaken. He had only three weeks, and he had to argue complicated State issues with which he had had only slight contact for 16 years. In addition, he had reasonably formidable opposition, led by the popular Attorney General Albert Ottinger, who was expected to wean away the normally Democratic Jewish voters. Party leaders made things more difficult by insisting that he spend much time in New York City, where he felt he was not needed. He was able to rescue only ten hectic days for the crucial upstate tour. And he had to breathe some spirit into his own staff. Long before Roosevelt reached New York, he had received Louis's strong advice: ". . . insist on limiting speeches to the four big cities with a radio hookup and generally make your campaign on the never mind me, vote for

---

[1] Quoted in *Personal Letters, 1905–1928*, pp. 647–8.

[2] Quoted in Ernest K. Lindley: *Franklin D. Roosevelt: A Career in Progressive Democracy* (Indianapolis: The Bobbs-Merrill Company; 1931), p. 21.

Al basis that will have the advantage of avoiding the necessity of debating on state issues with practically no preparation." Louis suggested that Lehman be given the major campaign chores: "He wants to relieve you of all routine work as Governor, and it is a grand time to start now." [3]

Roosevelt would have none of this. In a round of New York City speeches, he unveiled his program: a constitutional amendment committing the State to public power development; reform of the criminal codes and of local government; scientific study of the State's agricultural problems. The power issue he had inherited from Smith; the rest grew from his own experience, and Louis's, and it reflected their old preoccupation with the rural Democracy. As he headed west on the Erie Railroad, it became clear that polio would not restrict this seasoned campaigner. He made extemporaneous speeches in numerous small towns of the southern tier during the four days it took him to reach Jamestown at the far end of the State. He returned along the New York Central, with major speeches in Buffalo, Rochester, Utica, Syracuse, and Albany. Moving slowly, he reached the small towns along the way by automobile. By the time he reached Troy he could safely remind his delighted audience of the "sob stuff" about his health so liberally peddled by Republican editors. Taking several minutes to describe the hectic tour, he buoyantly told his partisans: "Too bad about this unfortunate sick man, isn't it?" [4]

As Howe had advised him, he campaigned more for Al than for himself, so much so that another of his aides back in New York urged him to remind the voters that he was running for office too. But there was no avoiding this strategy. Wherever he dug into State issues, he found himself running on the Governor's record, in a campaign already blueprinted by Smith and Ottinger. Religious prejudice was a major problem, underlined sharply by a public warning from the Democratic leaders of Chemung County that their area would cut both Smith and

[3] Howe to Roosevelt, October 2, 1928, Group XIV, FDRL.
[4] Samuel I. Rosenman (ed.): *The Public Papers and Addresses of Franklin D. Roosevelt,* 5 vols. (New York: Random House; 1938), I, pp. 53–4.

Ottinger because of Klan influence. The religious issue could hurt both sides. Smith might lose Protestants, Roosevelt might lose Jews, Ottinger might lose Catholics. Roosevelt spent much of his time in reasoned, careful appeals for tolerance. And then he lost his temper, furiously repudiating the support of any intolerant person: "May God have mercy on your miserable soul!" [5]

National issues were prominent largely because Ottinger raised them. When his opponent boasted of Coolidge economies, F.D.R. slapped back with the charge that the costs of national government had risen, by prewar standards. When Ottinger claimed that Smith's administration had been inefficient, F.D.R. noted that the Governor had reorganized the antique system he had inherited; Harding and Coolidge had been content merely to talk about reform. At Rochester the Republican candidate boasted that the protective tariff was the key to prosperity and warned that the Democrats would "scuttle" it. Roosevelt dismissed the tariff argument as "old hash" and defied the Republicans to show what they had done about agricultural depression. The national conflict, he said, was between "progress" and "reaction." When Ottinger promised that Hoover would abolish poverty with such projects as Boulder Dam, Roosevelt turned to ridicule. Would the great engineer accomplish the revolution with statistics? Roosevelt continued to challenge the "beauty sleep" of the Coolidge administration. But the core of his campaign was the broad reform program with which Smith had long been identified. [6]

The most striking issue was water power. Republicans had supported private construction and operation of electric power facilities. Smith had sponsored public production and distribution. The party stalemate in the State Legislature had lasted for nearly 20 years. Roosevelt himself had stood for public ownership since 1912, and he followed Smith's steps without hesitation. He attacked the Republican-proposed 50-year leases as outright gifts to private interests. Ottinger, he noted, was a mem-

[5] Rosenman: *Public Papers*, I, p. 38.

[6] *The New York Times*, October 19, 20, 1928; Rosenman: *Public Papers*, I, pp. 16–30.

ber of the Water Power Commission which was trying to "steal" the people's property for private corporations. And he attacked the "consummate nerve" of the commission in planning to authorize leases on the St. Lawrence only a month before its term of office expired. He deftly compared Ottinger on New York water power with Ottinger on the Boulder Dam: ". . . [it] depends very much on whose baby has the measles." [7] Ottinger protested that his views had been deliberately misrepresented. But he could promise only more scientific study; F.D.R. promised action.

Roosevelt made a major bid for the labor vote, indicting Republicans for "perjury," reading his own party's record and Ottinger's personal dossier of anti-labor votes. He spent much time defending himself against charges that his proposals were "radical." [8] Citing precedents for public ownership in the post office and the state highway system, he fondly looked back to the time when he had been called "radical" for favoring a 54-hour law, factory inspection, and employers' liability laws. When Hoover warned of "socialism," Roosevelt answered coolly that the candidate was in the "panic" stage of the campaign. [9] Actually, of course, it was a mild program, looking more to study than to action and containing few specific promises. The only really embarrassing issue was prohibition. He dodged the question of legalizing wine and beer, but could not avoid the issue of the re-enactment of a State prohibition enforcement law, and he took uneasy refuge behind the legal argument he had urged upon Smith four years earlier. He wrote one old friend: "Our grandfathers would turn over in their graves, if they could see the system of double jeopardy which has gone into effect in so many different States. . . ." [1]

On the whole, Roosevelt's readaptation to State politics

[7] *The New York Times*, October 23, 24, 25, 1928; Rosenman: *Public Papers*, I, pp. 44–51.

[8] Rosenman: *Public Papers*, I, p. 43.

[9] *The New York Times*, October 25, 1928; Rosenman: *Public Papers*, I, p. 59.

[1] Roosevelt to Mrs. Richard Aldrich, October 25, 1928, Group XVII, FDRL.

proved easy. Many of the issues he faced were old ones, familiar since his days in the State Senate. He made it easier by limiting himself to Ottinger's attacks. More important, he had in this campaign for the first time the services of his politically astute advisor and facile penman, Samuel Rosenman. Roosevelt had long since learned to use his aides, and Rosenman found himself turning out drafts for speech after speech, pounding away on his typewriter in his hotel room while the boss slept. In New York Louis ran two vast propaganda factories, the Business and Professional Division of Smith's headquarters and their own Independent Committee for Roosevelt and Lehman, at the Biltmore Hotel.

Louis was in his element here. Dominating his staff, with little interference from F.D.R., he had ample range for his imagination and his crotchets. He hovered over his workers like an irascible grandfather, bellowing his orders, receiving the best work morosely. He gave them a bit of "unshirted hell" for every mild error, demanded the impossible constantly, but managed somehow to inspire a devoted, almost worshipful loyalty from his aides. The girls claimed to live in terror of his rage, but they knew he appreciated their work, and privately they gossiped about how "cute" he looked. They fondly dubbed him "the little boss" and, in gayer moments, "Felix the Cat," and eagerly adopted the nicknames he caustically assigned them. The faithful Margaret Durand became permanently the "Rabbit" when she tried to wigwag him a signal behind the back of a visitor. Lela Stiles boasted years later of his giving her the official title "Chief Inspector of New Speakeasies." And they worried about his hacking cough, his interminable work, his careless lunches—an apple and a glass of milk. More important, they worked for him like inspired demons—frequently overtime, sometimes all night. "Rabbit" solved her dating problems by bringing her fiancé back to the office to work for Smith in the evenings, and Lela got up at 5 in the morning to send out Special Delivery letters to visiting department store buyers whose names were listed in the early morning editions.[2]

[2] Stiles: *Howe*, p. 178.

Lela and Rabbit would eventually go to the White House with Louis, and so would a score of others from this 1928 team: James A. Farley, Edward J. Flynn, Grace Tully, Margaret Le-Hand, Louise Hachmeister, Raymond Moley, as well as Henry Morgenthau, Jr., Franklin's old Dutchess County friend. And both the Roosevelt and Howe families pitched vigorously into the campaign work. Eleanor, now an able and dedicated professional, filled a heavy routine of speaking engagements in New England and New York, and kept a close check on Dutchess County. Their oldest son Jimmy, away at Harvard, was one of the major speakers at the frequent rallies of the Massachusetts College League for Smith. In Fall River Grace Howe discovered for herself the delights of practical politics which so engrossed her husband.

The Roosevelt team worked within the larger context of Smith's own staff. There was sharp rivalry and suspicion between Louis and the Governor's woman-of-all-work, Belle Moskowitz. Smith himself ignored them. Even Roosevelt had had to beg abjectly for a five-minute appointment with the candidate early in the national campaign, and some of their best plans were dampened when their memos remained unanswered in Al's office. In addition, there were troubles within Louis's own team. Howe jealously guarded his intimate relationship with his boss; many of his colleagues feared that Louis would ruthlessly destroy any potential competitor. But Howe, viewing his own interests as identical with Franklin's, thought of himself as mediator and moderator of the recurring tempests of rival ambitions and ideas. During one controversy between Farley and Morgenthau, he wrote to Roosevelt: "Not that I claim for one minute to have done this for Henry's sake, but it did seem wise to prevent friction in your own organization. However matters seem quieted down and . . . all parties to the quarrel will kiss and make up and pass a unanimous resolution that the entire trouble was my fault,—so that's that. . . ." [3] Louis still had his basic sense of humor. Suddenly recognizing in mid-letter that he was pontificating, he could warn his boss: "Yes, I am aware that any

[3] Howe to Roosevelt, October 22, 1928, Group XVII, FDRL.

opinion in which I concur . . . [is] considered by me the
consensus of everybody else's opinion. . . ." [4]

Louis concentrated on the type of campaigning he and Roosevelt had long since made their standard operating procedure:
daily news releases, masses of form letters sent to lists of political Committeemen, businessmen, and professional people. And
Louis managed the vast information-gathering apparatus which
had become his special pet. His staff read hundreds of newspapers, posted clippings in scrapbooks, and made elaborate
summaries of editorial opinion for Roosevelt and himself. They
digested the thousands of letters which poured into headquarters into daily reports for the candidates and strategists, and
ground out the hundreds of letters which could not be handled
with the standard forms. A typical "Roosevelt letter" might be
drafted by a secretary on information provided by Belle Moskowitz, edited by Louis, and signed by one of the practiced
"forgers" who had been delegated to copy Roosevelt's signature.

Louis was on his own completely once Roosevelt had started
off on his gubernatorial campaign, but he had plenty of guidance in the tactics he and his boss had worked out for their
crusade to sell businessmen on Smith. It was a campaign of
personalities rather than issues. Hoover, they insisted, was "not
temperamentally fitted or able to handle a great many problems
at the same time." [5] On the other hand, Smith had shown himself a superb administrator and a "great human engineer." [6]
Hoover was a weak man who had remained silent through
Harding corruption and Coolidge inaction. Smith was a dynamic
warrior who had forced William Randolph Hearst out of New
York politics. Smith would be friendly to business, but Hoover
would stand for the centralization of power and the constant
harassment of the businessman. To a New York manufacturer
they wrote: "Mr. Hoover has always shown a disquieting desire
to investigate everything and to appoint commissions and send
out statistical inquiries on every conceivable subject under
Heaven. He has also shown in his own Department a most

[4] Ibid.
[5] Roosevelt to Irving Hiett, September 5, 1928, Group XVII, FDRL.
[6] Roosevelt to William Loeb, September 21, 1928, Group XVII, FDRL.

alarming desire to issue regulations and to tell businessmen generally how to conduct their affairs. . . ." [7] This was the same Roosevelt who a few short years before had blasted Hoover's unwillingness to provide just this kind of statistical service for the construction industry, and this was the same Roosevelt who, within a few short weeks, would be stumping the State on a program of publicly owned electric power. But no one exploited the inconsistency.

Yet, on most matters, their Smith campaign had been positive in attack, artfully vague in commitment. Roosevelt had criticized the Kellogg Pact for superficiality; he had proclaimed that something must be done about Latin American suspicion of the United States, and he had asked Sumner Welles to write a pamphlet on the "Crime Against Our Neighbors," but he had refused to go beyond the general statement of his *Foreign Affairs* article. He had thumped cautiously for a "scientific tariff," had lambasted Republicans for their lack of a farm policy, yet had offered nothing except dire warnings that the country could not continue with "industrial prosperity and agricultural ruin." [8] Now it all fitted nicely into the campaign he found himself running upstate, especially his heavy correspondence on the liquor issue and on the "unspeakable . . . whispering campaign" [9] about Smith and Popery. Long before he faced his rural New Yorkers, he had promised that Smith would bring "another experiment which, if not noble, will at least be practical. . . ." [1] He had repudiated the Klan publicly, blasted the politicking of Protestant leaders who opposed so sharply the activity of Catholics in politics: ". . . that does not appeal to me as being the kind of American fair play that we preach about." [2] And he had read the scriptures to at least one southern clergyman: "Let him who is without sin cast the first stone." [3]

[7] Roosevelt to Ward Melville, September 21, 1928, Group XVII, FDRL.
[8] *Beacon Standard,* September 6, 1928, quoted in Carmichael: *F.D.R.: Columnist,* p. 122.
[9] Roosevelt to E. J. Cornish, October 3, 1928, Group XVII, FDRL.
[1] Roosevelt to Frederick Landis, October 5, 1928, Group XVII, FDRL.
[2] Roosevelt to Josephus Daniels, July 26, 1928, Group XVII, FDRL.
[3] Roosevelt to W. J. Carpenter, n.d., Group XVII, FDRL.

As Roosevelt greeted his enthusiastic upstate audiences and Louis ground out his relentless stream of letters associating Roosevelt vaguely with Wilsonian liberalism and internationalism, they both became gradually intoxicated with the signs of a new spirit in the State. Louis boasted that in a week they had raised $100,000 more for Roosevelt's gubernatorial campaign than Smith had been able to dredge up for his entire 1926 operation. Roosevelt assured the State's National Committeewoman: ". . . the situation upstate looks better to me than for many years." [4] In his own Dutchess County the situation was appalling. Regarding the county committee, Louis suggested: ". . . invite them to a picnic on the banks of Wappingers Creek. By offering them free food or free anything, they would all come and then I would invite them, one by one, to a private conference behind the bushes and drop them into the creek with weights around their necks like so many sick kittens." [5] But farther upstate there seemed to be life, "even in the Black Republican counties." [6] There was a chance, but it would be close, so close that they feared corruption in the vote counting. On election night, as the returns came slowly in, Roosevelt personally called the sheriffs in certain crucial counties, and Edward J. Flynn bluffed publicly at 2 a.m. by threatening to send hundreds of lawyers to check the upstate returns. No agents were sent; there was no need. Roosevelt, the pinch hitter, carried the State with a margin of over 25,000. But Smith had lost New York by over 100,000, trailing F.D.R. in every county except New York and the Bronx. The rebel of 1911 had become the accredited leader of his party. The old East Side professional who had forced him to make this race stood glumly in the shadow of the reluctant champion he had helped to create.

[4] Roosevelt to Elizabeth Marbury, October 22, 1928, Group XVII, FDRL.

[5] Howe to Roosevelt, October 22, 1928, Group XVII, FDRL.

[6] Roosevelt to Elizabeth Marbury, October 22, 1928, Group XVII, FDRL.

16

⋙-⋙-⋙-⋙-⋙-⋙-⋙-⋙

The Governor and

His Team

*I believe that in the future the State . . .
will assume a much larger role in the lives
of its citizens. . . . Now some people are
going to say this is socialistic. My answer
to them is that it is "social," not "socialistic."* (Franklin D. Roosevelt,
December 30, 1928) [1]

JANUARY 1, 1929, was a day of triumph and regret, for Franklin
Roosevelt, for his friends, for New York Democrats generally.
Deeply uncertain in the fall whether he was ready physically
for the Governorship, Roosevelt stood in the jammed Assembly
Chamber at Albany, radiating the confidence the campaign had
restored to him. There seemed no flickering of regret that his
ambition had robbed him of the cherished hope to walk again,

[1] *The New York Times*, December 30, 1928.

no trace of bitterness because the timing of his march toward the White House had been perhaps disastrously disrupted. Refreshed by an active six weeks' vacation in the Georgia sun, he stood a buoyant symbol of a new regime in a hostile house.

Nearly everyone at the crowded inauguration faced him with regrets and deep suspicion. Public tokens of tension abounded. The shouts from the gallery were for Al Smith, not F.D.R. Smith's sentimental farewell, tactfully arranged to precede the formal inauguration, made the festive occasion seem a funeral for the Democracy. Al's graciousness could scarcely veil the bitter frustrations of the preceding month. To the man who had dominated State government for ten years, who had been a leader of the New York Democracy for 20, this was perhaps a worse defeat than the November election. The smiling, imperturbable protégé who waited to succeed him had quietly undermined the entire structure of Smith's Albany influence. It had been done politely but thoroughly. There had been more than enough devoted, almost dogged praise for Al and his regime. There had been ample promises that the new administration would build upon the foundations he had laid—in fact it had to. And Roosevelt had wisely kept Smith's department chiefs. But it was clear that it would be a *new* regime. When Al had suggested that Roosevelt reappoint the tough, efficient Robert Moses as Secretary of State, F.D.R. had quietly chosen Edward J. Flynn, the Bronx leader who had been impressively effective during the campaign. Moses "rubbed him the wrong way," Roosevelt was reported to have said. Roosevelt had conferred with Al only briefly on essential matters of budget and legislative program, and he had firmly refused the services of Belle Moskowitz. This dynamic one-woman brain trust of the Smith camp had been expected to link the two administrations, but Franklin, Eleanor, and Louis Howe all feared her domination. Suspecting that Smith planned to stay in Albany despite his pronouncements that he was through with politics, Roosevelt pushed aside a Moskowitz-drafted inaugural address which Al brought him. He would be no part-time puppet. Only three days before the inauguration, Smith warned the State that he would remain in public life out of gratitude to his party and his

247

friends. He was beating a retreat to Manhattan, not yet bitter, but more than a little confused at the strength of the candidate whose aid he had so ardently begged.

For the county chairmen and State Committeemen who had trudged up State Street through the sleet and slush, there was more uncertainty than regret. Roosevelt had been careful to consult the regulars on appointments and plans. He had made a special point of inviting them to Albany for the ceremonies and for what were widely advertised as top-level conferences. The professional presence of Ed Flynn and Jim Farley was reassuring, but the untested aristocrat seemed an uneasy trade for the sure professionalism of the reliable Smith. And there were many who could still remember Roosevelt's maverick performances of 15 years before.

The most immediately significant people at the inauguration were the Republicans who controlled both houses of the Legislature. Their guarded promises of co-operation with Roosevelt were little more than the conventional posture of detachment suitable for the new Governor's testing period. It was suggestive of the future that the Republican-dominated Senate found the Assembly Chamber so jammed with visiting Democrats that they were escorted down the aisle and directly out again long before the ceremonies started.

The uncertainty and confusion extended even to the new Governor's personal staff. Herbert H. Lehman, the intelligent and reliable administrator whom Smith had designated as Lieutenant Governor, was faced with a dual dilemma. He was loyal to Smith, but attracted to Roosevelt. He was uncertain about the nature of his new job. He would not be *de facto* Governor, as perhaps Smith had wished, but Roosevelt would leave him in charge for lengthy vacation periods. Lehman faced the uneasy future of a pinch hitter, always available, frequently on the spot at crucial moments and with little notice, but without continuing responsibility or power.

Others might be expected to have similar misgivings. The department chiefs had all grown up under Smith. Even the advisors on whom Roosevelt had begun to rely heavily had been tied to Al: Flynn, Rosenman, Frances Perkins. Roosevelt had come to the Governorship abruptly, with no time to develop a personal team. He could count as firm political intimates only Basil O'Connor, his law partner, Henry Morgenthau, Jr., the indefatigable Howe, and Eleanor Roosevelt herself. But "Doc" O'Connor didn't want to pledge his life to politics and was already more involved than he liked with Roosevelt's business affairs. Mrs. Roosevelt was leading four careers, with her family, her furniture business at Hyde Park, her teaching at the Todhunter School in Manhattan, and her work for the Women's Division of the State Democratic organization. Now she would have to spread her time even more thinly as she dashed back and forth from Albany, to Hyde Park, to New York, with occasional side trips out of the State for political or family reasons.

To Roosevelt personally, the first challenge had not been the personnel but the program, which had to be spelled out in the brief weeks between November and January. The general outlines of the situation were clear. Roosevelt must implement Al's program, build on it, and extend its direction, but he must add something distinctively his own. Franklin Roosevelt could never become President merely as Al Smith's heir. His lack of experience was an asset. He had the freedom of not being committed to anything in detail, but he did have a reservoir of ideas which were deeply rooted in his early State experience and which had been fed by his years with Wilson. That these were general— some thought them merely instinctive—proved also an advantage. The politics of the moment dictated a gentle sparring with public opinion and with the Republican leadership. As Rexford Tugwell has suggested, F.D.R. could be fairly dogmatic on some matters that were either so generally supported that the Republicans had to agree or so extremely partisan that they never would. But on most issues of importance, he had to be careful not to create specific targets for the opposition. He might prod, suggest, and question, while he patiently tested the limits of the possible and bought time for the construction of specific programs.

The hastily drafted campaign speeches had done scarcely more than skim the cream from his own experience and from

Rosenman's fat file of Smith's experience. Roosevelt had drawn on his own frustrations with local and county government when he had preached extension of Smith's administrative reforms to the local level. His old progressivism had been resurrected in his adoption of the water power crusade. His—and Osborne's and Howe's—preoccupation with the crime crusade had come into play when he had spoken for prison reform, law enforcement, and judicial reorganization. His own experience on the Taconic Park Commission had proved useful when he had come to stress development of the park system of the State. Even on labor issues, where he had simply parroted the now habitual demands of the Democratic Party, it had been his carefully exaggerated pro-labor record in Albany and Washington that had made him seem one of the boys.

Much of this suggested that Roosevelt was merely a more cultured Smith. But in one notable respect F.D.R. departed at once from Al's preoccupations. His romantic attachment to the rural countryside asserted itself immediately, as did his ancient hope for the upstate Democracy. Under Roosevelt the problems of agriculture would not be left to the Republicans; under Roosevelt there would be a determined drive to rid the party of the urban stigma which had done so much harm to both the upstate Democracy and Smith's national appeal; under Roosevelt the party would shuck off the bipartisan deals which Smith had been widely reported to have concluded with Republican stalwarts north of the Bronx.

F.D.R.'s campaign appeals to the farmers had been nearly as vague and insubstantial as his other remarks, but their general tenor suggested that his views had matured considerably since the war. The old crusade against the market men was left quietly alone. From the dramatic eight-year farm depression and from his own experience at Hyde Park, he had learned to look more deeply at the fundamental problems of soil misuse, erosion, and crop surpluses. He was beginning to grasp the need for production as well as marketing controls. He saw new reasons for his old demands for conservation practices. The appalling number of tax sales in the rural counties dramatized not only the inadequacy of the ancient tax structure, but also the need to re-establish farm prosperity on a level equal to that of other areas of the economy.

If the campaign had been general, Roosevelt's inaugural address was almost lofty in its evasion of the problems. The future was more specifically spelled out in the Annual Message the next day. He maintained his mood of co-operation and declared his independence of Smith: "Let us all at this session rid ourselves forever of that blighting dread of following in the rear guard of another's triumphal procession along the road to better government. . . . It is of small moment who first points that road." [2] This was good propaganda and good tactics, but it hardly concealed the personal ambitions of the Governor whose program was so specifically associated with the Democratic Party's traditions. Now he demanded immediate action on water power. He sought to arouse a bipartisan crusade to cut down waste and corruption in local government. He urged the Republican Legislature to fulfill the whole catechism of Democratic labor promises and demanded a comprehensive reform of the State's judiciary. To all this were added conventional statements on public works, grade crossing removal, and education, as well as suggestions for initiative and referendum on constitutional amendments and for a four-year gubernatorial term.

All this was good Democratic dogma, as was, for the moment, the balanced budget he promised. But the major feature of the message was Roosevelt's proposal for a crusade on rural maladjustments. Here was an issue of infinite possibilities. It was close to Roosevelt's heart, and it was intimate to his ambitions. In solving New York's farm problems, he could make his most effective bid for midwestern and southern support in 1932 or 1936. Further, he had the Legislature on the spot with this matter. Refusal to co-operate might blast their solid upstate Republican monopoly. Co-operation under Roosevelt's leadership might give the Democratic Party at least a wedge with which to split the rural Republican bloc.

F.D.R. had moved to take the initiative on agriculture im-

[2] *Public Papers of Governor Franklin D. Roosevelt, 1929* (Albany: J. B. Lyon Co.; 1930), pp. 39–47.

mediately after the election. From Warm Springs he had appointed a large informal committee to study rural problems and make preliminary recommendations. This group cut across interests by including working farmers as well as college people and pressure-group representatives. It was overwhelmingly Republican. The committee had already made some preliminary recommendations, and Roosevelt now announced that he would appoint a formal advisory commission. He forecast the directions they would take with veiled references to the need of tax readjustments, of narrowing the margin between producer and consumer prices. And he announced straightforwardly the ultimate goal—parity for the farmer with the rest of the producing community. This would be the first major objective of his administration.

At Warm Springs also, Roosevelt had begun to bring together a new kind of advisory team. Up to now his political staff had contained mostly men of junior rank, skilled in political maneuver and public relations, or available for the endless "legwork" of political life—Marvin McIntyre, Steve Early, Dwight Hoopingarner, Tom Lynch. But it must have been shockingly clear to Roosevelt in the mornings after election that the governorship would require more expert advice on a wide range of technical problems. He sought immediately a group to act as regular intellectual foils in policy discussions, men whose loyalty and intelligence were unquestionable, whose ambitions could not compete with the Governor's. For the permanent nucleus, he had to turn at first to Rosenman, Lehman, and young Henry Morgenthau. There was no man of genius here, none of great imagination. Roosevelt himself had more than enough of the latter for all of them. But there was in this small group a considerable range of experience, a good deal of common sense and sound judgment. Their job would be that which Louis always insisted was the main one with Roosevelt, to "hold him down." And F.D.R. was already learning to rely for more technical matters on "experts" from business, from the colleges and universities, not treating them as council or cabinet, but consulting them individually, and carefully holding the coordination of their efforts in his own hands. Thus he turned for much advice on farm problems to the able staffs of the State Colleges of Agriculture and Home Economics at Ithaca, and for other problems he came to rely almost immediately on the more efficient members of the staff Smith had left him. He soon proved his own sound judgment of men and women as he began to winnow out the less helpful ones and to consolidate the positions of the strong members of the team. Almost invariably he went to Frances Perkins for advice on labor, to Colonel Frederick Stuart Greene, Smith's Commissioner of Highways, for almost all engineering matters. Mark Graves, Al's Secretary, became Tax Commissioner and was often consulted. For advice on prison and justice problems Roosevelt turned increasingly to Ray Moley.

Louis Howe might have been expected to move to Albany as number one man in the "privy council," [3] as Roosevelt began to call it, but there was really no job for him here. Unwilling to carry on the routine duties of secretary, he was not technically prepared for a major department job. More important, Howe was simply not qualified to dominate the policy-making machinery in State government. Suddenly and sadly his beloved boss had begun to move beyond him. Having bet his whole career on Roosevelt, he now could see clearly that he must share his work and his influence and his boss's friendship with others. He recognized the necessities, and he played a major role in bringing others into the team, but he was endlessly jealous of the power he exercised. Threats to his own position were confused with the dangers to his beloved Franklin's future that might lay in the advice of other ambitious men who were flocking to the standard. Having controlled access to Roosevelt almost absolutely for 14 years, Louis did not enjoy the prospect of holding the fort in New York while Franklin faced the world alone in Albany. Once nothing could be done without Howe's knowing it. Now almost anything might happen. Louis could still argue so bitterly with Franklin that the entire office staff would listen in as he cussed the Governor out. They would remember sharply this gnarled little man's calling the Governor

[3] Raymond Moley: *After Seven Years* (New York: Harper and Brothers; 1939), p. 22.

"pighead" or shouting into the phone: "Can't you get anything into that Dutch skull of yours?" or "I hope to God you drown!" [4] But the boss could hang up the phone and make his own decisions.

Howe had always been a jack-of-all-trades in the Roosevelt camp. He would continue to be number one man, the only one who had access to Roosevelt day and night, and on any problem he wished. He would continue for the rest of his life to involve himself in everything that interested him, to meddle in the most eminent and the most petty matters. He could be trusted implicitly with the charting of general political strategy, with the supervision of publicity, and particularly with the artful handling of much of Roosevelt's mail. And he would be useful, as he always had been, for the subtle undercover approaches and preliminary investigations which often preceded the public actions of the Governor. Yet even on the political side there were new and serious limits to the role he could play. He and Roosevelt would continue to be joint quarterbacks in the game, but the job was much too big for them to handle alone.

Dealing with Tammany, trying to rebuild the upstate Democracy and to shift the allegiance of the machine from Smith to Roosevelt, supervising press relations, analyzing trends of public opinion, building a nation-wide network of Roosevelt supporters for a Presidential nomination, maintaining liaison with Washington Democrats—all this was a task for a large crew. Furthermore, Louis was not particularly acceptable to regular politicians, and his personality increasingly disqualified him for any public role. His contempt for the exuberant mannerisms of politics, for modes of dress and manners, all made it essential to find a more suitable spokesman for the Roosevelt cause. And his chronic illness weighed upon him more and more heavily. He could no longer climb a flight of stairs without wheezing pitifully. He was racked constantly with the hacking asthmatic cough which sapped his vitality. And his physical misery often broke through in unexpected ways. He would grouse mercilessly at his staff until hardened professionals were cussing without

[4] Stiles: *Howe*, p. 161.

restraint. Visitors would find him hunched in the messy gloom of his office like some gruesome spook. Even the most important guests would sometimes be ignored completely as Louis sat slumped over his desk in abject misery. Strangers and friends alike often thought him hostile, or merely rude.

Sometime between election and inauguration, Louis and Franklin worked out their new pattern of operations. Louis's major responsibility would be the drive for the Presidency and Roosevelt's national politics generally. This could be managed more discreetly from New York than from Albany, and in Manhattan Howe could also double as city contact man for the Governor in handling personally the constant problems which would lead later chief executives to set up elaborate midtown outposts of their Albany offices. Louis continued to live in the 65th Street house and to work from the Crime Commission office for the next four years, but he spent virtually full time on F.D.R.'s affairs. Letters on national politics were systematically sent down to the city for him to answer. He often pitched in on speeches, and he personally replied to most of the Governor's mail on problems of crime, education, and minority groups. Although he had little to do with the formal operation of the State government, he flitted into Albany regularly, usually once a week, and had a room of his own in the rambling old Executive Mansion.

Working with Roosevelt was a joy, but an expensive one. Only Louis and Missy LeHand had any real security in the Roosevelt ménage. Those who lasted with him would be those who sensed instinctively the boundaries of his reserve, who respected his deep religious feelings and petty superstitions, his strong sense of family loyalty and the seldom-spoken fears which grew from his disability. They would be the ones who never forgot for an instant that he was the boss, who knew that the immense compliment of being in Roosevelt's family could be earned only by unquestioned loyalty beyond the threshold. F.D.R.'s trail would be littered with the broken ambitions of men who had once thought themselves indispensable. For many the most difficult part of the job was the absolute subordination of all personal concerns to the boss's needs and ambitions. No one in the Roosevelt staff made plans which conflicted with his. Louis often broke his promises of outings with Hartley or week ends with Grace when politics or the Governor's itinerary interfered. Sometimes desperately sick, as he was in May 1931, when Sara Roosevelt's illness called Franklin to Paris, he would hang on in New York and put off his sadly needed "drying out" period until the boss returned.

Others on Roosevelt's staff would learn what Louis had mastered years before. Sam Rosenman, uncertain about taking the job of Counsel to the Governor, would read of his appointment in the newspapers and have Roosevelt tell him glibly: "I made up your mind for you." [5] Margaret LeHand, Grace Tully, and others would literally give up everything in the outside world to devote themselves to their 24-hour, seven-day jobs, going South when the boss did, working all night when it was necessary and sometimes when it wasn't, even relaxing for cocktails when he did and drinking what he chose. Busy young university professors would soon find themselves spending hundreds of hours at night and over week ends at the expense of their own professional work to "educate" and to ghost for this smiling and redoubtable taskmaster. For those who could not bend to the inexorable demands of a Roosevelt-centered world, there could never be a full measure of the rewards which he meted out.

There were compensations aplenty to match the sacrifices. In fact, Roosevelt's close associates seldom voiced, or even felt, the personal price they paid. Most rewarding for many was the simple pleasure of working for the man. He might badger them remorselessly—he was almost childish in his teasing—but his paternalistic concern for their health and their families was sincere, and it touched them. He knew that Louis's mania for work was partly the compulsive result of his own demands, but he tried constantly to pry the little man away from his office for a rest at Warm Springs. He constantly referred to himself as "Father" with his secretaries. Father knew best, but Father would also take care. Life with this father was demanding, but

[5] Samuel Rosenman: *Working with Roosevelt* (New York: Harper and Brothers; 1952), p. 31.

it was pleasantly human and downright interesting. His deb-
onair and relaxed attitude toward responsibility might drive
them to distraction on occasion, but it would fill the office and
the house with an air of sunny gaiety. There was joy with this
man, and also there was power. The secretary or aide or brain
truster who earned his confidence won the privilege of immense
influence. This was heady wine to ease the moments of frustration. Perhaps it was the subtle blend of power and helplessness
in the remarkable man that cemented their loyalty. Roosevelt
could seldom express the deep-felt gratitude his staff earned
from him. The salutations "Dear Old Louis" and "Dear Old
Sam" were the highest marks of his affection; few received
letters begun like this. He expected his intimates to read from
his actions the deep affection in which he held them—and they
did. A dozen years after his death, the firm barriers of respect
and devotion would still seal off much of his personal life to the
inquiring historian. The man *must* have been, on occasion,
angry or peevish or vindictive. He *was* inordinately demanding.
But for Rosenman, Morgenthau, and Tugwell, for Grace Tully
and Lela Stiles and a score of others he was a genial father or a
gentle brother, to be loved and to be honored.

For Louis Howe, his beloved Franklin was by 1929 a hopeless
blend of protégé, boss, and son. One of Louis's own secretaries
sensed long before the Presidency that Louis must have loved
the man deeply because he cussed him out so thoroughly. Even
Louis could not have explained their relationship. In fact, he
would have considered any explanation an unbearable impertinence. Love, admiration, ambition, pride, and self-interest
were so inextricably woven into their relationship that it perhaps
didn't much matter where one began and the other left off.
Franklin and Louis no longer had to explain to each other.
Instinctively, like a perceptive parent, Louis knew the recesses
and ridges of Roosevelt's personality. Unfortunately for Howe
sometimes, Franklin and Eleanor knew him equally well. They
were immensely devoted to his personal interests, deeply re-
spectful of his advice, but they had long since learned how to
bypass him gently when the time came. They knew they could
rely on him, for Howe had already paid the price of loyalty

until there was no turning back. By 1929 everything else in Louis Howe's life had receded before his consuming passion to see Franklin in the White House.

Now Louis searched for the key men with whom he could work amicably, who would be free of all suspicion of disloyalty, who could lead the army they must build. He particularly wanted to check the influence of Sam Rosenman. Louis viewed Rosenman with the same suspicion he had Belle Moskowitz and saw in the Governor's Counsel the most dangerous competitor to his own influence. Roosevelt himself wanted an effective ambassador to the machines. It was clear from the start that the current State Chairman, M. William Bray, would have to go. He was neither energetic nor particularly pro-Roosevelt. But it would take nearly two years of careful maneuvering before he could be eased out. Meanwhile Ed Flynn could be depended on to give Roosevelt a strong base in New York City, while at the same time increasing the influence of the Bronx organization against that of Manhattan's Tammany.

Both Roosevelt and Howe found themselves turning increasingly to James A. Farley, the young, hard-working secretary of the State Committee who had learned his politics in Rockland County and in the Assembly and who had served with unusual vigor and devotion during the 1928 campaign. While Farley was indebted to Smith for his chairmanship of the New York Athletic Commission and for his role in the campaign, he was not one of Al's inner group. Throughout 1929 "Big Jim" was immensely active in the crusade to build the upstate Democracy, and he was effective. He fitted most precisely the major vacancy on the Roosevelt team. Superb in personal contacts, he was a master of the systematic friendliness which cements political relationships. He had already developed to a peak the subtle arts which would mark his career: the command of names and faces and incidental information that made him seem everyone's friend; the habit of the follow-up letter after every meeting, no matter how petty; the relaxed, easy conversation. All this was systematic, but it was effective because it was sincere. Farley genuinely liked people. Big Jim was immensely ambitious and limited in his command of public issues and policy, but neither of these characteristics was a handicap, for he had, momentarily at least, marked out a career in organization politics which could not threaten Roosevelt's own ambitions. Jim's limited vision of public affairs was carefully matched by an immense humility. Farley knew his shortcomings—he carefully avoided any interference in matters of policy or program. Here was the supersalesman Roosevelt needed to supplement the efforts of his shadowy plotter, Louis Howe.

Howe's and Roosevelt's analysis of the New York State political situation and their tactics in dealing with it were essentially the same ones Louis had been using since 1907. The major disease was "urbanitis." The cure: to build a healthy, active upstate Democratic organization. The methods: feed Democratic news to the rural press to offset the dominant Republican bias, choose able and vigorous county leaders, then tie them to Albany with a mass of personal correspondence and with patronage. The whole structure could then be cemented with lively and frequent personal contacts between State and local leaders. Meanwhile, a similar approach must be more subtly used to build the national Roosevelt organization. This F.D.R. himself never discussed. He could rely on Howe. Besides, he knew the dangers of appearing too eager for the Presidency too early, and in politics he was superstitious.

Early in 1929 Roosevelt and Howe began to evolve a master program aimed at winning support in upstate New York. There would be no anti-Tammany crusades like those of the callow progressive years, but the old desire to free the New York Democracy from Manhattan domination would direct the subtle alchemy by which the Smith program was to become Roosevelt's. F.D.R., Morgenthau, Rosenman, and others would hammer out the platform of power, parity, and public service which would appeal to the farmers and the upstate middle class. Howe, with Farley's help, would try to breathe vitality into the rural machines.

Roosevelt had hardly reached Warm Springs before Louis had started in on his own task. Finding his office pleasantly flooded with hundreds of congratulatory telegrams and letters, he thought immediately of the tactic they had used after the

1924 convention. A form letter was hastily telegraphed for Roosevelt's approval. F.D.R. returned it considerably tightened up, with more punch, but with Howe's ideas substantially intact. Practically a rewrite of the 1924 letter, it stressed the need for more effective organization, stepped hard on any talk of Presidential candidates, and solicited the views of the party faithful on what should be done in the future.

Howe checked the letter with Smith's National Chairman, John Raskob, to avoid unpleasant repercussions, and then set his writing machine in motion. During the rest of November it ground out over 2,000 copies, in various versions, of this subtle reminder of Franklin Roosevelt's leadership. Each letter was individually typed and signed with F.D.R.'s carefully forged signature. Copies went not only to Roosevelt's correspondents but also to all delegates and alternates to the Houston Convention, to county chairmen throughout the country, and to Democratic winners and losers in Congressional races.

Replies came in by the hundreds and from all over the country. Again, as in 1924, they were as variegated as the hybrid membership of the party. Hungry for evidence of the trends, Howe searched them exhaustively. Young Lela Stiles, a Kentucky newspaperwoman who had worked for him during the campaign, was set the task of digesting and classifying the comments. She eventually compiled a huge volume, organized by States and accompanied by a colored map, showing at a glance the apparent reasons for the 1928 defeat. Howe and Roosevelt studied the digest with care. Although both the limited size of the sampling and the nature of the respondents could provide no true cross section, there was nothing else available, except newspaper editorials, to suggest the drift of sentiment. For the most part, these letters reflected the obvious. Roosevelt found much in them to support his own strong feelings about prohibition as an issue, about the dangers of sectionalism, about the need for a progressive appeal and for the solution of the farm problem. There was also much flattery. Inevitably many of those who bothered to reply did so largely to express their personal support for F.D.R. in 1932.

Always preoccupied with the importance of press relations,

Howe had hardly wriggled out from under the letter-writing chore before he had reorganized his personal clipping service to provide a prompt, inclusive daily survey of editorial opinion throughout the country. The coverage was also expanded to include a daily clipping of papers throughout New York State on a variety of legislative issues. Louis also sent copies of F.D.R.'s inaugural address to the editors on the Crime Commission newspaper list, to supplement the truncated press association reports. He thought, he said, that papers throughout the country would be interested since the address dealt "largely with problems of equal interest to every State of the Union." [6]

Roosevelt chose to launch his campaign for a revived upstate Democracy personally during the festive inaugural period. He addressed the county chairmen at a banquet on the night of January 2. Speaking in the mood of non-partisan co-operation which he had set the day before at the State House, he slipped easily over to the need for dramatizing the Democratic Party's constructive contributions. Before the evening was over, he had authorization for a new press bureau in Albany and a committee to raise $100,000 to finance the revived activity.

This was the sort of thing for which Howe had been agitating for 20 years, and he dived actively into the organization of it. He chose as manager William J. Crawford, an old hand at Albany news. When Crawford proved slow in getting the show started, Louis helped him organize a schedule of stories and arranged to check with him twice a week. By early May a blueprint had been worked out. There would be news notes on the Governor's doings and on legislative and party matters, texts of Roosevelt's speeches, and editorials, mostly by Howe. In addition, prominent Democrats throughout the State and various department heads, such as Morgenthau and Perkins, were drafted to provide special articles which would dramatize in the course of the year the entire legislative program.

Meanwhile, Roosevelt and Howe planned every maneuver possible to bypass the press and reach upstate voters directly. The State Committee contracted early in January for a monthly

[6] Form Letter, Group XXXVI, FDRL.

State-wide radio hookup, and Roosevelt made a number of broadcasts throughout the spring. During the summer F.D.R. used his leisure for a politically effective "official" inspection tour of State institutions. He cruised along the Barge Canal on a State yacht, making side trips to schools, hospitals, and prisons, meeting people everywhere, and constructing a happy picture of himself as a busy chief executive, energetically seeking the facts while others vacationed.

By early fall of 1929 an elaborate strategy had been worked out to stimulate local organizations for the legislative elections. Regional meetings were set up all over the State to bring together county leaders and the Democratic members of the Legislature. There were pep talks, tactical planning sessions, briefings on legislative and campaign issues. Jim Farley and Maurice Bloch, the minority leader of the Assembly, managed these affairs. Although Chairman Bray boycotted most of them, Farley's lengthy reports and summaries for Howe reflected an immense optimism about the tactic. Meanwhile, Louis telephoned indefatigably from his New York cubbyhole to leaders he personally knew throughout the State. This activity was designed as much to arouse enthusiasm as to build a "confidential campaign fund for Assembly candidates"—his ostensible excuse for the pitch.

This political maneuvering was played out against a backdrop of increasing acrimony between the Republican Legislature and the Democratic Governor. The mood of pleasant cooperation had been shattered by a bitter struggle over the new Executive Budget, and was gracelessly buried in the recriminations which followed armed rebellions at two New York State prisons in the spring, the national disaster of the stock market crash in the autumn, and growing evidence of Tammany corruption.

17

Baptism under Fire

For all practical purposes this year's Legislature consisted of the chairmen of a few committees who in most cases have themselves been acting under orders from others. . . . (Franklin D. Roosevelt, April 3, 1929) [1]

THE Executive Budget system which Smith had relentlessly forced upon the New York Legislature had important ramifications. The Governor's staff would now write the budget; the lawmakers could only delete items. If they chose to make their own appropriations, they would have to do so separately and face the responsibility of providing the additional revenues. If the system worked, the lines of responsibility from department heads to the Governor would be firmly established. There would be no more log-rolling by civil servants with the legislators, and the committees would lose much of their power to control the executive branch from behind the scenes. The Executive Budget had resulted from a bipartisan crusade first

[1] Rosenman: *Public Papers*, I, p. 547.

launched by Charles Evans Hughes, but it immensely enhanced the power of a Democratic Governor in a State where
Democrats seldom controlled the Legislature, and it proportion-
ally truncated the power of the rural Republicans who con-
ventionally controlled the committees. It was Roosevelt's challenging task to pilot the first such budget through a grimly
reluctant Legislature. Success would enormously advance his
prestige; defeat could destroy him.

The Republican leadership faced sorry alternatives. It dared
not co-operate in promoting Roosevelt, yet it dared not attack
the widely popular concept of the Executive Budget. Instead,
it consigned the document to committee, where the leaders
could discreetly nibble at the 400-page tome, looking for faults
to exploit. Meanwhile, Senate Majority Leader John Knight
announced a great crusade for "the people" against a "despot." [2]
This hotheaded political oratory camouflaged a decision to sub-
vert the budget rather than attack it. The first step was a self-
righteous pruning of the "political appropriations"—$5,250 for
Jim Farley's Athletic Commission, for example, and $112,000
for a new police force in Bob Moses's Long Island Park system.
There was much virtuous consternation at the $23,000,000 in-
crease—less than 10 per cent of the $250,000,000 budget, and
most of it designed for overdue expansion of State hospitals,
prisons, schools, and parks. The legislative committees slashed
$3,000,000 and shifted nearly as much to supplemental ap-
propriations to make the total savings appear to be $6,000,000.
They also inserted some items, increased others. Meanwhile the
lawmakers found their best opportunity for criticism in the
large number of lump-sum appropriations. Smith's administrative reorganization was still going on, and precise, item-for-item
estimates were all but impossible in several areas. The easy
escape to lump sums seemed to underline the Legislature's
charge that the Governor was trying to "usurp" its functions.

The issue was not of Roosevelt's making—but he liked it. It
had forced Republicans to break the peace and harmony in a
way which made possible a dignified rebuttal on constitutional

[2] *New York World*, March 28, 1929.

grounds. Roosevelt maintained the studied composure of a man with the law on his side and allowed the opposition to blunt its effect with wild, unprovable charges. While they attacked his integrity, he posed, in a series of messages and statements, as the worried defender of separation of powers. When he received the emasculated Budget Bill, he set it aside for a time while he peppered the opposition with special messages on farm relief, tax reduction, school support, study of old-age pensions, and a St. Lawrence Power Commission. When he *did* veto the entire block of lump-sum items, it was against a broadly publicized backdrop of his own proposals and the Legislature's inaction. He followed up at once, burying the lawmakers under nine separate major proposals within ten days, and he offered them a fiscal alternative, a new supplemental budget replacing the lump-sum items with hastily contrived itemized lists.

Even so, the Republicans sensed a victory. When they adjourned they left Roosevelt a supplementary budget with an amendment providing for itemization of lump-sum items by a committee of three: the Governor and the Republican chairmen of the legislative fiscal committees. Roosevelt would have to sign abjectly, they supposed, or face the unpopular alternative of calling a special session while unpaid State employees agitated restlessly for justice. And the Republicans welcomed the possibility of a legal test, which they were sure they could win. Yet Roosevelt also sensed the makings of a political coup. He had sought the legal advice of "Doc" O'Connor and of the distinguished Republican George Wickersham. With the Legislature safely out of town, he vetoed the construction items only, and prepared for a test case in the courts.

The opposition screamed "duplicity" and "politics," but the legal issue was clear; it demanded solution. Roosevelt insisted that legislative designation of persons to help itemize the budget was usurpation of the executive duty to make administrative appointments. If, on the other hand, the function was really legislative, it must be carried on by the whole body, not by one or two members. The Republicans claimed simply that Roosevelt was usurping the Legislature's responsibility, since the law did not specifically give him power to itemize lump-sum ap-

propriations. In June the Governor lost a split decision in the
Appellate Division, but in November he won unanimous approval in the Court of Appeals. He had demonstrated a strength
of purpose and a tactical skill which the opposition had hardly
expected. Now he drove the lesson home with comic gentility:
"I trust that instead of constant bickerings and efforts to throw
monkey wrenches into the machinery, we shall have better
cooperation and a clearer understanding of the governmental
powers in Albany." [3]

This was not the only legislative defeat. Republicans had
been forced into an almost ludicrous scramble to outdo Roosevelt on his own favorite grounds, the crusade for farm relief,
and Roosevelt had outmaneuvered them at almost every major
point. A Republican-sponsored agricultural conference made
fewer headlines than the Governor's Advisory Commission.
During the legislative session Henry Morgenthau, the commission's chairman, submitted five detailed reports embodying
recommendations with which Roosevelt kept the Legislature
under constant fire: tax relief, agricultural research, market
study, reforestation, and simplification of local government.
Roosevelt went to the farmers directly with radio talks and
speeches at Syracuse and Cornell. When the Legislative Committee on Agriculture politely asked the Governor to testify, he
stole their thunder by recommending precisely what they intended to do anyway—the setting up of their own advisory
commission. By the end of the session there was a remarkable
record of achievement but considerable confusion as to responsibility. The majority had invariably substituted its own imita-
tions of the Governor's bills—but the substance was there. A
gasoline tax had been reluctantly approved and the rural towns
had been freed of 35 per cent of their highway building burden.
County expense for grade-crossing removal had been reduced
from 10 to 1 per cent. Additional funds had been approved for
training rural schoolteachers and for subsidizing the schools
themselves. Farm co-operatives had been freed from franchise
taxes, and the purchase of land for reforestation had been

[3] Quoted in Frank Freidel: *Franklin D. Roosevelt: The Triumph* (Boston: Little, Brown and Co.; 1954), p. 95.

authorized. Roosevelt had been defeated only on setting up a study of local government and on his most vulnerable demand, income tax reduction. The Legislature had countered this with repeal of the State real estate tax, which appealed more directly to farmers. Roosevelt could only protest plaintively that the counties might destroy the taxpayers' saving by raising their local levies.

As it was, Roosevelt's imagination ranged well ahead of this limited program. He was already proposing to his rural constituency a broad program of regional planning: "I look for the day when throughout the length and breadth of the United States, zones will be established for the production and consumption of whatever the soil within that zone is best fitted to raise and whatever the local demands of consumption require. . . . It is time for us, who are in business or in governmental positions, to regard this task as our own and to realize that the farm problem is not confined to wheat, corn and cotton. . . ." [4] Louis Howe had caught the farm problem's immense political potential. He and Morgenthau planned a sweeping program of publicity. "The idea," Howe said, was to ". . . impress the public with the fact that, while the Legislative Commission is out of business, the Governor's Commission is working all summer in the further help of the farmer." [5]

In the rest of his program Roosevelt was less successful. The Legislature was not so vulnerable and there were no wonderfully powerful farm pressure groups to help. But he was dramatic. On the power issue he could only set the stage with the right scenery. Assuming that the Legislature would approve public *production* of electrical power, he offered a "compromise," a group of public trustees to plan and negotiate for private *distribution* of the power: "I want to give business this big opportunity to participate in a public service." [6] But, knowing he could not win, he warned cleverly that the only alternatives were "exploitation by the private interests, or . . . com-

[4] Rosenman: *Public Papers,* I, pp. 139–40.
[5] Howe to Roosevelt, May, 1929, Group XII, FDRL.
[6] Rosenman: *Public Papers,* I, p. 177.

plete public ownership and operation." [7] For the rest, he chose
to make his case to the people. "Measures which are in no sense
political are being murdered in committee rooms without full
and fair consideration and without a record vote," [8] he charged.
He damned the 100-minute session in which the Assembly Judiciary Committee had killed 250 separate bills. Over a State-
wide network, he documented the "broken promises" of the
Republican Party, pointed with glee to the fact that Republican
legislators had appropriated $33,000,000 more than his budget
had suggested, and sympathized elaborately with Republicans
who felt "the lash of the party whip" [9] on their backs. He
blocked hundreds of special interest bills, more than any other
Governor had, and he spanked the majority over and over
again in his veto messages. Even when he signed their bills, he
slashed at them—"a toddling step in right direction," [1] he said
of one. In fact, the Legislature had been forced to grant much
more than he might have expected, but through it all he had
made them look as reactionary as the "Black Horse Cavalry"
against which Charles Evans Hughes had tilted so valiantly.

Once the bills were out of the way, it was safe for Roosevelt
to escape to Warm Springs. Lehman became Acting Governor,
constitutionally, as soon as Roosevelt left the State. This was
useful, and F.D.R. would remove himself gently from many a
hot spot during the next four years by his laconic reminder:
". . . when I am out of the State I possess no authority to act
as Governor." [2] But Lehman was untried, and Roosevelt still
wondered about his loyalty. He was haunted by the fear that
Smith might try to reassert his leadership through the Lieutenant Governor, and he worried about Lehman's being invited to a
National Committee Finance Conference when he had not
been. The reason was obvious: Lehman was a multimillionaire;
he was not. But he sent Louis to "inquire" about the meeting
and to "offer his services" to Lehman. The banker handled him

[7] Ibid.   [8] *Public Papers, Governor, 1929*, p. 693.
[9] Rosenman: *Public Papers*, I, p. 547.
[1] *Public Papers, Governor, 1929*, p. 269.
[2] Roosevelt to Howe, September 28, 1929, Group XII, FDRL.

tactfully, and Louis came away reassured and a little surprised. Although Roosevelt had carefully ordered Louis not to discuss "state business," Lehman himself had taken Howe into his confidence on several urgent official matters.[3]

The Lieutenant Governor proved immensely loyal, superbly efficient, and most agreeably astute in politics. He saved Roosevelt from many a crisis. He was assigned by the Governor to stop Republican criticism short by making recommendations for improvement of the State's business methods. But Herbert Lehman was not a puppet whose lead strings could be pulled from Warm Springs. He took his responsibilities seriously and often had a strong influence on policy during his chief's absence. A striking case in point was Roosevelt's determination to call a special session of the Legislature to pass a bond issue for hospital construction. Lehman warned him that the session would be hard to justify, in view of predicted revenue increases. Roosevelt was able to skip out from under the jam easily by announcing that a special session was out of the question because the Republicans wouldn't pass the bond issue anyway. Then, having blamed them for killing the bond issue, he went on to commit them to building the hospitals from cash income in the next year.

While Roosevelt was learning to trust Lehman's judgment, he had also organized his office to decentralize much of his routine work. He soon revived the system he had used so effectively in Washington of having subordinates prepare "a reply for the boss's signature." Rubber stamps were used in the Albany office to route the letters quickly. Louis handled his share personally now. He gleefully told his staff that he opened the "personal and confidential" mail at the New York house first, but he returned his drafts of replies for Roosevelt's signature. He had closed his forging operation on Inauguration Day, telling his staff that it was much too dangerous to copy a Governor's signature, and he sent the more difficult letters back for Roosevelt's personal attention on the basis of his own penciled suggestions. Louis knew precisely how far he dared to go. Typical of his occasional

[3] Howe to Roosevelt, May 6, 1929, Group XII, FDRL.

doubts was the note he sent Roosevelt on a particularly difficult
letter from a Bronx Colored Voters Club: "He will be hurt if you
do not answer it and we have to remember our southern breth-
eren if you do. . . . I am sending it to you, asking you to take
it up with me when I come up and see if we can work up a
general form with which to address the anxious colored breth-
eren." [4] Yet Louis could subtly short-circuit his boss on occasion.
When Roosevelt sent him, in the summer of 1929, a rambling,
ambiguous statement denying his Presidential ambitions, Louis
chopped it into a blunt pronouncement that the Governor was
not a candidate and released it a month earlier than Roosevelt
had planned.

Yet Louis had difficulty controlling his boss when Roosevelt
was absent. While he tried to hush Presidential talk, F.D.R.
merrily embarked on a spring and summer of busy speech-
making. In April he had shared the spotlight at the National
Gridiron Dinner with President Hoover and the Chief Justice
and had been greeted with the chant:

> *Oh, Franklin, Franklin Roosevelt*
> *Is there something in the name?*
> *When you tire of being Governor?*
> *Will you look for bigger game?* [5]

Hitting the commencement circuit in June, he implied over and
over again what in private he stated bluntly—if the States did
not respond to the social demands of modern civilization, the
country would face socialism or economic oligarchy.

Then, precisely at the right moment, he was presented with a
specific incident by the Morgan banking house and by State
Republican Chairman H. Edward Machold. Early in June *The
Times* published the first reports of a Morgan-sponsored power
merger in which Machold's own company would participate.
Roosevelt set Howe to work on an elaborate undercover investigation, and Louis saw immense possibilities. He was worried

[4] Howe note on letter: Eugene McIntosh to Roosevelt, January 21, 1929,
Group XXXVI, FDRL.
[5] *The New York Times*, April 14, 1929.

that the press might pillory F.D.R. for not having stopped the "power trust," and he even saw hopes that a little pressure on this matter might lead Machold to "whip the Legislature into line" for the Governor's own bill. He went cautiously to Herbert Bayard Swope, an intermediary for the power interests, and threatened a request for an official opinion on the legality of the merger from Republican Attorney General Hamilton Ward. Howe had done a little legal research of his own and had discovered that power holding companies might be exempt from both the existing anti-trust laws and the rulings of the Public Service Commission. If Ward might be expected to find the merger legal, then a mere threat to Machold might be the best bet, and he begged his boss: "Think it over!" [6]

But Roosevelt would have no deal, and he shortly dispatched his formal inquiry to the Attorney General. There was more here than simple opposition to monopolies. If his plan for public production and private distribution of electrical power succeeded, the proposed merger would be, perhaps, the State's only customer. Ward's reply was ambiguous. It took a month of waiting to get a firm opinion that the merger was legal. Meanwhile, Louis had a second "friendly" meeting with the "Morgan people" and told them "that the whole situation could be very much improved . . . if the new consolidation . . . would make a formal statement of their approval of your proposed legislation. . . ." He implied that they need not worry about Roosevelt's speeches assailing profits as high as 8 per cent—this kind of detail could be worked out later. Louis naïvely boasted that they were "almost convinced." [7]

But within days Roosevelt decided to make the Morgan interests a target for open assault. At Tammany's Fourth of July celebration he called for a new Declaration of Independence and a new American Revolution against the barons of big industry. He followed this line throughout the summer, preaching his power program, publishing letters from upstate mayors documenting the high costs of electricity, and earning national pub-

[6] Howe to Roosevelt, June 14, 1929, Group XII, FDRL.

[7] Howe to Roosevelt, June 24, 1929, Group XII, FDRL.

licity from *The Literary Digest* for "The Roosevelt Fight on Morgan Super-Power." [8]

Meanwhile, Louis helped him to similar headlines in the war against crime. Howe had already put him on record for a little "Scotland Yard" in New York. Now, with the annual Governors' Conference in the offing, they set out to make some use of President Hoover's newly appointed Federal Crime Commission, under the chairmanship of George W. Wickersham. Howe had hoped for an appointment to this distinguished body. He failed, but he did get from Wickersham a hand-written, personal letter containing an unguarded demand that the States undertake a larger "share of the burden" of enforcing the Eighteenth Amendment. Roosevelt's speech at the Governors' Conference was largely a conventional demand for study, for State crime commissions, and for uniform criminal laws. But he stole some of Hoover's thunder by reading verbatim Wickersham's personal letter, and he pandered shamelessly to states' rights: ". . . there is a tendency, and to my mind, a dangerous tendency, on the part of our national Government, to encroach, on one excuse or another, more and more upon State supremacy. The elastic theory of interstate commerce, for instance, has been stretched almost to the breaking point to cover certain regulatory powers desired by Washington." [9] F.D.R. managed, in the process, to push the Governors into a violent controversy over prohibition. Then, having let the cats out of the bag, F.D.R. quietly stepped aside and watched them eat each other up. It was all very useful for a man with many enemies athwart his road to the White House.

But he was not through with the problems of crime. Two weeks after boasting about his State's leadership in crime control, New York's "Siberia," Clinton Prison, erupted in a violent rebellion of 1,300 prisoners. Guns, hand grenades, and tear gas brought them under control. But in another week there were four escapes from the ancient Auburn penitentiary in the midst of another armed rebellion and a $250,000 fire. Here was shock-

[8] *The Literary Digest*, CII (September 28, 1929), pp. 10–11.
[9] Rosenman: *Public Papers*, I, pp. 373–6.

ing evidence of the impact of miserable crowding, the lack of work programs, the poorly trained and poorly paid guards. Roosevelt directed an investigation, but he was strangely unwilling to seize the initiative, and he was confused. He could not agree with the Republican chairman of the State Crime Commission, Senator Caleb Baumes, who blamed the riots on the mollycoddling of prisoners. Roosevelt tended himself to blame the compulsory life term for fourth offenders, which Baumes had pushed through the Legislature. On the other hand, he distrusted the confusion among professional penologists, whom his old friend Felix Frankfurter wanted him to assign to a broad investigation of prison philosophy and administration. As a result, he chose the middle road, a conference of politicians and the chairmen of various prison reform groups, and during the fall, Baumes's Commission and Roosevelt's Conference settled down to a bitter race to steal the initiative in the 1930 legislative session.

Meanwhile, much of the unfortunate publicity was offset by Roosevelt's careful inspection tours of prisons, hospitals, and State schools. While he talked with officials, Eleanor Roosevelt sought out the kitchens and crannies. He supplied newsmen with a running commentary on the "shocking" conditions they found. While thus loading the guns against an economy drive which threatened his construction programs, he preached the doctrines of farm relief and public power to eager audiences throughout the State. And he systematically flattered Republican town and village officials. Howe's publicity machine ground out letters to the press, giving the taxpayers of each county Morgenthau's precise, dollars-and-cents estimates of the amounts they personally would be saved by farm relief laws. The whole structure was capped in mid-September with F.D.R.'s radio report on a State-wide network.

By late August, Roosevelt had placed the issues before the people. He could safely sit out the campaign at Warm Springs. He had no wish to be caught defending Mayor Jimmy Walker against Republican Fiorello La Guardia and the popular Socialist Norman Thomas. Walker's reputation for wine, women, and corruption was the talk of the town. But Roosevelt also had no

intention of disrupting the tie with Tammany on which his legislative leadership depended. He quietly named an intermediary
with the Tammany leaders, ignoring Thomas's charges that his
liberalism was fake and La Guardia's demands for a broad investigation of Tammany corruption. Roosevelt was incredibly
lucky. Louis rushed back from a Nova Scotia fishing trip to help
Farley heal a dangerous breach in the upstate Democratic
organizations. The Republicans' own organization proved lackadaisical. When La Guardia concentrated on the unsolved mur-
der of gambler Arnold Rothstein and demanded an investigation, Lehman quickly took the heat off with a statement to the
press: "I can take no action unless specific charges . . . are put
before me. . . . So far as I can see I have before me only a
campaign speech by a candidate." [1] Roosevelt backed him up
with a demand to La Guardia to put up or shut up. And the
fateful stock market crash held off just long enough. Neither
Louis nor Franklin had foreseen it. As late as December, Roosevelt could refer to it lightly as "the recent little flurry down
town." [2] Had it come earlier, he might have paid at the polls for
his failure to hedge against the crash with State action. As it
was, Jimmy Walker rolled to a massive victory—500,000 votes
more than La Guardia. This was the last gasp of the insouciant
twenties. Trifling Democratic gains throughout the State made
possible Roosevelt's usual claims of sweeping victory.

He looked forward to the 1930 legislative session in fine fettle.
Although he expected stalemates, perhaps this did not matter.
His program was popular. And the stock market crash made 1932
look like a good Democratic year after all. There had been much
pleasant if dangerous talk about his Presidential future. On December 10 in Chicago he crashed into the national headlines
with a spectacular performance—three speeches in one day—a
performance that could not be misunderstood. He might protest
because "well-meaning but silly friends will talk about my
throwing my hat in the ring. . . ." [3] Yet that was precisely what
he was doing as he flailed against high tariffs and aligned him-

[1] Howe to Roosevelt, September 27, 1929, Group XII, FDRL.
[2] Roosevelt to Howe, December 1, 1929, Group XVIII, FDRL.
[3] Roosevelt to P. H. Callahan, December 5, 1929, Group XII, FDRL.

self with the western progressives whom a reactionary Senator had labeled the "sons of the wild jackass." In the Bible, Roosevelt noted, it was an ass who had been chosen by God to lead Balaam aside from disaster. He sniped at the "new craze for consolidation and combination, . . . the recent wild speculation and senseless inflation." He posed cheerfully as a "farmer" —his tree farms were incessantly useful—and he proclaimed: ". . . if the farmer starves today we will all starve tomorrow." [4] As Franklin boarded his train for a quiet Christmas at Hyde Park, Louis's mimeograph ground out copies of the speeches to be mailed to the Democratic members of Congress.

[4] *The New York Times,* December 11, 1929.

18

>>>->>>->>>->>>->>>->>>->>>->>>

Victory in New York

> . . . *Progressive Government, by its very*
> *terms, must be a living and growing thing*
> . . . *if we let up for one single moment*
> *or one single year, not merely do we stand*
> *still, but we fall back in the march of*
> *civilization.*   (Franklin D. Roosevelt,
> *October 3, 1930*) [1]

As F.D.R. rode home from his Chicago triumphs, the Auburn penitentiary broke out in another revolt which exposed how little had been done since the riots of the previous summer. Only the day before, *The Times* had demanded that Roosevelt match words with "works." [2] Now, in an ancient Auburn rookery, the Principal Keeper lay dead and the warden was being held as a hostage by the besieged rioters. Again Lehman saved the day. Despite the brutal facts, he announced at once that there would be "no compromise." [3] His courage paid off. Roosevelt followed up Lehman's statement by sending a special investi-

[1] Rosenman: *Public Papers*, I, p. 399.
[2] *The New York Times*, December 11, 1929.
[3] Ibid., December 12, 1929.

gator to Auburn and within four days had the emergency recommendations he needed. Three days before inauguration,
Lehman, who had carried on the negotiations with the Republican leadership, took to the public the emergency programs for
better food, clothing, and guards and for camps to relieve the
crowding and make possible segregation of hardened criminals.

Roosevelt faced the Legislature with confidence. He offered
co-operation but he taunted them relentlessly. The prison troubles resulted, he said, from their "false economy." The "banking laws . . . [were] woven so loosely as to permit the escape
of the meanest of all criminals." The eight-hour-day law was a
"counterfeit." [4]

The core of his program was the power issue. He already
knew that the Republican leaders were ready to compromise on
a Power Commission to study and negotiate, and he quietly expanded his demands to include State ownership of the transmission lines as well as the generators. He had been working
hard on the power question in his own special way: reading
some, listening more—to George Norris, to Cordell Hull, to the
New Republic's Stephen Raushenbush and General Electric's
Owen Young, to his conservative uncle, Frederick Delano, and
to Smith's old advisors in the great crusade. He had come finally to rely on a corps of university brain trusters, Harvard's
incisive Felix Frankfurter, William E. Mosher of Syracuse,
James Bonbright of Columbia.

One approach to the power question was through tighter public utilities regulation. In December Roosevelt had sharply advocated in the *Forum* "the prudent investment" theory of measuring proper utilities income for the purpose of rate-setting.
This measure would tend to lower rates; Roosevelt had advocated this since 1912. He was strongly supported by Frankfurter and Mosher, but he had little immediate hope for support in his own State. The public utilities investigating
commission set up the previous year was dominated by the
Legislature's own men. Roosevelt thought them totally "reactionary," [5] and he set about using his three-man minority for

[4] *Public Papers, Governor, 1930*, p. 29.
[5] Roosevelt to Felix Frankfurter, July 5, 1929, Group XVIII, FDRL.

the public power cause. He had many weapons: Mosher worked
on the need for more electricity; George Warren of Cornell
studied rural electrification; and Morgenthau's Agricultural
Commission conducted talks with power companies about it.
Roosevelt strengthened his hand with public demands for governmental development of the St. Lawrence, Muscle Shoals,
Boulder Dam, and a St. Lawrence River Bridge. He was already playing with the idea that public power might furnish a
"yardstick" with which the performance of private companies
could be measured. He was impatient at arguments that the two
could not be precisely compared: ". . . the fact remains that
where there is government operation the household consumer
pays less in his monthly bills." [6]

Louis tackled the job of comparing consumer rates for the
public power area of Ontario and the private power area of
New York. The idea had come from the State Conservation
Department, but Roosevelt was enthusiastic. He told Howe to
get at the study "P.D.Q." "It would be my idea," he said, "to get
comparative bills for three types of people: (1) the very small
householder who has perhaps only five rooms; (2) the larger
householder with perhaps nine or ten rooms; (3) the small
storekeeper or garage owner. . . ." [7] This might not be scientific, but it would be more effective politically than all the statistics and legal arguments the brain trust could accumulate.
Howe also built lists of groups and individuals who had made
complaints to the Public Service Commission. They might help
when the moment came.

Roosevelt suspected that his enemies' show of co-operation
was only a dodge to bail the dangerous issue out of politics for
the 1930 election. There were even signs of a "deal"; he was approached by one promoter with a request that the forest preserves be opened to power projects in return for support by
business of a study commission. But the power interests had
chosen weapons of which Roosevelt was truly a master. He had

[6] Roosevelt to Frederick A. Delano, November 22, 1929, quoted in Elliott Roosevelt (ed.): *F.D.R.: His Personal Letters, 1928–1945* (New
York: Duell, Sloan and Pearce; 1950), p. 90.

[7] Roosevelt to Howe, October 7, 1929, Group XXXVI, FDRL.

the advantage of decisive action. He controlled his team, while the unwieldy Republican organization was torn within itself. He received all their approaches with polite, ambiguous interest. When he quietly increased his demands by striking out for publicly owned transmission lines, they were incensed. And they lost again in an angry day of attack on the Governor. Roosevelt simply pinioned them for narrow politicking. They were plagued further by their own Suffolk County leader, W. Kingsland Macy, who wanted to seize the initiative by "dumping" [8] the whole problem in the Governor's lap. Convinced that Roosevelt was insincere, that he merely wanted to keep the pot boiling, the Legislature authorized a $200,000 study. They assumed Roosevelt would turn the measure aside with more "skillful obfuscation." [9]

They had misjudged their man badly. They soon discovered that Roosevelt's intellectual elasticity seldom extended to giving up the ultimate goal or the political initiative. After a late evening council of war, the Governor issued a triumphant victory statement. He had quietly turned their mandate to study his suggestions into a directive to write a proposal along Roosevelt's lines. Republican leaders were appalled to hear that they had admitted defeat, that their bill constituted "a definite approval of . . . a sincere effort on the part of the State to develop, through a State agency, the great electrical power of the St. Lawrence River." [1] Their bluff called, they could do little except pay up. F.D.R. rehearsed his "victory" in public speeches, wondering aloud and at length why the legislators had forgotten to include a statement guaranteeing consumers "the lowest rates compatible with a fair and reasonable return on the actual cost. . . ." [2] Under his whipping, they eventually did even this. Within three weeks of the inauguration, they had lost every advantage, political and substantive. Roosevelt's commission was put promptly to work.

But the Governor had only begun. He demanded a legislative resolution protesting against the Federal Court's right of juris-

[8] *The New York Times*, January 8, 1930. [9] Ibid., January 2, 1930.
[1] Rosenman: *Public Papers*, I, p. 178. [2] Ibid., I, p. 184.

diction over rate-making. He sounded the trumpet for states'
rights, and ridiculed the pretensions of inexpert lawyers when
they acted as special masters for the courts. "The special master
becomes the rate-maker; the Public Service Commission becomes a mere legal fantasy." [3] The Legislature meekly com-
plied. Roosevelt went on to challenge the Commission's own
concept of its role. It should not be judicial and "objective," he
said; it should be the protector of the public interest. It should
stand firmly for the "prudent investment" theory of measuring
corporate wealth, rather than allowing a loose migration in the
direction of accepting the corporation's own rough estimates of
replacement value or the even more swollen market value of
the stock and bond issues. An unpopular telephone-rate rise
gave him his chance. He demanded action of the lackadaisical
Public Service Commission, which accepted lower court decisions without appeal. Early in February its chairman resigned
in bitter protest against the Governor's meddling. This was the
best of luck. Roosevelt appointed a respected veteran of public
utilities regulation in the Hughes era—Milo R. Maltbie. Maltbie's investigations put a large crimp in the telephone rates, and
he stepped up the Commission's activities sharply.

But when the Legislature's Public Service Survey Committee
finally reported, Roosevelt found himself for once outmaneuvered. The committee beat his minority report to the press and
stole most of his thunder. They whipped the Public Service
Commission for inaction, agreeing with Roosevelt that it should
not be quasi-judicial, and thus putting to waste the weeks that
Louis Howe had spent developing material to support this very
position. And they espoused, as Roosevelt himself sometimes
had, the doctrine that rates should be set by contract between
the Commission and the companies. In fact, they left only the
"prudent investment" theory for Roosevelt's minority to advocate. But the 26 measures introduced to implement the report
were insignificant and largely technical. Roosevelt might dismiss
the majority report as a "wishy-washy document." Frankfurter

[3] Ibid., I, p. 235.

might protest that it had lacked the courage to adopt the "conclusions of its own analysis." [4] But for the moment, the Governor was on the run. Under a pitiless barrage from the corporate lobbies, the rate-making provisions of the bills were weakened until they provided only more options for the Commission. Roosevelt was tempted to capitulate with a bill of his own for rate-making through contract. It took all of Frankfurter's vigorous persuasion to keep him from thus easily giving up the battle for "prudent investment." In fact, the Governor made little progress. He did approve over 20 "feeble bills," [5] but he vetoed the rate-making bills with the caustic comment that the majority had believed "the utility lions . . . [could] be charmed into lying down with the consumer lambs." He stoutly affirmed that "without state authority capable of curbing the carnivorous impulses of the lions," they would "lie down only with the lambs inside." [6] He took his case to his State-wide radio "classroom." There must be a return to the "original" idea of basing rates on "the actual cash put into" [7] the corporations. He used tellingly the neat figures Louis had brought together. The hypothetical family Howe had dreamed up would pay $19.50 in Albany, $6.93 to Dunkirk's publicly owned power service, and less than $4.00 to the Provincial system of Ontario, for the same service.

The substance of the utilities dispute would plague Roosevelt for the rest of his career, but the political battle was working out well. He had emerged from the skirmishes with the issues nicely set up for the 1930 election, and he was giving his party in the Legislature a program on which to stand. Regular Monday luncheons provided the setting for what the Republicans sourly dubbed "The Governor's School for Legislators." At these "Turkey Cabinet" meetings, Roosevelt and his department chiefs briefed their legislative henchmen, and tactics were worked out. But this leadership could do little more than increase the nuisance value of Democrats in the Assembly and Senate. Roosevelt knew he could get action only by selling his program to the public so well that the Republican majority

[4] Quoted in Freidel: *The Triumph,* pp. 116–17.
[5] Rosenman: *Public Papers,* I, p. 246.
[6] Ibid., I, p. 255.   [7] Ibid., I, p. 242.

would have to steal part of it. This he did with notable success
on the prison issue. He swamped the Legislature with speeches
and research reports advocating his emergency program. He
added demands, worked out by Samuel Lewisohn and Raymond Moley, for a separate parole board. He once beat Republicans to the headlines so closely that they accused him of
stealing their own report. He laughed it off. The scramble for
credit was working beautifully. He could, in one breath, give
them generous credit for action, and, in another, jab them unmercifully for "sitting here . . . month after month without action, while a small group of leaders were trying to make up their
minds what to do." [8] He won his program—with a Republican
label on it. In turn, he accepted a new study committee, loaded
with Republicans, but even this was a victory, for Lewisohn became chairman, and the committee's report proved just the kind
of thorough, professional analysis for which prison reformers
had been agitating.

His program of "education" paid off in other ways. Having
vetoed a Judicial Reform Commission loaded with lawyers, he
got a new one with the lay representation he demanded. The
Legislature finally approved a hospital bond issue, a more comprehensive multiple-housing law, a reforestation amendment.
The Farm Relief program grew: more State aid for maintenance
of dirt roads and snow removal, for agricultural research, pest
control, and upgrading dairy inspection procedures. He was
balked only on his regional marketing schemes and on labor.
But for the workingman's cause he had not tried very hard. It
would be a "long, hard, up-hill fight." The best he expected was
to build a party record which would "get the support of the real
liberals and progressives." [9] The Legislature did approve a mild
extension of workmen's compensation coverage and a new 48-
hour law, with a half day off, for women. For the rest, he was
content merely to repeat the conventional demands and to
avoid using the National Guard in strikes.

[8] Quoted in Freidel: *The Triumph*, p. 120.
[9] Roosevelt to Rose Schneiderman, May 12, 1930, quoted in Bernard Bellush: *Franklin D. Roosevelt as Governor of New York* (New York: Columbia University Press; 1955), p. 201.

The problems of the burgeoning depression seemed hardly to touch him. He had been asking for a new program of old-age security, not a dole but a system of planned savings for retirement, a dignified program to remove the misery and disgrace of the poorhouse, but he used none of the emotional fire or sprightly tactics he had for agriculture. In 1930 he docilely approved a provision for State payment of half the costs of local old-age welfare expenditures. It would do no good, he noted, unless county officials chose to enlarge their programs. Yet he regarded it as a step in the right direction even though, in fact, it was opposed to his own program.

Publicly he ignored mounting unemployment, though from time to time he checked the available statistics with Frances Perkins. The depression, he expected, would be a short one. In March, when real alarm began to spread, he talked glibly of seasonal unemployment and the business cycles. He was content to advise local officials to collect better statistics, co-ordinate their employment and welfare activities, and start a few local construction projects. With almost incredible naïveté, he told newsmen that he depended on industrial leaders to solve this problem with "the same good will as they have overcome so many other adverse conditions, such as industrial accidents, industrial diseases, child labor, long hours, etc." [1] When he did act, it was merely to set up a committee on the "Stabilization of Industry for the Prevention of Unemployment" to make a long-range study. He called for facing "this unpleasant fact dispassionately and constructively as a scientist faces a test tube of deadly germs, intending first to understand the nature, the cause and effect. . . ." [2] There was no sense of urgency.

He had little to offer except the Boy Scout principle—let each employer do a good deed daily. As late as October 1930, he still emphasized the need for renewed confidence and private investment. However, he was happy to do what he could to increase President Hoover's embarrassment in the crisis. When Frances Perkins contradicted President Hoover's cheerful predictions, he chuckled and was delighted when Frankfurter sug-

[1] Rosenman: *Public Papers*, I, p. 449.   [2] Ibid., I, p. 448.

gested that they pillory Hoover for a naïve statement in March
that the problem would disappear in two months. Roosevelt
began to collect data from Miss Perkins and others to make his
rebuttal stick when the time came. Yet when he did drive spikes
into Washington's pollyanna position, at the Governors' Conference in June, he betrayed his own deep confusion. He blasted
Hoover for deserting the "law of supply and demand" with a
"new theory that, although a man cannot pull himself up by
his bootstraps, a nation can." [3] At the same time he demanded
extensive unemployment and old-age insurance and warned
that public works programs must be kept within balanced budgets. Yet he then boasted of his own co-operation with Hoover,
citing his State's $20,000,000 budget increase and carefully fail-
ing to note that this was a sheer accident of his reform programs,
not positive planning against depression. He really worried, not
about depression in general, but about the familiar charges that
industry was leaving New York because of the high costs of welfare. He was forthright. He would "rather have the industries
go" than allow the "breaking down" [4] of the welfare programs.
But he assigned Louis to dig out the facts. Howe was soon
frustrated in his search and suggested a preliminary gambit: in
the reply concentrate on those taxes that hit finance. It was
necessary "only to point out that wicked Wall Street is paying
the freight to excite three cheers from every farmer." If this
didn't work, they would have to "think out some ingenuous
answer." [5]

Bank closures were in the headlines as often as unemployment in 1930, and they came closer to Roosevelt's door. Here
the Governor was inhibited not only by a failure to recognize
the emergency but also by a petty yet deep dislike for Robert
Moses. Moses had been appointed by Lehman as Moreland Act
investigator of the scandals surrounding the closing of the City
Trust Company the previous December. He had done a striking
job of bringing the culprits to justice and working out a com-

[3] Quoted in Freidel: *The Triumph*, p. 139.

[4] Roosevelt to W. J. Crawford [January 1930], quoted in *Personal Letters, 1928–1945*, p. 99.

[5] Howe to Roosevelt, June 16, 1930, Group XII, FDRL.

prehensive reform program. Lehman had also helped the new Banking Commissioner, Joseph Broderick, to reorganize the City Trust. Together they had saved Roosevelt much grief. But the Governor buried the Moses report, setting up instead his own investigating committee, loaded with the bankers. He conspicuously left Moses out of it. As he might have expected, the report was conservative and sharply opposed to Moses's demands for reorganization of the banking laws. It was largely a moral problem, the committee insisted. Good men would run good banks, and good men could not be created by laws. Roosevelt easily accepted the mild recommendations of these sound men of business whom he trusted so deeply. But within six months he would have shocking evidence of their failure to grasp the problems. By October he and Lehman would be deep in their harried attempts to save the mammoth but shaky Bank of the United States. In December Broderick would have to close this giant which served 250,000 New Yorkers. The subsequent criminal charges would jar the entire banking community. Roosevelt could share the blame with his Commissioner and with the Republican Legislature, but he could not shift it. Only Robert Moses could claim to have spoken out clearly and in proper time.

Luckily for Roosevelt, the Bank of the United States did not collapse until after the 1930 campaign, on which his future was staked. He faced three campaigns in one: he must be re-elected Governor on his own record; he must beat the Republicans on their chosen issue of Tammany corruption; and, as everyone knew, he must also run for President—two years early.

Since his annual radio report to the people in March, every move in the Roosevelt camp had been aimed at the first Tuesday in November. He played the fatherly administrator, taking gentle pride in his victories over the "antiquated" Legislature and in saving the State from the pet bills of "my friends of the other party." To hear him tell it, the Governor had always won. Machold and Knight must have seethed, if they tuned in, to hear him say: "The policy is that a direct agency of the State . . . shall build a dam, generate the electricity and see that it is sold

to the consumer at the lowest possible rate . . . ," and to hear
him boast: "This year we deposed the czars of the budget." [6]

Much of his time and attention went into the third campaign,
the fight for the Presidency. He continued to play his little game
of ignoring 1932—"That date has become a positive nightmare
to me and the whole family" [7]—but every move was made with
an eye on the farmers and states' righters of the South and West.
Louis and Franklin had decided that he was safe in the Northeast, with the mantle of Smith and his own record. The job was
to dramatize him as the farmer's friend and to heal the wounds
of the 1928 debacle. Early in March he took to the radio to
thump for states' rights—or "home rule," as he preferred to call
it. He inveighed pleasantly against the "doctrine of regulation
and legislation by 'master-minds'. . . at Washington. . . ." [8]
He wept poignantly for the western farmers who suffered from
the "rich and powerful industrial interests of the East." And he
resurrected John C. Calhoun himself: "The moment a mere
numerical superiority by either States or voters in this country
proceeds to ignore the needs and desires of the minority . . .
that moment will mark the failure of our constitutional system." [9] Six weeks later he reached for a national audience again
with a blast at the monopolists. And later the same evening the
maverick western Senator Burton K. Wheeler boosted him as
the "General" who could lead "a reunited, militant progressive
party" [1] to victory in 1932. The Governors' Conference also
served him well, although Republicans ungenerously hoped
that his early-blooming boom would be blasted by frost.

Then, having kindled vast enthusiasm, Roosevelt dampened
it shrewdly. The nation had been reminded. Now it was time to
build the massive majority in New York that would give him a
first mortgage on the White House. In July and August he would
listen and plot while Republicans wore themselves out with
speaking. He studied Louis's press clippings, picked up the

[6] Rosenman: *Public Papers,* I, pp. 548–9, 553.
[7] Roosevelt to Nicholas Roosevelt, Group XII, FDRL.
[8] Rosenman: *Public Papers,* I, p. 571.   [9] Ibid.
[1] *The New York Times,* April 27, 1930.

smallest matters in State administration which might cause trouble, fretted nervously about the campaign literature. He even suggested a cartoon—a luckless man with his pockets turned inside out—"Are you carrying the Hoover banner?" Louis delighted in calling it "Franklin's two-bits" for the campaign.[2] When Lehman was on vacation Roosevelt stayed close by on Van Lear Black's yacht—safely within the three-mile limit—to "save" Republican John Knight "from the responsibility of the Governorship." [3] And he fretted about Al Smith. He had been playing up to the old warrior with pleasant little letters ever since the 1928 defeat, but the response had been cool. There had been a moment of danger in the spring when newsmen cultivated the rumor that Smith wanted to be a member of the Water Power Commission. The reporters had put a fine edge to their badgering at the annual Correspondents' Dinner, when Roosevelt and Smith had listened together to the bitter little ditty:

> *What's Al Up to Now Boys?*
> *What's Al Up to Now?*
> *Franklin will make*
> *An awful mistake*
> *If he names Al Water Power Commissioner.*
> *Al doesn't like water*
> *But he does like power;*
> *And he'll say to Franklin D.*
> *"Just leave the whole thing up to me";*
> *Back to Hyde Park*
> *Frank will embark.*
> *What's Al Up to Now?* [4]

[2] Memorandum, August 19, 1930, Group XVIII, FDRL.

[3] Roosevelt to Herbert Lehman, July 29, 1930, quoted in *Personal Letters, 1928–1945*, p. 137. When the Governor and Lieutenant Governor were both out of the State, the President *pro tem.* of the Senate became Acting Governor.

[4] "Breaks and Outbreaks," Program of the Albany Legislative Correspondents' Dinner, March 30, 1930, Personal Papers.

Al had taken him off this hook, and Louis had cheerfully gone around to see Smith to work out a formal exchange of letters designed to "stop the wagging tongues." [5] Tammany itself helped. Smarting from Smith's rebukes, the machine refused him a place in the State convention delegation. Louis was delighted: "quietly arrange a vacancy . . . from Hyde Park district," he told his boss.[6] But Al received a hundred offers of proxies, accepted none, and sailed into the Syracuse convention with no legal status, to nominate Roosevelt and to excoriate Tammany. No one dared challenge him.

The one thing about which Roosevelt did not have to worry was organization. He was surrounded by loyal and experienced professionals. The Executive Committee was safely dominated by Lehman, Farley, Howe, Rosenman, and Howard Cullman. Cullman would raise the money with the help of "Uncle Henry" Morgenthau, the aged angel of the New York party. Farley, now State Chairman, would ride herd on the upstate machines; Ed Flynn would handle the City from his Bronx bailiwick; Frank Polk, Wall Street lawyer and old friend from Wilson days, would go after the businessmen. The Women's Division under Eleanor Roosevelt and Mary Dewson planned a gigantic campaign. And Louis took for himself the radio and movie division. Early in the summer he canvassed radio stations to find the ones with the biggest audiences, bargained for time, and made plans for a novel movie campaign. He arranged motion picture coverage of Roosevelt's inspection tours and eventually produced a documentary film, *The Roosevelt Record*, which was shown in over 200 theaters and was distributed for viewing at small meetings by five Movietone soundtrucks.

Louis planned, as usual, to be top co-ordinator in fact if not in name. He cut red tape ruthlessly when it irritated him and showed a fine contempt for the vouchers and procedures of Cullman's office, until the unhappy financial expert tagged him

[5] Roosevelt to Alfred E. Smith, June 18, 1930, quoted in *Personal Letters, 1928–1945*, pp. 132–3.

[6] Howe to Roosevelt, August 30, 1930, quoted in *Personal Letters, 1928–1945*, p. 142.

the "rudest" as well as the "most loyal" man he had ever known.[7]
But Louis could carefully isolate himself from the complicated
frictions of headquarters, as he regularly did in the affairs of the
Women's Division. He could terrify his office staff, and then relieve the tension nicely with an executive order signed, "Colonel
Simon Ananias Lothario Legree Howe." When his girls presented him with a gift, he would reward them with one of
"Louis Notting Howe's" original verses about the "perfect secretary's" arrival in Heaven:

> . . . He found the golden streets a-buzz
> With violent agitation—
> St. Peter was accused of graft,
> "We want investigation!"
>
> It seems there recently had come
> Into these realms of light—
> Through some Recording Angel's slip—
> One "Macy" and John Knight. . . .[8]

The organization ran with smooth precision, and matters
looked hopeful when Republicans had been reduced to the disgrace of conducting a public search for a candidate. "We're looking for a sap, to come and take the rap, just a big easy mark for
the Tammany cat,"[9] someone wrote. But there were two problems which constantly worried Roosevelt. Either Tammany corruption or the liquor issue might destroy him, and he dared not
delegate these knotty puzzles even to Louis Howe. The Tammany mess might be ignored for the moment, but the liquor
issue had to be handled at once. Roosevelt had been trying to
take it out of politics for six years, without success. Louis had
also been scratching at the problem. In May he suggested one
last evasive maneuver. Call a national conference of State commissioners to work out a new program, he said, but make the
call a pious explanation of the "fact" that temperance was com-

---

[7] Quoted in Stiles: *Howe*, p. 131.   [8] Ibid., pp. 133, 137.
[9] Albany Legislative Correspondents' Dinner Program, March 20, 1930,
Personal Papers.

ing gradually with technological change; make it a noble out-
burst against the "hideous mistake" of the Volstead Act and an
appeal to moderate leadership against the extremists of both
sides.[1] But Roosevelt thought this was too cumbersome; the
whole issue made him impatient. He complained peevishly of
the "perfectly fool stories" that said he was writing a wet plank
for the platform,[2] and warned upstate news czar Frank Gannett
that he had little faith in tinkering with symptoms. "I think we
need a new doctor!"[3] Early in September he took his stand in a
public letter to Senator Wagner.

He stood for repeal of the Eighteenth Amendment. It had not
increased temperance; most New Yorkers were against it, he
said. But the statement was craftily designed to make him appear damp rather than wet, and a states' righter who wanted
home rule on this explosive matter. It was a gamble, but perfectly timed—early enough to prevent Republicans from pin-
ning him down and taking the credit, early enough to hope
that the grim ghost would be driven off before 1932. And Roosevelt had made a decision his party would support. The Republicans had not. Their ticket featured a wet Governor and a
dry Lieutenant Governor. Roosevelt gaily tagged the G.O.P.
"an amphibious icthyosaurus, equally comfortable whether wet
or dry."[4] Louis himself wrote the epitaph for Caleb Baumes,
the dry candidate:

> *Should dear old Baumes be forgot,*
> *Who did so much for crime,*
> *Who though he tried to be half dry,*
> *Was all wet all the time?*[5]

But Roosevelt's kit of political magic could hardly make the
Tammany Tiger disappear, and the track of the cat would
cross his path at every turn, right to the door of the White
House. He needed the New York City vote, the co-operation of

[1] Howe to Roosevelt, May 23, 1930, Group XII, FDRL.

[2] Roosevelt to Herbert Lehman, July 29, 1930, quoted in *Personal Letters,
1928–1945*, p. 136.

[3] Roosevelt to Frank Gannett, August 14, 1930, Group XII, FDRL.

[4] *Public Papers, Governor, 1930*, p. 755.   [5] Personal Papers.

Democratic legislators, and his State's powerful block in the 1932 convention. If he joined the Republican hunting party, the Tiger might deny him all three. Yet he could hardly afford to be blackened with the machine's unparalleled corruption. The only hope was that Tammany might fear Republican investigation more than it did Franklin Roosevelt. The only certainty was that it could not be ignored, for, under the incompetent leadership of Tammany's John Curry and Mayor James J. Walker, city officials were raiding the treasury with a carelessness and stupidity that defied explanation. One Borough President made away with over half the price of a $16,000,000 sewer contract. Police in Brooklyn openly disposed of traffic tickets on the spot—they carried rubber stamps of judges' signatures. Jimmy Walker merrily vacationed in Europe on a letter of credit provided by a "paper" bus company which had recently been given a franchise. There were rumors that judgeships were being sold on the open market.

It was here that the mess began to ooze across Roosevelt's desk. He had quietly left to Tammany the city patronage—perhaps, he thought, a small price to pay for the freedom they gave him in Albany. But one of his judges had disappeared after closing his bank account. Republican Federal District Attorney Charles H. Tuttle produced evidence that another Tammany jurist had accumulated $250,000 in "fees" for arranging pier leases. There were incessant demands for State investigation. Roosevelt warned the opposition "that if they insist upon a spring and summer orgy of investigations, we had better do a good job and investigate everybody and everything—upstate, downstate, Republican officials, Democratic officials. . . ." [6] But the Legislature had no intention of allowing him to play the traditional New York game of investigating the other party's backyard, and they had no intention of doing the job themselves. Instead, they authorized the Governor to investigate. Roosevelt was ready for them. He posed as guardian of civil liberties, home rule, and due process of law, explained patiently that Governors could intervene only when specific charges were

[6] Roosevelt to Paul Block, January 24, 1930, quoted in *Personal Letters, 1928–1945*, p. 104.

presented in matters over which they had control, and stalwartly refused to become a "czar" in defiance of the Constitution. His veto message challenged the Legislature to run its own "general fishing expeditions."[7] And he chuckled with delight when the Republican leadership first demanded a special session on the matter, then denied that they had ever asked for it.

Roosevelt's gamesmanship was adequate for dealing with legislative leaders, but Tuttle soon cornered him with the case of a Tammany magistrate whose wife had mysteriously loaned $10,000 to a Tammany leader the day her husband had been appointed. Although city officials refused to testify and the case seemed about to die, Roosevelt was furiously pummeled in the press by people of the stature of Walter Lippmann and Rabbi Stephen Wise. Forced to act, he did so with unexpected zeal. He assigned the case to the Republican Attorney General, asked a Republican Supreme Court Justice to call a blue ribbon jury to hear the arguments, and demanded that the Appellate Division conduct a broad investigation of the magistrate's courts and that the ambitious crusader Samuel Seabury be its counsel. It was all within the strict limits of the law with which he had been defending his inaction throughout the year, but politically it was dangerous. He had committed himself to a solution in which either Tammany or the Republicans could embarrass him.

They both did. Attorney General Hamilton Ward made newspaper headlines by continuing demands for more power. He wanted just the kind of "general fishing expedition" Roosevelt feared. John Curry and sixteen of his Tammany leaders refused to sign waivers of immunity when called to testify. And the Republicans nominated Charles H. Tuttle for Governor. Roosevelt moved at once. He gave Mayor Walker 24 hours to bring his lieutenants into line. They came in meekly, but limited their waivers to their "public acts." Roosevelt pressed no further, but privately he complained: "Never in Anglo-Saxon civilization have Grand Juries asked people not suspected of crime to waive immunity . . . the danger to our constitutions and our per-

[7] *Public Papers, Governor, 1930*, pp. 171–2.

sonal liberties has always become too apparent." [8] Instead, he arranged for Wagner to damn Tammany corruption publicly in his keynote address at the State convention. Tammany had to take it, and they had to get out and fight. Their 17 per cent increase in New York City registration was a token of their desperate hope that Roosevelt would at least be better than Tuttle.

Tuttle and Roosevelt campaigned as if they were in different States. Tuttle had two issues: corruption and prison riots. Roosevelt preferred the pose of the hard-working statesman and defender of the Constitution. He promised to labor over the State budget, meanwhile giving Tuttle two weeks to tell his story unopposed, and he confided wickedly to newsmen: "Probably he could tell all he knows in two hours." [9] He talked incessantly of his administration's policies, and wondered publicly whether Tuttle was running for Governor or for District Attorney. As the campaign progressed, his harried advisors began to realize that the Governor's tactics were sound. Farley's observers reported little enthusiasm at Tuttle meetings upstate. Some were bored with the old story; some wondered what had happened to "Hoover prosperity"; others brutally asked why the Federal Attorney hadn't stayed in the City to do something about the mess. Tuttle had failed to arouse the white heat of public resentment that he needed.

But F.D.R. was worried about the nation, not New York. The law was on his side, but from a moral point of view he had painted a weak and irresolute self-portrait. He resolved to strengthen the lines of his image, but only when it was too late for Tammany to knife him on election day. Three days before the canvass, he stood white with anger and emotion, before a cheering city audience in Carnegie Hall. He blasted corruption, blurted out his resentment of Republican distortions, and promised that any crooked judge still in office would be ousted "by constitutional means, not by inquisition." [1]

[8] Roosevelt to W. Russell Bowie, October 9, 1930, quoted in *Personal Letters, 1928–1945*, p. 148.

[9] *Kansas City Star*, October 8, 1930.

[1] *Public Papers, Governor, 1930*, p. 837.

For the rest, Roosevelt merely sharpened the stereotype he had so neatly constructed in Albany. He had worked out the strategy with Howe, Rosenman, and O'Connor early in September. They must identify with rank-and-file Republicans while isolating and attacking "Republican leadership." They must ignore Tuttle. They would attack both Republican "obstructionism" in Albany and Republican "incompetence" in Washington. Sometimes the mask slipped. A Kansas reporter wrote: "That budget is an engrossing thing. . . . I never saw so many financial authorities in one place before. I am struck with awe. If I had seen them in Madison Square Garden, I would have taken them for politicians." [2] But for the most part the façade was handsomely preserved. Howe neatly spiked new whispering campaigns about Roosevelt's health by arranging $250,000 worth of insurance and making a public show of the medical examiners' reports. Roosevelt stumped the State for two weeks, unfolding their strategy and scoring Tuttle's errors. When the District Attorney accused him of giving the New York grand jury a "wooden hatchet," he retorted: "Their weapons are the scales of justice and the sword of justice." [3] When Tuttle was quoted as wanting to "get down among the people," Roosevelt remarked: "I know the people will be properly flattered. . . ." [4]

It was an easy campaign. The machinery ran with efficiency: the Republicans played Roosevelt's game smoothly, seldom challenging his pertly warped description of his victories. He quoted Hoover's pathetic prophecy: "The poor man is vanishing from among us . . . ," and charged: ". . . if Washington had had the courage to apply the brakes . . . the fall from the heights would not have been so appallingly great." [5] Yet no one asked why the Governor of New York had done nothing to fend off the crash. He noted with pride the big public works program, and no one questioned his hint that he had planned this program to offset unemployment. He appealed at last for unemployment relief, saying: "It is not a matter of party. It is a matter

[2] *Kansas City Star,* October 8, 1930.
[3] Rosenman: *Public Papers,* I, p. 403.   [4] Ibid., I, p. 403.
[5] Ibid., I, p. 405.

of good citizenship and good Americanism." [6] And he read with pleasure an endorsement from the American Federation of Labor, which he had obtained only after an expedient change of mind on the prison labor issue. He demanded repeal of the "tragic failure," prohibition, and turned to Louis's old argument that a "mechanized society" could not tolerate intemperance.[7] In Machold's Syracuse he thumped for cheap electricity while party workers distributed Louis's little campaign pamphlets showing a nearly empty kitchen and the slogan: "Under Governor Roosevelt's plan most of these empty spaces will be filled." [8] In Albany he punched at the Republicans on the Utilities Survey Committee. They knew as much about the subject, he said, "as my granddaughter does." [9] When Hoover sent a squad of distinguished Republicans to help the harried New Yorkers, Roosevelt blasted them with ridicule. Two of them were defeated gubernatorial candidates: "The people of this State who repudiated them are the best judges of whether or not any man is fit to be Governor." And he ticked off the achievements of his administration like a litany, climaxing each item with the identical note about these Republican visitors: "They tell the people of this State that that does not count!" [1]

Roosevelt told his Carnegie Hall audience: "Cheerfully and confidently I abide the result." [2] And well he might. He made Jim Farley tone down to 350,000 the proposed prediction of a 600,000-vote majority, but he secretly guessed 437,000 in a newsman's poll. The results were astounding. He had beaten Tuttle by 725,000 votes, doubling Smith's best record. He had even carried upstate New York by 167,000. He had outrun every candidate in 59 counties; he had polled higher than the Democratic registration in every county outside the City. A cold second look would have shown that he had much help—from 181,000 Prohibition ticket votes, mostly taken from Tuttle; from a scared Tammany, a disorganized G.O.P., a depression, a colorless opponent. But there was little tendency to take that cold

[6] Ibid., I, p. 412.   [7] Ibid., I, pp. 417–18.
[8] Group XXXVI, FDRL.   [9] Rosenman: *Public Papers*, I, p. 429.
[1] Ibid., I, 436–40; *Public Papers, Governor, 1930*, p. 835.
[2] Rosenman: *Public Papers*, I, p. 444.

second look. Friends and enemies alike were content to assume
that Roosevelt would be nominated in the Presidential race still
two years away.

For F.D.R. himself there was a major lesson that others often
overlooked. He had faced down the old habit of fighting New
York campaigns in the Tiger's cage. Political corruption was a
dead issue; he had caught sight of new vistas of social and
economic reform. Louis Howe saw this more clearly than others
as he parodied the election in one of his little skits:

> *Shall Charlie Tuttle be forgot,*
> *To history left unknown?*
> *He banked on the reformers' votes,*
> *And they all stayed at home.*[3]

[3] Personal Papers.

19

Relief and Reform

> . . . *the Republican party's claim that it*
> *is the father and mother of all prosperity*
> *has been so completely exploded that we*
> *cannot even find the shattered remnants*
> *of the child, in order to give the remains*
> *a decent burial.* (Franklin D. Roosevelt,
> *October 31, 1930*) [1]

THE DAY after the stupendous victory, Jim Farley astonished the
newsmen at his Biltmore headquarters with an astounding bit of
political bravado. Instead of the conventional post-election release, he had written: "I do not see how Mr. Roosevelt can
escape becoming the next presidential nominee of his party,
even if no one should raise a finger to bring it about." [2] But
Farley was uneasy. He had not checked with his boss, who at
the moment was on the Albany train, chuckling at the gay
badinage of Rosenman, O'Connor, and his secretaries about the
White House and 1932. Farley called the Governor as soon as
F.D.R. had made his triumphant way through the 5,000 cheer-

[1] *Public Papers, Governor, 1930,* p. 827.
[2] James A. Farley: *Behind the Ballots* (New York: Harcourt, Brace &
Co.; 1938), p. 62.

ing people who had waited to greet him in the chill, windy rain
which swept down State Street. Roosevelt was warm and nonchalant: "Whatever you said, Jim, is all right with me." [3] Then
he calmly issued to newsmen a new version of his familiar chant:
"I am giving no consideration or thought or time to anything
except the duties of the Governorship. . . . you can add that
this applies to any candidacy, national or otherwise, in 1932." [4]

It was all dramatic and quite safe. Louis Howe had known
precisely what he was doing when he and Jim had worked out
the bold prediction. They could be repudiated, if necessary.
But, in any case, Roosevelt was the front-runner, whether he
liked it or not. He could no longer play the dark-horse. His
friends must now work to beat down the gang of competitors
who would descend on them.

Roosevelt's greatest danger lay in Albany. He had thrown
enough challenges at Republicans to trip himself up a dozen
times. And the depression, which proved so useful for hanging
Hoover, might crucify a Governor of New York during the next
two years. Roosevelt recognized at last that this was no ordinary
cyclical recession. Well aware that he was already late, he kept
the Highway Department under constant pressure to speed
construction projects, and Frances Perkins worked at creating
emergency relief committees in the larger cities. But still they
lagged behind Senator Wagner, who was already calling for a
great national public works program.

Within ten days of the election, Roosevelt made a gesture by
reappointing his stabilization commission, and giving it a more
immediate but vague mandate to co-ordinate relief. He knew he
must do something, but he had little idea what, for he was ham-
pered by three deep personal dilemmas. He was beginning to
see that the State must spend money or people would starve,
but he still believed that governments, like individuals, must
pull in their belts and economize during depressions. "We must
share now out of what we have, not out of what we expect to
have some day in the future." [5] Secondly, he was committed to
states' rights and to local home rule within the State, but New

[3] Ibid.   [4] *New York World,* November 6, 1930.
[5] *Public Papers, Governor, 1931,* p. 765.

York communities were facing bankruptcy, and he was beginning to sense that the problem cried for national solution. And
last, he was uncertain about the extent and pace of the crisis,
and was chronically torn between the impulse to act and the
need to study.

Yet when he faced the Legislature in January, he betrayed
little sense of urgency. He knew that relief expenses had
mounted 73 per cent in a year, that 48 of the 54 cities had exceeded their budgets, but he boasted: ". . . wherever the State
can find a place for a man to work, it has provided a job." [6] He
asked appropriations only for his "Emergency Commission's"
operations. While he sought to stimulate employment, he used
a heavy hatchet on the departments' budgets. Giving jobs with
one hand, the government would take them away with the
other. And strategic departments, like labor, insurance, and
banking, were seriously hamstrung in the moment of greatest
crisis. Roosevelt was no more able than Hoover to cut loose
from the hallowed image of the balanced budget and gamble
with deficit spending, which neither he nor his constituents
understood. As tax revenue fell off, his budget hatchet became
sharper.

But if Roosevelt was conservative, the Legislature was blind,
refusing even his mild request for committee study and coordination. Roosevelt settled back. His pace was that of a tortoise
in a crisis which raced like an antelope. But he fumbled along in
the right direction. His conference with six nearby Governors in
January was a case in point. It produced nothing immediate,
but it gave Frances Perkins a chance to educate them. While
national leaders repeated their worn exhortations to keep working and smiling, Miss Perkins employed bright young university
and labor union economists to brief her Governors on the facts
of unemployment, public works, and social insurance. Leo Wol-
man, William Leiserson, and particularly Paul Douglas made a
striking impact.

Miss Perkins's school for Governors by no means revolution-

[6] Rosenman: *Public Papers*, I, p. 103.

ized Roosevelt's own thinking, but it did prod him along, and
he picked from the economists' arguments the new ideas that
fitted his own experience and cast of thought. For some time he
had been seeing the depression as a problem of overproduction,
brought on by excessive consumer credit. He had moved along
with this idea in a context set by his experience with the American Construction Council and its objective of industrial self-
regulation. In March 1930 he had written a western banker:
"Is there any possible device to be worked out along volunteer
lines by which the total wheat acreage of the nation could be
gradually decreased to the point of bringing it in line with the
actual national consumption figures?" [7] Now, shortly after the
Governors' Conference, he confided to his brother-in-law his
feeling that excessive production and consumption should be
curbed in periods of prosperity, and hinted that control over
consumption as well as production must lie with the industries
themselves. He was attracted by one economist's idea that in-
stallment buyers be allowed to abandon their purchases to the
vendors if they could not keep up the payments. This, he
thought, would make for more careful selling. And he asked
hesitantly: "Would it be possible for the automobile manufacturers to present a plan to prevent both dangers and at the same
time make it a part of an unemployment insurance plan?" [8]

He showed a similar confidence in private management and a
similar confusion about specifics in his awkward handling of
unemployment insurance. He had come out for insurance rather
than doles, and for employee contributions, as early as the
spring of 1930. He believed in a private insurance program, and
he was compulsively anxious to demonstrate that it could be
sound business. To an insurance man he wrote: ". . . the little
tin god I worship is called 'actuarial table.' In spite of the
ghastly mistakes of the fifty-seven other varieties of nations in
installing the old age pension insurance, we might profit from

[7] Roosevelt to A. N. Mathers, March 11, 1930, quoted in *Personal Letters, 1928–1945*, p. 108.

[8] Roosevelt to G. Hall Roosevelt, February 24, 1931, Group XVIII,
FDRL.

their mistakes and discover something which an actuarial table fits." [9] To the public he explained that unemployment insurance was the next natural step in the growth of a great industry which had won public confidence by the "reduction of the problem of risk to a business basis" and by "keeping up with changing conditions." [1] But insurance-man Roosevelt was soon pushed off balance. Republicans Seabury Mastick and Irwin Steingut introduced a bill for compulsory unemployment insurance. Frances Perkins supported it openly, as did Professor Joseph Chamberlain, one of the economists at his Governors' Conference, and Sidney Hillman of the Amalgamated Clothing Workers' Union. But business groups bitterly protested, and even the A.F. of L. dragged its heels. The legislative majority embarrassed him further by introducing a bill authorizing private companies to undertake this business if they chose. Their bill squared nicely with Roosevelt's public statements, and it might take the heat off the Legislature while leaving the companies free to do whatever they wanted. Roosevelt vetoed it, yet he had no alternative to offer. His own request had been conservative. He wanted a commission of experts to study the question, and had had to accept a joint legislative commission with only one Roosevelt appointee. The commission produced only a request for more money for a larger study program. The lone Roosevelt man among them could only protest in rage. F.D.R. had to leave Albany with a record of achieving nothing on the issue which he himself had raised.

Insurance for the future might be postponed, but a record of achieving nothing to mitigate the darkening crisis of the moment proved increasingly intolerable. By June 1931 Roosevelt knew he must stop trying to study academically and start studying by action. He warned: ". . . new and untried remedies must be at least experimented with." [2] And again: "A new economic and social balance calls for positive leadership and definite experiments which have not hitherto been tried." [3] The

[9] Roosevelt to S. N. Eben, November 15, 1930, Group XVIII, FDRL.
[1] Rosenman: *Public Papers*, I, p. 454.
[2] *Public Papers, Governor, 1931*, pp. 740–1.   [3] Ibid., p. 734.

human problem had swept in upon him, but the political and economic answer was still sadly vague. Yet answer there must be in the summer of 1931 for human, economic, and political reasons. There were a million unemployed in the State; New York City alone would need at least $20,000,000 for relief in the coming winter. And Roosevelt was about to lose whatever credit for leadership he had already garnered. Pennsylvania Republican Gifford Pinchot had called a special Governors' Conference on unemployment. President Hoover had for six months been challenging talkative Governors like Roosevelt to avoid Federal intervention and save "self-government" in the United States. Roosevelt had not a single substantial measure to match against his frequent calls for making the States the "experimental laboratories" of the nation. He might boast that Pinchot "has made me look one hundred percent conservative!" [4] But early in August he prepared for action. The Republican leadership, almost incidentally, gave him his opportunity. They demanded a special session of the Legislature to authorize their legislative investigating committee to grant immunity to Tammany leaders and thus compel them to testify on New York graft. Roosevelt had to act now or face the grim winter without a program.

F.D.R. quickly called the session, recommending the legislation they wanted, and then confronted the Legislature with a ringing demand for a $20,000,000 Temporary Relief Administration. There was to be no dole. Work would be created; if necessary food, clothing, and shelter would be provided. Local officials would expend the funds under the guidance of a three-man State Commission. The budget would be balanced with an increased income tax: ". . . it is the duty of those who have benefited from our industrial and economic system to come to the front in such a grave emergency and assist in relieving those who under the same industrial and economic order are the losers and sufferers." [5] There were other marginal recommendations: allow counties and cities to borrow money for public works;

[4] Roosevelt to Elizabeth Marbury, June 9, 1931, quoted in *Personal Letters, 1928–1945*, p. 195.
[5] Rosenman: *Public Papers*, I, pp. 465–6.

allow veterans to collect bonuses for which they had failed to apply under a 1924 law; spread employment by limiting those on public works to a five-day week.

All of this was accompanied by a new statement of philosophy toward which F.D.R. had been groping for two years. "The duty of the State toward the citizens is the duty of the servant to its master," he proclaimed in phrases Rosenman had drafted for him. "One of these duties of the State is the caring for those citizens who find themselves the victims of such adverse circumstances as makes them unable to obtain even the necessities for mere existence . . . aid must be extended by Government, not as a matter of charity, but as a matter of social duty. . . ." [6] Mild as the dogma would seem 25 years later, it was a sharp break with tradition and ideology in 1931. But the Legislature challenged neither the principle nor the urgency of the need. Instead, the majority concentrated on politics, seeking a plan to keep the machinery of relief beyond the Governor's control. Roosevelt reacted sharply. He would accept no measure which placed its administration with the Republican-dominated Department of Social Welfare and with the rural governments. He would not leave the lid off the pork barrel with an unlimited guarantee to match local welfare expenditures. He would not allow the Legislature to force him into deficit spending by voting appropriations without taxes. But he would not face the winter unprepared. Instead, he boldly threatened the Legislature with continuous special sessions until they gave in. The result, after two weeks of wrangling, was a Republican bill which in all important matters followed Roosevelt's line.

In the process, Roosevelt sharpened both the image of himself as a responsible public leader above politics and the stereotype of Republican opportunism and obstructionism. He moved immediately to strengthen the impressions. Choosing as head of the Commission the widely respected executive of R. H. Macy and Company, Jesse Straus, he left for Warm Springs, conspicuously giving Straus an independent hand in setting up

[6] Ibid., I, p. 458.

the structure. Straus chose as executive director Harry L. Hopkins, a professional social worker, director of the New York
Tuberculosis and Health Association, unknown to both Roosevelt and Democratic politics.

Hopkins moved with lightning efficiency. By paying well
above the going rate, he accumulated a staff of trained welfare
officers. By early winter the monumental job was well in hand.
At the end of February nearly 160,000 persons were receiving
relief. Sadly enough, the challenge outstripped even the ambitious total estimates of the summer. Faced early in March
1932 with over 1,500,000 unemployed, with over 100,000 de-
serving applications for relief which could not be honored, with
the prospect that the $20,000,000 would be used up long before
June, Roosevelt was finally forced to relinquish his cherished
articles of faith. He might speak frequently and wistfully about
his dreams of decentralization and rural relocation, of bringing
back the virtues and security of nineteenth-century agrarian
life. He had to act to solve twentieth-century problems.

In February 1932 Roosevelt joined, at long last, the growing
procession of Governors demanding a Federal Emergency Relief Act. Throughout the same month he smoothed the way with
the Republican leadership for an extension of the State's Temporary Relief Administration. They squeezed out $5,000,000
more to carry the load until November—it didn't quite last.
Almost as reluctantly as the Republican Legislature, Roosevelt
finally had to accept deficit spending—a $30,000,000 bond issue
for relief which he asked the voters to approve in the fall. Meanwhile, he moved farther and farther from his early "economy"
drive. He resisted sternly the pressure-group demands to cut the
already low salaries of State employees, to chop to the bone
State operations in non-emergency areas. Roosevelt's program
had been dramatic when it had finally been put into effect, but
it had been too little and too late. Unemployment continued
to mount sharply; relief expenditures always lagged.

A similar slowness plagued his reaction to the other dramatic
aspect of the depression of 1931–2, the near collapse of the
State's financial institutions. The enormity of the situation had
been brought home to him even before his second inaugura-

tion, when his Banking Department had closed the Bank of the United States. This institution had handled a great many small "thrift accounts," and its closing hit especially hard at the Jewish community of the City and the workers in the garment industry. Roosevelt appeared all the more lax because both the reasons for the Bank's collapse and the belated action of his Commissioner made this seem a shocking repetition of the City Trust Company disaster two years earlier. The Governor had been as slow as the Legislature to learn the lesson. His own knowledge of banking was superficial, his faith in the banking community still unshaken. He temporized for the moment and was bitterly attacked in the press. He refused the Moreland Act Investigation which Socialist Norman Thomas demanded, as well as the summary removal of the Banking Commissioner and the public grand jury investigation for which Republicans clamored. But Roosevelt was sadly petty when he blamed the Legislature for failing to provide protection for thrift accounts, protection which he himself had not requested. He promised Thomas that he would demand such protection, but privately he shared the bankers' fears that new laws might cause new panics as depositors lost confidence. He searched desperately for something the bankers themselves would support. Finally at the end of March he lost patience with the financial community's "blocking all reform." [7] Late as it was in the legislative session, he could do little more than rescue his own reputation. He sent a special message damning both bankers and legislators and demanding protection for thrift accounts. The leadership co-operated nicely with his public relations program by stifling the bill in committee.

Roosevelt did strengthen his Banking Commissioner's staff, and when Broderick was made the scapegoat in charges of neglect of duty, Roosevelt went out of his way to support him. But in substance the Governor was conservative. He strongly opposed suggestions for insurance of bank deposits. He was inordinately slow to act on the popular demand for laws to regulate the issuance of fraudulent stocks. Only his vigorous Com-

[7] Ibid., I, p. 537.

missioner, George Van Schaick, saved his administration from
similar embarrassments with the insurance business.

Meanwhile the broad program of reform was dissipated by
public preoccupation with the crisis and shattered by legislative intransigence. Roosevelt's own enthusiasm seemed sapped
by defeat, and by the broader challenges of 1932. Despite deepening rural hopelessness, he even vetoed some agricultural appropriations for economy's sake in 1931. There were small victories. Roadblocks to special farm credit facilities were at last
removed. The crusade to which Louis Howe had committed
him 20 years earlier was finally won with an Agricultural Marketing Law which included bonding of the commission merchants. But his only major victory was the land-retirement program for conservation. This multi-purpose project had been
generated from Roosevelt's own passion for forests. It was a
partial answer to the lack of voluntary crop control, and it an-
ticipated the gradually evolving program which would characterize his New Deal in Washington. The State forests would be
extended, and there was money for a scientific land-use survey.
Strangely enough, the opposition he had to fight was not the
Legislature's but Al Smith's. Singling out the clause which allowed selective cutting in these "producing" forests, Smith took
to the hustings to blast Roosevelt's plan as a pork barrel
for lumber barons. F.D.R. professed dismay at these "un-
Smithsonian" speeches, but the situation was clear to him who
would read. In his broad programs Roosevelt had been pushed
beyond the balanced-budget, businesslike progressivism into
which Al had long since settled. It was scarcely less clear that,
as Al wept for the forests, he kept one ear thoughtfully tuned
to the Presidential music of 1932.

If the time for agricultural adjustment had passed, the time
for labor reform had not yet come. Of all the broad programs
he suggested, Roosevelt saw through the Legislature only an
eight-hour-day requirement in highway contracts and a five-day
week for State employees, both parts of the T.E.R.A. package.
But his four Annual Messages made good reading for the labor
unions; they allowed no confusion about where the blame for
inaction lay.

There were other sharp defeats. For two years Roosevelt had pressed vigorously for reform of the State's antique and appallingly intricate structure of local government, with its overlapping villages, towns, counties, and special districts. He became bitter when 39 counties raised their budgets despite the new patterns of State aid, and he threatened that the State might refuse any longer to act as a "collection agency" for these officials who had "shown that they are not to be trusted." [8] But it was hopeless. The Republican leadership had no intention of blowing up the structure upon which their power was built. And they balked also at his demands for professional boards of health to replace the patronage-ridden local agencies, and at his arguments for further strengthening of the Public Utilities Commission.

But despite all the inhibitions that partisan deadlock and Presidential fever could impose, there were two victories. The battle of prison reform was easily won as the Lewisohn Commission led the way to new prisons, to replacement of the old Baumes law with open-ended sentences for habitual offenders, and to a broad new parole program. For their work, Roosevelt himself received the Distinguished Service Medal of the National Committee on Prisons and Prison Labor in 1931. He might have shared the credit more generously with Howe and with Lewisohn, but he had helped to turn the tide from vengeance to rehabilitation. Prisons, he was fond of noting, were designed to return citizens to society, rather than to cage them permanently.

The other victory—on public power—was more distinctively Roosevelt's and more arduously won. In mid-January 1931 the Power Commission rewarded him with an ambitious and optimistic report. A St. Lawrence dam was feasible; water power would cost less than half the cost of steam-generated electricity; the objective would be the lowest possible consumer prices, arranged by contract with the distributor to avoid judicial intervention and delays. But the legislative leadership elected to stage in the Senate the same kind of maneuver by which they

[8] *Public Papers, Governor, 1932,* p. 556.

had hoped to beat Roosevelt a year earlier. To force a veto, they amended the measure by appointing the personnel of the St. Lawrence Power Development Commission in the text of the bill. Roosevelt would not authorize a Commission chosen by the enemies of public power, and in this he was on sound political ground, for he had prepared his constituency in advance. They had not. While he attacked the leaders for bad faith and servitude to the private interests, Rosenman managed a quiet telephone and telegraph campaign by the Governor's staff to bring in resolutions and letters of support. The replies flooded in. Then Roosevelt tightened the screws with the threat of a radio speech. Amidst nasty argument and recriminations, the Legislature voted down their leaders' amendment on the day of the threatened address. Two Republicans had deserted to give Roosevelt the victory by three votes. His radio report became a joyous paean to the power of public opinion.

But the battle, hard won in New York, was lost in the political morass that lay between Albany and Washington, for the matter involved international negotiations with Canada. President Hoover stood staunchly on the proposition that no State could be consulted until the Senate had given its consent to the treaty. Roosevelt and his Power Authority pestered Washington with letters, visits, and public appeals for the clearance they needed. Roosevelt earned the plaudits of public-power Senators like Robert La Follette, Jr., and George Norris, but he gained nothing tangible. In July when the treaty was finally signed, it became an issue in the Presidential campaign. It was no longer a constructive program for the people of New York.

· V ·

FOR THE VICTORS: "TRIUMPH AND TRAGEDY"

20

Planning the "Draft"

Franklin D., Alfred E.
One for each and each for one
'Til the Presidential run;
Franklin D., Alfred E.
Love no longer—hope is stronger
Each for ME.
(Program, Albany Legislative
Correspondents' Dinner, *1931*) [1]

THE MORNING after the 1930 election, Will Rogers quipped: "The Democrats nominated their President yesterday." [2] But Louis Howe had already spotted the lowering clouds which promised gales of a strength to swamp their bravely rigged craft. Roosevelt might play at his little game—"I have seen so much of the White House ever since 1892, that I have no hankering, secret or otherwise, to be a candidate" [3]—but he invited a parade of far-flung politicians to Albany for little talks. And Louis organized the "Friends of Roosevelt" to provide the

[1] Personal Papers.
[2] *The New York Times*, November 6, 1930.
[3] Roosevelt to Mrs. Caspar Whitney, December 8, 1930, quoted in Freidel: *The Triumph*, p. 167.

money, office space, and personnel for a hard two-year campaign. After Ed Flynn had insisted he could not play the "easy
mixer," they singled out Farley to be their public spokesman.
Farley might boast that Roosevelt's nomination was inevitable,
but they all knew that the draft they planned must be carefully arranged.

By January Howe and Farley had begun their first basic maneuver, the building of a vast correspondence network to exploit in the future. Louis used invitations to the inauguration
for this purpose; Farley used a State Committee press release,
and then sent out their first pamphlet, a statistical demonstration of Roosevelt's vote-getting powers. By March Louis's new
office on the seventh floor of a Madison Avenue building resembled the letter-writing assembly line he had pioneered during earlier campaigns. There were so many eager bandwagon
drivers that he had to prepare a form letter for aspiring founders
of Roosevelt Clubs. Flynn and Frank C. Walker raised the
money. Old friends of Roosevelt were hit hard and frequently:
James Gerard, Edward M. House, "Uncle Henry" Morgenthau,
Laurence Steinhardt, Basil O'Connor, John Mack, and Jesse
Straus. There were new contributors, but not many: William H.
Woodin and William A. Julian, for example. Louis was not always helpful in this. He snubbed Joseph P. Kennedy, but the
Boston millionaire contributed anyway—and generously.

Publicity was much easier to get, sometimes too easy. Early
in 1931 Roosevelt himself had to cold-shoulder a friend of a
friend who wanted to write a "biblious-ography" of him:
". . . he may see me for fourteen and a half minutes. . . . I
doubt if I could give him the other half minute." [4] He and Howe
had careful plans they did not want endangered by competition. Ernest K. Lindley was about to start on his *Franklin D.
Roosevelt: a Career in Progressive Politics*. Lindley was a brilliant and friendly reporter who received much help from both
Louis and Eleanor. F.D.R. himself censored some of the incidents in the original manuscript, but he had good reason to be
grateful. Lindley turned out a model of friendly objectivity,

[4] Roosevelt to Livingston Davis, February 13, 1931, quoted in *Personal
Letters, 1928–1945*, pp. 175–6.

more effective than a dozen of the conventional, mawkish campaign biographies. More carefully inspired was the arrangement with Earl Looker. A Republican friend of the Oyster Bay Roosevelts, he challenged the Governor to submit to a physical examination to assure the nation that he was fit for the Presidency. Howe may have put him up to it; certainly Roosevelt was delighted. The doctors provided new affidavits of his buoyant health, and Roosevelt gave Looker the run of the Executive Mansion to observe at first hand the strenuous Roosevelt life and the warm human incidents that would enliven his story. Louis ordered 50,000 reprints of Looker's dramatic article in *Liberty*. This led to a quiet arrangement among Roosevelt, Howe, Looker, and the magazine. *Liberty* would buy a 400-word article every two weeks over Roosevelt's signature; Looker would write them; Howe would furnish material and enlist the aid of men like Harry Hopkins. In 1932 Looker turned out his own immensely helpful book, *This Man Roosevelt,* and a year later, *The American Way: F.D.R. in Action.* Meanwhile, a national public read "Roosevelt's" terse professional pieces on taxes, crime, and relief. And another member of Howe's staff helped Sara Delano Roosevelt put together her tender little memoir, *My Boy Franklin.*

All this was grist for Howe's mill. But he had to supply his own copy for the form letters which gradually moved from his desk to the correspondence machine. In addition, his office produced a supply of pamphlets: *Franklin D. Roosevelt—Who He Is and What He Has Done; Roosevelt and Human Welfare; Labor, Unemployment and Care for the Aged; What Roosevelt Is Doing About It;* and scores of others. This campaign, however intense, was only a first step. The real problems were to corral significant leaders in the West and South, to quiet the prohibition issue, to build up the importance of the farm question, and to pull as smoothly as possible away from Al Smith and John Raskob.

Roosevelt had made a good start with his polite letters on farm questions and power problems, and his winsome wooing of the Georgians. Louis had carefully cultivated Cordell Hull, Thomas J. Walsh, Key Pittman, and others in Washington. But they lacked the contacts to bridge the broad gap between Manhattan and the Great Plains. Louis knew only a few Senators; Farley was unknown in the West; Flynn was suspect as a machine politician. They turned, not too hopefully, to Colonel Edward M. House, the ghostly puppeteer of Wilson days. There developed a helpful comedy of confusion. House thought Roosevelt and Howe naïve; they might amount to something under his guidance. Howe thought House bombastic and limited in influence, but he could be useful if carefully watched. Howe flattered the old Colonel relentlessly, letting him hope that he could make and master another President before his life was over. House bubbled with enthusiasm for this new little manipulator: "It is a joy to cooperate with him for the reason that he is so able and yet so yielding to suggestions." [5] It would be months before he would realize that he was working on the periphery of a well-organized machine. His letters to the old Wilson and McAdoo leaders were immensely useful in preparing the way for a switch to Roosevelt in the Convention after the first ballots for the native sons, but he brought no delegation firmly into camp. His own state remained pledged to John Garner, the Speaker of the House, shattering the image of his power. The Colonel could no longer manipulate his Texan puppets from the genteel seclusion of his Manhattan writing room. Roosevelt and Howe consulted him on speeches, press releases, and personalities, but they carefully undercut his subtle attempts to replace Jim Farley with one of his own satellites.

And there were other dangers, beginning with a string of amateur and premature Roosevelt Clubs which smacked of being rackets or of ties to the Ku Klux Klan. Howe wanted to send professionals to take them over; instead Roosevelt flattered them, and later some of their leaders plagued him with charges of bad faith at the height of the campaign. The team handled the dangerous gymnastics of National Chairman John Raskob and his aide Jouett Shouse much more shrewdly. Roosevelt avoided taking issue with them when they advocated just the kind of national strategy conference he had proposed

[5] Edward M. House to Roosevelt, March 23, 1931, quoted in *Personal Letters, 1928–1945*, p. 201.

in 1922 and when they promised Hoover their party's co-
operation on anti-depression measures. But he moved sharply
when Raskob tried to commit the National Committee to a
wringing-wet, economically conservative program. Louis had
no trouble enlisting Cordell Hull's coterie of powerful southern
Senators. Roosevelt and Howe had no intention of losing on
liquor or blunting their attacks upon the economic philosophy
which Raskob shared with the Du Ponts, the Mellons, and the
President. While Roosevelt sharply warned Raskob in personal
letters, Texan Tom Connally trumpeted the Senators' public
defiance of any National Committee with the impertinence to
make promises for the party. And Al Smith helped by leaving the old New York regulars with the firm impression that
he had abandoned his Presidential ambitions. When Farley left
for the National Committee meeting at which Raskob hoped
to commit the party to his program, Jim could boast of having
enough votes and proxies to beat the National Chairman by two
to one. It was almost overdone. When Arkansas Senator Joe
Robinson broke into an angry personal attack on Raskob, Al
Smith himself had to intervene to save the meeting from becoming a shambles.

Roosevelt spotted the danger at once. As he congratulated
Farley he warned: "The thing we must work for now is the
avoidance of harsh words and no sulking in tents." [6] He could
afford to be careful. The well-publicized meeting had seemed
proof of a solid alliance between industrial New York and the
Hulls, the Connallys, the Harry Byrds, and the Carter Glasses
of the South. For a time in the spring of 1931 the path to the
White House seemed strewn with flowers. In March and April
the supposedly disinterested Jesse Straus issued the results of
two polls, one of the 1928 Convention delegates, one of business
and professional men. Roosevelt led everywhere. Undoubtedly
this was part of Louis's bandwagon propaganda, for there were
careful gaps in the publicity. No one pointed out that New York
had been left out of the polls, that less than half the Houston
delegates had replied, that Smith was still strong in the North-

[6] Roosevelt to Norman Mack, March 9, 1931, Group XII, FDRL.

east, and that there was no hint of the necessary two-thirds support. But Louis knew the facts. As he played with the figures from his Straus polls, he probed busily west and south. He sought the advice of their old North Carolina pro-McAdoo friend, Daniel C. Roper: "He fairly purred like a cat . . . ," [7] Louis reported. He and Eleanor cultivated visiting friends from the West. Louis warned his associates to be careful in answering letters from Negroes and to make sure in Texas and Arizona "that the wet Catholics do not leap on the band wagon first. . . . If that happens we will not get any of the independent and Republican drys who are at present most kindly disposed. . . ." [8] He spent weeks arranging for a display of fireworks to pop spectacularly in the month of June.

The first item was the Governors' Conference, followed soon after by a love-feast Colonel House had arranged for F.D.R. with the Massachusetts leaders. But here the aging puppeteer had pushed his doddering influence to an unhappy test, appreciating neither Irish Boston's fierce loyalty to Al Smith nor the intricate dangers of meddling in the feud between Mayor James M. Curley and Governor Joseph B. Ely. To make matters worse, Louis had been cultivating Jim Curley for years. Curley boarded Roosevelt's train in New York and showed up at the party dinner with the candidate firmly in tow. In this murky atmosphere, House's skyrocket fizzled erratically. Roosevelt didn't yet understand the danger; but powerful Senator David I. Walsh announced at once that Massachusetts would be for Smith. Roosevelt was committed to supporting Curley in a hopeless party vendetta in the Bay State if Smith chose to play his cards. There was no retreat and little hope of victory.

Louis's major contribution to the summer's fun was a masterpiece—a coast-to-coast sales trip by Jim Farley. Farley's previous plans to visit Elks Lodges in his capacity as National President of the B.P.O.E. gave them an elaborate pretext for the trip which appealed to Louis's love of intrigue but which fooled no one. Farley would test the reaction to New York's

[7] Howe to Roosevelt, May 12, 1931, Group XII, FDRL.   [8] Ibid.

three "sons"—Roosevelt, Smith, and Owen D. Young. Secret meetings would avoid the danger of wasting time on independents, dry Republicans, and amateurs. Farley must sell Roosevelt to the men who, in Louis's phrase, "carried the guns"; when he could not sell, he must test the temper of the resistance. Howe worked out the itinerary and prepared the way with a sheaf of personal letters. Roosevelt approved it point by point during a Sunday-morning conference late in June. In 19 days Farley stopped in 18 States and wrote as many detailed reports for Roosevelt and Howe. There was little time for Elks—or for much appraisal in depth. His optimism mounted with every stop. And he proved a phenomenal salesman, fencing expertly when the leaders were against his man, shattering with his personal abstinence and contagious friendliness the stereotype of New York politicians so grimly confirmed by Tweed, Croker, Charlie Murphy, and Al Smith. He found most of his "key" men anxious for a winner and attracted to the dynamic Roosevelt. His chief problem was to discourage politely the innumerable native sons. "Governor, the presidential job must be a great one," he wrote Roosevelt, "judging from the way they are all anxious to have it." [9] But even with opponents he smoothed the way for friendly rapport in the Convention crises. He was justly proud. In Missouri, after having defied Howe's orders to stay away, he had turned a potential trap into a Democratic love-feast. Roosevelt was elated. Even Louis was pleased: "He has a wholesome breeziness of manner and a frank and open character which is characteristic of all Westerners . . . he gives a distinct impression of being a very practical and businesslike politician . . . he is winning his spurs. . . ." [1]

Farley returned home ready for a prophecy that would make the world think him a "fit candidate for the insane asylum." [2] But he and Howe were both naïve to assume that delegations could be tied up this early, and this cheaply. Some of his "key" men turned out in the battle to be not hardened and devoted legionnaires but merely camp followers dragging along in the

[9] Farley: *Behind the Ballots*, p. 86.
[1] Howe to Edward M. House, August 17, 1931, Group XXXVI, FDRL.
[2] Farley: *Behind the Ballots*, p. 85.

dust at the rear and watching slyly for a better prospect. And sometimes Farley misunderstood. He reported, for example, that Arthur Mullen of Nebraska was firmly in the Roosevelt camp. Mullen himself supposed that he was still astride the fence. But Farley had done much good and no harm. With southern Senators or western politicos he proved to be a warm, appealing symbol of Roosevelt realism, humanity, and honesty.

Other agents were sent to Texas and California. And the correspondence machine ground on inexorably under Howe's direction. Only occasionally did Louis pass on to Roosevelt a particularly tough letter from a big name. Only very occasionally did he confess defeat, as he did with a note to Farley: "Around and around and around goes the buck—from you to Franklin, from Franklin to Sam, from Sam to me; and as this letter is addressed to you I promptly wish it off on you. If you are not a farmer you ought to be by this time, and you must learn and read all you can about the great throbbing, agricultural heart of the West." [3] Through the summer Roosevelt and Howe sought the magic balance they needed between Raskob, who controlled the national machinery, and the rural leaders on whom they pinned their hopes. Raskob hinted of new attempts to use the National Committee. Hull suggested they start writing platform material. He may have wanted to tie Roosevelt down to positions the South wanted, but Louis was delighted at the opportunity this gave him for further contacts. Roosevelt sent him off for several conferences during October and November with Hull, Pat Harrison of Mississippi, and Thomas J. Walsh of Montana. They made guarded approaches to favorite sons. And Wilson's old Attorney General, A. Mitchell Palmer, finally came up with a statement on which they generally agreed. But through it all Roosevelt signed nothing, said nothing. Even his unsigned memorandum for the Senators was carefully vague. He was worried about rivals, not platform reveries, as the winter months came on.

The rivals were numerous. Louis was concerned about Newton Baker of Ohio, a dangerous competitor for Wilson's mantle.

[3] Howe to James A. Farley, October 21, 1931, quoted in *Personal Letters, 1928–1945*, p. 225.

He toyed with running "a dummy man in the Primaries with the understanding that his delegates were really going to vote for you." [4] But the most slippery situation lay in Manhattan. Smith, Raskob, and Jersey's Frank Hague were busily at work to stop Roosevelt at any price. There were doubts about Smith's personal ambitions; there were no doubts about his hostility. Roosevelt watched Smith's erratic trail with mounting concern. The grapevine brought in rumors of a half-dozen candidates: Baker, perhaps, or Owen Young, Cox or Chicago banker Melvin Traylor or maybe Albert Ritchie of Maryland, the handsome, ambitious pet of Raskob's "wringing wets." Roosevelt was cautious. When there were rumors that Bernard Baruch was talking up both Ritchie and Roosevelt, Franklin confided to the foxy old financier his worries about *other* friends who "emit innuendoes and false statements behind my back with the blissful assumption that they will never be repeated to me." [5] But Louis could thrust hard, as he did when he warned Shouse that "we" would consider his planned visit to Alabama a hostile act.[6] Journalists stirred the boiling pot with gossip that Roosevelt had called Smith a "rotten Governor," that Smith had tagged him a "crackpot," that Baruch had labeled Roosevelt a "boy scout Governor." [7]

"Frank" and "Al" kept up the façade of their uneasy friendship. There were pleasant little letters about nothing of importance. There was a conference in New York on the State budget that fall. But the veneer was dangerously thin. Roosevelt protested that Smith would not answer his letters about politics. His Insurance Commissioner reported a violent tirade against him by the angry old warhorse. Louis confided to a reporter that Franklin had been told that he could have the nomination if he would make Al his manager and accept a little guidance in the White House from the man in the brown derby. Roosevelt, Louis said, had pounded the desk with fury and shouted: "I'll

[4] Howe to Roosevelt, September 12, 1931, Group XXXVI, FDRL.

[5] Roosevelt to Bernard Baruch, December 19, 1931, quoted in *Personal Letters, 1928–1945,* p. 244.

[6] Howe to Jouett Shouse, November 19, 1931, Group XXXVI, FDRL.

[7] Quoted in Freidel: *The Triumph,* pp. 236–7.

be damned if I'll do it!"⁸ Al was hurt and angry. He protested
to a mutual friend: "By God, he invited me to his house . . .
and did not even mention to me the subject of his candidacy."
And again: "Do you know, by God, that he has never consulted
me about a damn thing since he has been Governor?" When Atlanta publisher Clark Howell tried to persuade Smith that he
could not destroy his party's chances if it needed Roosevelt as a
candidate in order to win, Al snapped out: "The Hell I can't!"⁹

There was much to belie Farley's persistent public promises
of a first-ballot nomination. And not all the trouble was outside
the Roosevelt camp. House was trying to undercut Farley. Even
Louis was beginning to worry that "Big Jim" might be keeping
things from him. Characteristically, he sent word of his uneasi-
ness through Mrs. Roosevelt. Jim was more understanding of
Louis's human weakness than most of their associates; he
quickly and gently mended the breach. The job was getting
too big for both of them to handle. Joseph Guffey of Pennsylvania was put to work ironing out difficulties in Ohio and Kentucky; Robert H. Jackson of New Hampshire worked expertly
in New England and the Middle West. Other Senators were enlisted—Wheeler of course, and Clarence Dill of Washington,
drawn by Roosevelt's stand on the power question. Louis himself latched on to newsman Cornelius Vanderbilt, Jr., and dragooned the millionaire away from a Florida vacation. "Neil" was
soon traveling constantly for them.

In January real obstacles appeared. Raskob threatened to poll
the party's financial angels on their attitude toward prohibition.
"Mollie" Dewson returned from the West with sober warnings about States Farley had thought firmly in hand. Again
there was a desperate scramble for proxies in the National
Committee meeting; again Raskob backed down from his threat
to make prohibition *the* issue. Roosevelt had to warn his own
friends not to spoil the game by attempting to commit the National Committee to their own position. The coalition was strong
enough to stop Raskob; it was dangerously weak on anything

⁸ *Boston Post*, April 19, 1945.
⁹ Clark Howell to Roosevelt, December 2, 1931, quoted in *Personal Letters, 1928–1945*, pp. 229–32.

else. Farley had to accept Chicago as the Convention city, although the hall could be packed with a hostile mob. And when Roosevelt finally announced his candidacy in mid-January, to take advantage of early primaries, native sons sprouted everywhere. Here was all the raw material for a stop-Roosevelt movement. Even those who had fought Raskob's control of the platform might well fight Roosevelt's control of the nomination. Harry Byrd of Virginia and "Ham" Lewis of Illinois had been friendly. George White of Ohio and Jim Reed of Missouri were non-committal. No one could predict the shenanigans of Oklahoma's colorful demagogue, "Alfalfa Bill" Murray. Newton Baker's friends found Roosevelt's placid generalizations on foreign policy too weak. Al Smith simply waited.

Worse yet, powerful forces in the press attacked viciously. On January 1, William Randolph Hearst lashed out at visionaries like Baker, Smith, and Roosevelt who had deserted Hearst's pet brand of jingo nationalism. The next day his nationwide newspaper chain launched a boom for John Garner, the Speaker of the House. Louis was shocked; he had thought Garner would be with them. The loss of California and Texas—90 votes—could mean disaster for Roosevelt on the first ballot. To win Hearst's support would require an abject retreat from Roosevelt's old internationalism. But this was made infinitely more difficult by the attack which Walter Lippmann unleashed in the *Herald Tribune* a week later. Lippmann's rapier sought out the heart of Roosevelt's weakness. Caricaturing the Governor as a master of the art of carrying water on both shoulders, he rasped: "Franklin D. Roosevelt is a highly impressionable person, without a firm grasp of public affairs, and without very strong convictions . . . an amiable man with many philanthropic impulses, but he is not a dangerous enemy of anything. . . . He is a pleasant man, who, without any important qualifications for the office, would very much like to be President." [1] Louis wrote his boss: "I do not think there is anything we can do about it but I would advise you to read the article." [2] Nor was this all. While Roosevelt wriggled unhappily between

[1] *New York Herald Tribune,* January 8, 1932.
[2] Howe to Roosevelt, n.d., Group XII, FDRL.

Hearst and Lippmann, Samuel Seabury dumped the whole problem of Tammany corruption on the Governor's desk. This was monumentally dangerous. Seabury had precisely the kind of specific evidence Roosevelt had unctiously demanded for two years and precisely the kind of case in which Roosevelt could legally act by removing Tammany's County Sheriff, Thomas N. Farley. But F.D.R. needed Tammany delegates at Chicago, and John Curry had bluntly refused to commit them.

Faced with fatal threats in California, Texas, and New York, Roosevelt temporized while Farley garnered early victories in Alaska and Washington, and Louis released three more "Straus" polls. Roosevelt was buffeted by advice. Louis insisted he "sit tight" on everything. House demanded a strong position on both Tammany and the League of Nations. Farley wanted an adjustment with Smith. Roosevelt could not please both Hearst and Lippmann, both John Curry and Rabbi Wise. Attempts to negotiate with Hearst failed. He chose to appease the good Rabbi and the Baron of San Simeon. With Howe's reluctant agreement, Roosevelt dramatically repudiated the League of Nations in a speech before the New York State Grange on February 2. This was no longer Wilson's League, he said. It was "a mere meeting place for the political discussion of strictly European political difficulties. In these the United States should have no part." [3] He softened the blow to the internationalists with an appeal for tariff revision and an international trade conference to please his southern friends, but Hearst had all he could possibly want. The attacks from San Simeon slacked off. Roosevelt's oldest friends were incensed. Mrs. Charles Hamlin summed it up cryptically: "I am devoted to Franklin but he ought to be spanked." [4] Yet they had no place to go except to Newton Baker; most of them followed Roosevelt meekly, but in grief.

The Tammany issue took less soul searching, but it proved more dangerous. Early in February Smith announced his own candidacy. Two weeks later Roosevelt removed the sheriff

[3] *Public Papers, Governor, 1932,* pp. 551–2.
[4] Mrs. Charles Hamlin to Josephus Daniels, March 1, 1932, quoted in Freidel: *The Triumph,* p. 254.

from office. He tried to cage both Seabury and the Tiger with this one definitive act. But the ringing announcement Ray Moley had penned for him brought more trouble. While pushing aside most of Seabury's evidence, he had firmly stated that public officials whose bank accounts or standards of living were clearly in excess of their salaries owed "a positive public duty . . . to give a reasonable and credible explanation. . . . The State," Moley had him say, "is a just but a jealous master." [5] The Seabury Committee's files were full of such cases, including that of Jimmy Walker himself. Rabbi Wise and the Reverend John Haynes Holmes clamored at once for more scalps. And Roosevelt, jittery with work and tension, deeply disturbed by John Curry's insistence on an uninstructed New York delegation which the Governor could not control, blundered into one of the most ill-tempered mistakes of his career. His public letter to Holmes and Wise questioned their "good faith," accused them of wanting more "personal publicity," and went on to counsel that, if they "would serve their God as they seem to serve themselves, the people of the City of New York would be the gainers." [6] Louis was incensed—he always blamed Rosenman for letting the boss get out of hand. The tone and the words were inexcusable and stupid. But no draftsman could be blamed for the letter. There was no magic mirror by which Roosevelt could be made to appear to Tammany a subtle sympathizer and to its enemies a moderate but sincere reformer. The letter could hardly have come at a worse time. For between the end of March and mid-June there were over 35 crucial conventions and primaries to be managed.

[5] Rosenman: *Public Papers*, I, pp. 582–4.

[6] *Public Papers, Governor, 1932*, pp. 292–3; Roosevelt to Holmes and Wise, March 30, 1932, Group XXVIII, FDRL.

21

>>>->>>->>>->>>->>>->>>->>>-<<<

The Road to Chicago

*I am not speaking of an economic life
completely planned and regimented. I am
speaking of the necessity, however, in
those imperative interferences with the
economic life of the Nation that there be
a real community of interests. . . . I
plead not for a class control, but for a
true concert of interests.*

(Franklin D. Roosevelt,
April 18, 1932) [1]

THERE WERE early victories to follow those in Alaska and Washington: New Hampshire, North Dakota, Minnesota, Georgia.
Tom Pendergast sent word that Missouri would be held in
reserve for Roosevelt behind its native son, Senator James Reed.
Farley was buoyant. But the victories were costing too much.
Even in North Dakota they had had to send Senator Wheeler,
Neil Vanderbilt, and two aides to press a last-minute fight
against Murray's violent populism. New Hampshire had cost
them $12,000 of Louis's cherished war chest; even so, Smith's
strength in the cities was ominous. There were limits to this

[1] Rosenman: *Public Papers*, I, p. 632.

sort of thing and Roosevelt wrote ingenuously to Maine: ". . . a little backbone among our friends there would go a long way. As you know, one cannot send money when one has not got it and . . . in New Hampshire . . . they are handling practically all their own financing." [2]

Elsewhere, there was more trouble. Howe had to send Homer Cummings to Kentucky to work his way through the elaborate intrigues between Roosevelt's man, Judge Robert Bingham, and the Governor, Ruby Lafoon. Senator Alben Barkley became their candidate for convention keynoter and Kentucky fell into place. Lafoon was so happy that he made Louis Howe a Kentucky Colonel. Howe dragooned Farley into a similar chore in Iowa, which Jim thought firmly in line. Louis's sour caution paid off, and Farley's last-minute work saved them from another uninstructed delegation to sap their first-ballot strength. Maine fell easily into line, but Smith boasted openly that he had six northeastern states, two thirds of the Pennsylvania delegation, and a second mortgage on Garner's votes. Tom Pendergast suggested an elaborate deal with Al.

Roosevelt was neither so naïve nor so desperate as to attempt to make a deal with Smith on the eve of the New York Convention. But he was forced to another compromise on Convention arrangements. He agreed by phone that the Committee could "commend" Shouse as Permanent Chairman as well as Barkley for Temporary Chairman. This was vague. Inevitably Shouse insisted that "commend" meant the same thing as "recommend." Roosevelt claimed it meant nothing at all. It did mean, however, that he must control the Convention from the first moment. Even friendly, native-son, and uninstructed delegations might be a liability if they failed to accept discipline in the initial skirmishes.

Louis was pessimistic; his own political map early that spring had shown only nine states firmly for Roosevelt. He had been uncertain even about Maine, New Hampshire, North Dakota, and Minnesota. He had crossed off as hopeless not only Delaware, which they later won, but also Massachusetts, in which

[2] Roosevelt to Elizabeth Marbury, February 29, 1932, Group XII, FDRL.

he was fighting hard. Roosevelt would allow himself none of this defeatism. In fact, his easygoing confidence may well have fed the dangerous self-satisfaction which plagued the headquarters. Yet there were warnings even he could not ignore. Wisconsin, Arkansas, and Nebraska came into line in late March and early April, but the big delegations were escaping. Illinois's mammoth block was carefully husbanded behind native son "Ham" Lewis. He had no hope of winning, but Chicago's boss, Anton Cermak, was ready either to support Smith or block Roosevelt, to create an atmosphere for deals. Roosevelt's own State was largely lost. He might salvage 30 to 40 votes from the delegates chosen by district primaries, but there would be no unit rule. The big tests on April 26 in Massachusetts and Pennsylvania resembled the situations in New York and Illinois more than they did the neat little maneuvers in North Dakota.

As late as March 11 Roosevelt had been able to refer easily to "Governor Smith's active or inactive candidacy," [3] for Al had made clear only that he would accept support. It may have been Roosevelt's own ill-conceived challenge in the Bay State that made Smith a major candidate. Here Louis's caution and judgment deserted him. Or perhaps he had no alternative. Exaggerating the importance of Roosevelt's sweeping primary victories in Maine and New Hampshire, and listening to Joe Guffey's excessive promises for Pennsylvania, Howe insisted the Smith boom was "largely a fake." Perhaps he thought to clinch the race by puncturing this little balloon. Roosevelt's old college friend, Larue Brown, sought to bring Curley and Governor Ely together. Meanwhile, young James Roosevelt toured the State and acted often as his father's spokesman. There were notable blunders. When Jimmy indiscreetly promised a Worcester audience that his father would call a special session of Congress for the repeal of prohibition, Louis hauled him back to New York for a blistering rebuke. But when Curley himself blasted Smith as a mere stalking-horse without serious pretensions, no spanking from Howe could cure the damage. Al

[3] Roosevelt to Josiah W. Bailey, March 11, 1932, quoted in *Personal Letters, 1928–1945*, p. 263.

came out in the open as a fighting candidate. Much too late they
realized that Curley's interest was parasitic—he hoped to ride
to victory on Roosevelt's coattails. By mid-April they knew they
were licked in Massachusetts, but they did not foresee the three-
to-one repudiation of Roosevelt that was to give Smith all of the
State's 36 votes. The same day, the Pennsylvania primaries
proved Joe Guffey almost as poor a prophet as Curley. He had
promised Howe 66 of the 78 votes. Roosevelt got slightly
over 40.

Meanwhile, Rhode Island and Connecticut, which Howe had
assumed were firmly in hand, joined the Smith parade. At
Providence, despite Louis's constant week-end conferences, he
was finally put off with the assurance that the State would be
for Roosevelt "in spirit." Louis could only bring the whip out of
the closet and hope. The *Providence Journal* noted: "It is reported in New York quarters close to Roosevelt's headquarters
that the New York Governor's supporters are not at all keen
about 'spiritual support'. . . that those who cannot make up
their minds while Smith is marking time will be made to realize
their mistake if Roosevelt is elected. . . ." Louis's bombastic
bluff was called. Under J. Howard McGrath, the State Chairman, the Rhode Island convention chose a solid Smith delegation. In Connecticut, overconfidence again put the Roosevelt
team to a test with Smith which they lost. The misery increased
with the prospect that Boss Hague would line up New Jersey
for Al. Later Howe himself would complain of Curley's inefficiency and failure to keep promises.[4] If Louis were ever threatened with overconfidence, he might well remember the New
England disasters that spring, although he plaintively protested
that the fight in Massachusetts had been essential to encourage
Roosevelt supporters in Pennsylvania. Thus while Smith and
Raskob had made F.D.R. the favorite of the West and South,
Roosevelt and Howe had undoubtedly helped to hand the industrial Northeast to Smith.

By May Roosevelt could be sure of slightly over 300 delegates, but he needed 460 more. Smith had almost 225 in his

[4] *Providence Journal*, April 8, 1932; Howe to Elizabeth Marbury, President's Personal File (PPF), 3279, FDRL.

pocket. Throughout the month delegates from southern States rolled in to help fill the breach: Alabama, West Virginia, Tennessee, both Carolinas, Delaware, under the guidance of friendly Senatorial machines. In Florida Roosevelt had to face only his favorite whipping boy, Alfalfa Bill. He had already swamped the unkempt populist eight to one in West Virginia. Of Mississippi they could never be sure until the test of the Convention. Its traditions insisted on the very thing Raskob wanted, an uninstructed delegation. Senator Pat Harrison hoped to hold it under a unit rule by a slim, one-vote majority. Louisiana was even more uncertain. It was held firmly in the unprincipled hands of Huey Long. The "Kingfish" had always distrusted Roosevelt, but he had been won over tentatively by the blandishments of Senators Burton Wheeler and George Norris, whom he much admired. Republican Norris might put Louisiana in Roosevelt's hands, but F.D.R. would have to keep it there. Anything could be expected from the demagogue at Baton Rouge.

While the South was smoothly filling the breach in Roosevelt's lines, the crucial western tests had to be faced with the handicap of new headlines about Tammany graft. Voters were beginning to wonder, as Seabury turned up the evidence, why Jimmy Walker should have received such handsome bonuses from businessmen, $26,000 in one case, $23,000 in another. When one of his obscure law clerks disappeared leaving a $700,000 bank account, there were more questions. But Roosevelt was saved from the worst. Walker himself was not called to the stand until after most of the major delegations had been chosen.

California was a blow, even though half expected. Smith and Garner had turned what had seemed a sure thing for Roosevelt into a bitter three-way struggle. "Cactus Jack" won narrowly with the help of McAdoo's immense prestige and Hearst's money and newspapers. He took all 44 votes under a unit rule. Roosevelt could only hope that he would not be party to a "block" movement. But the small western States—South Dakota, Nebraska, Wyoming, Arizona, New Mexico, Montana, Oregon, Nevada, Utah, and Idaho—fell into line almost as easily

as the South, thanks to the hard work of the "key" figures Farley
and Howe had chosen. Even in Colorado the bitter factional
fight went their way. It would be one of the minor ironies of
the Convention that the unit rule compelled Kansan Jouett
Shouse to vote for Roosevelt while Connecticut's Homer Cummings had to vote for Smith. By the end of May the larger part
of the Roosevelt strategy had been vindicated. He had the
South, except Maryland and Virginia, and much of the West.

But he had lost the two big blocks. Smith had taken the
Northeast. F.D.R.'s reliance on the fading Colonel House had
cost him Texas, and in turn California. Despite Roosevelt's ob-
sequious bow to Hearst, Garner would come to the Convention
strong and serious. He held the key to the situation, as popu-
lous Ohio and Indiana fell into the uncertain bargaining posture
which Cermak's Illinois had already assumed. While Farley had
been a whirlwind success with the tight little organizations of
the West and South, he proved naïve with these tough urban
bargainers. He would go to the Convention convinced that he
could swing both Indiana and Ohio, but he had got little more
than all other candidates had from these key States—a polite
hearing and pleasant gestures designed to prepare the way for
a jump in any direction. In Indiana he misunderstood the situation completely and bet on the weak, friendly State Chairman, when old Boss Tom Taggart and Governor Paul McNutt
were actually in control. In the powerful Northwest, only Michigan was sure. Here Louis had worked directly with Hall Roosevelt, Eleanor's brother, and with the enthusiastic Mayor of
Detroit, Frank Murphy.

While Farley surveyed the field sprouting with native sons
and bargaining bosses, looking for a way to vindicate his first-
ballot predictions, Roosevelt was increasingly distraught at the
mounting challenge of speeches and issues. Farley and Flynn
could not help here. Louis's command of economics was rudi-
mentary. Rosenman doubted personally his own command of
national problems. In fact, it was Rosenman who abruptly
warned F.D.R. one evening in March that they would be in
an appalling mess if they had to start a campaign at once.
Throughout the winter, Roosevelt had turned on occasion to

House, Baruch, or Hull for counsel, but each of these men was identified with a special brand of opinion and none could do the necessary legwork. Furthermore, each was a strong man in his own right. Baruch and House could be dangerous. Placed on the first team, they would insist on quarterbacking the whole game.

But Raymond Moley was pre-eminently available. At the moment, he was superbly demonstrating his ability to put Roosevelt's vague concepts into ringing phrases. Roosevelt liked him and was immensely pleased with the speeches he had written. Moley had carefully cultivated Louis Howe, dropping across Madison Avenue frequently to chat with him. And Moley had two other essential qualities: he was ready to work without limit and he could get along with both Howe and Rosenman; in fact, both claimed him as a protégé.

When Rosenman suggested that they build a core of scholars around Moley, Roosevelt objected. Could professors keep secrets? Could they work in harness? But the idea was hardly new to a Governor who had so assiduously used Cornell, Columbia, and Harvard. There was little as an alternative. Roosevelt insisted on New Yorkers—he wanted them easily available. Moley turned naturally to his younger colleagues at Columbia. There were several distinctive things about the group he assembled. They were young, unanimously imaginative. They were drivers, and idealistically hopeful for the future. They were not all eager Roosevelt supporters at first, but Moley was after ideas, not politicians. Their ideas varied widely. The conservative and "practical" Moley had chosen Adolph Berle to specialize in financial matters. Berle was co-author of a sprightly and incisive study of corporations which was about to be published; he favored major economic reforms of which Moley had serious doubts. Rexford Tugwell, an agricultural specialist, also demanded fundamental economic changes. There were numbers of others, mostly temporary, for example Lindsay Rogers, who advised on the tariff. Rosenman and O'Connor went over Moley's list first, and then those left on it were introduced to Roosevelt one or two at a time in long evenings of questions and answers at the Executive Mansion. Some of them were rapidly weeded out as they proved unable to work with Roosevelt or unattractive to him. Others would fall by the wayside, like Rogers, who made the fatal mistake of sending Al Smith and Franklin Roosevelt the same memo. F.D.R. found himself publicly embarrassed at having said the identical words Al had used shortly before.

The group worked secretly through April and May. Roosevelt gloried in the heady stimulation of their long confabs. They slaved hundreds of hours on lengthy research reports and memoranda, and later on speeches. Moley rode herd on them; much of their advice reached the boss only through him. But they all recognized that their chief value lay in the interminable general discussions which prevented the boss from being left at the mercy of any one advisor. In the fall, Louis Howe would catch their spirit in his sardonic tag, the "brains trust." James Kieran would make the tag stick when he used it in a newspaper story.

As their files on various subjects filled, Roosevelt proved himself an apt and sympathetic pupil. The professors viewed their genial boss with paternal concern. They thought him too uncritical. Moley protested that Roosevelt knew little economics and that his intelligence was the kind that "skips and bounces through seemingly intricate subjects. . . ." He confided to a close friend: "There is a lot of autointoxication of the intelligence that we shall have to watch." [5] But Moley played a major role in his boss's evolving candidacy, which he did not himself appreciate at the moment. One of his brief radio speeches for F.D.R. featured two of those sprightly phrases which became fighting symbols of the campaign and helped focus its direction: "These unhappy times call for the building of plans that rest upon . . . the forgotten man at the bottom of the economic pyramid," Moley had Roosevelt say. And then: "No nation can long endure half bankrupt. . . ." [6] The first had been taken from the arch-philosopher of American capitalism, William Graham Sumner. But Sumner's "forgotten man" had been the gentleman of property. Moley gave the old refrain a new and

[5] Moley: *After Seven Years*, p. 11.
[6] Rosenman: *Public Papers*, I, p. 625.

powerful meaning. The second was merely a happier wording of an old Roosevelt idea, that farm bankruptcy was everyone's business.

As important as the phrasing was the shift in emphasis. Roosevelt had pushed aside only a week earlier a long memo from Baruch counseling balanced budgets, economy, and a limited, self-liquidating public works program. Instead F.D.R. had adopted Moley's emphasis on the restoration of farm purchasing power, loans to small banks and homeowners, tariff revision and reciprocal trade agreements. These were old ideas with wide popularity.

The timing made the "Forgotten Man" speech. It came midway in a crucial schedule of State conventions and primaries which hinged on the farmers and the big eastern cities. Within a week Jefferson Day Dinners would provide a forum for a broad range of anti-Roosevelt spokesmen. In fact, it was Roosevelt's enemies who made the magic phrases stick. Al Smith broke into a tirade against "any demagogic appeal to the masses of the working people of this country to destroy themselves by setting class against class, and rich against poor." [7] Cox, White, and Ritchie orated listlessly about economy and tariff cuts. Roosevelt blandly joked with reporters about Smith's "terrible attack . . . on Alfalfa Bill Murray." [8] He could well afford to be smug. His enemies had unanimously tagged him as the only serious candidate who dared appeal to the common man. Smith, at least, might have known there were more of these than any other kind.

Yet much of Roosevelt's future would depend on the way he followed up the "Forgotten Man" speech. Old friends of the Wilson days urged him to be careful. In a speech at St. Paul on April 18 he chose to appeal broadly for national unity, perhaps to blunt the edge of the class-consciousness of which he had been accused. He called for "a concert of action, based on a fair and just concert of interests," to replace the "panic-stricken policy of delay and improvisation" in Washington. This was "soothing syrup" for those alarmed by Roosevelt's "dema-

[7] *The New York Times,* April 14, 1932.
[8] *The New York Times,* April 15, 1932.

goguery," and the speech was heavily flavored with the American Scriptures, from Jefferson to Theodore Roosevelt. There was even a pious refrain from Lincoln: ". . . let us renew our trust in God and go forward without fear and with manly hearts." But for those who would read there was fair warning of things to come: "The plans we make for this emergency . . . may show the way to a more permanent safeguarding of our social and economic life to the end that we may in a large number avoid the terrible cycle of prosperity crumbling into depression. In this sense, I favor economic planning, not for this period alone, but for our needs for a long time to come."[9]

At Oglethorpe University, a month later, he added full harmony to the tune he had sung at St. Paul. There must be programs to increase the consumer market, to raise the nation's purchasing power. There must be "bold, persistent experimentation."[1] This was a novel speech, drafted for him "on a dare" by Ernest K. Lindley, who had been criticizing his speeches. But it was a masterly job of phrase-making; it fitted Roosevelt's line precisely. And the brain trust was already preparing him for a back-flip on agriculture which would become clear only after his nomination. As late as May 24 he was standing publicly for "getting surplus crops out of the country without putting the government in business."[2] By late June Tugwell and Moley had persuaded him to espouse the "Voluntary Domestic Allotment" concept, a combination of crop controls and direct subsidies which would dominate the New Deal's agricultural program.

Meanwhile he must deal with Mayor Walker. Subjected to two grueling days of testimony on May 25 and 26, Jimmy Walker put on a glib, evasive, almost obscenely irrelevant performance. He disowned his unfortunate clerk, asked the world to believe that $250,000 of businessmen's favors were mere evidences of friendship, blamed the system and the laws for his troubles. While the press demanded that Roosevelt act, the Governor himself was haunted by hallucinations. Seabury, he fretted, was after *his* scalp, not Walker's. Republican money

[9] Rosenman: *Public Papers*, I, pp. 627–39.   [1] Ibid., I, p. 646.
[2] Roosevelt to *Collier's Weekly*, May 24, 1932, Group XII, FDRL.

and influence had managed the whole show. In public he could only berate the investigator for not taking action himself. Seabury had to reply and he did, a bare three weeks before the National Convention, with a 15-count indictment sent directly to the Governor. He made no recommendation. It was Roosevelt's mess now. F.D.R. sent the charges to Walker for reply six days before the Convention. This made it easy for Jimmy to do him the only favor possible and delay until after the Convention. Roosevelt could have hoped for nothing better. His best posture was clearly that of a responsible Governor, *in the process* of doing justice.

By early June their Convention arrangements were ready. Farley would be "field-marshal," a title given him later by enemies. But Louis was chief of staff, and Farley well knew that every major decision must be cleared with him. Both knew that F.D.R. was the real boss. Roosevelt himself would not go to Chicago. It was difficult for him to move about in a mob; there were immense advantages in being insulated in Albany, where he could decide at leisure and with reflection. Louis came up with a solution that gave him some of the advantages of both presence and absence. A private wire was strung from the Executive Mansion to Louis's hotel room in Chicago. Through an attached loudspeaker, Roosevelt could talk directly with individuals and groups; but there would be no record of the talks and no eavesdropping.

Farley spent the last precious days on the road in a harried search for crucial delegates. Louis holed up in his Madison Avenue retreat to watch the late correspondence and iron out the myriad details of Convention plans. He sent each Roosevelt delegate a signed portrait of F.D.R. and, more important, a one-and-a-half-minute phonograph record with a personal message from the Governor. Louis had written this cordial little pep talk, which was designed to let Roosevelt's friendly voice carry him personally to the delegates: "We are in a safe majority in the coming convention if we stand together. . . . I hope history will point to your wise action at Chicago and your determination to make our country a land of equal opportunity for all—rich and poor, strong or weak—at the beginning of a new era of equality and prosperity for these United States." [3]

But Howe was frantic with suspicion and worry as the supreme crisis of their career approached. He saw dangers everywhere. One assistant was sent to the Chicago Convention Hall to stake out three rooms for Jim Farley's conferences, so that two could be locked up on either side of the meeting room to provide insulation against eavesdroppers. He was ordered to stay in the rooms night and day to prevent their being pirated by the opposition. Fearful of sabotage, Howe arranged for his faithful switchboard operator, "Hacky," to handle the Roosevelt telephone lines at the Congress Hotel. His own son, Hartley, and his secretary, "Rabbit," would act as doorkeepers for his personal headquarters in Room 1702. Other widely separated suites were reserved for Farley and for Ed Flynn. Confidential liaison would be maintained by messengers who dashed up and down in elevators and through the complicated corridors of the Congress Hotel to elude newsmen and enemy spies. Secretaries were briefed on the dangers of dating men who might be working for a rival. Secret lists were drawn up of men in the various delegations who might be "relied on" to help in emergencies. Some were designated to keep tabs on the anti-Roosevelt coalition. Daniel C. Roper, for example, consulted regularly with his old friend William G. McAdoo in the Garner camp.

Howe's passion for cloak-and-dagger preparations was sometimes funny, but there was no nonsense about its purpose. He had long since built up an elaborate card file on enemy delegates which might be used to probe their weak spots at a crucial moment. The terse evaluations might sometimes be inaccurate, but they were decisive and sharp. On the three-by-five pink cards which summarized Garner's Texas, some of the great figures of the day were nailed down like butterflies. Tom Connally, for example, later to be Roosevelt's chairman of the Senate Foreign Relations Committee: "Politician—no conviction—Friendly, but non-committal. . . . *Tremendous* influence

[3] Howe to Roosevelt, June 3, 1932, Group XII, FDRL.

—Key man—Delegate at Large—Fears N.Y. situation." And Jesse Jones, fated to be a conservative anchor through 12 Roosevelt years: "Money—Houston Chronicle, owner of—For himself first, last and all the time—Ambitious—Promises everybody everything—Double-crosser. . . ." [4]

There was also a positive and genial side to the planning. Delegations were met at the train by Roosevelt representatives, and Jim Farley's official headquarters on the main floor of the Congress featured all the gay claptrap of buttons, pretty girls, comfortable furniture, plus a gigantic map portraying the Roosevelt States—there was an impressive splash of Roosevelt real estate. But the cynical would note with Al Smith that it represented a lot more area than votes.

Roosevelt himself was left free to fuss with the acceptance speech which Moley, Rosenman, and their aides had been preparing for weeks. Meanwhile, a final strategy session was called at Hyde Park on June 5 to make the crucial Convention decisions, which had to be agreed upon by all the varied Roosevelt groups. Homer Cummings came up from Washington with Senators Hull, Dill, Wheeler, and Walsh to represent the South and West. Guffey sat in for the crucial Pennsylvania delegation. Farley, Ed Flynn, Bob Jackson, and, of course, Roosevelt and Howe completed the group. Careful and broadly representative as the discussions were, the decisions of this meeting were loaded with dynamite.

Convinced that Shouse as Permanent Chairman would maneuver to kill the Roosevelt boom, they stood firm for Barkley as keynoter and Thomas J. Walsh as Permanent Chairman. Arthur Mullen, who had engineered victory in Nebraska, was their choice for floor leader. Hull would be their candidate for chairman of the platform-writing Resolutions Committee, and Bruce Kremer of Montana, who had wanted to be floor manager, they named for chairmanship of the Rules Committee. Senator Robert F. Wagner and author Claude Bowers were selected as possibilities for making the nominating speech. Finally, and almost fatefully, a tentative decision was taken to

[4] Group XXXVI, FDRL.

fight for the abolition of the two-thirds rule, which had been a one-third veto on Presidential nominations since the age of Jackson and Van Buren.

There was trouble at once. Shouse screamed that Roosevelt had broken his promise on the Chairmanship. No amount of explanation would convince Al Smith's friends that they had not been buffaloed by a smooth master of slippery semantics. Both candidates for the honor of nominating Roosevelt escaped the dangerous distinction—Wagner was afraid of Tammany; Bowers was afraid of Hearst. F.D.R. turned sentimentally and in desperation to John Mack, the Poughkeepsie lawyer who had nominated him for State Senator 22 years before. But the most dangerous Hyde Park decision was the challenge to the two-thirds rule. As the delegates converged on Chicago, they gossiped that Roosevelt was weakening. Some came to the crowded Loop hotels raging about his conspiracy to steal the nomination unfairly, about his impertinent tampering with sacred party traditions.

22

"Happy Days Are Here Again!"

This is more than a political campaign; it is a call to arms.
(Franklin D. Roosevelt, *July 2, 1932*) [1]

ON MONDAY, June 20, as the delegates streamed into the muggy, sun-baked, lake-front hotels, Big Jim's first-ballot predictions sounded like empty boasts. Al Smith called them "Farley's Fairy Stories." [2] Roosevelt was the front-runner, the man everyone must beat. The prize seemed more tantalizing than ever after the Republican renomination of Herbert Hoover the week before. Any candidate could win, they thought. And Roosevelt's prime argument had always been that only he had the breadth of popularity to rescue his party. Garner announced himself for repeal and economy, against "socialism and com-

[1] Rosenman: *Public Papers*, I, p. 659.   [2] Stiles: *Howe*, p. 176.

munism."[3] The unkempt old demagogue from Oklahoma, Alfalfa Bill Murray, called up the ancient spirit of the populists and Bryan. Impeccable and dignified Albert Ritchie sought the party's approval for sound conservatism. He looked more like a President than any man since Harding. The covey of old-fashioned bosses maneuvered for a bargain. And Al Smith sailed into Chicago, nattily tailored and topped with a cocky straw hat, full of wisecracks, ambition, and resentment. Smith meant to stop Roosevelt; he meant to have the Presidency. While Raskob, the businessman-politician, ignored the depression, thumped for repeal, and challenged Roosevelt to a fight on the two-thirds rule, Boss Cermak's machine distributed gallery tickets to the loyal Chicago infantry who would hiss Roosevelt, cheer Smith, and transform the Convention Hall into a raucous circus, on signal.

Farley, Flynn, Howe—all amateurs at National Convention maneuvering—faced the same tough professionals who had run the 1920 show, turned Madison Square Garden into a shambles in 1924, and nominated Smith at Houston in 1928. And their own friends were a strangely undisciplined rabble: the raucous maverick from Louisiana, the calculating conservatives from Mississippi, the dry but dissatisfied farmers from the Great Plains.

But Roosevelt's enemies lacked unity. "The Allies" agreed only on stopping F.D.R.; like wolves in a pack, they would turn on the first to fall. Hearst distrusted F.D.R., but he despised Smith and feared Baker. McAdoo wanted Garner, but of the two men who had crucified him in New York, Roosevelt seemed preferable to Smith. Virginia was uneasy about Roosevelt progressivism, but again, Al was worse. And though Smith yearned deeply to stop his treacherous protégé, he would do nothing to help a Garner, a Ritchie, a Baker, or a Harry Byrd. With it all, Smith had lost his touch. His tactics and his manner made him, in the end, one of Roosevelt's best allies at Chicago. The champion of the city masses had become the darling of Du Pont. He appeared recklessly in evening clothes at the Convention arena

[3] Quoted in Arthur M. Schlesinger, Jr.: *The Age of Roosevelt: The Crisis of the Old Order* (Boston: Houghton Mifflin Co.; 1957), p. 297.

and made it clear, as H. L. Mencken wickedly wrote, that he had "ceased to be the wonder and glory of the East Side and becomes simply a minor figure of Park Avenue. . . . His association with the rich has apparently wobbled him and changed him. He has become a golf player." [4] Yet there was still enough of the East Side boy here to feed the ancient rural prejudice. Even professionals found too much bitterness in his wit, too much vengeance, too much ruthless ambition. And if the unresolved Walker mess hung over Roosevelt like a pall, it completely enveloped Smith, as he hobnobbed with Tammany friends and with the bold little Mayor himself.

Farley fully expected an early break to start the avalanche he had predicted. But breaks must be engineered, and he experimented carefully with the two weapons that might blast out the landslide. He dangled the Vice-Presidency, with caution, in several directions at once, and, with Roosevelt's approval, explored carefully the prospects of abolishing the two-thirds rule. Then he lost control of his own show for one hectic, almost fatal, afternoon. At the first meeting of Roosevelt delegates, Huey Long took over with a ranting demand for abolition of the rule. Cummings, Hull, and Josephus Daniels chimed in. There were others. Farley was distraught. He suspected now that his forces would disintegrate if he persisted; but he dared not muzzle the meeting. "Bewildered, confused and pathetic," [5] he let the violent controversy boil to a vote. By nightfall, the bickering, undisciplined meeting and the decision to fight for majority rule were common Convention gossip. It seemed for the moment that Roosevelt himself had given his enemies the only issue that could cement their unwieldy bloc. The press was deluged with statements from distinguished Democrats—Smith, Davis, Cox, Carter Glass, Sam Rayburn, McAdoo—on the sanctity of the two-thirds rule. Baker growled ominously of the "moral flaw" [6] in a nomination gained this way. Newsmen predicted a dark-horse candidate.

Roosevelt was cool. He told Farley to let the controversy simmer a while. But when Louis arrived next morning, he insisted

[4] Quoted in ibid., p. 303.   [5] Mary Dewson, quoted in ibid., p. 299.
[6] Quoted in ibid., p. 299.

on a retreat. On Monday F.D.R. issued the inevitable statement
from Albany that took Farley off the hook. He believed in majority rule, said Roosevelt, but he would abandon the fight in
this Convention.

There were no more major blunders. Farley and Flynn had
learned much that disastrous afternoon. In addition, the necessity for consulting Louis Howe helped to mature their decisions. Always suspicious and pessimistic, Louis checked their
enthusiasm and naïveté. And all of them were more careful to
clear things with their distant boss.

Even so, there were plenty of problems. With the Convention
about to split open, Farley worked around the clock, greeting
delegates by the hundreds and escorting them to Howe's seventeenth floor bailiwick where a carefully briefed Roosevelt could
greet them by name and chat with them over the telephone
amplifier. Farley's phenomenal memory for names and faces
and efficient planning paid off here. Yet they waited for the
crucial tests on Tuesday morning with deep anxiety. A defeat on
any one of them could beat Roosevelt before the first ballot.

Their lines held. Disputed delegations from Louisiana and
Minnesota were seated. They won the chairmanship for Walsh
by nearly a hundred votes. The platform was a striking Roosevelt victory. Hull shepherded through the committee the carefully balanced document on which they had worked. It threw
the spotlight on the depression and blasted the Republicans as
architects of disaster. The program swayed safely between action and laissez-faire. Democrats would stand for "sound
money," economy, removing government from business, a "competitive tariff." Yet Democrats would also stand for public
works, federal relief, unemployment and old age insurance,
regulation of the financial markets and of public utilities, conservation programs, and for "a continuous responsibility of government for human welfare." Walter Lippmann, who had castigated Roosevelt for carrying water on both shoulders, praised
the committee for "the best job in . . . at least twenty years." [7]
But the Convention cheered largely for repeal. On Roosevelt's

[7] Walter Lippmann: *Interpretations, 1931–1932* (New York: The Macmillan Co.; 1933), p. 308.

orders, Farley stood aside while they voted a wringing wet plank. The Smiths and the Ritchies boasted stridently of their empty victory on an issue F.D.R. had sensed long ago was dead.

By the afternoon of Thursday, June 30, the Convention was exhausted but had hardly commenced its work. Then there began the endless orgy of oratory, the mad confusion of the demonstrations. If nominations were decided by applause meters, Smith would have been chosen on the spot. Governor Joseph Ely's nominating speech was a masterful performance. Cermak's mob provided a steady overtone of shrill noise to reinforce the boisterous crowd; confetti and gaudy signs and hundreds of waving white handkerchiefs studded the smoky cavern and the organ boomed and shrilled with "The Sidewalks of New York."

In comparison, the Roosevelt show had been mild and disappointing. All the tricks had been prepared; when John Mack finished his colorless speech, a vast portrait of Roosevelt unrolled from the galleries and the organist swung into "Anchors Aweigh," Roosevelt's own choice for a theme song. Delegates marched and cheered but with little help from the balcony crowds. Back in the Congress Hotel, Louis lay hunched up on his bed, wheezing and coughing, miserable with tension, while he listened to the Convention hullabaloo. Irritated beyond all containment as "Anchors Aweigh" boomed from the organ over and over again like a dirge, he whispered huskily to Ed Flynn: "For God's sake, tell 'em to play something else." And then remembering the suggestion that had come from some of his secretaries, he rasped: "Oh, tell 'em to play 'Happy Days Are Here Again.'"[8] Howe had found the mood music of the campaign.

But Louis, gasping for air in the close hotel room, and Jim Farley, collapsed from sheer exhaustion on a cot in his Convention Hall headquarters, were desperately worried. All week long they had been maneuvering to gain the delegates needed for a first-ballot victory. Their Vice-Presidential bait had brought hardly more than a nibble. Ritchie and Harry Byrd

[8] Stiles: *Howe*, pp. 181–2.

had refused the prestigious but vacuous honor. The most important prospect seemed Garner. He had been approached from all quarters, through Hearst and McAdoo and Sam Rayburn and Missouri's Senator Harry Howes. Yet Rayburn still insisted that Garner be given a real chance to test his strength. Farley faced a first ballot with only a dream of the spontaneous bandwagon switch which might turn the tide. Should he play for time and postpone the balloting until the next day? Did he dare risk the loss of delegates who might see this as a sign of weakness? As the floor leaders gathered around Farley's cot, they pressed for a ballot. Howe was at a loss in this crucial moment; at any rate, Roosevelt himself must decide. From the little sitting room of the Executive Mansion in Albany, where he had been listening all night to the Convention noise, chain-smoking, nervously smiling, F.D.R. told them to go ahead.

But the flood of oratory went on and on. Delegates squirmed and talked and prowled about in the muggy, trash-strewn auditorium, sweltering under the lights, groggy and irritable with sheer fatigue, their eyes smarting from the clouds of cigar smoke, their ears numbed with the interminable booming of the organ and the shrill cacophony of the seconding speeches. At 4:28 a.m., the first ballot began. Farley moved tensely about the hall, jotting down the vote, as challenge after challenge dragged the count out for nearly two hours. But the break never came. Roosevelt polled his monumental block of 661¼ votes, but this was over a hundred short of two-thirds. Farley appealed to McAdoo, then to Cermak, but his first-ballot predictions drifted off into the Chicago smog as the sun began to shine eerily down on the disheveled delegates.

Almost by inertia, the Convention found itself in a second ballot. Farley held on, but he could produce only six more votes. He had told Sam Rayburn the night before that he could hold his bloc together for three ballots, maybe four or five. Now the opposition clamored for the crucial third, and Jim dispiritedly wondered whether he could ever go back to New York. Huey Long and Alabama Judge Leon McCord were assigned to keep a mutinous Mississippi delegation in line; it held by one vote. Farley dredged up 16½ more votes. At 9:15 the exhausted

mob shoved its way into the hazy morning sunshine and strag-
gled back to the hotels. To most of the tired professionals it
seemed clear that Roosevelt had been stopped.

There would be no sleep, except catnaps, for Jim Farley,
heading back to the Congress in a cab, or for Louis Howe,
stretched out in abject misery on the floor in 1702. They had
less than 12 hours to make or break their boss, and the opposition was working feverishly within their own bailiwick. Mississippi might desert. Worse yet, Arkansas might bolt, and this
might commence a mass retreat in the alphabetical voting.

There was serious disagreement among Roosevelt's advisors
on how to blast the log jam. Howe insisted that Garner would
never retreat; Harry Byrd was the only hope. Farley thought
that only Garner could turn the trick. At last, after a whispered conference, with Farley stretched out beside Howe on
the carpet, Louis agreed with him. The Garner bloc was rigid,
devoted, encouraged now by some third-ballot gains. It would
be hard to crack, but it was the best hope.

Yet suddenly the cracks began to appear on all sides. Farley
and Harrison had a hasty morning conference with Sam Rayburn. The enigmatic Texan would say only: "We'll see what
can be done." [9] Meanwhile in Washington Garner fretted over
the dangers of a deadlocked Convention; he wanted the Democrats to win more than he wanted to be President. And from
San Simeon, Hearst sent word to the Speaker that Roosevelt
must be chosen to stave off Smith or Baker. But Garner was
making the great decision of his career, and he took his time
while he refused all telephone calls, lest he have to talk with
Smith leaders. Finally at 3 p.m. he called Rayburn to release
his delegates to Roosevelt. At 6, Rayburn faced a Texas caucus
more rabid for Garner than Garner himself. There were arguments, shouting, tears, and a close ballot—54–51 for Roosevelt. Rayburn hastily adjourned the caucus before the rabid
Garner men who were working on other delegations could return. It was close, but enough, under the unit rule. Meanwhile,
Roper and Hull were working on McAdoo. And Louis Howe,

[9] Farley: *Behind the Ballots*, p. 145.

unsure even now, maneuvered feverishly to bring Virginia into
line.

The break was one of the best-kept secrets of Convention history. That night the delegates dug in for another long riot of
ballots and contentions, and the wiseacres among the press men
glibly predicted an open race. But when California was called,
McAdoo strode to the platform to explain their vote, while the
loaded galleries jeered and hooted. He was grimly smug as he
nailed the rivets into Al Smith's coffin. California's 44 votes
were for Roosevelt. Everyone knew that this meant Texas also.
Cermak rushed to put his Illinois and Indiana blocks on the
right side. Ritchie gave in stiffly, but properly. Only the East
Side Warrior strode grimly from the Convention after holding
his 190½ votes to the sad conclusion.

In an ordinary Convention this would have been the climax
and the end. But Roosevelt intended to make this an extraordi-
nary year—to begin the campaign at once. Early Saturday
morning F.D.R., his family, and Sam Rosenman climbed into
a tri-motor plane and took off from the Albany airport under
lowering skies. Sharp-eyed reporters had queried the Governor
about the plane they had spotted there the day before, and he
had joked that he intended to go to Chicago on a five-place
bicycle, with his boys doing the peddling, "Papa" handling the
steering, and Sam Rosenman trailing behind on a tricycle. Roosevelt carried with him one of his most carefully prepared
speeches. Moley's brain trust had been working on it for weeks.
Rosenman had stayed up all night polishing, editing, roughing
out a peroration. And the Governor, who had gone over it again
and again, buffed and cut and sharpened it as they flew through
the turbulent storms along the lake shores.

In Chicago the waiting delegates nominated Garner for Vice-
President. Cactus Jack did not particularly want the honor. He
thought the Speakership more important. And there had been
no specific deal, despite Farley's agile auctioning of the spot
in several directions. But Farley, Howe, and Roosevelt had
decided that the honor belonged to Garner if he wanted it, and
Big Jim smoothly pushed aside a swarm of minor aspirants in
the Roosevelt camp.

The mood of the Convention had changed. The more agile and realistic of Roosevelt's opponents were rushing into camp lest they be ostracized later. Charley Michelson, the keen publicity man of the Democratic National Committee, showed up in Howe's rooms at once. Michelson had done more than any other man to keep Democratic pressure on the Hoover Administration. Louis had long since quietly advised him that they wanted his help when F.D.R. won. He was, as Howe well knew, too good a man to lose. And Bernard Baruch strode briskly into 1702 to make a last appeal for Ritchie for Vice-President and then to offer his services and advice to the winner. Louis's aides were shocked to see their little boss welcome the wily old operator with a smile and hand over a copy of Roosevelt's speech for Baruch's comments. But Howe had no illusions; he knew that this was the time for healing wounds. In any case, Baruch was more useful as an uncertain camp follower than as a sworn enemy. In fact, Howe's welcome may have been genuine. Louis's suspicion of the progressive extremes to which Moley's crew seemed prey, his firm belief in "balance," may well have made him happy to have conservatives like Baruch and Harry Byrd aboard to reef the sails and hold the skipper down.

Yet there were some bitter hold-outs. The night of the nomination Roosevelt posters were ripped and defaced. One disgruntled Garner man protested it was a kangaroo ticket, stronger behind than before. Al Smith and his New York cohorts left before their Governor could arrive. But even Smith would have received a welcoming smile in the Roosevelt headquarters. Roosevelt himself arranged for Justice Bernard Sheintag to go up to Harmon to meet Al's train and persuade him not to blast the ticket when he met newsmen at Grand Central Station.

But Howe's major worry in this moment of victory was not the old enemies trooping into camp or slinking out of town to nurse their wounds. It was Franklin himself. Even now, Louis could not unwind from the nervous tension which had driven him through the long ordeal. He demanded that the entire acceptance speech be dictated over the wire to his secretary, and as he read it, he grumbled and cussed. He might have expected as much from Rosenman and Moley! In his mingled fear and jealousy he lost all sense of proportion. He never doubted that he alone could dash off a better speech than the one that had emerged from weeks of work by the team of Moley, Tugwell, Berle, Rosenman, and Roosevelt. As F.D.R. slept soundly among his miserably airsick family and the Convention waited restlessly for the tardy, storm-buffeted plane, Howe dashed to his desk to draft out a proper speech for his boss. His stenographers rushed to keep up with the scrawled sheets of lined yellow paper he tossed them.

If there was any doubt that Roosevelt was a strong candidate, the scene at the Chicago airport should have dispelled it. The mob which met him as he emerged from the plane, leaning carefully on his son's arm, was wildly enthusiastic. This was one demonstration Tony Cermak didn't have to arrange; yet Chicago's Mayor was there to put himself in the Roosevelt limelight. But it was big, beaming Jim Farley and nervous, sober Louis Howe who sat on either side of their champion in the large white touring car that took him through the mobbed Chicago streets. As they rode, Louis thrust his new speech confidently into Franklin's hands. Roosevelt protested—"Dammit, Louie, I'm the nominee!" [1]—and then, sensing that this was important to Howe, he leafed through the pages as he waved and shouted and smiled to the people who would elect him.

On the platform at the auditorium Franklin D. Roosevelt stood triumphant, gripping the speaker's desk firmly with one hand, to steady himself on the uneasy prop of his braces, waving genially to the crowd, smiling, ever-smiling—and before him on the desk lay two speeches. Behind him stood Louis Howe, victorious, jubilant, and Ray Moley, anxiously waiting to hear the words that had been burned by hard work into his brain. Only half a dozen men in the entire mob realized that F.D.R. commenced with Louis's first page and then smoothly slipped into the manuscript he had carried from New York. For

[1] Quoted in James Roosevelt and Sidney Shalett: *Affectionately, F.D.R: A Son's Story of a Lonely Man* (New York: Harcourt, Brace and Co.; 1959), p. 226.

the party and for the country this was a call to action, a crusade against Depression and Misery.

It was a partisan speech, designed to whip tired politicians into frenzied crusaders: "We will break foolish traditions and leave it to the Republican leadership, far more skilled in the art, to break promises." It was a hopeful speech, holding out the promise of relief and action to a dismayed and distraught people: "Let us now and here highly resolve to resume the country's uninterrupted march along the path of real progress, real justice, of real equality for all of our citizens great and small. . . ." It was a careful speech, inviting co-operation, eschewing extremes, dictating moderation: "To meet by reaction that danger of radicalism is to invite disaster. . . . I invite those nominal Republicans who find that their conscience cannot be squared with the groping and the failure of their party leaders, to join hands with us, here and now. In equal measure, I warn those nominal Democrats, who squint at the future with their faces turned toward the past, and who feel no response to the demands of the new time, that they are out of step with their Party. . . ."

It was a prophetic speech: its promises to farmers and workers and businessmen of relief and economy, action and laissez-faire, betrayed all the dilemmas of the "balanced" path he had dictated for the platform and which he would seek to follow in Washington. But it was not the dilemmas and the ambiguity that the country remembered. It was the striking symbolism of the moment—the confident smile and warming voice of the man whose cruel steel braces and halting walk were visible signs of the adversity he had mastered; the lilting rhythm of "Happy Days Are Here Again"; the indelible promise of the words which had slipped almost by accident into the manuscript: "I pledge you, I pledge myself to a new deal for the American people." [2]

[2] Rosenman: *Public Papers*, I, pp. 647–59.

23

Triumph of a Lifetime

> *You and Jim have done more than elect a President. You have created a new party that ought to hold power for twenty-five years.*
>
> (Raymond Moley *to* Louis Howe, *November 12, 1932*)[1]

THE CAMPAIGN began in Chicago, with Roosevelt's speech at the National Committee Dinner, with the long midnight conference in which F.D.R. outlined to Moley the broad dimensions of the strategy. It was firmly built on the organization and on the material for speeches which Roosevelt's team had been developing for two busy years. Even tentative itineraries and topics for speeches had been sketched out by Louis Howe and discussed with Roosevelt. Yet the campaign began with fundamental and unresolved dilemmas which had been foreshadowed by the contradictions inherent in the platform and the acceptance speech. Roosevelt stood at a crossroads in logic.

To the right lay the path of sound money, retrenchment, and laissez-faire, the path which Bernard Baruch, Joseph Kennedy,

---

[1] Quoted in Freidel: *The Triumph*, p. 370.

and Harry Byrd were following. To the left and slightly to the rear ran the road to a trust-busting, low-tariff, inflationary paradise, to the restoration of the old America, a road marked out in the speeches of western Senators like Wheeler and loud rabble-rousers like Long and in the quiet scholarly memos of Felix Frankfurter. And off in front, winding uncertainly over the hills, lay the unmarked trail of the economic planners who had accepted the bigness of American organization and hoped to tame that bigness in the public interest by the countervailing power of big government. Here Tugwell and Berle sought to throw a little light on the shadowy and uncertain path. Roosevelt would soon be hemmed in by what Arthur Schlesinger, Jr., has called this "triangle of advice," but for the moment he would temporize. June and July were for enthusiasm and harmony.

There were political crossroads which must be passed immediately. Farley was made National Chairman. Moley was given to understand that he had major responsibility for ideas, issues, and speeches. He and Farley soon came to terms; each would mind his own business: Farley's to get the votes, Moley's to help Roosevelt develop the issues. Howe's position remained typically ambiguous. While Farley presided over six floors of the central headquarters in the Biltmore Hotel, Louis held forth across the street in his own private headquarters. While Farley developed a correspondence list of 140,000 names, Louis answered tens of thousands of letters addressed to Roosevelt himself. And Howe held the purse strings so firmly that Joe Kennedy, whom he disliked, refused to be on the campaign committee because he thought it wise not to have a "dissenter" in Louis's office.

Farley thought he had the same deal with Howe that he had with Moley. He should have known better. Louis spent most of his time studying the trends, but he could be expected to meddle with anything and everything. It was a miracle wrought of their mutual respect that the two old kingpins of the machine were able to work smoothly together, through continuous and cordial personal chats. Farley made a point of keeping Louis informed of everything. Louis in turn never

double-crossed him. But F.D.R. made it clear at the start that
every major decision must eventually come to his own desk.

The first of these major decisions was the nature of the campaign. Roosevelt's advisors were all but unanimous for a quiet,
front-porch affair. Garner put it sharply: "All you have got to
do is to stay alive until election day." [2] Howe agreed. He always
saw more danger of error than hope of gain. But now he lost
again to his buoyant boss. Roosevelt ruled firmly for an aggressive, coast-to-coast appeal. He would make himself the symbol
of action and hope—to create the confidence that he would need
when the battle was won. Although he ordered his headquarters never to mention his health in any way, he knew he must
stop short the subterranean rumors of his disability. And he
sensed more clearly than anyone around him the vast reservoir
of votes that education and depression had made available to
the first man with the wit to go to the people directly, over the
heads of the old organizations. While he made full use of the
radio he had mastered so well—and blessed Howe and Farley
for their traditional and superbly efficient organization work—
he set out to dominate the campaign personally, and everywhere. Besides, he loved campaigning: the excitement and
tension, the cheering crowds, the genial talk with old politicos,
the faces at the station platforms, the little incidents that made
him feel at home with the nation's people.

His mind lay more with action in the coming March than
with persuasion this fall. He must offer hope and direction. He
must fight against the bitterness which hung across the nation
like a pall, the witless hunt for scapegoats, the burgeoning violence: ". . . the chief thought to get across is that . . . I am
willing to try things out until we get something that
works. . . ." [3] But for the moment scapegoats could be politically useful: "Another four years of Hoover's inept leadership,
or rather complete lack of leadership, will spell disaster for the
country . . . ." [4] And he would remember constantly that the

[2] Quoted in Schlesinger, Jr.: *The Crisis*, p. 416.

[3] Roosevelt to Floyd Olson, September 5, 1932, Group XII, FDRL.

[4] Roosevelt to Dave H. Morris, June 6, 1932, quoted in *Personal Letters,
1928–1945*, pp. 281–2.

middle of the road was the safest place to travel as long as the
road seemed to be heading slightly upward. "To accomplish almost anything worthwhile," he had written, "it is necessary to
compromise between the ideal and the practical." [5] For the
moment, he went fishing. As he cruised along the New England
coast, newsmen caught for the nation a vignette of the exuberant, superbly healthy Roosevelt relaxing with his vigorous boys
as a good American father should.

If Roosevelt could relax, no one else on the team could.
Moley, Tugwell, and Berle were holed up in their paper- and
book-strewn apartment, working against time on memoranda
and studies which would become F.D.R.'s speech reservoir.
They were reinforced by the cocky, exuberant, sometimes violent Hugh Johnson, Baruch's personal donation to the campaign.
Howe and Farley were even more harried. The organization
job was monumental, despite their long experience and planning. Frank Walker raised the money—eventually each party
would spend between $2,000,000 and $3,000,000. Walker and
Farley brought in an amazing number of the "fat cats" who
had financed the Ritchie, Garner, and Smith drives: Baruch,
Pierre DuPont, Hearst, Raskob, as well as the original Roosevelt-
millionaires, Kennedy, Woodin, and Vincent Astor. Much of the
work at headquarters was managed by the Senators. But Garner
was little help. Cactus Jack retired to Uvalde to fish, hoping
only to keep up with Roosevelt's changing ideas and avoid mistakes. Louis was delighted at this, and sent an agent down to
watch the Speaker's infrequent statements to the press. One
of the by-products of Garner's silence was the Republicans'
strange assumption that he was more radical than Roosevelt
himself.

Great care was taken to attract the special groups, especially
the women. Mollie Dewson's "grass-trampers" were organized
for house-to-house canvasses from Maine to California. Howe
supported them, but it was expensive, and he groused morosely
as he totted up their mounting clerical expenses. Teamster Dan
Tobin led a labor group; Louis Johnson of the American Legion

[5] Quoted in Drew Pearson and Robert S. Allen: "How the President
Works," *Harper's Magazine*, CLXXIII (June 1936), p. 10.

plugged Roosevelt with the veterans, although F.D.R. refused to come out for a bonus. George Norris, Harold Ickes, Donald Richberg, Henry Wallace, and other ex-Republicans and Bull Moosers organized the National Progressive League for Roosevelt. Frankfurter kept a close watch on this group.

In Howe's personal headquarters the emphasis was on anonymity. The daily news digests flowed inexorably out to Roosevelt and all the key figures of the campaign. The candidate himself became a little bored with it. Swamped with work and paper, he sent down an order before the end of August not to bother him with more editorials. A bigger task was the digest of the mail. Thousands of pieces were reduced to succinct summaries, handwritten letters were translated into typescripts, and the most important summaries were sent to Roosevelt. Louis collected a coterie of skilled ghost writers to produce thousands of "personal" letters. They studied the Roosevelt style and the Roosevelt speeches and gambled that they could get away with posing as Roosevelt. Eventually Louis added it all up: 65,000,000 pieces of literature, over 3,000,000 personally addressed letters, and 5,000,000 buttons had been sent out from his headquarters and Farley's. Nearly 500 releases were fed to the newspapers. And all of this furious activity ate up a payroll of $26,000 a week, plus an uncounted horde of volunteered hours. Over 600 people bumped against each other in the frantic, organized confusion at the Biltmore.

But this was only the command post. Roosevelt, Howe, and Farley had decided at once to throw most of the responsibility to the State and county Committees, no matter what heartaches this might cause to some original Roosevelt boosters who now found their enemies in power. They had learned from searing experience not to buck the organization unless there was another ready to take its place. Their chips were firmly placed on Cermak to carry Illinois, on Taggart to deliver Indiana, on McAdoo in California. They might boast of reforms. For example, they sent out the literature in small lots to insure distribution, but it was the official committee chairmen whom they called to headquarters for small regional meetings, where Farley told them bluntly that they were responsible for their

States and just as bluntly assured them there would be no undercutting by rival clubs. Louis quietly sent out personal agents to check on their activities, but there was no toying with insurgents.

The prime operation was the Governor's train. This was Roosevelt's own pet. He dictated the kind of cars he wanted and loaded the staff with his family: James to escort him on the innumerable and painfully awkward trips to the back platform; Jimmy's wife and Anna to help greet the women; Louis's old Navy aide, Marvin McIntyre, to run the staff. Moley would be chief policy advisor. McIntyre would maintain liaison with headquarters, but even Louis would find it difficult to reach Roosevelt personally when he wanted to argue. It was all dramatic and it was all familiar. In a sense, it was the opening night for which 1920, 1928, and 1930 had been dress rehearsals.

As Howe and Farley put together their intricate machine, Roosevelt and Herbert Hoover wrestled with a summer full of problems. Roosevelt's were the more easily solved, although not even Howe knew what his boss would do with Jimmy Walker. No matter what he did, Roosevelt would lose votes; but in the best Roosevelt tradition he turned the mess to some advantage. During the long days of public hearings Walker squirmed unhappily, and Roosevelt's stature grew with his relentless, dignified cross-examination. The little Mayor resigned on September 1. The Roosevelt luck had held. He got the credit for disposing of Walker; he avoided the onus of actually discharging him. Tammany growled but it dared only the petty gesture of denying Sam Rosenman a judgeship. Roosevelt tartly warned John Curry: "I have a long memory—and a long arm—for my friends." [6]

Hoover's problems were less easily pushed aside. The depression could not be resolved within the boundaries of his economic faith. He had been pushed into action by a relentless Democratic Congressional majority, but his action had been weak: a Reconstruction Finance Corporation, a grimly inade-

[6] Roosevelt to Samuel Rosenman, September 30, 1932, quoted in *Personal Letters, 1928–1945*, p. 302.

quate plan to purchase crop surpluses. He had resisted Federal relief for the unemployed and the strident demands of Wagner and Garner for public works programs. He had become the symbol of inadequacy in crisis; his record was indelibly written. Roosevelt had a supreme advantage; far from Washington during the crisis, he had avoided making commitments as to how he would meet the national problem of depression. Hoover must stand firm; Roosevelt could maneuver. More immediately embarrassing was the Bonus Army—10,000 to 11,000 men, women, and children camping in a crude jungle of board and tin-can shacks, long after hope of a bonus had fled. When argument and railroad fares failed to budge them, the President turned to the Army. He thought he saw a Communist conspiracy; General Douglas MacArthur thought he saw the face of revolution itself. Tear gas, bayonets, and tanks held in reserve did the job. But the picture of veterans' wives and children pitifully fleeing before gas-masked troops earned them new sympathy. The photos of an impeccable and stern MacArthur, standing in his cavalry boots and pants with his swagger stick carelessly swinging by his side, aroused new resentment against the luckless and humorless President.

While Hoover fretted with deep anxiety, Roosevelt utilized every resource to embarrass him further. First came a public telegram, inviting the President to help in "cutting red tape and eliminating formalities" on the St. Lawrence project and to get this "great public work" under way at once.[7] Hoover was furious; he slapped back with a cold, proper, impolitic refusal. But Roosevelt seldom gave opponents free advertising by mentioning their names. It was always the Republican "leadership" he attacked, as he did in Columbus on August 20. "I proposed to show that this leadership misunderstood the forces which were involved in the economic life of the country, that it encouraged a vast speculative boom, and that, when the reckoning came the Administration was not frank, not honest, with the people. . . ." And then he went on to the kind of inspired attack that the sober, worried Hoover could never match:

[7] Rosenman: *Public Papers,* I, pp. 203–5.

A puzzled, somewhat skeptical Alice asked the Republican leadership some simple questions:

"Will not the printing and selling of more stocks and bonds, the building of new plants and the increase of efficiency produce more goods than we can buy?"

"No," shouted Humpty Dumpty. "The more we produce, the more we buy."

"What if we produce a surplus?"

"Oh, we can sell it to foreign consumers."

"How can the foreigners pay for it?"

"Why, we will lend them money."

"I see," said little Alice, "they will buy our surplus with our money. Of course, these foreigners will pay us back by selling us their goods?"

"Oh, not at all," said Humpty Dumpty. "We set up a high wall called the tariff."

"And," said Alice at last, "how will the foreigners pay off these loans?"

"That is easy," said Humpty Dumpty, "did you ever hear of a moratorium?"

Much of this could be quoted against him in later years, but it served its present purpose. And he shifted sharply to the damning indictment made by stringing together, in relentless series, the President's optimistic predictions of October 25, 1929, to December 2, 1930: "the Administration did not tell the truth. . . . That was the measure of the Republican leadership." [8]

If Hoover was angered by the attacks, he might well have been confused by Roosevelt's pious straddling of the real problems. At the end of July, F.D.R. had preached relief *and* balanced budgets, "saving in one place what we would spend in others." [9] Now, in Columbus, he rang the changes on Hoover's own faith: ". . . Government, without becoming a prying bureaucracy, can act as a check and counterbalance to . . . oligarchy so as to secure the chance to work and the safety of savings to men and women. . . . We must make American indi-

[8] Ibid., I, pp. 669–84.   [9] Ibid., I, p. 663.

vidualism what it was intended to be—equality of opportunity for all, the right of exploitation for none." [1] At the same time he promised bluntly a wide spate of banking and stock-market reforms and maintained just as bluntly that this was a domestic crisis, not an international one, as Hoover kept insisting.

This was all very sprightly, and Roosevelt found agreeable support among businessmen for his Columbus speech. He toured New England triumphantly, and the tough old Jersey dictator, Frank Hague, symbolized the campaign reunion of dissidents with the mammoth demonstrations he staged for the candidate.

It was the West about which Roosevelt worried. He carefully cultivated the widely divergent press barons, Robert McCormick and William Randolph Hearst, and pushed aside Louis's warning to stay out of California, where a single misstep in the tangled web of State politics might endanger him. He agreed to let Flynn come along to watch him, but he would go. He met scores of farm-State leaders, had Morgenthau and Tugwell canvass others: inflationists, sound money men, surplus dumpers, crop controllers, protectionists and free traders, advocates of loans and mortgage moratoria, Farm Bureau, Farmer's Union, farm machinery producers, Senators. There was no consensus. His own record was spotty enough to hang him. He had fuzzy commitments to dumping surpluses—his *Liberty* article on the subject was republished in book form during July. He had damned government speculation in surpluses only months before in *Collier's*. He had gestured vaguely toward crop controls at Chicago. But he had one advantage. The voters' only alternative was Hoover, whose vetoes of the farmers' McNary-Haugen bill hung like an albatross about his neck. Roosevelt made the most of it. His master speech to the farmers at Topeka on September 14 was phrased vaguely. It could satisfy no one; it would drive no one away. Twenty-five different collaborators had helped to mix this bland and harmless brew.

And yet it was strong on the attack, summarizing wickedly

[1] Ibid., I, pp. 669–84.

Republican farm policy: " 'One third of you are not needed.
Run a race with bankruptcy to see which will survive.' . . . It
has been reactionary policy since time immemorial, Help the
few; perhaps those few will be kind enough to help the many."
For the future Roosevelt promised only golden objectives without embarrassing discussion of details: reorganization of the
Agriculture Department, lower interest payments, renegotiation of mortgages, narrowing the farmer's price gap, reciprocal
renegotiation of tariffs. And on the surplus, he would "compose
the conflicting elements of these various plans . . . gather the
benefits of the long study . . . coordinate efforts . . . [for the]
restoration of agriculture to economic equality with other industries." [2] He would avoid all the problems: the program must
be self-financing, avoid European retaliation and new bureauc-
racies, and be "insofar as possible, voluntary." Beyond the vague
phrases of the first western speech he would not go.

Like Henry Wallace, many went away deeply disillusioned.
But for ordinary farmers it was the note of deep concern that
counted, and the genial platform talks at the little tank towns
where they could see the candidate in person. The pattern un-
folded: the smiling, confident, friendly figure, making folksy
small-talk about farm problems and local friends; the well-used
jokes, always fresh to his listeners, about his "little boy Jimmy"
towering bald-headed above him; the handshakes and pleasant
remarks about gifts passed from the crowd; and the genial wave
as the train slowly pulled away. The big speeches seemed almost incidental to the more serious business of these little
friendly sessions with the American people.

And often the big speeches were in fact innocuous, less
significant for what was said than for the impression of concern
and competence conveyed by the speaker. At Salt Lake he gave
a thoroughly unobjectionable analysis of transportation problems, with vague promises of government aid and better planning. Seattle received a succinct argument for reciprocal tariffs.
But as he neared progressive California, the bailiwick of Re-
publican-maverick Hiram Johnson, he stepped up the pace. In

[2] Ibid., I, pp. 697–711.

Portland, on the Columbia River, he spoke out bluntly for public power and for a "national yardstick" to check the private utilities. In San Francisco, he reached the progressive peak of his campaign in a speech built largely by Adolph Berle. If the frontier had created American individualism—as Frederick Jackson Turner had once taught Franklin Roosevelt at Harvard —it seemed clear that the end of the frontier demanded the beginnings of national planning.

> Our last frontier has long since been reached. . . . Our task now . . . is the soberer, less dramatic business of ad- ministering resources and plants already in hand, of seek- ing to reestablish foreign markets for our surplus produc- tion, of meeting the problems of underconsumption, of ad- justing production to consumption, of distributing wealth and products more equitably, of adapting existing eco- nomic organizations to the service of the people. The day of enlightened administration has come.

And the planning must bring "balance, even though it may in some measure qualify the freedom of action of individual units within business." [3] This far Roosevelt was willing to go with Berle and Tugwell, but no farther, for the moment. The vital commitments were left open. Who would do the planning? What would be the techniques? Whose concept of "public interest" would win out?

Quite as significant were the issues he ignored: foreign policy and labor especially. Even so, Roosevelt feared that he had gone too far. And Howe prodded him incessantly. Louis was worried about Hoover's insistent promises that Democratic radicalism would destroy the American economy and bury American individualism. He was infuriated over the San Francisco speech. He had wanted Roosevelt to use instead a Hugh Johnson draft emphasizing economy and sound money. Louis had haunted Roosevelt throughout the whole western trip, telephoning him at station after station. Failing to persuade Franklin personally, he had egged on western politicians to press Roosevelt to follow a more conservative line. And the boss

[3] Ibid., I, pp. 742–56.

was warned by others that the farmers might not be ready for the sharp blasts he had sounded against the tariff. Moley carried two tariff speeches, one for reciprocal trade agreements, one for a 10 per cent reduction. Roosevelt airily told him to "weave them" together.[4] And then he ordered a new one drafted with the help of western high-tariff Senators. Out of this hapless attempt to marry the unmarriageable came an almost silly speech at Sioux City which promised reduction but not too much, reciprocal trade but no foreign dictation, larger foreign trade but no danger to domestic interests.

In Detroit Roosevelt seemed to be retreating from his San Francisco speech. It was an ideal forum for a firm stand on unemployment. Instead, he gave the labor crowds an innocuous Sunday sermon on the "philosophy of social justice."[5] Back in New York, he faced the relentless badgering of Howe, Johnson, and Baruch. By October 6 he had capitulated. In a radio address he recast his appeal for business reforms in terms of cooperation, "a concert of interests." Two weeks later he used a polished version of the Johnson speech which clashed sharply with much that he had said and much that he would do. He blasted Hoover's "reckless and extravagant" deficit spending, his penchant for "Federal control." His own promise was reckless: a 25 per cent reduction in the cost of Federal government operations. He fell in meekly with the recent demand of Calvin Coolidge and Alfred E. Smith: "All the costs of . . . Government must be reduced without fear and without favor." Only one exception would be made. No American would be compelled to continue in "starvation and dire need."[6] Six days earlier he had called again for Federal relief; now he insisted it must be put into effect within a balanced budget. In his one inspired moment of the campaign, President Hoover lashed out that this glib crusader was only a "chameleon on plaid."[7]

The President, who had thought Roosevelt would be easy to beat, knew by September that his own case was hopeless. He

[4] Moley: *After Seven Years*, p. 48.
[5] Rosenman: *Public Papers*, I, pp. 771–80.   [6] Ibid., I, pp. 807–10.
[7] Quoted in James MacGregor Burns: *Roosevelt: The Lion and the Fox* (New York: Harcourt, Brace and Co.; 1956), p. 144.

was bitter, and he was anxious to vindicate his administration and his faith. He was bitter at Roosevelt's insouciant hedge-hopping, at what he considered to be misrepresentation of his record, at a candidate who seemed to get his speeches from an assembly line of ghost-writers. He was bitter at the easy manner he could not match, the flippant tone which seemed to make sport of a deadly crisis, and at the artful attacks on the concept of individualism to which he was so deeply committed. He saw all about him the grim threat of socialism—in the loose promises of his arrogant opponent, in the violence that whipped across the prairies, in the bonus mob which had clamored at the very gates of the White House.

He carried much of the attack alone. He chose to do it in a way that left him exhausted, stumbling, humorless, grumpy. He wrote his own speeches—nine of them—in longhand. He worked far into the nights, worrying incessantly about the affairs of state that he must manage while Roosevelt was free to carp and caper. He seemed to carry the entire weight of the world crisis on his own sturdy, competent shoulders, but he neared collapse as he stumbled through speech after speech, almost pathetically sincere, doggedly determined, before a nation which would not listen.

At times he nearly threw Roosevelt off balance. During his second western trip, F.D.R. had fallen into mentioning Hoover by name, answering some of his charges, ridiculing others. Sometimes the technique worked, as in Baltimore, when he reached far back into the days of Charles Evans Hughes to attack the " 'Four Horsemen' of the present Republican Leadership: The Horsemen of Destruction, Delay, Deceit, Despair . . . this 'Black Horse Cavalry.' " [8] But sometimes he nearly lost control. Having questioned Hoover's motives and intelligence, he was outraged when Hoover questioned his. Once in Boston Moley had to argue passionately to keep him from making the irate reply he had planned as he listened in wrath to a Hoover radio speech.

If it had been a campaign of logic, both candidates would

[8] Rosenman: *Public Papers,* I, p. 832.

have been disqualified: Hoover because his impeccable reason-
ing was based on abstract assumptions which had little rele-
vance to the crisis he faced; Roosevelt because his agile mind
jumped hither and yon to establish his "compromises" with his
conflicting advisors. It was a campaign of personalities, moods,
and sympathies. Roosevelt sensed this. He made himself the
symbol of confidence, determination, and action. His very uncertainty about specifics seemed to promise moderation, balance, and careful evolution of policies. Meanwhile Hoover
seemed the prototype of stuffy inaction, fatigue, irresolution,
rigidity to principle, inadequacy in action. Hoover, the immensely sensitive human personality, appeared to the world as
a prophet of dogma, insensitive to crying human need. Roosevelt, the gay, secure, often careless aristocrat, worked his way
into the hearts of millions with a smile, a gesture, and a promise
of deep concern.

Hoover was defending a blueprint of society which he feared
would be repudiated. F.D.R. was enlisting the confidence,
enthusiasm, and faith which the new administration must have.
In Boston on October 31 he stated: "We are through with
'Delay'; we are through with 'Despair'; we are ready, and waiting for better things. . . ." [9] In New York on November 3:
". . . we want to get for the American people two great human
values—work and security. To achieve this end I invite you all.
It is no mere party slogan. It is a definition of national need. It
is a philosophy of life." [1] In Madison Square Garden two days
later: "The next Administration must represent not a fraction of
the United States, but all of the United States. No resources of
mind or heart or organization can be excluded in the fight
against what is, after all, our real enemy. Our real enemies are
hunger, want, insecurity, poverty and fear. Against these there
is no glory in a victory only partisan." [2]

At Hyde Park on election eve Roosevelt was jubilant over the
coming victory, suddenly sober at the monumental challenge he
had worked so long to face. The next night he would sit for
hours in the Biltmore Hotel, checking the returns with his
closest friends and staff members. Only Louis Howe was miss-

[9] Ibid., I, p. 855.   [1] Ibid., I, p. 860.   [2] Ibid., I, p. 862.

ing. Strangely but typically, in this moment of impending crisis, Louis was full of gloom, not even now trusting the pleasures of self-confidence. He sat in his deserted headquarters among the tag-ends of the campaign he had planned for years. Grace Howe had come down from Fall River, fresh from her months of work as a director of the Roosevelt-Garner Committee and a key worker in the local campaign. Hartley was there to help him celebrate the victory. But Louis could only smoke and growl and hope as he nervously watched the isolated early leads of the Republicans. When at last he was convinced of victory, there was a quiet family celebration before he was finally pushed across the street to join the jubilant mob. Louis hated to be in the limelight, although he yearned for it. But standing on the platform in the ballroom of the Biltmore with his beloved Franklin and Jim Farley, he could secretly revel in the words of the man whom he had helped become President. "There are two people in the United States more than anybody else who are responsible for this great victory," said Roosevelt. "One is my old friend and associate, Colonel Louis McHenry Howe, and the other is that splendid American, Jim Farley." [3]

[3] *Time,* XX (November 21, 1932).

24

>>>->>>->>>->>>->>>->>>->>>->>>

Preparing
for the Challenge

I am just a handy man. . . .
(Louis Howe, *1933*) [1]

THE LOWERING SKIES and the chill March winds could throw no damper on the thousands of exuberant Democrats who crowded Washington to cheer and gawk at Franklin Roosevelt's inauguration. For weeks to come they would mob the Post Office auditorium, thirsting for recognition after 12 years of Republican hegemony, pressing their claims on Jim Farley's hopelessly slim patronage list. Yet for the millions who waited by their radio sets to hear the new President's speech, for the other millions who had somehow struggled through a ghastly winter without work, this was a time of testing, a moment of uneasy hope held carefully in check by skepticism learned of hardship.

The scene on the Capitol steps was a link with the past: the

[1] Quoted in Jerome Beatty: "Here's Howe," *American Magazine*, CXV (March 1933), p. 69.

grave, bearded Chief Justice who himself had so narrowly missed this prime honor 16 years before; the unusually solemn Roosevelt bending stiffly to kiss the ancient Dutch Bible of his ancestors; the rows of lifted faces stretching across the plaza to the Library of Congress; the expectant tension of the moment. But the speech itself was a call to arms, a promise of hope, a link to the future. Roosevelt and his aides had caught the mood precisely, the mood of confidence they had worked to build and preserve through the harried, dangerous months.

That winter, depression had stalked more deeply each day into the heart of America. Hoover's desperate hope that the corner had been turned had been cruelly shattered by the vaulting unemployment statistics, by the rumbling undertones of discontent which broke into evil maelstroms of violence. In the farm country the accelerating tempo of the mobs hinted of revolution. On the city streets one could read the dangerous impatience of despair in hungry, hopeless faces. Governors and Mayors, bankers and industrialists whispered uneasily of "Red Armies," of the need for toughness. The financial system of the whole nation seemed on the edge of collapse; on February 14 the Governor of Michigan closed his State's banks.

Roosevelt had sensed the explosive quality of the moment. During the campaign he had confided to a friend that he thought Huey Long and Douglas MacArthur the most dangerous men in the country—the prototype of the demagogue and the prototype of military authority. These men represented the hideous alternatives to which a nation might turn from its agony of inaction. Eleanor Roosevelt noted soberly that the greatest inaugural applause was for her husband's guarded promise that, if Congress did not accept the challenge, he *would* act. On February 15 in Miami F.D.R. himself had lived through a moment that made starkly clear how close the nation was to that margin where irrational accident could spark disaster. Joe Zangara, the pain-crazed psychotic who sprayed Roosevelt's car with bullets, had narrowly missed killing the President-elect. As Roosevelt drove toward the hospital cradling the fatally wounded Tony Cermak in his arms, he displayed that masterly discipline with which he was to face the crises of a nation as firmly as he had the senseless, unexpected brush with death.

Yet Roosevelt had done little to relieve the tension of that bitter winter. No period of transition had been so potently fateful since the country had waited through four critical months for the inauguration of Abraham Lincoln. Hoover, the President with responsibilities but with little power and no prestige, worked unhappily to the point of exhaustion. He sought to solve the problems of the European debt defaults, of the mounting bank crisis, and of the shattered economy; he sought to blueprint an international economic conference. But Europeans knew he could not carry through. There was no whip to lash the politically bloodthirsty lame-duck Congress. His strong faith in individualism continued to impose limits on possible government action. In desperation he turned for aid to the President-elect. Roosevelt was polite, concerned—he came three times to Washington to confer—but he was adamant. He would not dissipate on the Hoover administration the public confidence he must have to launch his own programs. He would not bind himself to policies he had not evolved and could not manage. He would not precipitate a premature Congressional battle that might lay his own house in shambles before it was well founded. And personal bitterness made it hard for the two men to talk, impossible for them to trust each other. Roosevelt thought Hoover was trying to saddle him with repudiated policies; Hoover thought Roosevelt was playing politics with the nation's security. In any case, co-operation was impossible. Roosevelt had not evolved his own policies, and insofar as he had commitments, they clashed sharply with Hoover's. Hoover wanted a blueprint now; Roosevelt wanted freedom to experiment. Hoover believed the solution lay abroad; Roosevelt was convinced that recovery must come first at home.

What Roosevelt did do, with monumental success, was to preserve the faith which vague commitment or partial action might have shattered. No President-elect had received so spontaneous a vote of confidence. Almost 500,000 people had sat down to write their enthusiastic response to his victory: on the stationery of business and labor organizations, on bond paper expensively engraved with coats of arms and well-known initials, on the modestly impressive paper of the New York clubs, and on lined and porous sheets torn from dime-store pads. In their enthusiasm lay a challenge made even more urgent by the terrifying drift of events that winter. The smiles that lighted millions of faces as the call to action boomed in firm accents through the nation's radios were for a man and a mood that promised to wrench victory from the very teeth of disaster. The millions knew he would do something and do it well. But not even Roosevelt knew precisely what he would do.

As he turned from the reviewing stand for the "family party" at which his cabinet were sworn in, the new President faced terrifying disabilities. Despite all the mobs of Democrats roaming the Washington streets and milling about in expensive and sweaty confusion at the three Inaugural Balls, his administration at the moment consisted of a mere handful of men. A corporal's guard, they were suddenly in technical command of a vast bureaucracy staffed with civil servants and Coolidge and Hoover appointees. Yet he must take prompt action in the banking crisis. The new Congress was already divided and confused. Some wanted inflation, some a sound gold dollar. Some wanted a 30-hour week, some employment guaranteed. Some looked for a new Mussolini, some for a new Jefferson. Roosevelt's own advisors were a warring rabble playing for position, swamping him with their bickering advice. For them the months between the election and the inauguration had been a nightmare of insecurity and confusion. Working hectically to build a skeleton staff, they had worried about their own futures, worried about the tangled web of ideas that spun in giddy confusion around Roosevelt's desk, worried about the studied carelessness of their ebullient boss who seemed able to relax with such disconcerting ease at Warm Springs and on Vincent Astor's yacht.

Moley was a case in point. Uncertain whether he wanted to be in Washington, still yearning vaguely for the classroom, he suddenly found himself the "packhorse" of the Roosevelt train. Fighting against an appointment as Assistant Secretary of State

—a mere cover for his destined role as advisor to Roosevelt—
he promised himself that he would stay only for a few days,
then only for a month. Yet the prospects were intriguing. The
brain trust had been dissolved, as Moley had planned it should
be. He worked without the limits which Tugwell, Berle, and
Johnson had provided. They had joined the growing throng
who showered Roosevelt with memos and notes and privately
drafted the bills they hoped would fill the vacuum on March 4.
There seemed no one but Moley to give direction to all this, to
put some organization into the guerrilla army of idea men. He
had aimed to get as much legislation as he could through the
lame-duck session, so that Roosevelt could have six or
seven easy weeks for settling into the White House. The boss
had already assigned economy-minded Swagar Sherley and
Lewis Douglas to work on the budget. Now Moley brought together Wallace, Tugwell, Morgenthau, and M. L. Wilson to
draft a farm program. He set Berle and others to work on
mortgage relief and transportation. He assigned Samuel Un-
termyer and Charles Taussig to work on securities legislation.

Nevertheless, there were rude shocks in store for Moley.
Congress produced nothing but bickering; Roosevelt refused
to intervene, except for a haphazard attempt to marshal votes
for unemployment relief. Much of Moley's time went into fruitless tilting with Hoover. Worse yet, Moley recognized for the
first time the essence of the Roosevelt management technique.
The boss would consult people with several points of view, trust
no one completely, and hold the reins firmly in his own hands.
Moley had assumed that he was "*de facto* minister for the moment"; [2] he soon learned that he was only one among many.
Many times in the next three months he would be exasperated
to find that Roosevelt had given the same job to three, four, or
five different men or groups of men. He put this down to absent-
mindedness. But with Roosevelt it was purposeful. This technique could provide a busy President with the crosscurrents
of thought which the brain trust had afforded in a simpler day.
It defined the alternatives for his personal decision; it left his

[2] Moley: *After Seven Years,* p. 83.

staff in healthy insecurity. No one made Roosevelt's decisions
now, not even Louis Howe.

But there were times during that fall and winter when Moley
was convinced that Howe had more authority than he should.
Louis himself was uneasy about Moley's influence and his own
position. Despite 20 years with Roosevelt he could not allow
himself the pleasures of security. He must have known that
Roosevelt would have a place for him, yet he could joke uneasily after election: "I guess I've worked myself out of a job." [3]
F.D.R. himself said lightly: "The only job that Louis really
wants is to be an Admiral. When we were in the Navy Department, he was furious because many navy officers made him
stand back to let them enter the elevator first. He wants to be an
admiral so he can go down there and push them all out of the
way." [4] Farley was convinced that Roosevelt never bothered to
tell Howe that he would be Secretary to the President. Louis
may have been posing for Farley, but there were deep reasons
for his fears. Roosevelt's affairs had mushroomed so that no one
person could hope to keep track of all. And Louis was seriously
limited in the role he could play. He had none of the social
philosophy or crusading spirit to match a Tugwell, a Johnson,
or a Wallace at policy-making. He could not build a personal bailiwick as head of a department, like a Harold Ickes or
Frances Perkins. He no longer had the stamina to handle the
President's appointments or press relations; these tough jobs
went to the aides they had groomed for many years, Marvin
McIntyre and Stephen Early. And his position in the Roosevelt
camp had subtly and dangerously changed. For 20 years he had
been above the broiling rivalries of lesser Roosevelt aides and
advisors. Now he found himself fighting as sharply as Moley in
the battle for Roosevelt's mind and power; for the first time
he was in peril of being identified with one faction instead of
managing them all from above.

Throughout the four months of transition Louis had consistently supported the conservatives in Roosevelt's camp. If

[3] Edwin C. Hill: "The Human Side of the News," *Boston American*,
May 31, 1933.

[4] Beatty: "Here's Howe," p. 69.

Howe had had his way, the cabinet would have contained
Owen D. Young of General Electric and Carter Glass of the
conservative Virginia machine, as well as Cordell Hull, whom
Roosevelt did support. There would have been no Ickes, no
Henry Wallace. His motives were mixed, and largely it was
politics he had in mind. For 20 years he had viewed issues and
men as raw materials for putting Franklin in the White
House; now he saw them as tools to use for keeping him there.
He knew better than most the sad fragmentation of the Democratic Party, the broad differences of opinion throughout the
country. He had, like most old Progressives, a commitment
against Wall Street. But, as someone noted, he would have
bowed to J. P. Morgan three times a day if that had been
necessary to advance Franklin's career. Now he feared the extreme opinions, the reckless experimentation of his new allies.
He thought men like Henry Wallace too radical, the old Bull
Moose Republicans who had trooped into camp practically useless. When someone suggested Ickes for a major post, Louis
growled: "There isn't any such name!" Although, in fact, he
had himself enlisted Ickes's co-operation in the campaign.[5]

His own progressivism was romantic, vague, vestigial of the
Teddy Roosevelt-Hughes days. He broke through his customary
caution when he told a Columbia University audience in January that the new administration would be "liberal without being
crazy." In more detail than he had ever dared before, he promised:

> There will be . . . less government in business and less
> business in government. . . . Governor Roosevelt believes
> in keeping the different functions of government separated.
> He believes that the legislative, executive, and judiciary
> branches of the government should keep to their particu-
> lar places. . . . Eventually, I think, I hope, that the voters
> of the country will have taken a natural division of thought,
> and we will have a government where liberals will stay in

[5] Quoted in Raymond Moley: 27 Masters of Politics in a Personal Perspective (New York: Funk and Wagnalls; 1949), p. 139; Henry Wallace
to Author, December 6, 1961.

power until they get radical and conservatives will have the power until they become reactionary.[6]

Roosevelt had sounded like this on occasion in the past. But Louis had never before gone to the public as he did now in casting his vote against the Tugwells, the Berles, and the Wallaces of his boss's army.

Yet Howe had certain assets which none of his colleagues in the loose Roosevelt organization possessed. He knew Roosevelt better than anyone else; he saw him more frequently and without witnesses; he could talk with F.D.R. about anything at any time. He could sense the boss's direction more quickly than others. And, as Roosevelt well knew, he was a skillful critic. He had his own weakness for an occasional flashy idea, but he and Roosevelt were seldom enthusiastic about the same one. And he knew his main value was in being able to "sit on Franklin's toes."[7] His last words to John Garner, at the end of his life, were: "Hold Franklin Down."[8] Most important, he had Roosevelt's loyalty and understanding. His White House job was soon tailored to his strengths and limitations.

As *the* Secretary to the President, Louis was given an inside office where he did not have to meet the public but would be immediately available to the boss at all times. Roosevelt was sensitive to Howe's thin sensibilities. McIntyre and Early were commissioned *Assistant* Secretaries although, in fact, they were supreme in their special fields. F.D.R. did nothing to dispel the myth that Louis was the mastermind of the regime. In fact, the President delighted in promoting Howe's passionate anonymity. The mystery of his position, the intimacy, the President's evident respect for him, set Louis free to meddle wherever he wished. As he had been for 20 years, he remained Franklin's trouble shooter. In the end he was both more influential than he might have been expected to be and less influential by far than he wanted to be.

[6] *The New York Times,* January 18, 1933.

[7] Beatty: "Here's Howe," p. 69.

[8] Quoted in John Gunther: *Roosevelt in Retrospect* (New York: Harper and Brothers; 1950), p. 85.

All this became clear in the hectic months before the inauguration. At first Louis had trouble adjusting to the new shape of things. He continued relentlessly to use the letter-writing machinery. As the letters piled up by the hundreds for Roosevelt to sign, the harried boss wrote him tartly: ". . . this business must stop! . . . What I do want is this . . . 'The Governor has asked me to convey' etc. . . ."[9] But Louis insisted that, some way or other, every letter of congratulation must be answered.

He learned more about his restrictions in the heady business of cabinet-making. Roosevelt warned him at once that no one would make commitments except the President. But Louis shopped, maneuvered, and conspired eagerly, soon discovering that he must share even this job with Moley, Farley, Flynn, and O'Connor. Outside this charmed circle there was relentless pressure from all sides. And they worked within complex limits set by Roosevelt himself. The familiar prescription would be honored—balance, recognition of the faithful in the For Roosevelt Before Chicago Club, careful investigation to prevent future embarrassments—but there was more: this would be no back-shelf cabinet of prominent but useless characters. He wanted men he liked working with. There would be no has-beens to bring the taint of past defeats—no Coxes, Smiths, or McAdoos. And he must be the first President to appoint a woman to the cabinet.

Louis undertook at once to manage the State Department appointment. He wanted Cordell Hull, whose dignity and caution he admired and whose claim on their gratitude was boundless. Roosevelt was not difficult to persuade, though Moley and several Senators objected. Hull, they said, knew nothing of foreign policy except for the "one string" on his bow, reciprocal trade.[1] This may have seemed an asset to a President who intended to run his own foreign affairs. Louis worked to pave the way. He undertook to line up Roosevelt's old friend William Phillips as Under Secretary to relieve the Hulls of expensive entertaining. When newsmen spread the rumor that Moley was being placed in the State Department to keep an eye on Hull,

[9] Roosevelt to Howe, December 14, 1932, Group XVIII, FDRL.
[1] Moley: *After Seven Years*, p. 114.

Louis deftly blocked Moley's effort to explain. He would have
no public airing of the humiliating fact that Hull was to provide a title and office space for Roosevelt's personal advisor.
Louis investigated personally the background and qualifications of Sumner Welles, whom Roosevelt intended for Assistant
Secretary for Latin American Affairs, and smoothed Secretary
Hull's ruffled feathers at not being consulted in the choice of
his own assistants. But Louis also played a dangerous game with
this most important of posts by using it to pay a political debt.
Owen D. Young was given to understand that *he* could be
Secretary of State. Young pleaded his wife's illness and quietly
refused. The debt was paid without damage, yet the fact remained that Louis had been willing to risk the prospect of a big
business executive in the premier cabinet post.

Much of this elaborate game was played out while Roosevelt
was cruising along the coast. Moley and Howe kept in touch
with him by radio messages, sent in code to confuse any eavesdropping newsman. The Treasury appointment proved complex. Roosevelt's and Howe's choice was the aged Carter Glass,
the Senate's financial expert since Wilson days. Glass kept them
in suspense for weeks while he sought a bargain to commit
Roosevelt against inflation and to insure the appointment of the
Morgan Bank's Russell Leffingwell as Under Secretary. Roosevelt dodged on inflation; on Leffingwell he was adamant. He
liked this old personal friend, but he could not afford the Morgan taint. Louis was deeply distressed, although he recouped
rapidly when Moley bounced into his Madison Avenue office
one afternoon to suggest William Woodin. Howe was delighted
to find here a man who was both a loyal Roosevelt partisan
and a sop to the "big boys" of business. Roosevelt agreed, but
Glass kept meddling in the matter, pushing for another favorite,
Swagar Sherley. Howe and Moley finally had to invent a code
to warn the absent Roosevelt of what was going on: "Prefer a
wooden roof to a glass roof over swimming pool. Luhowray." [2]

Some appointments were easily arranged, growing naturally
from the unspoken commitments of Roosevelt and Howe during

[2] Quoted in ibid., pp. 121–2.

the pre-Convention campaign: Thomas J. Walsh for Attorney
General (Homer Cummings would succeed him when the
Senator died, hours before inauguration); Claude Swanson for
the Navy (it was essential to make way for Virginia's Harry
Byrd in the Senate); George Dern of Utah to represent the
West (he ended up in the War Department, after everything
else had been arranged); Frances Perkins for Secretary of Labor;
Farley for Postmaster General. But here Louis undertook to
meddle. He pressed on Farley the more lucrative Collectorship
of the Port of New York. Was he really concerned about Jim's
flattened pocketbook or was he trying to keep his friendly
rival out of Washington?

Often it was Roosevelt himself who frustrated Louis's elaborate plans. Howe was angry when the Commerce job went to
McAdoo-man Daniel C. Roper. Roper was an old friend, but
Louis had practically told Jesse Straus the post was his for the
asking. Key Pittman had to be denied a cabinet post because
he was more useful on the Senate Foreign Relations Committee.
Louis was incensed when Roosevelt personally reserved Interior and Agriculture for the western progressive Republicans,
yet he loyally pitched in to help land Hiram Johnson or Senator Bronson Cutting, only to be enraged when the boss chose
Harold Ickes "on impulse" [3] after the briefest of conversations
and then stubbornly refused to discuss the matter. Wallace was
just as bad from Louis's point of view, but Tugwell argued for
him and Roosevelt had been deeply impressed by the Iowa
editor's talk during the campaign. In consequence, Louis
had to salve the hurt feelings of their old friend Henry Morgenthau, Jr., denied the post despite all his efficient hard work on
New York's farm problems.

Meanwhile Louis was swamped with a welter of work on details. He checked the status of the various commissions, advising Roosevelt which positions must be filled and which could be
left for the moment. He worked out arrangements for the Governors' Conference which would be held in Washington shortly
after the inauguration. He studied the White House staff lists

[3] Moley: *27 Masters,* p. 139.

to make room for their own aides. By later standards it was a small personal entourage: Missy, Rabbit, Tommy, and Tully— Margaret LeHand and Grace Tully to work for the President, Margaret Durand for Howe, and Malvina Thompson for Mrs. Roosevelt. There were sentimental touches. Howe brought over from the Navy Department their old Negro messenger of World War days. With Louis, McIntyre, Early, and retired Admiral Christian Peoples, the White House would look for the moment as if they had just moved over from the old Navy Building across the way.

They were all swamped with the task of making a mass of lesser appointments. Many were put off, after a Warm Springs conference in which they decided to use patronage as a lever with Congress, but much of their difficulty lay with the reluctant appointees. An amazing number of hard-working Roosevelt campaigners wanted no part of the hectic confusion of government responsibility. Rosenman insisted on remaining in New York to pursue the judgeship on which his heart was set. Tugwell was happy to be Assistant Secretary of Agriculture, Johnson would soon find a place in the yet-unsketched N.R.A., but Berle resisted the blandishments of department positions that would steal him from scholarship and teaching. Frankfurter refused to be Solicitor General. Like Ed Flynn, he delighted in influence and hated entanglement in administration. He would prefer being advisor and master employment manager for young lawyers seeking government jobs. Vincent Astor, Frank Murphy, Frank Walker, all refused appointments. Joseph P. Kennedy was reluctant, but others proved too anxious, and here the embassies proved useful. Jesse Straus went to Paris, Breckenridge Long to Rome, and Claude Bowers to Spain, where he could write in leisure and dignity. Jim Curley was neatly sidetracked from exercising influence with a polite offer of the Ambassadorship to Poland. He didn't want it, but he could not well resent it.

For Louis McHenry Howe there were deep rewards in these crowded months before the crisis. He still buried himself in work and worry; he still prowled about his cluttered office and wandered the crowded, lonely streets at night before he sought retreat in his room with its dim lights and relieving incense. He still found comfort in his endless Sweet Caporals, his endless small bets on the horses. But now for the first time he seemed to the world to be an important person. After years of seeking space in the columns of the austere *Times*, it was exhilarating to have Adolph Ochs's feature writers pounding up 65th Street to interview him, to probe his early life, to arrange his formal portrait for the Sunday supplements. He took care with the image he created for them. Forgotten were the sad, hard days in Saratoga, the abortive years with Osborne. The dailies painted saccharine pictures of his dogged devotion and self-sacrifice and suggested artfully that his influence knew no limits. The despairing, part-time reporter of 1910 was billed as a successful, experienced editor and newspaper owner.

He still had his sense of humor. He could laugh, as he had in 1931 when Roosevelt gave him a formal certificate of appointment—"Louis McHenry Howe, General Goat." [4] He could be flip when reporters, that same year, gave him a tin sword and cocked hat in honor of his Kentucky Colonelcy. He took ghoulish delight in the adjectives newsmen spun out to describe his careless dress and quaint physiognomy. He gleefully answered the phone for days as "the mediaeval gnome," [5] after Edward G. Hill tagged that label on him. When *The New Yorker* ran a profile of him in the spring of 1932, he wired Eleanor Roosevelt: ". . . have sent the grey suit to be pressed. The tie is a slander. . . ." [6]

Yet there was a new pride now. Despite his jokes he subtly encouraged the growing practice of calling him "Colonel Howe." He carefully fed the story about his passion for anonymity. He was especially careful about his dress and appearance. Reporters and friends were fond of gossiping behind his back that he looked like a comic-strip character in striped pants and morning coat and winged collar, but for Louis there was no nonsense in this. He was aware of the funny figure he cut. He could still joke grimly with reporters that he and Mrs. Roosevelt were running a contest to see which could find the ugliest news

[4] Personal Papers.   [5] *Boston American*, May 31, 1933.
[6] Howe to Eleanor Roosevelt, April 25, 1932, Group XXXVI, FDRL.

photo of himself. But he also knew that a secretary to the President ought to look the part. When he sat for his formal portrait or stood in full-dress outfit beside Franklin Roosevelt at formal dinners, there were no Sweet Caporal ashes drifting aimlessly down his white vest front.

He allowed himself no smile of triumph in public, but he took a quiet glee in the recognition that flooded his way. There was no mistaking his profound feeling of satisfaction when the Executive Committee of the Democratic Finance Committee presented him and Farley with enormous loving cups in recognition of their achievement, or when he joined F.D.R., Farley, Garner, Walker, and Moley at a dinner for the President-elect given by the National Press Club. His office was flooded with telegrams and letters congratulating him personally. If he ever needed his innate sense of modesty and inadequacy to hold him in check, he needed it now. His correspondence told him over and over again that he had been the real wire-puller at Chicago, that he had made a President. Phrases like "Warwick," "Colonel House," "President-maker," sugar-coated the letters of transparent flattery. Even Frank Polk's personal note implied a compliment: "My heart bleeds for Franklin and yourself, for what the office seekers will do to you both will be nobody's business." [7]

Perhaps most welcome were the notes from the handful of people who knew how far he had come in 20 years, how much of a struggle it had been. Grace's cousin, a Vassar College librarian, assured Louis that only his motives were beyond question among the ambitious men around Roosevelt.[8] His nephew, who had grown up with him in the Regent Street house, asked now what more could a man want than having helped to give the nation F.D.R.[9] His boyhood friend, Clare Knapp, remembering graphically the hungry years of haunting the printing offices for jobs, wrote two days after election: "It was swell and were I near you I should be tempted to place a light, chaste kiss on that leather—or should I say leathern—map of

[7] Frank Polk to Howe, November 18, 1932, Personal Papers.
[8] Fanny Borden to Howe, November 20, 1932, Personal Papers.
[9] Harry M. Hall to Howe, March 13, 1933, Group XXXVI, FDRL.

yours. Jack Walbridge mentioned the fact that you were a former *Saratogian,* so what more can you ask . . . ?" [1]

Louis knew his role precisely, and if he was ever swept off his feet by the flattery, it was only for a moment. Yet sometimes he did seem to slip in his adjustment to this new and strangely public life. He accepted two speaking engagements during the interim. His radio talk in February on prohibition and crime went well and caused no trouble. He carefully checked his facts with government agencies in advance. His radio voice proved surprisingly dignified, deep, and impressive. But his speech to the School of Journalism at Columbia proved a dangerous blunder. He forgot himself so much as to be frank and bitter. Inviting the students to crusade for clean and efficient government, he attacked the subservience of rural newspapers with a zeal and venom drawn deeply from his own experience. And he shocked the nation with his unparalleled display of directness: "You can't adopt politics as a profession and remain honest. If you are going to make your living out of politics, you can't do it honestly." He went on to explain that you had to have an independent income to avoid the temptations of privilege and power. But *The Times* featured headlines: "Politics as Career Assailed by Howe. Roosevelt's Advisor Declares an Honest Living Cannot be Made from it." [2] Within a week his desk was scattered with clippings: from New Bedford, the question: "What about Coolidge, Al Smith and Roosevelt himself?" From Fort Wayne, the hint that when Howe said F.D.R.'s administration would be "liberal without being crazy" he had illustrated nicely his charge that you couldn't be honest in politics. [3] No one knows what Roosevelt said to him.

The rewards were many and varied. Louis could now sit happily at the Legislative Correspondents' Dinner in Albany, the butt of many of the sketches rather than the anonymous author of them. He would find a cartoon in the program show-

---

[1] Clarence Knapp to Howe, November 10, 1932, Personal Papers.

[2] *The New York Times,* January 18, 1933.

[3] *New Bedford Standard-Times,* January 25, 1933; *Fort Wayne News-Sentinel,* January 23, 1933.

ing Louis and Franklin fussing over the cabinet: "Plenty of Pieces But They Don't Fit." He would enjoy even the snide probing in the "Lehman Lullaby":

> *Oh, Frankin D., you'll say has charms*
> *On which we ever love to dote—Oh*
> *I'd like to take this deficit*
> *And cram it down his precious throat.*[4]

There must have been real satisfaction, although he spoke of it to no one, in the honors that came to Grace Howe in the wake of his victory. In January Grace was elected Secretary of the Massachusetts State Committee. More important was the new prestige which their role in the inauguration sharply sketched. Only he, Grace, Hartley, Mary, and her husband were to share the seventh-floor wing of the Mayflower Hotel with the Roosevelts and their family. And Grace Howe in Fall River received a personal note from the future First Lady which outlined their busy Inauguration Day. Would she and her children join them at prayers in St. John's church at 10:15? Would they lunch and have tea at the White House and be with the President in the reviewing stand? Would she join Eleanor at the Ball that evening? And on Sunday would they come to the same church they all used to attend together? [5]

Louis would hardly have been noticed, unless you looked for him, as his beloved Franklin read the Inaugural Speech. His slight, almost pathetic figure in unaccustomed formal clothes was tucked away in the Capitol stands among physically bigger and more prominent men. But Louis did not intend to go unnoticed. The one symbol of his new prestige which he allowed himself was a sand-brown Lincoln roadster. This car betrayed both the thirst for recognition and the nonchalant sporting air which he coveted but so often repressed. He would never drive it much. Illness would keep him from behind the wheel —one old friend insists the car was so big that Louis could never see through the windshield. But on many a sunny afternoon

---

[4] "Foam, Sweet Foam," Program, Albany Legislative Correspondents' Dinner, February 23, 1933, FDRL.

[5] Eleanor Roosevelt to Grace Howe, February 23, 1933, Personal Papers.

Eleanor Roosevelt would take time out to drive him about town or through the Virginia countryside in this gaudy symbol of his achievement. And it would become the wonder of Horseneck Beach when Louis arrived there with his White House chauffeur. But the real satisfactions for this nervous, worried little man were the challenges of more work and more mystery and the quiet sense of power. There was practically no precedent for his role.

Louis McHenry Howe would sit in guarded seclusion at the right hand of power. Louis Howe would live in the room Abraham Lincoln had used. The small-town boy from Saratoga would drift easily into the President's bedroom in the morning, squat carelessly at the bottom of the bed and swap gossip, arguments, blunt and cynical jokes with the President of the United States. Louis Howe would drift like a mysterious wraith through the White House. Some strong men feared him; others knew they must deal with him. Little went on without the touch of Louis Howe's gnarled, experienced hands.

25

Trouble Shooter
in the White House

> *His hand will appear for an instant, al-
> most haphazardly, in the most unexpected
> situation. He seems to roam at random.
> He alludes to himself as "the dirty job
> man." He takes onto his shoulders trouble-
> some affairs which fit in no one's else de-
> partment. . . .*
>
> (Ernest K. Lindley, 1933) [1]

SOMEHOW the promise was turned to action in 100 days of
more excitement, more confusion, more heady intoxication than
sophisticated Washington had ever known. In the quality of
its tenseness, it was like the fateful weeks when Lincoln faced
the rebel armies across the open Potomac with a hostile Maryland behind him. But there was a difference—Roosevelt's
Washington was a city alive with the excitement of hope and

---

[1] Ernest K. Lindley: *The Roosevelt Revolution: First Phase* (New York:
Viking Press; 1933), p. 291.

filled with ideas. The Roosevelt crusade had drawn to Washington an army of idea men such as the cynical old Capital had never before entertained. Perhaps it was partly F.D.R.'s suspicion of the tired party hacks that did it; more likely it was the unparalleled invitation to experiment which his speeches had contained. Whatever the cause, F.D.R.'s captains found hundreds of eager recruits from the law schools and the universities, from business and journalism, falling over each other to fill the gaping ranks of the administration. Their pockets bulging with memoranda, even with drafts of proposed legislation, they worked night after night to fill in the preliminary sketch of Roosevelt's New Deal. On Capitol Hill wide-eyed new Democrats and hardened oldsters jostled each other with a score of prescriptions for depression, a hundred pet projects which victory must now bring to fulfillment.

The first steps had been planned largely by Moley and Woodin on the eve of the inauguration itself: the closing of the banks throughout the nation and the proclamation controlling gold exports. The orders were issued after a cabinet meeting Sunday afternoon. Congress would meet on Thursday, March 9. Woodin and Moley had until then to find a permanent solution for the momentarily propped-up financial structure. It was typical of the new mood that Roosevelt placed public confidence first, reform second; that Republican Treasury officials stayed on to work in a team with Woodin and Moley; that Roosevelt eschewed nationalization of the banks and dictated co-operation with the bankers themselves. While harried Treasury officials kept at their incessant calls to check the health of the nation's banks, Woodin and his advisors came up with a plan for enlarging the money supply through new Federal Reserve Notes rather than the widely suspected printing-press money, for controlling the flow of gold, and for reopening those banks that were solvent and liquid and the careful liquidation of those that could not open. On Thursday afternoon, March 9, Congress rushed the bill through with hysterical enthusiasm and with only a typed copy. In eight hours it was law.

All thought of adjournment in the crisis was now gone. The enthusiasm was too important to waste. In any case, the

13,000,000 unemployed and the collapsing farm economy would not wait. While Senator Hugo Black pushed for a 30-hour week and Senators Costigan and La Follette pressed again for direct relief payments, the products of Moley's informal interim committees were finding their way into legislative hoppers. Wallace's group came up with a formula for agriculture, Berle's task force produced drafts of securities and transportation regulations, a score of ambitious idea men worked at the amorphous concept which emerged as N.R.A. And Lewis Douglas, now Director of the Budget, rode herd on the balanced-budget clique who prepared the Economy Bill which the President commended to Congress on Friday, March 10. Wallace and Tugwell were implementing the Topeka farm speech; Berle and Johnson were spelling out the new pattern of regulation which F.D.R. had forecast in his San Francisco Commonwealth Club Address. Douglas was Pittsburgh-minded. And Roosevelt? He happily planned to follow all the leads of his campaign, to have action and planning, and to have economy too. When the time came, he would explain to the nation that you could have both a balanced and an unbalanced budget: balanced in the regular operations, momentarily unbalanced in the temporary emergencies of relief.

By the first of the second week the banks were reopening. There were signs of renewed confidence everywhere. But the Senate boggled badly at the economy bill, which lowered government salaries and threatened major cuts in veterans' pensions. The only hope lay in lightning action. If the veterans' lobby were given time to catch its breath, no Congress could withstand it. Roosevelt's prescription was an inspired bit of the kind of offhand action which Moley so much feared and Howe so much loved. At the White House supper table on Sunday night F.D.R. talked the problem over with Howe and finally said: "I think this would be a good time for beer." [2] This was an inevitable step, which Congressional Democrats would greet with hoops of joy. But it was the timing that counted. Louis scurried out to get a copy of the Democratic platform.

[2] Quoted in ibid., p. 91.

Together they worked out Roosevelt's brief message requesting the legalization of light wine and beer by redefinition of the amount of alcohol that "non-intoxicating beverages" might contain.

That night Roosevelt went to the people with his first Fireside Chat. Speech-writing was still in its infancy in the White House. This one evolved from a draft sent over by Charlie Michelson at Democratic headquarters. But then Roosevelt had stretched out on a couch and quietly dictated the finished Chat himself, trying desperately to visualize the ordinary people who would hear it. Sometimes he said he had been thinking of his farmer friends back in Hyde Park; sometimes he said it had been written for the workmen outside his window tearing down the reviewing stand. But people all over the country sensed it had been written for them on this first quiet Sunday night of the New Deal. Will Rogers cracked that it explained banking in such simple terms that even bankers understood it. And the plea for help from all the people was inspired: "Let us unite in banishing fear. We have provided the machinery to restore our financial system; it is up to you to support it and make it work. It is your problem no less than it is mine. Together we cannot fail." [3]

On Monday morning a Senate sobered by the superb radio performance, its thirst whetted by the special message on beer, pushed the economy bill to the floor. By Wednesday, Beer and Economy had become law. And so the pace continued. Catching the mood of enthusiasm, Roosevelt and Howe pushed one of their own pet hobbies to the fore, and on March 31 the Civilian Conservation Corps was established to take young men off the cities' streets, to do something about the preservation of the forests and the land. On April 19 the nation left the gold standard, a gesture to Congressional inflationists, although the President himself would hesitate for months to use the new currency control powers he was given. In May the pace became dizzying: on the 12th came the Emergency Farm Mortgage Act; the F.E.R.A., a Federal relief system; and A.A.A.,

[3] Rosenman: *Public Papers,* II, p. 65.

385 *Trouble Shooter in the White House*

the Agricultural Adjustment Administration, with its mandate to set crop quotas, make benefit payments to farmers, and finance the elaborate plan by taxes on food processing that consumers would eventually pay. Shortly thereafter Jesse Jones's Reconstruction Finance Corporation, under pressure from the South and Roosevelt himself, would commence supporting cotton prices by making loans against the surplus. On May 18 George Norris's ancient dream was pushed through Congress easily with the President's enthusiastic support: a regional corporation for unified planned development of the Tennessee Valley resources, T.V.A. On the 27th the Truth-in-Securities Act; on June 5 the gold clauses in both private and government contracts and bonds abrogated, a further slip away from the old standard. On June 13, the Home Owners Loan Corporation, to refinance home mortgages. On one monumental day, June 16, the Railroad Coordination Act, the Farm Credit Act, the Glass-Steagall Banking Act, and the National Industrial Recovery Act. N.R.A. would prove the most challenging essay ever made at massive industrial planning without dictatorship. Built on an ideal concept of universal co-operation, it would prove the most monumental administrative and public relations task that Washington had ever faced. Eventually even the old tiger, Hugh Johnson, would flunk the test it posed. But for the moment its defiant Blue Eagle, soon plastered on store fronts and underwear, flaunted by gay, day-long parades, claimed by both unions and management, would be the symbol of a people determined to rise from the vortex of disaster.

In this welter of ideas, of ambitious, devoted, and bickering men, there was plenty of initiative and drive. But badly needed were traffic cops, amateur psychologists, and roving trouble shooters who could solve more problems than they raised. Inevitably Howe's personality and position pushed him into all three roles. For one thing, he could save immense amounts of time for his harried boss. As Jim Farley noted: ". . . he was able to take care of . . . many visitors who were content to see him instead of the Chief Executive because the close relationship between them was so well understood. Louie was an excellent 'buffer,' and his natural tendency to say 'no' and to turn over a proposition in his mind a thousand different times before giving his assent was a wise safeguard on many important occasions."[4] During the first harried year, he received scores of groups presenting demands to the President and sent them away reasonably happy. One case in point was the delegation of the Association of Unemployed College Alumni, which descended on the White House on May 4. Louis mustered his best paternal manner and lectured them gently, reminding them how much of their program was already part of the administration's plans. They went away talking about his "fatherly sermon."[5] A more brutal task, specifically assigned him by the President, was to quiet the mob which had been picketing the White House all day at the height of the tension over the Scottsboro case. While Colonel Ed Starling's Secret Service mingled with the picketers, Louis met their delegation and explained as best he could the limits of the President's influence. This sort of thing was his strong point. He had been anxiously heading off trouble for Franklin Roosevelt for 20 years.

His most successful coup was his handling of the new Bonus Army. Roosevelt could afford neither a second Battle of Anacostia Flats nor the indignity of a President haggling with a mob. He would not spike his economy program by giving in to their demands to restore reduced veterans' benefits to their original level. On April 29 Louis held in his hands a carefully worded letter from the "Veterans' Liaison Committee," explaining that the large groups then on their way to Washington from all over the country would be orderly and disciplined and "should be treated as any other group holding a Congress or Conference at the capital of the nation"[6]—but with one difference. The Committee "respectfully" requested that the government both house and feed this particular conference. Louis at first tried to persuade them to send a delegation of only 200 to represent the veterans back home. The Committee replied within three days that they knew this would not work and

[4] Farley: *Behind the Ballots,* p. 351.
[5] *New York Herald Tribune,* May 4, 1933.
[6] Veterans' National Liaison Committee to Roosevelt, April 29, 1933, Group XXXVI, FDRL.

asked a conference with District of Columbia officials to assure them that they would not be "molested or harassed" [7] by the police. Roosevelt now backed down, and Howe informed the Committee that facilities would be provided. Veterans' Administrator General Frank Hines was directed to set up a camp at Fort Hunt, Virginia, across the river, for 6,000 men, and Howe got a special executive order for him to cover expenses. Meanwhile the veterans protested that the V.A. must not be allowed to make a list of delegates and that they would govern themselves and guarantee order, discipline, and cleanliness.

While the new Bonus Marchers put on their demonstrations under the watchful eyes of a restrained Washington police force and presented their petitions to Congress, Louis cast about for a formula to break the jam. He and Roosevelt finally hit upon the new C.C.C. Louis quietly presented his veiled ultimatum to the Veterans' Committee. He would provide facilities at Fort Hunt for a few days more. If they wanted to stay longer, he could accommodate 1,200 enlistments for work in the Civilian Conservation Corps, and Fort Hunt would be turned into a training camp for them.

Meanwhile, he played his master card one rainy, muddy spring afternoon. He innocently asked Eleanor Roosevelt to take him for a drive. As they rode toward Fort Hunt, Louis explained that she was going to visit with the veterans for the afternoon. At the camp, Louis pushed her out to go it alone; he would stay in the car and sleep. He had no worries; he knew well both Eleanor Roosevelt's easy adaptability to challenge and the immense warmth of her human sympathy. It was no gamble to guess that, alone, she could break the tensions which a dozen official inspection parties would only sharpen. This sort of thing drove the Secret Service to anguish. Soon afterward they would give Louis two pistols, one for Eleanor and one for himself. Eleanor loyally carried hers, although she was always uncomfortable about it. Louis used his with elfin glee to wave in front of surprised visitors. But Eleanor Roosevelt needed no plainclothes man, no gun. As she quietly mingled

[7] Veterans' National Liaison Committee to Roosevelt, May 2, 1933, Group XXXVI, FDRL.

with the orderly mess lines and trooped into the hall to talk with
the old veterans while they ate, she was accepted, respected,
and welcomed with unconcealed surprise and with dignity.
The moment was nostalgic. She talked of France in 1919;
they sang the old war songs. She visited the hospital, poked
into some of the other buildings. Later someone said: "Hoover
sent the Army. Roosevelt sent his wife." [8]

Gradually the marchers dispersed, into the C.C.C. or back
home. Louis's secretary cheerfully wrote to Grace that he had
amazed official Washington with his handling of the veterans.[9]
In fact, it was so well done that it became a virtual invitation to
still another Bonus March in the spring of 1934. This time,
with the pressure off, Howe was sharper. The government had
decided in 1933, he told the "Provisional Rank and File Committee," that there would be no more free conventions at government expense. But he would make one last exception—because no public announcement of the new policy had been
made. Facilities would be available for ten days and no
longer. This last march went off, again without major incident,
and 568 of the 1934 crew joined the C.C.C. When Louis called
for a complete inventory in January 1935, Frank Hines would
be able to tell him that 2,663 of the 1933 group had joined
C.C.C., that a third of them had left within five months, that
only 15 per cent stuck it out for 13 months, that only 3½ per
cent were still left in the organization. Their work had been
satisfactory. There had been no problems.

More important in the long run was Louis's work with individuals—hundreds of them. Mysterious, vaguely yet obviously close to the President, he could seem to speak for Roosevelt in a way that satisfied many. Not knowing the precise range
of his influence, the scattered captains and camp followers
feared him and went out of their way to consult him. No one
man could ride herd on the mounting and changing personnel.
Louis didn't try to, yet somehow he knew what was going on.

[8] Quoted in Arthur M. Schlesinger, Jr.: *The Age of Roosevelt: The Coming of the New Deal* (Boston: Houghton, Mifflin Co.; 1959), p. 15.
[9] Margaret Durand to Grace Howe, May 12, 1933, Personal Papers.

And he sometimes intervened directly. When he wished to place Katherine Blackburn, librarian of the National Committee, in Moley's office, a word to the Professor was enough. Farley would later insist that Louis never intervened in the vast patronage operation which he ran from the Post Office Department. Louis was happy to pass the headaches to Jim, but he did refer a steady stream of job applicants to him, and he knew that his suggestions would be respected. Morgenthau would remember vividly that, when he became Secretary of the Treasury, it was Louis who had supported him in getting rid of the politicians who had crept into the Treasury Department under Woodin's easy regime. Louis acted as personal agent for southeastern Massachusetts and Rhode Island. He would forward with his blessing scores of appeals for aid of various kinds from Grace Howe to the various Washington agencies. He knew and cared little about the ideas of the men he helped to screen. He judged their personalities and balked particularly at arrogance, at the kind of uneasy ambition that might lead to disloyalty. Sometimes he let old snap judgments and grudges intervene. And Roosevelt did not always give in to him. When Moley wanted to take newsman Herbert Bayard Swope to the London Economic Conference, Louis fought against it and enlisted McIntyre and Early in the battle. But the President supported Moley.

Louis had enough weapons in his arsenal to do the most nasty and delicate jobs. More than once Roosevelt assigned him to fire subordinates when he didn't relish the unpleasantness himself. More than once Louis was delegated to salve the wounds of injured politicians after others had pushed them to the point of danger. When a securities bill drafted by Felix Frankfurter's team was sent to Congress to replace one on which Huston Thompson had worked for many weeks, it was Louis who was told to somehow make Thompson happy. Louis had his own realistic appraisal of the ruthlessness of politics. He told Morgenthau once: "Henry, when you have been in Government service as long as I have, you will recognize that coordinators come and coordinators go, and that furthermore sometimes it is good business to place so much work on a man that he cannot handle any of it." [1] But he could be relied on to understand the need to make even sacrificial lambs reasonably happy.

His smoothing tactics did not always work with those who had watched him operate from the inside. Moley had no illusions when Louis used one of his tested techniques to grease the skids for his departure. Louis's first gambit, put to Moley directly, was that the problem of administration of criminal justice desperately needed this crime expert's personal attention for three months. Moley balked—he had already made plans for leaving the administration—but he gave in a few days later when Roosevelt himself presented a more dignified plan for easing the pain. Moley had long since come to suspect that Louis Howe did not love him; he did not like Louis more for having to undergo the expert treatment which he had so often seen worked on others.

Howe's own prime aim was to prevent friction. No one could have managed this completely with such a dedicated, ambitious, egotistical, dynamic gang of leaders. But he worked nobly at it. Some he never understood and seems not to have dared to touch—Henry Wallace, for example. With others he had such long-standing rapport that a word here and there would keep things smooth. With Jim Farley there were no problems as long as Louis sat in the White House. But for others he provided almost an official wailing wall. Consider the case of Harold Ickes. Through April and early May he haunted Howe's office with his problems over the Governorship of Hawaii and the regulation of oil production. He didn't know how deeply Louis had distrusted his appointment; he assumed at once that Howe would push the boss in his direction. On June 16 he turned to Louis to help him at a two-and-three-quarter-hour conference in which he sought to commit Farley and his staff to a high standard in Public Works Administration appointments. He went away happy. A few days later he turned to Louis with one of his chronic fears—that others were undercutting his authority. This time it was the temporary head of

[1] Henry Morgenthau: "Diary," September 27, 1933, quoted in Schlesinger, Jr.: *New Deal*, p. 545.

the P.W.A. On June 17 Louis called him to assure him that both he and McIntyre had made it clear that Secretary Ickes was the real boss. Ickes was realistic enough to suspect that the President in fact had not made up his mind on the "final setup for public works." [2] But Howe had clearly established himself with the "old curmudgeon" to the point where he could hope to stave off trouble before it exploded in public. Louis came to like Ickes genuinely. But the Secretary of the Interior was a hopelessly gullible mark for flattery. By August he could confide to his diary: "As I have seen more of Colonel Howe lately, I have come to have a very high regard for him, and he has had no hesitation in indicating to me that both he and the President had a very good opinion of me, of which, of course, I am very glad." [3] Ten days later Ickes found his way into Louis's den to unload his worries about the violent newspaper attacks and the anonymous letters that he and his wife had been receiving. His enemies were trying to "break my morale," he said.[4] Quite obviously they had won their game. But Louis calmed him down. Harold was simply having to take his turn at receiving the abuse of which Moley, Johnson, and Louis himself had already had their share. This was one of the jobs one had to do for the President, he quietly pointed out. As late as January 1935 Louis would welcome Ickes in his upstairs bedroom and work arduously to smooth down the ruffled feathers of this violent, competent, suspicious gamecock. Ickes might have been less happy had he known how gleefully Howe could bounce into the White House cocktail sessions to tell the assorted company his latest Ickes story.

Or consider Howe's operations with Henry Morgenthau. He had known Morgenthau almost as long as Roosevelt had. He had no illusions that "Young Henry" possessed either the drive or the flair of a Moley or an Ickes. But Howe knew well both Morgenthau's loyalty and his durability. They were friends. They had both known Roosevelt intimately in other days; they both knew the lash of Franklin's sharp, little personal jokes and

[2] Harold L. Ickes: *The Secret Diary of Harold L. Ickes: The First Thousand Days, 1933–1936* (New York: Simon and Schuster; 1953), p. 55.
[3] Ibid., p. 78.   [4] Ibid., p. 82.

of his impatience. Morgenthau went to him in times of trouble. And Louis helped when it was in Franklin's interest to do so. He eased Henry's disappointment at losing the Treasury post and helped him slide gently into the Farm Credit Administration. He helped keep political hacks out of the Treasury Department after Morgenthau became its Secretary. He backed Morgenthau in a fight with Ickes and Farley over a New York public works project where scandal threatened. Louis helped him to get rid of the indiscreet subordinate who had been partly responsible for the trouble and to put contract awards in the reliable hands of Christian Peoples. This was easy, because Farley was vulnerable and because Howe trusted implicitly the retired admiral with whom he had worked 25 years before. But Louis was cautious even with Morgenthau. Henry might have noted that his old friend was carefully standing clear from his deepening vendetta with Ickes over Interior's "secret" investigation which had led to uncovering the New York mess. Henry did *not* know that Louis went out of his way to assure Ickes that he was not supporting the Treasury in the fight. Twenty years later Morgenthau would recall romantically that Louis had told him: ". . . you are the first man to go into the Roosevelt Cabinet who earned it." [5]

Louis was a master of ambiguity when it was useful. He was also a master of meaningless sympathy when action was dangerous or premature. Louis was merely sympathetic when Rex Tugwell tried to involve him in the messy civil war that divided the Department of Agriculture between "reformers" and price stabilization men. There was little either he or Roosevelt could do once the feud had reached the shooting stage. He was sympathetic, but he did nothing to save reformers like Jerome Frank from Wallace's inevitable purge. Sometimes his skill left him. It happened more and more as illness gripped him firmly in 1934. When Adolph Berle supported Fiorello La Guardia against the regular Democrats in New York, Louis sealed him off from access to the White House and ordered him to get Jim Farley's stamp of approval first. Louis distrusted La

[5] Interview with Henry Morgenthau.

Guardia. Berle had other lines to Roosevelt and was soon back in the charmed circle; Louis had done nothing to smooth this crisis, which he apparently saw as stark, unforgivable disloyalty. Sometimes, as he became more ill, his chronic gloom and suspicion deepened into frenetic fretting. Early in 1934, when Ickes and the Coolidge-appointed Comptroller General got into a bitter public squabble, Howe insisted on a long conference with Ickes about it and then sent two notes into the Executive Council meeting during the course of one morning. Ickes complained: ". . . one would think from his attitude that the Administration is about to crack right in two." [6]

Yet Howe's short temper and deepening gloom were neither progressive nor steady even in the later months. His was often a stabilizing force. In July 1934 when San Francisco was gripped by a bloody "general strike," Cummings and Hull wanted Roosevelt to turn back from his Pacific vacation cruise and use force to break the strike. Hiram Johnson saw "Revolution"; Hugh Johnson ranted that the unions must "run these subversive influences out from their ranks like rats." It was Louis Howe who turned the balance to Frances Perkins's wise and moderate counsel with a radiogram to Roosevelt: "Only danger San Francisco strike is that Mayor is badly frightened and his fear infected entire city." [7] For the President to return, they said, would bring on real panic.

As the size and complexity of the administration increased, Louis became more and more restive with the vendettas and confusion, the overlapping authority, the proliferating coordinators who created new conflicts that required coordination. He was personally and deeply interested in the relief programs, for example. He threw his whole weight behind Harry Hopkins's insistence on work programs rather than a dole. He mediated between Farley and Hopkins on the question of politics in relief, between Hopkins and Ickes on their divided responsibility for public works. But he soon complained that F.E.R.A. was a madhouse of confusion. He was particularly con-

    [6] Ickes: *Diary*, p. 141.
    [7] Quoted in Schlesinger, Jr.: *New Deal*, p. 392; interview with Frances Perkins, December 1961.

cerned over the criticism that Hopkins was wasting money with reckless haste. A couple of weeks after the 1934 election, when Hopkins sent him a draft of a speech summarizing the relief achievements, Louis pressed him to include a long paragraph which would have committed F.E.R.A. to a careful audit and full public report of its statistics. "I believe that every public official concerned with administering public funds owes it to all of our citizens not only to be prepared at any time to account to the last penny of the public money placed in his hands," he wanted Hopkins to say, "but to let the people know from time to time without waiting for any particular demand, the essential statistics. . . ." [8] But as the President moved in January 1935 toward even heavier relief spending and toward strengthening Hopkins's role as its administrator, Louis quietly retreated.

It was similar with N.R.A. Neither Roosevelt nor Howe could check the ebullient General Johnson as he rode off with astounding vigor in several directions at once. Sometimes it seemed as if the President himself had been quietly kicked upstairs by this tough old bundle of nervous energy who could storm into the White House without an appointment, demand Roosevelt's signature on a batch of codes the President had never seen, and rush out wildly to catch a plane. When real trouble threatened, Howe was often assigned to it. But whenever he meddled in the unwieldy organization, he was caught in a morass of difficulties no one could master. In August 1933 he worked out the guide lines by which government contractors could be compelled to meet N.R.A. standards without losing money. Here he labored with old friends from Navy days—Admiral Peoples, John Hancock, Silliman Evans; the orders and appropriations were soon arranged. But as late as October he was still embroiled with the Budget Bureau on specific cases. He sat occasionally for the President on the Industrial Emergency Committee, through which Donald Richberg tried to co-ordinate N.R.A. policy after Johnson's departure. But his major brush with the Blue Eagle occurred because he was an old journalist.

The attempt to write a "code of fair competition" for the

[8] Howe note on copy of Hopkins's speech to Annual Conference of Mayors, Chicago, November 23, 1934, Group XXXVI, FDRL.

newspaper industry ran at once into the owners' charges that proposed labor regulation would endanger "freedom of the press." Louis was torn between old friends among the publishers and Mollie Dewson, who protested bitterly at newspaper exploitation of child labor. His influence favored the publishers. Under heavy pressure from many sides, Johnson weakened the code, but he wrote sharply to Louis that there was no constitutional guarantee of the right to exploit labor any more than there was a guarantee of freedom to publish a newspaper in a firetrap or a pest house.[9]

Louis backed away, only to become completely involved in a hard fight between the owners and Heywood Broun's new American Newspaper Guild in the fall of 1934. A Hearst reporter and Guild member had appealed to the National Labor Relations Board; his paper insisted the case belonged before the Newspaper Industrial Board, set up under the N.R.A. code. This was important. It would decide the fate of a rankling struggle between Richberg and Francis Biddle, chairman of the N.L.R.B., over jurisdiction and over the majority-rule principle of union recognition which the Labor Relations Board had espoused. It went far beyond the newspaper world to all the areas where N.R.A. labor boards had been set up. The problem lay in an ambiguous executive order providing that N.L.R.B. "may" refuse to hear cases for which other machinery existed.[1] With Richberg and Biddle at sword point, with both organized labor and the powerful press barons involved, and with the struggle featured daily in the newspapers, Howe hastened to find a compromise to quiet the dangerous furor. He worked out with Richberg and Biddle an executive order to bar N.L.R.B. from cases for which there was code machinery, except where the N.R.A. board did not constitute a "fair and impartial" body.[2] Industry attorneys dashed the compromise to bits with their refusal to accept its provisions on appeals. In January 1935 the whole mess blew up. As strikes proliferated,

[9] Hugh Johnson to Howe, November 17, 1933, Group XXXVI, FDRL.

[1] Draft of letter: President to National Labor Relations Board, Group XXXVI, FDRL.

[2] Howe draft, Group XXXVI, FDRL.

Richberg warned that the N.L.R.B. would destroy the whole N.R.A. machinery. Biddle pressed for decisions on specific cases. Publisher Roy Howard demanded the intervention of the President himself. Louis worked patiently: "Will you let me know very frankly why you are not willing to talk with N.L.R.B.?" he wrote one of the principal warriors. "It would help me understand the situation a little better." [3] But meanwhile he worked on a letter with which Roosevelt would finally cut the knot in Richberg's favor. This did nothing to build F.D.R.'s rapport with labor, yet nothing could save N.R.A. itself. In February a Supreme Court decision knocked out its labor section; in May another ruling shattered the remnants of the shaky structure. But in time Roosevelt's reputation with the workingmen would be saved by the strong insistence of Senator Wagner and Frances Perkins on a new National Labor Relations Act.

Roosevelt was fond of telling his cronies that Louis knew nothing about economics. His knowledge of foreign policy was equally limited. Yet during the first year of the New Deal he dabbled haphazardly in both, to the wrath of everyone else involved. The prime instance was the mismanaged debacle of the London Economic Conference, inherited from Hoover. During the preliminary talks in Washington between Prime Minister Ramsay MacDonald and Roosevelt, Louis had been constantly about, relieving the tension of the moment when there had been little hope of progress. MacDonald, who had hoped to enlist Roosevelt's aid for Britain's return to the gold standard, had been hopelessly muzzled by F.D.R.'s own desertion of that venerable standard while the British were still en route to America. There was a major crisis in the offing which neither Roosevelt nor Howe seemed to understand. Certainly Louis was more interested in talking with MacDonald's daughter Ishbel, and they exchanged sprightly cables and letters: "Yours for bigger, brighter and more interesting crime." [4]

Outside their tight little group, Roosevelt was buffeted by advice, irresolute in decision. Caught between the demands of monetary stabilization abroad and his vague interest in mone-

[3] Howe to Howard Davis, January 21, 1935, Group XXXVI, FDRL.
[4] Howe to Ishbel MacDonald, June 26, 1933, Personal Papers.

tary manipulation at home, between Hull's concept of free trade and Key Pittman's demands for protection, his mind cluttered with fear of the New York bankers, Roosevelt sent off to London, under Hull's uneasy guidance, a warring delegation with ambiguous instructions. He sapped Hull's enthusiasm by deciding, after the Secretary left, that tariff reform would be shelved for the moment. Then he doubled the damage by insulating himself from all expert advice.

While Treasury officials shuttled back and forth between Washington and New York, where Woodin lay desperately ill, Roosevelt went fishing. As he fished and relaxed with his boys, he turned the whole business over in his mind and had second thoughts. When Moley dropped in unexpectedly by Navy plane, he cautiously agreed to let the Professor go to London with vague instructions to stress long-range projects such as raising the world price level. Meanwhile he had warned Hull that the administration must have complete freedom of action in raising American prices. This alone was enough to make Hull doubt he could work out the international currency stabilization the European powers wanted. Moley's arrival added only bitterness. Hull stepped aside, already suspicious of the Professor and hoping he would hang himself, and Moley worked out a careful stabilization agreement, broad enough, he thought, to gain Roosevelt's approval. But F.D.R. was having third thoughts now as he watched the activities of N.R.A. and A.A.A. and as he noted that his public warnings to Hull had been followed by further drops in the value of the dollar and further rises in domestic prices.

At Campobello he found eager support from Howe and Morgenthau. There was no one to play the devil's advocate, as Louis had so often boasted he did. No one knows precisely what he said, but Louis did argue sharply that Moley's plan must be overruled. Perhaps, as Moley suspected, Howe was too much impressed with the uncertain barometer of the money market. More likely, he listened to the quickening tempo of western inflationary demands. These were politically important. Perhaps his ancient fear of Wall Street came to the fore—or his newer fear of Moley. Morgenthau added nothing to the decision, but he approved. Neither of them could be expected to admire what was going on in London. Hartley Howe, in London on a press assignment, had written his father that the delegation had gained little prestige—"In the more frivolous diplomatic circles our chief delegate is apparently referred to as 'Miss Cordelia Dull,'. . ." [5] Old Henry Morgenthau, in more dignified language, had written his son that the situation was hopeless, that only strong Presidential action could save the conference.

Roosevelt would probably have sent anyway the cold rejection of the stabilization plan which blasted Moley's hopes. But he would not stop there. Aboard the *Indianapolis* on the way home he wrote out in longhand the most biting, devastating message of his career, pillorying the conference for its "singular lack of proportion and a failure to remember the larger purposes for which . . . [it had been] called." [6] He read it to Howe and Morgenthau. They suggested no changes. Louis did nothing to tone down the contempt, to give it the sophisticated "Roosevelt touch." The "bombshell" message demolished a conference already undermined. John Maynard Keynes, Winston Churchill, Walter Lippmann, and Russell Leffingwell might praise his call for long-term planning, but Europeans in general were incensed at the tone, disillusioned at the contents. The decisions had been made hastily and published ineptly. But they had been made. The United States would seek recovery at home first. And there was another result in which Louis may have felt a quiet satisfaction. Moley's position had been endangered. The grease had been applied to the skids before the Professor reached home. Someone had left on Hull's desk a copy of a private memo from Moley to Roosevelt containing an insult to Hull's ability which could not be misinterpreted.

That summer the President turned to Howe in desperation to carry out odds and ends of diplomatic chores. Some of these were harmless enough—for example, an investigation of nitrate

[5] Hartley Howe to Howe, June 9, 1933, Personal Papers.

[6] Rosenman: *Public Papers*, II, pp. 264–5.

supplies to help in negotiations with Chile. But the Seventh Inter-American Conference at Montevideo in December 1933 was a different matter. Here Howe not only acted as Roosevelt's liaison with Hull but also meddled personally and deeply in the negotiations.

Montevideo created a major problem for the administration. The Good Neighbor policy, so repeatedly stressed by the President, must be strengthened. American leadership must be reasserted in a new and more acceptable manner. But the decision to seek recovery first at home tied the hands of American delegates. There was no tariff relief program for Hull to bargain with; there were no specifics to spell out the genial spirit of which Roosevelt spoke so warmly. And, despite their long conversations, F.D.R. feared that Hull might go too far and commit the United States to action he might have to repudiate. He wanted no more London incidents. Louis would be set to watch.

In August Howe began to demand Latin American trade statistics for the White House to study. When Hull was about to leave, Louis was assigned to give him a final warning. As the Secretary remembered it years later, Louis came to him on behalf of the President and said: "We don't think you need to undertake much down at Montevideo. Just talk to them about the American Highway from the United States down through Central and South America." [7]

In fact, it was much less casual than this. Howe personally drafted a directive for Hull, warning him not to discuss specifics and limiting him to arranging the agenda for the next conference. Roosevelt himself publicly restricted the delegation with a White House statement that it seemed "desirable for the United States to forego immediate discussions of such matters as currency stabilization, uniform import prohibitions, permanent customs duties and the like." He went on to stress innocuous matters such as "the organization of peace, international law, the political and civil rights of women, uniform legislation respecting bills of lading and exchange methods,

[7] Cordell Hull: *The Memoirs of Cordell Hull,* 2 vols. (New York; The Macmillan Co.; 1948), p. 319.

social problems, intellectual cooperation. . . ." [8] But his major
bid to distract the conference from more volatile items was his
offer of American aid for a survey of the international highway,
improved navigation, and air travel. As if this were not enough,
Louis undertook to tell Hull what he could say in his opening
speech at the conference and to direct from long distance the
delegation's public relations. In almost insultingly flip language
he told the Secretary of State to start out with "the usual kind
words about good neighbors, band of brothers, etcetera," to go
on with a strong emphasis on the need to speed up transportation and some mild and vague regrets that the world financial
crisis "makes it impractical at this time to reach definite conclusions on several of the suggestions which, two years ago,
seemed ready for action as well as discussion." He warned Hull
to avoid "like the plague" the Paraguay-Bolivia boundary
dispute, the recent Cuban revolution, tariffs, and currency
stabilization and suggested that women's rights was "safe:
. . . if you don't want to talk about anything else, you can just
let the women go to it for the rest of the conference. . . .
'Social Problems' seems safe," he went on, "and we can talk a
lot about what we have done on the child labor end of it. . . .
'Intellectual Cooperation' is safe, but we must watch that the
wild students do not slip something over on us . . . immediate
and careful study of the new plan to run a line down the inside
of the Andes rather than along the coast as first proposed. This
would keep the steamship people quiet. . . .

"We will try up here through our own news service to magnify
everything that is done about transportation in order to build
this up as the big achievement of the conference. It looks like
the only thing of importance that we can brag about when we
come home even if all goes well. . . ." [9]

If Hull was annoyed by this patronizing packet of advice,
he did not show it publicly. He and Louis were old friends. He
carried through a masterly performance, appearing everywhere
permissive, polite, deferential to his Latin colleagues, a fitting
symbol of the northern giant's new humility. But Roosevelt and

[8] Howe to Cordell Hull, November 9, 1933, Group XXXVI, FDRL.
[9] Ibid.

Howe could not leave him alone. Howe insisted that Under Secretary William Phillips send over to the White House all the telegrams exchanged between Hull and his department. On December 13 Louis drafted another directive for the Secretary, to be sent over his own signature with Roosevelt's approval. This one suggested that Hull offer the creation of a non-profit engineering corporation, financed by the United States, to build at once the desired radio beacons and landing fields. "Cannot urge too strongly," he said, "my personal belief that the psychology will have very stimulating effect." [1] Three days later he was wiring one of Hull's aides to get the "best possible play" [2] in the press if the Secretary made an offer of flying fields to promote the plan.

As it turned out, the conference fell well short of what Louis wanted and went well beyond him on other matters. Discussion of the transportation item led only to a study committee, but the conference insisted upon discussing the volatile matters they all had hoped to avoid. Hull's diplomacy was effective. He navigated carefully on the Bolivia-Paraguay dispute, on trade barriers, and gave in gracefully to Argentine insistence upon non-intervention. The results were a series of conventions committing the United States and its neighbors generally not to intervene in the domestic affairs of others and to seek the lowering of trade barriers, as well as agreements on women's rights, extradition, patents, and Pan-American radio frequencies.

Louis Howe took no more flings at diplomacy. Soon after the conference Roosevelt began to rely on the smooth expertise of Assistant Secretary Sumner Welles in Latin American affairs.

[1] "Suggested Cablegram to Hull to be signed by Howe," December 13, 1933, Group XXXVI, FDRL.
[2] Howe to Ulrich Bell, December 16, 1933, Group XXXVI, FDRL.

26

The Call of the Crusades

Of all the things that could be said about the President, I think he would be most pleased by Kipling's description of the German scientist in the Indian jungle: "He was a man who dreamed dreams and made them come true."

(Louis Howe, *1933*) [1]

LOUIS RANGED WIDELY and freely throughout the whole Administration, but his own deep enthusiasm went to three pet projects he shared with Eleanor and Franklin—the Civilian Conservation Corps, the anti-crime crusade, and the Subsistence Home Experiment.

C.C.C. was the President's special hobby, born of his lifelong passion for conservation and universal military service, his ancient love of the land and distrust of cities, the deep interest in Scouting he shared with Louis. He had explored the possibilities long before the inauguration, with a tree expert from Cornell, with Tugwell, and with the National Forest Service. He had foreshadowed it in his campaign. But, quite typically,

[1] Script for Radio Program, August 20, 1933, Group XXXVI, FDRL.

his mind ranged over only the broad outlines of the mammoth project. He knew only that he wanted a crash program to put 250,000 unemployed men and boys to work by the summer of 1933; they should do useful conservation work, be saved from the crowded, restless city streets, and be given the healthy, outdoor environment he loved so much. Characteristically he warned Moley a few days after the inauguration that he planned to "go ahead with this, the way I did on beer." [2] Moley was distraught at the thought of more Howe and Roosevelt free-lancing. The result was an elaborate deal in which C.C.C. was pushed through Congress as part of the public works and unemployment relief package.

There were protests: that it was dangerous to concentrate gangs of restless, unemployed men; that it would undermine the labor movement; that it was militaristic; that it smacked of "fascism, of Hitlerism, of a form of sovietism," as William Green insisted.[3] And it promised a hopeless administrative tangle. If the President wanted action, it must be taken by existing agencies, already engaged in uneasy rivalry. Roosevelt cut the knot by demanding one of those impossibly complex administrative systems which would merely perpetuate conflict but which might get things done in the interim. The Army would house and supervise the men—no one else could; the Forest Service, the National Park Service, the Army Engineers would dream up projects; the Department of Labor would recruit men; and a union executive, Robert Fechner, would co-ordinate the whole project. Roosevelt was both gay and ruthless. When Frances Perkins objected that she had no machinery for the job, the President simply insisted that she go ahead. Three days later she was ready. When someone objected to the overlapping authorities, he was merely flip: "Oh, that doesn't matter. . . . Fechner will 'go along' and give everybody satisfaction and confidence." [4] He knew that there would be no action if the problems were to be solved first, and he knew Fechner's im-

[2] Quoted in Moley: *After Seven Years*, p. 174.
[3] Quoted in Schlesinger, Jr.: *New Deal*, p. 337.
[4] Quoted in Frances Perkins: *The Roosevelt I Knew*, p. 181.

mense skill and patience from close observation during the war. In any case, Roosevelt had no intention of allowing the C.C.C. wars to reach him personally. He dumped the whole problem of police and management on Louis's desk. It nearly killed Fechner, it drove Howe to distraction, but it worked.

Between March 31 and the middle of June, 1,300 camps were established. By midsummer they had exceeded Roosevelt's own goal and had 300,000 men at work. But for over two years Louis would have almost daily business with the C.C.C. as he exercised Roosevelt's veto power over the endless details and sought to quiet the relentless squabbles before they broke into the press. His files were filled with detailed reports of camp directors. His simple "yes" or "no" scrawled on Fechner's press releases told the co-ordinator what he could and could not say. When scandal threatened in Rhode Island, Louis personally worked out the problem with Governor Theodore Greene. He personally studied the Army's flood-control projects so that he could press them for rapid action. And he trustfully turned to old friends in politics to see that "political influence" did not "creep" into the choice of educational directors throughout the country.[5] The personal diplomacy was endless as he manipulated Fechner, the Budget Bureau, the Army, and the civilian bureaus. Mostly he tried not to solve problems but to keep them from exploding. After a year and a half Fechner would still be badgering him to resolve festering conflicts. Fechner needed authority to remove unsatisfactory personnel appointed by Agriculture, Interior, and the Army, and to control purchases. He needed a policy to guide him on C.C.C. work on private lands and on requests for camps in Hawaii and Alaska. He needed higher salaries and a better educational program. Only occasionally did Louis have to rush to F.D.R. for help—to answer a speech by Secretary of War Harry Woodring about "economic storm troops,"[6] to lecture the Army on the cost of processing recruits. . . . Roosevelt's penciled note did the job: "This figure . . . is absurdly high—It must be greatly reduced.

[5] Howe to Guy Helvering, Louis Brann and others, February 8, 1934, Group XXXVI, FDRL.
[6] Quoted in Schlesinger, Jr.: *New Deal*, p. 339.

F.D.R." [7] After 20 months Fechner was still holding on; Howe
was still co-ordinating the co-ordinator; Frances Perkins, Harold
Ickes, and others were still going over his head to report to the
President. Roosevelt was delighted, for, with all its confusion,
C.C.C. was a genuine success in both geographic and human
rehabilitation.

C.C.C. was more than a job to Louis. Both he and Grace
viewed it as their personal crusade and their private preserve.
He bragged endlessly that "he and Franklin" had planned it
for years.[8] Despite his illness, Louis went out personally to inspect the camps in the Washington and Fall River areas. In
southeastern New England Grace Howe took the C.C.C. boys
under her protective wing, visited them often, carried their
complaints directly to the White House. The boys soon called
her "Mother Howe" and labeled one of the highways on which
they worked, "Louis McHenry Howe Boulevard." [9] But C.C.C.
created one disastrous incident which embarrassed the administration gravely and might well have destroyed Louis.

A Senate Committee digging into its complex affairs came
upon a contract for 200,000 toilet kits purchased for the Corps
without competitive bidding. The search for a culprit led to
the White House itself; Louis Howe had ordered the purchase,
said Fechner. And the contractor himself tightened the noose
around Louis's thin neck as he told a public hearing that he had
come to Howe at 3 p.m. and had had the contract in his pocket
by 6. Louis managed to squirm out. There was no evidence
against him on paper. He had simply referred the man to Fechner, he said, with a draft from the Bureau of the Budget explaining that C.C.C. had authority to buy the kits if it wanted
to. There the matter rested, and the committee exonerated him
nicely: ". . . there is no foundation for any criticism of you.
. . ." [1] But it was much too close for comfort. It was an old
Washington game he had been playing, and he was lucky that
he had learned to play it so well. The luckless Fechner had

[7] Roosevelt note on letter: Duncan K. Major to Robert Fechner, Group
XXXVI, FDRL.
[8] Stiles: *Howe*, p. 267.   [9] Interview with Mary Howe Baker.
[1] Morris Sheppard to Howe, March 7, 1934, Group XXXVI, FDRL.

long since been taught to take Louis's phone calls and cryptic notes as law. Now he was left to take the blame. Louis had learned years ago in the Navy Department that suggestions from the top could be relentlessly effective, but that responsibility for decisions was best left with subordinates. Yet in all the tangled web of C.C.C. mediation, co-ordination, and confusion, this was the only shadow of scandal to fall across the pale green walls of Louis's office, and this was a hastily treated matter in which he had not the slightest personal interest.

There was much more to criticize in the Subsistence Home Projects, and here Louis succeeded in compounding confusion rather than mastering it. At the start the idea appealed to everyone. Proposals for self-sufficient rural communities had come from a score of directions at once, from the little experiments of Quaker reformers, from the dreams of Rex Tugwell, Marcus L. Wilson, and Henry Wallace, and from Roosevelt's own New York State dream of solving unemployment by resettling surplus city population on the good green earth. Roosevelt was intrigued. Eleanor Roosevelt's enthusiasm was boundless after seeing for herself the desperate, grimy, hungry people of the West Virginia coal-mining towns. And Louis, already swamped with C.C.C. and dabbling in diplomacy, found himself caught up in the heady crusade.

The money was ready—$25,000,000 earmarked in the N.R.A. package. There was already a boss—the fund was controlled by Ickes's Public Works Administration. But late in the summer of 1933 Louis and Eleanor began to give their personal attention to the pioneer experiment in West Virginia. The main problem was to find work for the displaced miners who would live in the model community. Howe and Mrs. Roosevelt dreamed of a self-sufficient village, combining small industries and gardening. Louis canvassed the government departments for suggestions. Admiral Peoples thought the only practical thing the Navy could use would be paper products. Silliman Evans at the Post Office Department warned that almost anything they produced would compete with private industry or existing government manufacturing. There were reminders from William Julian, Treasurer of the United States, that both factory owners and the unemployed would resent any government experiments with new shops. But Louis had caught a vision too large for petty objections. He had already told a nation-wide radio audience that rural resettlement was "part of a very great and notable experiment . . . [to] revolutionize the manufacturing industry. . . ." It would ease the crisis of the choked and dismal cities; it would solve the problem of the part-time worker "who has now to go into the breadline whenever work is slack." [2] And he had invoked the Roosevelt blessing in public. By mid-September the Post Office Department had fallen into line, and Silliman Evans sent him specifications for all the furniture used in Federal buildings, as well as a humble promise to furnish blueprints for suitable shops to manufacture furniture, screen-line, twine, and lockboxes, "in our little village." [3]

The Division of Subsistence Homesteads had an official organization, with M. L. Wilson as Director. Within ten months 52 projects had been approved. But Wilson was hopelessly outflanked by Louis and Eleanor and their friends from Morgantown, West Virginia. Clarence Pickett, who was already experimenting with a project there for the Friends, was made Wilson's assistant. The Executive Committee consisted of Wilson, Eleanor Roosevelt, Howe, and Bushrod Grimes, who had been working with Pickett in West Virginia. Mrs. Roosevelt was chairman of the Committee on Admissions, which included Grimes and Silliman Evans. Evans and Howe were the Industrial Committee. Howe *was* the Electrification Committee, all by himself. Eleanor *was* the Population Committee. Grimes was the Resident Director at "Arthurdale." Wilson was virtually powerless in the eager rush to make the West Virginia experiment the show window for subsistence homesteads.

Louis used his influence with Harold Ickes to quiet the loud complaints of Hugh Johnson, and then proceeded to run the Arthurdale project from his White House office. By September 22 he had reports from Ickes on water supply, from the Justice Department on land condemnation, and from Grimes on

[2] Radio Script, August 20, 1933, Group XXXVI, FDRL.

[3] Silliman Evans to Eleanor Roosevelt and Howe, September 16, 1933, Group XXXVI, FDRL.

the broad outline of the plans, and he had set Grimes to work looking for lumber supplies. Meanwhile he toyed with plans to manufacture pyrethrum sprays and to revive the linen and flax industry in the United States. By mid-October they were ready to tell the public their plans. Ickes's press release was a masterpiece of promise and hope. There would be three types of projects: suburban communities like one planned near Dayton, Ohio; farm settlements with home industries like Arthurdale; farm projects in which some one member of the family worked in a factory. At Arthurdale houses would cost the government only $2,000; the Post Office Department would build a shop to manufacture some of its supplies there; there would be self-government patterned on the New England town meeting. Three days later Louis promised his radio audience an experiment with rural electrification and boasted: "Here is where we will have a chance to try everything once—and see how it will work." [4]

For a year Louis would be involved in every minute detail of construction, spending hours poring over statistics on concrete, electricity, crops, and lumber, personally negotiating with General Electric for pumps and refrigeration equipment, personally ordering prefabricated houses, personally shopping around to find out whether concrete blocks or hollow tiles were better suited for foundations. He was a whirlwind of activity on all the vast details which should have been handled by technical experts and managed by a full-time administrator, rather than by the President's secretary in his odd moments. And Eleanor Roosevelt watched even more carefully, inspecting the project over and over again, talking with friends like Elinor Morgenthau and Bernard Baruch, whose own suggestions were soon solicited. The complexity was confounded by the administrative pattern Wilson had chosen—a top government holding corporation, with subordinate but separate operating companies for each project.

There were comic moments. Louis found himself pictured on the cover of the G.E. Company magazine, solemnly contem-

[4] Radio Script, n.d., Group XXXVI, FDRL.

plating with Mrs. Roosevelt, David Lilienthal, and Eleanor's
friend Nancy Cook the new combination refrigerator and range
in which, the caption hinted, the Subsistence Home Project was
interested. And Louis's files became the repository for all sorts
of outlandish projects. The most touching was the full-blown
blueprint for "Louis Howe, Oregon," sent him with the pious
observation: "This coveted goal is possible through the power
and will of our President." If Louis read it, he found everything
a planner could want: the type of roses to be used in the
hedges; the inscription for a religious monument in the village
square; the dues for the "Louis Howe Welfare League"—50
cents a week.[5]

But the problems were monstrous and the worst one was of
his own making. Early in the fall he recklessly told the President
that he could get the work under way in three weeks and have
families under the roofs by winter. From that moment on he
was over his head in a hopeless struggle to make good. Prefabs
seemed the answer; he had studied them carefully for Navy
housing during the war. But the 50 houses he ordered turned
out to be flimsy summer constructions and, worse yet, the
wrong size for the foundations already laid. Yet there was no
turning back. By December 2 Ickes was beginning to sense that
something was wrong. "I understand these houses are only
about 10 feet wide and I am afraid they will look a good deal
like a joke. . . . I have a disturbed feeling about it."[6] When
Ickes did see them, he would be furious. But this was only the
sad beginning. Despite the rush, the first families could not
move in until April 1934. Louis's bland prediction of cheap
electricity crumbled before the cold statistics. They could not
possibly match the private power rates with less than 200 families. With only 50 at the start, their costs would be close to
double the going rate in the area. Water supply proved difficult. The Bureau of the Budget objected to the decentralized
corporate structure. Howe fumed and fussed, but finally accepted Ickes's formula for a central corporation with separate
project managers. Wilson resigned in public protest.

Meanwhile strategically placed Congressmen objected. Louis

[5] Group XXXVI, FDRL.   [6] Ickes: *Diary, 1933–1936,* pp. 129–30.

Ludlow, whose district included a factory which made postal supplies, blasted Arthurdale as "the death knell of individual liberty in America." [7] One Senator charged Mrs. Roosevelt with Communist ideas and made the reckless claim that she intended to unload the products of her own Valkill furniture factory on the projects. Louis tried to "straighten" it out [8] but the watchdogs of the budget, Daniel Reed, John Taber, and Andrew J. May, came to their colleague's aid. Louis was so scared by this time that he stepped on Eleanor's plans for community gardens and herds. This sounded too radical, although it made much more sense than the individual garden plots and personally owned cows upon which Ickes, Howe, and the miners themselves insisted. But no amount of last-minute maneuvering could save their plans. In June Ludlow killed the postal factory with a rider which the President could not veto. A filibuster on another matter stalled action in the Senate, and the House Appropriations Committee neatly blocked Louis's attempts to slip an appropriation into the deficiency budget.

On top of this, newsmen *did* go down to Reedsville to see for themselves, as Howe had once prematurely invited them to do. In August 1934 the *Washington Post* told the story with screaming headlines: "FLIMSY HOMESTEADS COST FANCY PRICE, BLUNDERS AT ARTHURDALE PUT BURDEN ON MINER AND TAXPAYER." [9] And there, for all to see, was the damning photograph of a tiny prefab house, set ridiculously on a foundation several sizes too large, with the chimney standing a lonesome ten feet from the house wall. Louis blandly explained to his radio audience: ". . . word came from the mining section of West Virginia that there would be at least fifty families compelled to sleep under tents during the coming winter. . . . It was then within two months of the first snows and it was decided to erect for the temporary use of these people quickly constructed but sufficiently comfortable winter quarters." But it was hardly convincing; he added the lame explanation that accommodations had been found elsewhere for the homeless, that the "temporary" struc-

[7] Quoted in Schlesinger, Jr.: *New Deal*, p. 367.

[8] File Memorandum, January 29, 1934, Group XXXVI, FDRL.

[9] *Washington Post Magazine*, August 12, 1934.

tures had been torn down and rebuilt into "permanent" homes, that the costs of experiment were bound to be high. These prototypes might run to "four, five or even six thousand dollars," but they would pave the way for homes any carpenter could build from government plans for $2,000."[1]

Eleanor helped. Reedsville was "a human experiment station," she explained. Like agricultural experiment stations, it cost more than an ordinary farm to run. But it would pay off in discovering "what is the highest level to which the family with an ordinary income can aspire."[2] Ickes sought to reassure Howe. "I like the way you handled the croaking critics. . . ." And Eleanor penciled on Ickes's note her own assurance: "Grand."[3] But privately Ickes spluttered about incompetence and mismanagement, blamed Howe for the "initial mistake," and protested that, since Mrs. Roosevelt had "taken the project under her protecting wing," they had "been spending money down there like drunken sailors."[4] He went to Roosevelt at last, but the genial boss would not mix in the family squabble. He put Ickes off with the remark—which he certainly did not expect to be recorded—"My missus, unlike most women, hasn't any sense about money at all."[5] And he went on to note fondly that Louis was no better. Others were more direct. One of Louis's radio listeners put it bluntly: either the official statements of the Subsistence Homestead Bureau were false or Louis himself was lying.[6]

Howe gradually withdrew from it all after the unfortunate publicity in the summer of 1934. Perhaps Roosevelt did intervene, or perhaps it was Louis's illness. Howe made suggestions on local government and cultural projects for the experimental communities, but he left to the professional manager the frustrating search for private industries to replace his much-lamented government-owned, community-run factories. In

[1] Radio Script, September 28, 1934, Group XXXVI, FDRL.
[2] Eleanor Roosevelt: "Subsistence Farmsteads—Reedsville Project," manuscript in Group XXXVI, FDRL.
[3] Harold Ickes to Howe, October 1, 1934, Group XXXVI, FDRL.
[4] Ickes: *Diary, 1933–1936,* p. 207.   [5] Ibid., p. 218.
[6] C. D. Beebe to Howe, October 16, 1934, Group XXXVI, FDRL.

the spring of 1935 the President placed the entire project in Rex Tugwell's new Resettlement Administration. The dream would remain part of the New Deal. Louis had helped to make it; and he had endangered it vastly. But there would be no more direct maladministration from Louis's little bailiwick.

If C.C.C. had been largely Franklin's pet and the Homesteads Eleanor's, Louis's own private hobby was the crime wave. He had no particular training in the area. He had read more mystery stories than scholarly studies of crime. He was, without doubt, merely an "armchair criminologist," [7] as Moley was fond of noting. But he did see the central issues, and he did appreciate the political urgency of doing something. The need was pressing in the spring of 1933, as the displaced rum runners turned their warped talents to a broadening horizon of rackets: kidnapping, protection, labor manipulation, dope smuggling, and infiltration of normally respectable businesses. And the kidnap-murder of Charles Lindbergh's son brought clamoring demands for national action. Howe saw the problem simply. Only Federal power could match the automobile with a gangster behind the wheel. Only Federal action could provide effective training of police in an age of scientific crime, of machine guns and sawed-off shotguns, of private armies. Only Federal resources were adequate to deal with men like Scarface Al Capone, who could rule Chicago from his Cicero hotel suite.

The crusade begun in the Crime Commission carried over to Louis's White House office. He wrote a popular article, "Uncle Sam Starts after Crime," [8] claiming for Roosevelt the original suggestion of a national law-enforcement agency. He prodded the Justice Department on its plans for new legislation. He opposed anti-lynching legislation for fear of a filibuster and opposed the death penalty for kidnapping, but otherwise he supported the Justice Department's broadly ranging plans to give the Federal government jurisdiction over crimes in interstate commerce and to provide Federal law-enforcement agents with weapons suitable for dealing with modern racketeering. He

[7] Moley: 27 Masters, p. 266.

[8] Louis Howe: "Uncle Sam Starts after Crime," Saturday Evening Post, CCVI (July 29, 1933), pp. 5-6, 71-2.

lobbied personally for their bills in Congress and then persuaded Roosevelt to put the whole weight of White House pressure behind the program in the spring of 1934.

On May 18 Roosevelt signed a group of statutes which was almost all that Howe could desire. Only one old crusade remained, his ten-year fight for a Federal training institution for police officers. When he pressed the matter with the Justice Department, he was lectured on the dangers of talking about a "Scotland Yard" and Homer Cummings expressed his fears of too much national action in a Federal type of government.[9] Howe took to the radio with some specific proposals and with a sharp blast at some of the law's most deeply held and ancient traditions. He wanted "swift, sure justice that cannot be defeated by the cleverest and most unscrupulous criminal lawyers," he told the nation. He wanted a national criminological laboratory, a preplanned system of roadblocks for trapping escaped criminals, a probationary system for lawyers before they would be allowed to practice criminal law, a system of jury decisions by ten- or eleven-man majorities to do away with the problem of the narrowly hung juries and jury bribing. He wanted better training for prison personnel—"Ninety percent of prison riots start from stupid wardens." [1]

A few days later *Harper's Magazine* appeared with a formidable blast against Roosevelt and Howe for conniving to saddle the country with a Federal secret police. Nonetheless, Louis went on to help stage an "Attorney General's Conference on Crime" in December. But illness again interfered, and by early spring of 1935 he had to relinquish any further ambitions in the anti-crime crusade. Yet much of what he had failed to gain was eventually achieved in the elaborate expansion of the F.B.I.

Louis's work as top policeman for the administration, as Roosevelt's ever-present "no" man, as the special friend of C.C.C., Homesteads, and the war on gangsters, seems in retrospect more than a full-time job for one ill and elderly man. Yet he had considerable routine responsibilities on the White House staff. He controlled the budget and the personnel of the

[9] Joseph B. Keenan to Howe, October 13, 1934, Group XXXVI, FDRL.
[1] Radio Script, October, 1934, Group XXXVI, FDRL.

executive office. Despite occasional skirmishes with his old friends, he learned to leave appointments and press relations to McIntyre and Early. But he would not give up the control of the correspondence. The incoming mail was a nightmare— literally, Louis claimed, for he often groused about his dream of riding in an airplane high above a white landscape, covered with letters flowing into the White House. Someone calculated that Roosevelt received more mail in six months than Hoover had in four years. On the average there were 6,500 letters a day. Louis complained that a man working at the rate of half a minute a letter could read only 2,800 in a solid 24 hours. The answer was, of course, the letter-writing machinery he had long since perfected. Roosevelt himself received the official matters which required his action as well as letters from old friends, Congressmen, important administrative officials, and major local politicians. Some of these could be handled with forms; others were quickly passed on with F.D.R.'s penciled chits indicating his intention. Yet Roosevelt kept a staff of secretaries busy with the work he himself dictated. There were no eight-hour days for Missy and Grace Tully. They worked until the day's stint was done, and often they returned to type speeches late at night.

Even so, this left great piles of routine letters and personal notes by the thousands which flooded into the Executive Office after each Fireside Chat. Louis's rule was simple. Every letter must be answered, and there must be none of the "Yours received and contents noted" business. The person in Kankakee or Keuka, Milwaukee or Atlanta who felt he knew the President personally must never be brushed off, even if his letter had to be signed by a White House clerk. Louis worked out a series of form letters with the "Roosevelt touch." A carefully trained squad of 25 to 30 girls went through the daily business of matching the forms to the letters. But Louis trusted no one completely. The finished products were channeled to his own secretaries, Lela Stiles and Lucille Flanagan. Sometimes he and Rabbit pitched in when the chore was heavy. Louis could be blunt when he spotted one that didn't fit: "This is a lousy answer." [2]

[2] Quoted in Stiles: *Howe*, p. 242.

Sometimes Louis's forms were sent in for the President's personal signature. It was a token of his success in managing the "Roosevelt touch" that old friends from Dutchess County would cherish 25 years later the little "personal" notes they had received from "Franklin," never guessing that hundreds of carbons of the same letter were reposing in the President's files.

Louis often sampled the mail himself, catching the drift of opinion to which his sensitive ear had always been attuned. Sometimes he had letters summarized for Roosevelt, although the boss had little time for this now. And Roosevelt was amused by the lists of strange salutations which Lela and Lucille culled from the mail for their boss: "Dear Buddy," "Our revered President, the most godlike ruler in the history of civilization," "Franklin Dillinger Roosevelt," "Dear Man," "Our Darling Ruler." There were more laughs in the quaint misspellings and original twists of unconscious humor the girls saved for him: "I am a widow. My husband deserated me"; "We are all rotting for you one hundred percent"; "My husband is an unable war veteran. His composition was cut off in 1934"; "I meant to wait to ask for your autograph till you left the White House, but I'm afraid now you never will"; "My wife is a handicap and has been for 27 years"; "I am a lady and I have intended for a long time to write and give myself up for some benefit." [3]

Roosevelt turned to Howe's office for summaries of documents that were too long to read. Applications for pardons, already carefully investigated by the Justice Department, were often handled in this way, so the President could see the whole case in a paragraph. They had instructions to underline the tag "dope peddler"; Roosevelt had a special distaste for this brand of crook.

The massive correspondence provided one barometer of public opinion, but Louis was never happy without the clipping service on which he had relied so heavily since 1906. Even in the White House he insisted there was much more to testing opinion than reading the half-dozen metropolitan, East Coast papers through which the President browsed at breakfast. Lack-

[3] Quoted in ibid., pp. 242–4.

ing both space and staff, he arranged for Katherine Blackburn to do the job in the Division of Press Intelligence which Hugh Johnson's N.R.A. agreed to accommodate. "Casey" issued a regular Press Intelligence Bulletin with summaries and excerpts culled from hundreds of small-town and city papers throughout the country. "Louis Howe's Daily Bugle" was soon reaching most of the major executives as well as the President himself. Louis was persistent in his demand that they know what was going on, even if they didn't particularly want to.

Yet of all the coats Louis Howe wore in his anomalous White House job, his favorites were a very old one and a very new one. He continued to be Roosevelt's personal political agent, gauging every move with a cautious glance toward 1934 and 1936, and he made himself a major Roosevelt spokesman in magazine articles, in speeches and radio programs, in interviews. The anonymous little manipulator had suddenly become a man of authority, sketching forthrightly, almost possessively, the benchmarks of his beloved Franklin's New Deal.

27

━━━━━━━━━━━━━━
⋙-⋙-⋙-⋙-⋙-⋙-⋙-⋙-⋙
━━━━━━━━━━━━━━

Spokesman and Strategist

> *If the President takes away from the strong man the right to hit the little man over the head with a club, is that too great curtailment of liberty? We must assure the little man's right not to be clubbed.*
>
> (Louis Howe, 1935) [1]

THIS WAS a brand-new Louis Howe, this confident, wise old spokesman, who sent reporters away with the distinct impression that Roosevelt without Howe would be inconceivable. There was a mixture of motives in this sudden search for the limelight he had always so carefully eschewed. The public appearances gave a healthy boost to his sagging ego. He could make money—real money—for the first time in his life. But there was something else. He could, he knew, add immeasurably to the effectiveness of the administration with his careful explanations of the New Deal in terms that would reach ordinary people like himself. Liberals never got their fair share of the headlines, he insisted. The administration should grasp

[1] Interview by Associated Press Correspondent with Howe, copy in Group XXXVI, FDRL.

every chance to reach the people. And there was nothing cor-
rupt in being paid; why should government officials do for
nothing what others were paid well for doing?

He had no illusions about his role. He did not try to create
policy with his articles and talks. He checked carefully with
the departments involved and relied on them frequently for
the complete material. In two years he produced eight major
articles for the *Saturday Evening Post, Liberty, American
Magazine,* and *Cosmopolitan.* His style was tighter, more pun-
gent than it had been 20 years before, but his articles still were
sprinkled with romanticized pictures, fictionalized conversations. Occasionally there slipped in a purple metaphor reminiscent of his old writing for the *Herald*— "the wolves who prowl
around the temples of high finance." [2]

Many of his pieces helped to shape the already growing
Roosevelt folklore: "The Winner"; "Behind the Scenes with the
President"; "The President's Mail Bag"; "Women's Ways in
Politics"; and "Uncle Sam Starts after Crime." [3] Here appeared
for the first time many of the stories of F.D.R.'s early career
that would be hashed over and over again in popular articles
for the next 20 years. The Roosevelt he portrayed was that
"perfectly impossible young man" [4] who refused to bow to the
bosses, who carried the noble banner of popular government
for 22 long years without relenting, without a slip. And Louis
gave the public behind-the-scenes glimpses of a typical day in
the President's life. In none of these did he play himself up.
Yet there was a curious hidden pride in what he wrote. Again
and again he boasted of Roosevelt's achievements which he
knew were his own: the news gathering, the propaganda and

[2] Howe: "Life More Abundant," *Cosmopolitan,* CXXIV (April 1934),
p. 106.

[3] Howe: "The Winner," *Saturday Evening Post,* CCV (February 25,
1933), pp. 6–7, 48–9; "Behind the Scenes with the President," *American
Magazine,* CXVII (March 1934), pp. 42–4; "The President's Mail Bag,"
American Magazine, CXVII (July 1934), pp. 22–3, 118–20; "Women's
Ways in Politics," *Woman's Home Companion,* LXII (July 1935), pp.
9–10; "Uncle Sam Starts after Crime," *Saturday Evening Post,* CCVI
(July 29, 1933), pp. 5–6, 71–2.

[4] Howe: "The Winner," p. 6.

organizational techniques of the campaigns, the crime crusade. And he practically ignored the larger matters which had actually been Roosevelt's to decide.

In his more serious efforts he sought to explain his boss's thinking, and always on the same unsophisticated level on which F.D.R. himself operated. He caught with great accuracy the major note of the particular moment; he followed with subtle finesse the changing emphases as policies evolved from the first hectic maneuvers. His only pre-election article played on the theme of Roosevelt's "forgotten man" speech and pictured romantically the limited Roosevelt and Hopkins experiment with relocating the unemployed on the farms. The sentimental, idealized sketch of a "typical" relocated family could do nothing but flatter farmers everywhere and remind distressed and jobless city men that this candidate thought in terms of the little man.[5]

In June 1933, when N.R.A. was being boosted off the ground with parades, Blue Eagles, and Hugh Johnson oratory, Louis struck the precise note of the moment with another variation on a Roosevelt theme: "Balanced Government—The Next Step." His concept of government ran back to Wilson and T.R.: "A government that will act as a sort of referee and see that no foul tactics are used by those in the lead to hold back or oppress others. A government that will give full scope for natural ability and willingness to work but which will prevent the abuse of acquired or inherited power." But he sought a bridge to the present. The task of government was to bring "harmony" among the interests. Unbothered by either mathematics or economics, Louis preached the dogma of "balance" among Agriculture, Industry, and Finance. And he went on to help stake out a Democratic first mortgage on the term "liberal." The Democratic Party would remain the liberal party. What of the Democratic conservatives? They would remain a small but effective brake on "the more enthusiastic and radical element."[6]

[5] Howe: "The Fight for the Forgotten Man," *Liberty*, IX (September 17, 1932), pp. 18–21.

[6] Howe: "Balanced Government the Next Step," *American Magazine*, CXV (June 1933), pp. 11–12, 84, 86.

This was almost straight Roosevelt, and it suited the mood of the N.R.A. But there was no mistaking Howe's emphasis. It was significant that he tempered his enthusiasm for "the more radical group," that there was nothing here for labor, that there were clear hints of a balanced budget, of lower taxes. It was significant that the liberalism to which Howe laid claim was a liberalism carefully in the center. And it was significant that there were few specifics. Master of well-manipulated platitudes and happy generalizations, he intended to lose no votes with his little excursions into print.

Yet within a few months Ernest Lindley would be writing of Howe: "Definite conclusions concerning the cause of the Nation's distress begin to escape from him. He has begun to use phrases familiar to the left wing of the brains trust. One suspects that he derives a sharp satanic pleasure from the consternation caused in the counting houses by the Administration's monetary policy."[7] In "Life More Abundant" in April 1934 Louis betrayed how much he had learned—though he may not have believed all of it—from the social reformers, the gold price manipulators, the industry regulators with whom he had been forcibly barracked for a year. Thumping the drum for unemployment insurance, for shorter hours and job security, for fair farm and consumer prices, for conservation, slum clearance, managed currency, and the dissolution of "wasteful and ruinous business competition," he sought to link the old individualism with the New Deal.[8] As early as November 1933 he had told the Progressive Education Association: "We talk about 'rugged individualism' and 'personal liberty.' My dear friends, both of those disappeared from the earth the day the first colony of cave men held a conference around a community fire."[9] Now, in April, he sought to set the milestones of progress in terms of a contrast between Teddy's "Square Deal" and Franklin's "New Deal." The Square Deal, he insisted, "was primarily aimed at giving him a chance, if he was wise enough and strong enough to accumulate at least enough material wealth to keep him a

[7] Lindley: *Roosevelt Revolution,* p. 292.
[8] Howe: "Life More Abundant," pp. 18–19, 104–6.
[9] Address to Progressive Education Association, Group XXXVI, FDRL.

jump or two ahead of the sheriff. . . . It was still every man for himself and the devil take the hindmost. . . . The New Deal," he claimed, "is the recognition that those who are regulated and governed in the interests of the common good are entitled to something far more than the mere right to struggle for existence . . . a true and proper social order must see that these are also given an equal opportunity to make life not only possible, but a pleasant thing, as well. . . . There may not be as many rich individuals, but there will be far less poor . . . ," he promised. And "the ultimate goal is the happiness of the individual as an individual." [1]

Just before Christmas 1933 he had taken the same plea to a national radio audience in a fuzzily philosophical mood and almost lyric language. The world was entering, he said, an age that would be greater even than the Renaissance. But it was an age with a new challenge and new demands. Man must learn to accept more regulation of his way of life in the interests of society than he had ever done before. Rugged individualism was absurd. The depression's blessing in disguise had been its lesson that people must help each other to help themselves. The goals, as he staked them out, were two. Industry must learn to keep up with the inventive mind of man. But even more important, man's soul must keep pace with his broadening intellect. Men must learn to use their leisure constructively, must learn to give as well as take.[2]

All of this was mystical and vague, the deeply idealistic sensitive Louis Howe breaking through the crust of tough political armor. The economics that lay behind it was still the folklorized dogma of the classic free market—"The law of supply and demand holds eternal," he would explain. And the solution seemed inevitable. Either the work and the capital must be spread and managed and organized or the nation would fall into "industrial stagnation" on the one hand or "hopeless inflation" on the other.[3]

[1] "Life More Abundant," pp. 18–19, 104–6.
[2] Recording, Cities Service Program, WEAF, December 15, 1933, Personal Papers.
[3] "Life More Abundant," p. 104.

There were public appearances too, for the first time in his career—his controversial speech to Columbia Journalism students, a more carefully guarded, off-the-record talk to Edward S. Corwin's American government class at Princeton, where he chatted about what really went on in politics. There was a prepared address for the Progressive Education Association that fall. Here he preached the responsibility of government for the care of its citizens who had been crushed by the system. "When the President started preaching that doctrine it was regarded in many quarters as a 'radical' idea. It ought to be as apparent as the Solar system and as unarguable as the virtues of the Ten Commandments." [4]

But it was on the radio that Louis Howe was most impressive. Here his wasted form, his deeply shadowed, parchment face could not distract. Here his voice came through, deep, resonant, cultured. Except for an occasional slurring of a phrase, he was almost as effective as Roosevelt himself. He had the same quiet mannerism of speech, the same friendly warmth, the same insinuating intimacy. Louis made his debut in February 1933 with a talk on the Secret Service. Then, late in April, Edwin C. Hill tried him out on the Socony Vacuum Hour, "The Inside Story of Names That Make the News." Louis crossed out of the script the totally inaccurate claim that he didn't care for movies or theater and the all-too-accurate statement that he read almost nothing except newspapers and detective stories, but he left alone the telling phrases that helped build his popular image: "diminutive and gnome-like"; "working and planning under cover like a benevolent mole"; "it would be absurd to call him a king-maker. Roosevelts come of a clan who crown themselves." [5] Within a month Myles Lasker had signed Louis for 13 weeks on an RCA Victor program.

Superficially, this was a question-and-answer program, with the skilled Walter Trumbull presenting to Louis the listeners' questions. In fact, it was carefully planned, with prepared scripts worked out jointly by Trumbull and Howe, with ma-

[4] Address to Progressive Education Association, Group XXXVI, FDRL.

[5] Script: "Inside Story of Names That Make the News," April 28, 1933, Group XXXVI, FDRL.

terials provided by the various government departments. Louis had an absolute veto over every spoken word. He cleared many of the scripts with the President himself and others with the particular departments involved. And while some attention was paid to questions sent in, the programs were largely geared to the administration's interests of the moment or to the material Louis was able to obtain. Yet there was some aura of spontaneity about it all, as Louis forthrightly refused to answer certain questions they had carefully planted to vary the pace.

Throughout the summer of 1933 Howe went on with these broadcasts. In December and again in the summer of 1934 he did several more for the Cities Service Hour. He was astonished at the $900 a program RCA was willing to pay. Ickes was even more astounded when he once filled in for Louis: ". . . the compensation was at the rate of $100 a minute, which, without being overmodest, I may say I regard as more than ample." [6] Before he was through, Howe had covered practically the whole administration, the securities exchange bill, the Farm Credit Administration, the London Conference, the Home Loan Bill, the banking legislation, N.R.A., the languishing Disarmament Conference, the anti-crime crusade, subsistence homes, and Latin America, F.E.R.A. and education, C.C.C., the Post Office, the Secret Service, and the Surplus Commodities Corporation. He proved himself an adept dodger, an effective explainer, a master of personalizing the most abstract matter and over-simplifying the most complicated. On the requirements of the truth-in-securities act: ". . . they include all kinds of little awk-ward matters which the promoter generally keeps down in the safe deposit vault for fear someone will find out, for instance how much salary the officers are getting, whether any of the money received is going to be used to buy some other stock which a director wants to unload at a fancy price, whether any-one is going to be on a preferred list and get the stock cheaper than anybody else. . . . It is a terrible list for a man with a bad conscience to face. . . ." [7] Or, in early June: ". . . the defi-nite trend towards better times was caused by the announce-

[6] Ickes, *Diary, 1933–1936*, p. 60.
[7] Script, n.d., Group XXXVI, FDRL.

ment that the budget would be balanced and balanced it will have to be one way or another. . . ." [8] On Roosevelt's London Conference message: "That's right, he almost always writes important messages in longhand first." [9] Of the moribund Disarmament Conference: ". . . it is saying nothing and sawing wood." [1] Of C.C.C., three months after the bill had been signed: ". . . we have turned 300,000 boys of an average age of nineteen, from despairing down and outers, to cheerful, optimistic young men full of determination to win the battle of life." [2]

He was sharp in rebuttal. When N.R.A. was labeled socialistic: ". . . no one can give me a definition of Socialism that will agree with anyone else's definition. . . ." [3] When Congress was pilloried for abdicating responsibility to the President: "I like to refer to this last Congress as the Congress that dared . . . it wasn't afraid of the dark." [4]

Sometimes he squirmed badly, as when he tried to explain Roosevelt's position on the London Conference. At moments like these he would load the script with folksy stories about F.D.R. or with little jokes. It was from Louis that the public got its pleasant little run-down on the President's cruise that summer: the anti-aircraft practice aboard the *Indianapolis,* the songs, dancing, and boxing by the crew, the Sunday church, the dignified little picture of a deeply worried President sitting down by himself in the Admiral's cabin to "put the position of our country beyond question" on the conference issues. [5] But usually he stuck to the safe materials given him by the departments. Only twice did he use his program to fight his own inside battles: once, when he sought to promote executive reorganization by telling the public candidly of some of the worst administrative confusions; again, when he pressed on the public directly the line he had "instructed" Hull to take at Montevideo. [6] His worst problem was time. Once he found himself sneaking

[8] Script, June 4, 1933, Group XXXVI, FDRL.
[9] Script, July 8, 1933, Group XXXVI, FDRL.
[1] Script, July 16, 1933, Group XXXVI, FDRL.
[2] Script, August 13, 1933, Group XXXVI, FDRL.
[3] Script, June 25, 1933, Group XXXVI, FDRL.   [4] Ibid.
[5] Script, July 8, 1933, Group XXXVI, FDRL.
[6] Scripts, August 13, 27, 1933, Group XXXVI, FDRL.

his script in to the President via Joseph E. Davies, who had an appointment: "Help! help help. This is the damn radio. . . . Will you be a good, kind, considerate President and glance over it before you and Joe get on the high affairs of State . . . ?" [7]

Yet Louis's attempts were not all to the good. Senator Arthur Vandenburg followed him up weekly with Republican rebuttals, charging him with every crime from misrepresentation to profiteering on his government position. The *New York Sun* wickedly told the world that Louis was making $100 a minute. He received masses of personal letters, many of them hostile. An old friend wrote bluntly: "You give us cake when what we really want is bread—some real honest to God facts about what the President is really striving to accomplish instead of a lot of gooey-hooey. If you think you are a radio speaker, just listen to your Boss the next time. . . ." Someone wrote: "I still like Eddie Cantor." Someone else wanted to know more about "kits" and less about "kittens," when he told one of his little jokes. Another: "The cheapest vaudeville wouldn't tolerate such drivel as this asinine act." Still another: "It is not fair to give broadcast facilities for such flapdoodle. Some people might believe it. . . ." And another: ". . . I was compelled to reach the conclusion that of all the jackasses who ever talked over the radio, you certainly were the worst one. . . ." [8] Yet the criticisms were mostly for the artificial staging, the "cuteness" of the stories, the occasional sentimental drivel into which he fell. And there was much praise. Significantly, this was for the substantive achievements of the administration, the note of hope and progress he struck.

Louis went well beyond his own resources to exploit the public relations possibilities of the White House. When Lorena Hickok suggested to Mrs. Roosevelt that she hold press conferences for the women reporters, Louis was delighted. He knew Eleanor Roosevelt's skills; he was confident of her ability to handle these informal mass interviews. But he spent much

[7] Howe to Roosevelt, August 4, 1933, Group XXXVI, FDRL.

[8] Letters to Howe in reaction to radio broadcasts, Group XXXVI, FDRL; for Howe's own realization that his early broadcasts were "rotten," see PPF, 324, FDRL.

time coaching her on the wiles of the press. He encouraged the Gridiron Widows' Parties, which Mrs. Roosevelt held for the women reporters, reporters' wives, and cabinet wives who were barred from the newsmen's annual dinner. This was good for press relations, but also it was fun. He helped with the skits and did much of the make-up work for them— his master coup was the First Lady disguised beyond all recognition as an apple woman. And he encouraged Eleanor in her active career, her inspection tours and speeches. As she began to write more frequently for magazines, he acted as literary agent for her. All this was both old friendship and good politics, for Louis recognized that Eleanor Roosevelt was an unparalleled asset to the administration. She would make thousands of friends her husband could never reach.

And while Louis enjoyed his new and dignified role as spokesman for Roosevelt, he continued to wear frequently his comfortable old jacket as political manipulator. Yet here also the White House made a difference. He never attempted after 1932 to ride herd on political planning as he once had. He was too busy with other things, he was too ill, and this job was now Farley's. Louis was happy to shuck off on Big Jim the innumerable details, the troublesome patronage, and to dabble himself in the larger matter of shaping the New Deal's image. He was delighted to "crawl out" from under the impossibly complex California situation.[9] And he could trust Farley. Shortly after the little man's death, Big Jim would write of him: "I shall never ask for a better friend than Louie Howe."[1] And 20 years later Farley would still speak of this strange little man with deep respect and emotion. While Howe was still active, Farley consulted him on all major decisions, checked with him the elaborate procedures for handling patronage, and kept him informed. Even when Louis became insulated from the world by desperate illness and hospital walls, Farley would go out of his way to help this old friend feel that he was still influential. And

[9] Howe to Harry Hopkins, March 5, 1934, quoted in Arthur Schlesinger, Jr.: *The Age of Roosevelt: The Politics of Upheaval* (Boston: Houghton Mifflin Co.; 1960), p. 115.

[1] Farley: *Behind the Ballots*, p. 303.

when Louis wanted to, he could make that influence felt. When there were politically dangerous headlines he could cut ruthlessly through the chain of command to warn personally an errant or clumsy administrator.

He was particularly concerned with the Congressional elections of 1934 and especially with the early campaign in Maine. He knew that this would be a barometer of Roosevelt's success. As he thought about it alone at Horseneck Beach, his old pessimism took over. Suddenly he was all work. He insisted that Farley send a skilled manager and a healthy infusion of money. He promoted a program of rallies, advertising, and sound trucks that the ordinarily impoverished Maine Democracy could never afford. From the beach he dashed off page after page of encouragement, pep talks, and orders to campaign workers in Maine. He invited Governor Louis Brann and his aides to Horseneck for a planning session, and one of them later wrote in amazement at the extent of Louis's precise information on the Maine situation.[2] Louis had been doing his homework in Casey Blackburn's files. But he went well beyond the local professionals. He pressed Roosevelt to announce a dramatic approval of the Quoddy Bay hydroelectric project. He demanded the award of a destroyer contract to the Bath Iron Works. Bath was not the low bidder, so he appealed to Roosevelt directly. "This makes me very tired! . . . I am so tired of the Old —— ring running the awards of the Navy Department that I get hot under the collar. Some one of these days the way these awards are handed out between themselves is going to make the Air Mail scandal look sick. I am now going out on the front porch and cool off, but I wish you could do something about it. . . ."[3] Roosevelt remained cool. This was another case of Louis's hysterics, and he replied blandly that to throw a contract to a high bidder was "indefensible."[4]

As it turned out, Louis need not have worried so much. The Maine election was a stunning victory. And Maine provided an apt forecast of the November successes. Still Louis worried

[2] Carter B. Keene to Howe, September 11, 1934, Group XXXVI, FDRL.
[3] Howe to Roosevelt, August 29, 1934, Group XXXVI, FDRL.
[4] Roosevelt to Howe, September 5, 1934, Group XXXVI, FDRL.

incessantly—about the Negro vote, about the grinding friction of the antique Indiana machine, about the "absurd" impertinence [5] of a premature drive for Governor Paul McNutt for Vice-President in 1936. But he could do little, as illness closed around him. By January 1935 he was so weak, so plagued by wheezing and coughing that he kept to his room most of the time. He wrote almost nothing, signed few letters, but he could still dictate, telephone, and confer happily as he sat hunched on his bed.

He was especially worried about Huey Long, whose obscene demagoguery was casting uncertain shadows over Roosevelt's own future. He could have little use for any man who tagged his beloved boss, "Prince Franklin, the Knight of the Nourmahal." He may have chuckled at Long's name for Ickes, "The Chicago Cinch Bug," but this was no mere personal vendetta. Regarding Long's trip into Kansas he warned Farley: ". . . we should stop the Huey Long Grand Tour, although I think it is too late here." [6] In February when Long blasted the President in a rambling, violent radio tirade, Louis turned the administration inside out, trying to find a way to stop this kind of enormity.

After April 1935 Louis was dangerously and constantly ill, but he would not give up. He could still muster the energy to telephone Harry Hopkins from beneath his oxygen tent, warning of dangers to the relief bill pending in Congress. He could still insist that Farley put off a much-anticipated Hawaii vacation. Someone must watch the shop, he said, while Congress was still in town: "I've done those things for Franklin for years—postponed vacations, canceled engagements, and everything else too numerous to mention. I wish you would do what I ask." [7] Farley did.

In August 1935 Louis finally was moved to the Naval Hospital. But even here, despite his isolation and exhaustion, the little old master made his influence felt. Cries for help still reached him from old friends, and he channeled them on, with the Rabbit's aid, to the spot in Washington where they would receive

[5] Howe to R. E. Peters, December 19, 1934, Group XXXVI, FDRL.

[6] Howe to James A. Farley, February 13, 1935, Group XXXVI, FDRL.

[7] Farley: *Behind the Ballots*, p. 300.

the most attention. At the end of September he dived frantically into a campaign to persuade Hopkins that W.P.A. money for airports ought to be spread widely throughout the small cities instead of being concentrated on the existing large fields. He warned: "I am told that claim will be made we are favoring some of the present monopolies to the exclusion of other firms wishing to get into the aircraft game. . . . It is full of political danger and had better not be made public at all. What changed your mind and the President's after we had thrashed this all out? Hope you will change your decision if possible before your return as we are going to need a good red herring in the President's absence to divert public attention from some things not so pleasant." [8] He even worked out a letter to be sent to Mayors throughout the country, offering Federal money for an airport to any community of 10,000 or more which would provide 66 acres of land. And he warned the President himself: "I feel you will lose the best chance to get support in many cities in which you are not strong." [9] He carefully prepared the plans for press releases at a timely moment. But the word never came.

Louis was tasting the bitter gall of enforced retirement. He complained pathetically to Steve Early in September that he was being left out of things and still talked politics with anyone who would come to him—with Bernard Baruch and Eleanor Roosevelt and Jim Farley, with Early, McIntyre, Henry Morgenthau, with the President himself on his frequent visits. He would not give up. He even planned seriously to have himself moved into the Biltmore in the fall of 1936, so that he could manage the campaign personally—this when it was evident to everyone except his desperately hopeful secretaries that he would never leave the narrow confines of his hospital room.

As the autumn of 1935 turned to winter, he began to lose touch with the day-to-day facts. But there was no weakening in his shrewd judgment of events or in his sharp eye for tactics. He came up with an idea for a Roosevelt Good Neighbor League which would organize "non-partisan" clubs all over the country. It was a sound gambit, designed to ease the shift of large num-

[8] Howe to Harry Hopkins, October 2, 1935, Group XXXVI, FDRL.
[9] Howe to Roosevelt, October 2, 1935, Group XXXVI, FDRL.

bers of habitual Republicans who wanted Roosevelt but couldn't quite bring themselves to wear the Democratic label. Farley was delighted to pick it up and set his headquarters machinery to organizing what proved to be an extremely successful operation.

In his last major interview in early October 1935 Louis Howe outlined the 1936 campaign for the Associated Press in shrewd and direct language. As he himself edited the release, it said:

"The campaign next year will see a far more intelligent use of the radio. There'll be less spell-binding, less soap-box stuff. The speeches will be comparatively few and important. There'll be more intention on both sides to keep the platform down to what they really intend to do. . . ."

Hearing how that sounded, the political sage interrupted himself with a cross between a snort and a chuckle, said, "No, I'll modify that to what they want people to think they intend to do!

"There'll be much more effort really to explain things on both sides. Torch-light parades once sufficed to settle issues. But now we have women voters, and women have an insatiable curiosity. What has been done and why will figure prominently.

"All the old issues have fallen down. Prohibition is out of the way, thank heavens. Tariff has simmered down to a compromise, both parties taking about the same attitude. States Rights—the Republicans are trying to steal our clothes on that issue!

"But go back through the President's speeches and you will see that he has preached a new doctrine in the relation of a government to its people. Fifty years from now you'll find it in the history books. Look it up. I won't be here.

"No, I'm asking you, because you're out and about, and I'm held in, if it isn't true that man's liberty is taken away from him at every turn—by every red and green stop light in every city. Lord bless you, you can't even sing in the bath-tub any more. There's not much in our lives but what is bound by law. . . .

"The Republicans are moving early—too early. They remind me of the boy who gets so eager he just has to buy a giant firecracker three days before the Fourth of July. On the night of the third, he can't stand it any longer, and gets up and fires it off. . . . There are times when I rejoice in possessing a sense of humor!" [1]

[1] Copy in Group XXXVI, FDRL.

28

━━━━━━━━━━━━━━━━━━━━━━
-≫≫-≫≫-≫≫-≫≫-≫≫-≫≫-≫≫-≫≫
━━━━━━━━━━━━━━━━━━━━━━

And Quietly Sleep

I have been as close to Franklin as a
valet, and he is still a hero to me.
(Louis Howe, *1935*) [1]

FOR LOUIS HOWE these were bitter years—these White House years of illness, of desperate weakness and appalling challenge, of gasping for breath itself at the very pinnacle of victory. "It is a curious twist of fate," wrote Jay Franklin in an unlovely moment, "which has placed the affairs of the world's wealthiest country in this crisis in the hands of two men, one of whom walks with difficulty and the other of whom has rotten internal workings. . . ." [2] But Louis himself was far from bitter; he had phenomenal reserves. In the spring of 1935 Ickes wrote appreciatively: "He has been going on his nerve, but he has had fine nerve." [3] Louis had lived with death for 20 years. He had learned to savor life fully, in sheer ecstatic defiance.

[1] John Keller and Joseph Boldt: "Franklin's on His Own Now—The Last Days of Louis McHenry Howe," *Saturday Evening Post*, CCXIII (October 12, 1940), p. 47.

[2] [Jay Franklin]: *The New Dealers* (New York: Literary Guild; 1934), p. 217.

[3] Ickes: *Diary, 1933–1936*, p. 320.

There was never a thought in the Roosevelt family of retiring Louis. It was as beyond comprehension as the banishment of one's own father into exile. There was a deep, abiding love among these three—Eleanor, Franklin, and Louis—a love seldom spoken of in their tight Victorian reserve, but commanding beyond all compromise. And the Roosevelts needed him more deeply than even they fully realized until he was gone. Franklin would search fruitlessly the rest his life for another who could provide the confident but sharply critical friendship, who could relieve the loneliness, who could say no directly, who was absolutely reliable.

Louis had moved into the White House with the rest of his adopted family, had taken half a dozen man-killing jobs into the shelter of his quiet inner office, and had never given them up completely. Fortunately there was no abrupt crisis. After the first intoxicating whirl of the 100 days, which had seemed to give even Howe's emaciated frame a shot of adrenalin, he simply faded imperceptibly. Gradually, and at an increasing pace in the summer and fall of 1934, the details drifted from his hands. No one supplanted or displaced him. But others—Early, McIntyre, Farley, Eleanor Roosevelt, and the President himself —moved in to fill the gaps. An immensely loyal secretary, Rabbit, learned to carry on most of the routines in Howe's own manner. As he became more and more ill, the President's orders went out that he was to be treated with respect. And he was, even when his erratic interventions seemed irrelevant or dangerous. He died with the plans for a campaign he would never see spread out around him, firm in his grasp of victory, assured of the respect he had earned.

There was real sadness for Louis only near the end. In the early months there were periods of mellow security and dynamic action. He seemed more at home in the White House than he had in any other lodgings. Always he had appeared to be camping out between trips. Now he settled into the nation's Executive Mansion like a traveling salesman who has at last retired to the home in the country for which he had worked a lifetime. The pomp and circumstance of living in this national goldfish bowl bothered him not a bit. He moved into the Lincoln

Room with an air of permanency and made changes at once. The room was soon cluttered with the junk of his profession. He carted his small bed to the little dressing room adjacent. He felt as if he were rattling around "like a pea in a pod" in the great high-ceilinged chamber where the patriarch had slept.[4] Louis was not used to grandeur, and he simply cut it down to size. But he made no secret of his pride at occupying the room where his own father's commander-in-chief had once thrashed out the problems of the great war. Louis Howe had come a long way since he had haunted Saratoga penny ante games to pick up grocery money.

His pride was curiously mixed with humility, but it showed through. He would reply in mock agony when someone reminded him that he was a "king-maker." Yet he made it clear to everyone in the rambling administration that he was a power to be reckoned with. To underestimate Louis Howe was to court disaster that might come from the most unexpected quarter. He had a long arm and many agents, and he was eternally suspicious of those who had opposed either himself or Franklin in the past—he didn't distinguish between the two. Even his closest friends were made to feel the whip of his importance. Jim Farley or Eleanor Roosevelt, whose aid he needed and valued, often found themselves barred from Louis's room at the times they suggested, only to be asked to call at another time more convenient to him. He could be absolutely exasperating, as he was when he once kept Frank Walker waiting until he nearly missed his New York train, and all because Louis was involved in the important business of checking the record of a race horse. Yet this little man could spend hundreds of hours helping friends, and even total strangers who seemed genuinely to need help.

His pride came through in petty ways on occasion. In his great, flashy Lincoln car he installed an enormous short-wave radio on the rear seat, because there was no other place for it. He joked about the gun the Secret Service gave him, but he carefully carried his credentials as a "Special Operative" of the

[4] Quoted in Stiles: *Howe,* p. 240.

Service until his death. He was grouchy about the house and office. Many of the White House servants thought him a terror. They took uneasily to being sent down to the office to "tell the President to go to Hell," even though Franklin would sit back and laugh hilariously at the long-familiar Howe rejoinder.[5] He groused about the meals. In fact, he was in actual physical distress much of the time. It was hard for a man with such contempt for ordinary human failings to maintain an equitable façade when he might be literally gasping for breath as he worked, when he had to lie down on a couch in his office for long intervals two or three times a day. Visitors were generally astonished that this exhausted, emaciated, gray little man could work at all. And his friends and associates knew that this man could be genial to a fault, a genuinely charming dinner companion, a warmly sympathetic human being, a gay and waspish jokesmith. He would protect his staff like a grandfather from outside criticism, quietly arrange to help them when they were ill, even sending Rabbit on a restful trip to Geneva when her as yet undiagnosed illness began to sap her strength.

The most natural butt for jokes the White House had ever seen, he had to put up with much insulting or sickening nonsense from the press. He had dished it out once; he could take it, but there were unbelievable extremes in the gaudy portraits of himself that he read in the newspapers. Jay Franklin told the nation that reporters in Albany had called him "Lousy Louis" and explained: ". . . Women adore him and cannot refrain from mothering this gnarled little gnome. . . . He once told a friend that he was hated by everybody, always had been hated by everybody, and that he wanted to be hated by everybody. You can see why women love him!"[6] One New York reporter dug up an outlandish story about a Jumping Frog business which presumably Howe and Ben Riley had run as boys back in Saratoga.

And he still remained the stolid butt of his boss's adolescent badgering. "Ludevic," the boss would tell visitors, never changed his socks. "Louis just wears his socks until they don't cover his

[5] Quoted in ibid., p. 282.
[6] [Jay Franklin]: *New Dealers*, pp. 216–19.

legs anymore." [7] He rode Louis mercilessly about his weakness in economics, his carelessness about money, and his antique Sweet Caporals. Howe took it all in stride. He had long since learned to protect his sensitive soul with a tough, cynical façade. And perhaps it seemed easy by contrast with those days at Horseneck Beach when he prowled restlessly about the house, out of cigarettes and too tired to walk to town, and Grace's familiar voice punctuated the salty air: "If I were a slave to a habit like that . . . !" [8]

He played up to his own caricature with a grim nonchalance. He would stroll down to work on a summer morning, a comic, coatless, suspendered figure in high black shoes, his loose shirt and trousers hanging limply on his sparse frame, his white sailor hat with its upturned brim set jauntily atop his head. When *The New York Times* printed a picture of Louis in his favorite beach costume—painter's overalls, white buck shoes, and an outlandish sailor cap with the brim turned down around his ears—Farley wrote him: "What the hell kind of makeup did you have on for this picture?" [9] He could be smooth and urbane at White House dinners, but in his own bailiwick the Sweet Caporal ashes "drifted aimlessly about," as every reporter was fond of noting. He would receive the President's visitors dressed like a harried country newsman. Louis Howe could have been popped back into the dingy city room of the *Saratogian* in 1933 and you would never have known that he had been away.

He could ride with the fun and make a little of his own. He was hardly in the White House before he had had engraved as formal calling cards: "Col. Louis Rasputin Voltaire Talleyrand Simon Legree Howe." [1] He finally became so tired of the kingmaker business that he told one patronizing visitor: "Oh, hell, it's no trick to make a President. Give me a man who stays reasonably sober, shaves and wears a clean shirt every day and I can make him President." [2] He could send on to the President one of the incoming letters which pronounced of Roosevelt: "He really

[7] Quoted in Stiles: *Howe*, p. 225.
[8] Interview with Mary Howe Baker.
[9] James A. Farley to Howe, July 19, 1934, Group XXXVI, FDRL.
[1] Quoted in Stiles: *Howe*, p. 224.   [2] Quoted in ibid., p. 251.

has only one honest-to-God-disinterested friend, Colonel Louis McHenry Howe . . . ," with the comment: "Dear FDR, Note marked paragraph. Even the cranks are for me. I am about to order a large hat." [3] They often enjoyed a kind of strained humor which for outsiders seemed a little dull. Consider Howe's reply to a garbled note from Missy LeHand: ". . . would you mind sending a little translation for a man without much education as to the exact meaning of your note that 'President is to taking it up.' I suppose this is some of the high brow talk you have been learning from the Brain Trust lately." And Missy's reply: "He says the following: 'The President's "taking up" means this—When the President dies he expects to go up, not down! When that happens he has a very large file which he is taking up to Heaven with him. He will spend the next thousand years going through the file.' " [4]

Sometimes the humor to relieve the tensions was nicely inane. Consider the dull report which traveled back and forth between Morgenthau and Howe with the endorsements:

> Dear Louis, What the Hell? Henry
> Dear Henry, O yeah? Louis
> Dear Louis, What do you mean oh yeah? Henry.[5]

Louis's ghoulish twist of mind made it inevitable that he would have Rabbit snag the telegrams of condolence and sympathy which came in when his death was momentarily expected in the spring of 1935. He signed the replies himself. But there were limits which he well understood. In the White House he tempered his language so that his "Mein Gawd" seemed mild beside the towering profanity of Steve Early. He gave his staff a tart lecture on decorum when some joker, during their swearing-in ceremonies, whispered "and Huey Long," as they swore to defend the nation from its enemies. And in the White House there

[3] Quoted in ibid., p. 264.
[4] Howe to Margaret LeHand, May 23, 1934, and LeHand to Howe, May 31, 1934, Official File (OF), Howe File, FDRL.
[5] Howe to Henry Morgenthau, February 10, 1934, Group XXXVI, FDRL.

were none of the flip comments on letters like the one he had written during the campaign: "I am sorry this letter was lost in the mail. The Governor would have loved to have plunged into the hot water that an answer would have involved." [6]

There were deeply sentimental rewards for the little man in his White House years. Perhaps the chief of them was the quiet joy of seeing his own family participate in the honors and pleasures of victory. They visited frequently at the White House. Grace carefully saved the mementos—invitations, cards, personal notes—and told newsmen proudly that it was F.D.R. himself who had come to Fall River to be godfather of her grandson, Bobby Baker. Hartley was Louis's special delight. Perhaps because he had been away so much while his son was growing up, he turned all his new resources to help the boy start on his career. Fresh out of Harvard, Hartley wanted to be a journalist —to Louis's "intense disgust," as he said [7]—but to his great pride, as his actions made fully clear. He set the boy off to a running start, sending him to England as an informal aide to a friend on the *Tribune* during the London Conference, providing him with letters to Prime Ministers and Ambassadors. In the fall of 1933 Hartley went to Montevideo as one of Hull's "assistants" and in May 1934 to the Geneva conference on narcotics in a similar capacity. But Hartley would not cash in on his father's influence and reputation. He did an effective job wherever he went, clearly anxious to leave no room for a charge that he was freeloading. He quietly refused to pander at the embassies and brought back unused the powerful credentials Louis had given him. His mother might snort angrily: "Hartley appears never to have set foot at the Chancellery . . ." [8] Her son had no illusions. He wrote her bluntly of his job in Montevideo: "My work is general odd jobs. . . ." [9] Meanwhile he went out to land a job with one of the press services, the beginning of a highly successful ca-

[6] Huey Long incident quoted in Stiles: *Howe*, p. 237; Howe note on Francis H. Kennicutt to Roosevelt, October 20, 1932, Group XXVII, FDRL.

[7] Quoted in Stiles: *Howe*, p. 238.

[8] Grace Howe to Howe, August 3, 1933, Personal Papers.

[9] Hartley Howe to Grace Howe, December 15, 1933, Personal Papers.

reer in journalism and public relations, a career of his own making, without the shadow of his famous father.

For Grace Howe the matter seemed different. Already well
established in Fall River and in Massachusetts politics, she
started on a career as unpaid political leader, relief administrator, social worker, and Roosevelt agent in southern Massachusetts. For the rest of her life she would be as busy as Louis had
ever been. Hard work and deep interest were the major keys to
her success, but her unusual entree to the White House proved
immensely helpful. She did not hesitate to use Louis's office and
Farley's and Eleanor Roosevelt herself to facilitate the endless
stream of special pleas with various government agencies. After
Louis's death his secretaries continued to help her from the
White House. Roosevelt appointed Grace Howe postmaster of
Fall River—an appointment which Grace promptly made easy
for him by coming out at the top of the Civil Service list.

"Mother" Howe became a major personality in Fall River and
a power to be dealt with. Her position was enhanced immeasurably by the inevitable assumption of newsmen that Louis
Howe's wife must be Roosevelt's personal representative in the
State. She did nothing to disturb this convenient and pleasant
impression; but, in fact, the tables were reversed. More often
than not it was Louis, and even Franklin himself, who represented Grace in Washington. But Louis was careful. He would
not speak out in a way that "would subject me to call before the
Congressional Committee for using my position improperly." [1]
This was a side of Louis's code which never ceased to astound
his friends and critics alike. He asked so little for himself; he was
almost inordinately squeamish about accepting gifts. He would
facilitate ordinary patronage requests from his wife precisely as
he would those of other political acquaintances who still "carried guns" in their districts. He would write and speak for
money, for he knew that, by the standards of commercial press
and radio, he had earned his rewards. But having worked for 20
years to smooth Franklin's path to the White House and to keep

[1] Howe to Joseph Hurley, October 3, 1935, Group XXXVI, FDRL.

from his door every wispy rumor of scandal, he would not now risk ruining either the President he had helped to make or the power he had gained.

For Grace Howe too there was much more to politics than mere possession of influence. Power was to be used, and Grace used it relentlessly and devotedly to help the people of her depression-ridden State and community. She fought insistently the battle of the disadvantaged, and she took her rewards from the penciled thank-you notes that jammed her files. She asked little for herself, and the single reward that her friends expected for her—membership on the Democratic National Committee—was not provided by Jim Curley, the man she had worked so hard to support.

For Louis, Fall River and the Beach remained largely a retreat for "drying out." Travel had become such an exhausting business by 1933 that he could no longer manage the quick week-end trips. He puffed and wheezed so painfully merely walking along a station platform that Eleanor Roosevelt arranged with stationmasters in Washington and New York to pick him up on one of the motor-driven baggage carts for the short trips from train to taxi. But the long summers at Horseneck Beach were restful and rejuvenating. Here in the apartment he had built for himself in the barn he could move at his own pace, without the noise and confusion of the younger people and the fear of keeping others awake at night. Here there was little of the sarcasm or the clowning he saved for town. At Horseneck he was a tired, more or less grumpy and very sick old man. Unable to sleep for any great period of time, he napped on a tarpaulin in the sun. He could still make the short trip out to his "Ship Rock" in the harbor, to lie in the heat for hours with a fishing pole in hand as an excuse. He puttered with his lathe and helped young Bobby with boat models. And he spent hours with photography. He tried his hand at painting with an airbrush, using the compressor he had bought for the boys, and he dabbled at linoleum-block prints.

He was often surrounded by young people. Hartley and his friends were there frequently, and Louis would preside at corn roasts and steak fries on the beach. Here there was no grumping about meals, for Louis had the full-time help of a faithful friend and aide, "Jere" Pacquette, who cooked most of their meals to his specific order in the kitchenette of his barn apartment or over the rough grill in the sand. Louis favored chops, steaks, eggs, and an occasional special treat of Lobster Newburg. He liked Martinis, and he was a perfectionist about his ceremonial crème de menthe each evening. Jere painstakingly cracked the ice in a canvas bag, frosted the glass and the straw, to serve this special delicacy in the style Louis insisted on amid the sand and dune grass of their rough retreat.

There was the inevitable racing news—and Jere's cat. Back on Phila Street, the house had been full of them, but in the doggy Roosevelt household Louis had had to be satisfied with his "cat's nest," a little arrangement of feline figures and colorful stones which he arranged and rearranged endlessly while he and Franklin talked. Louis liked cats, he once told someone, because they were so independent. He felt a kinship for their contempt of human beings. They would never faun and pander as a dog would. Now he spent hours gently stroking Jere's pet and pulling the wood ticks from its fur. Jere brought in daily five or six newspapers. There were always at least three radio sets on simultaneously at newstime, so Louis would miss nothing.

By 1934 Jere was also full-time nurse for his boss. Sometimes the job was agonizing. It took a full hour to get Louis up and going in the morning, another hour to set him back down again at night. There was an assortment of prescriptions like a drugstore shelf. Dr. Ross McIntyre sent young George Fox from the White House staff down to Westport at frequent intervals to check up on his aging patient. There was much tension. Louis seemed always at the portal of death: the constant gasping for breath, the danger of a massive heart attack, the agonizing fits of coughing which punctuated the night. Each evening a glass of brandy was set out beside his bed to provide a quick stimulant. But here, as in the White House, the ailing, grumpy little man made devoted worshippers of those who helped him. Twenty-five years later Jere Pacquette had nothing but praise for the lovable little personality whose whims and needs he had served. He would still think of Louis as a very great man who himself was always thinking of the little men.

By 1934 Louis had begun to achieve the gentle manner of an aged patriarch—"a wise old padre," someone said.[2] He had been desperately ill from January through March of 1934, confined to his bed in the White House with the grippe and pneumonia, which complicated his already haphazard breathing. The ever-present Sweet Caps did nothing to help. Louis would not even make the gesture of using a filter holder the way his jaunty but equally enslaved friend Franklin did. He probably sensed how ridiculous it would seem. And he could give up working no more than he could smoking. He was sometimes a little pathetic in his enforced isolation. Dictating a two-page letter to Frances Perkins in early February, he pleaded: "As this is the longest note I have written since the first of the year, I do hope you will read it personally and let me know how you feel about it."[3] He could still break out some old brandy for a little celebration with Harold Ickes and Franklin when the President came back from a cruise. When Admiral McIntyre ordered him not to get out of bed until noon, he simply called visitors to his room, complaining loudly about "their" having taken his trousers away and apologizing: "It's an outrage for doctors to make such a handsome man as I receive visitors before I get my makeup on."[4] When he was still under orders to stay in bed, he sneaked out to the Gridiron Dinner in April. Late in the summer he shocked everyone by showing up in Portland, Oregon, to meet the President after his Pacific cruise and join him in the auto and train trip home. This was Louis's last junket, and he made the most of it, appearing on the back platform with Franklin at the numerous stops, thinking always, as usual, of the coming election.

By January 1935 Louis Howe was facing his last crisis; it would last for 16 months. So weak now, so pitifully breathless and pain-ridden, he was confined to his room. Franklin called off for the first time in 13 years the much-loved Cuff Links re-

[2] Quoted in Marian Dickerman to Howe, n.d., Personal Papers.

[3] Howe to Frances Perkins, February 5, 1934, Group XXXVI, FDRL.

[4] *Boston Herald*, April 21, 1934.

union. Ickes found Louis one day propped up on his elbows and knees, the only position which seemed to bring a moderate degree of comfort, but Louis was ready to talk, and he had been dictating his letters in this strange position. Farley noticed the deepening black hollows under his eyes, the weakness, the faltering hands. In mid-March Grace came down from Fall River and Mary from Urbana. Eleanor Roosevelt canceled all her plans. The President put off his yachting trip. A special train quietly pulled into a siding and cabinet officers were alerted for the sad cavalcade to Fall River. As Mary turned from her father, who was unconscious and struggling for life in his oxygen tent, she wired her husband: "No hope beyond twenty-four hours." [5] This was March 19. About 5 o'clock Louis awoke and grumbled: "Why in Hell doesn't somebody give me a cigarette?" [6]

A week later he seemed miraculously his old wheezing, coughing, pugnacious self. The President finally went off on his cruise, but he insisted on daily bulletins so that he could rush back if there were danger. And no one could quite tell. On the 26th, Stephen Early informed the President that Louis had downed his coffee and Cream of Wheat. Meanwhile McIntyre and Early glumly argued about the relative political merits of two techniques in case Howe should die. Should they go ahead with the funeral and not tell the President? Or should they have him break his rest to come back for Louis's last trip? This was the kind of worry that only Louis Howe could have appreciated fully. In Early's shoes he would have been wondering about the same thing.

Louis had rallied, but he would never get downstairs to work again. Eleanor mothered him, as she had for years, bringing him sweaters like the ones she made for Franklin on her ever-busy knitting needles, watching his diet, and insisting on proper rest hours. During the long humid Washington summer, Grace came down from Fall River to live in the White House and watch over him. She read to him for hours on end. The little man could still

[5] Mary Baker to Robert H. Baker, March 19, 1935, Group XXXVI, FDRL.

[6] Quoted in Stiles: *Howe*, p. 279.

be difficult. Once when she quit in fatigue after hours of reading, he turned to her spitefully and said: "Don't you like to read to me?" [7] The forthright Grace Howe confided to his secretaries that she could have hit him over the head with the book, if he hadn't looked so pitiful.

Louis's mail began to take on a macabre look which he did not relish and from which the girls protected him for the most part. There were welcome cables and telegrams from old friends and distinguished acquaintances, from Dick Byrd, for example, and Ramsay MacDonald. But also there were grim requests for his favorite hymn. Someone decided it was "Now the Day Is Over." [8] Worse yet, there were hundreds of prescriptions of infallible remedies for this friend of the beloved President. Mostly they belonged to witchcraft or folklore. But Louis could still get about on occasion. He took a grim kind of pride in being able to manipulate one of Franklin's wheel chairs among the upstairs family rooms, so that his boss wouldn't always have to wheel in to him.

By mid-August the problem of caring for Louis in the White House became insurmountable. Certain urgent repairs provided the needed excuse and he was quietly moved to the Naval Hospital. Everyone expected him to raise the roof, and Eleanor Roosevelt went along to see that he was properly settled down. But the little man was more realistic than they sensed. He could face facts when he had to. He welcomed the cooling system which took some of the galling humidity out of the air, and he joked easily about missing the pushbutton bells he had used in the White House. But he would not face more facts than he had to, and he exploded loudly when he discovered there would be no telephone. Even the gentle Eleanor wrote to Grace that he was in a bit of a "tizzy-wiz." [9] Louis would not be cut off from giving the advice that he was certain would be needed. And the Louis Howe who had groused mercilessly when the Washington police had closed up his favorite bookie did not intend to be cut

[7] Quoted in ibid., p. 281.

[8] Margaret Durand to Joe Emerson, August 26, 1935, Group XXXVI, FDRL.

[9] Eleanor Roosevelt to Grace Howe, August 23, 1935, Personal Papers.

off from placing an occasional small bet on the nags. The President finally ordered a special phone for Louis to use only from 10 to 4:30. But this hopeful device for keeping Louis from calling the President in the early morning or the middle of the night did not always work. Hacky protested that she could not be caught between her boss and the President. However, Roosevelt would not curb Louis in a way that would hurt him, and he told the reluctant Hacky that some of Louis's ideas were "darned good" even now that he was isolated from great events.[1]

In any case, Louis did not intend to be put off. One day in September he sent a radio message via Steve Early: "Louis is feeling quote hurt unquote because he says the President promised yesterday and again today to talk to him dash he feels like he is on the outside comma cut off period. He wants the President to call him."[2] On another occasion early in November, prevented from using his own telephone, he sent his orderly downstairs to call Hyde Park to insist that the President call him back. The President did.

These were long months, but Louis never allowed them to be boring or despairing months. Many hours were filled with reminiscences mustered for the young naval corpsmen who attended him. He boasted moderately of his successes, but he left them feeling that he had a "nineteenth century mind-set." When he talked about economics it was in a manner from another world. He told them, as one remembered it: "You must limit production for the simple reason that the old profit must be reasonable. That's human nature. You can't pay labor too much, because that would mean a rise in prices and labor wouldn't be able to buy as much as she had before with her low wages." And, as they read to him hour after hour, he turned back to the old favorites of his boyhood: Kipling, Stevenson, Carlyle, Anthony Hope. From contemporary writings he wanted only Wodehouse and *Punch* and the omnipresent blood-and-thunder mysteries.[3]

The President came to see him often, creating moments of

[1] Quoted in Stiles: *Howe*, p. 292.
[2] Stephen Early to Marvin McIntyre, September 10, 1935, PPF, Howe File, FDRL.
[3] Keller and Boldt: "Franklin's on His Own," pp. 47, 131–2, 135.

their old spontaneous give and take, as if nothing had come to break their partnership. They would argue politics and joke about his ailments being "unconstitutional," or about the outrageous goatee which Louis had affected. Louis thought it made him look more distinguished. Most of his visitors thought he looked like a goat. Visitors generally found him bumptious despite his obvious discomfort and his having to lie on his stomach with his head propped on a pillow. Bess Furman recorded the anomalous scene in October:

> As he talked, with dry twists of humor, the hospital atmosphere faded quite away. For Howe, in pajamas gayly striped, made it clear that there was the busy office of the President's Number 1 Secretary. He had a telephone at hand, radio in reaching distance—a conference calendar even. . . . "The trouble is—dammit—they keep the clothes off me, and keep me down, because if I started out I can't stop," said the irrepressible Howe, in bed since the middle of March. . . .[4]

Louis did his best to make Bess Furman's picture a true one. He busied himself constantly with little things and large. He remembered Sara Roosevelt's birthday in September: "I probably know better than most people how much you have to be proud of."[5] And the elegant old lady healed the wounds of 20 years with her gentle reply: "I think I receive too much kindness but I am proud to feel that my 'one and only' is the cause and I always hope his father knows!"[6] Louis responded to the needs of his new friends, even pushing through to the President himself once to obtain a White House car for one of his corpsman whose mother was suddenly ill. He was concerned deeply about foreign policy and repeatedly warned Roosevelt against Mussolini, who he insisted would start another World War. He followed the debates on the arms embargo proposal in the fall of 1935 and

[4] Associated Press Interview, copy in Group XXXVI, FDRL.

[5] Howe to Sara Delano Roosevelt, September 20, 1935, Group XXXVI, FDRL.

[6] Sara Delano Roosevelt to Howe, September 24 [1935], Group XXXVI, FDRL.

inquired of the State Department about the details of the plebiscite in Memel. At home he was worried about the demagogues who had flowered in the pre-election months. He warned everyone who would listen about Father Coughlin and Huey Long. He thought the disenchanted Hugh Johnson almost as bad, and it took Bernard Baruch to cool him down and keep him from answering publicly Johnson's attacks on Roosevelt.

He intervened here and there as best he could to stop troubles of which the newspapers warned. He went over Ickes's head on a burgeoning crisis in the Subsistence Home Projects in Alaska, and sent up to straighten it out an old engineer friend whom he had cajoled over the telephone to leave his business for a few weeks. Later he boasted of the Alaska situation, "which Ickes ruined and I saved." [7]

But chiefly he was interested in the coming campaign. As winter came on, he planned it in more and more detail. Ickes was astounded to have Howe call him to the Hospital and insist on a long summary of P.W.A. activities complete with pictures. He dictated a long letter to Franklin about the State of the Union Message: "You have a lot to brag about, nothing to apologize for. Let 'em have it. They'll lap it up." He was optimistic: ". . . while the charlatan cannot fool all the people all of the time—a man who is desperately in earnest; who believes in what he is trying to do; who is trying to do what most of the people believe in as well;—will inevitably retain the confidence of the majority of the people all of the time." [8] He warned Farley vociferously of the dangers of the Liberty League, which Al Smith and Jouett Shouse had organized with Du Pont money and distinguished sponsors like John W. Davis, but he then agreed with Farley's diagnosis that the best thing to do was to ignore it and let them wear themselves out.

Meanwhile Louis ordered "Casey" Blackburn to get together the research material, the organization charts, and other data necessary for updating the 1932 techniques, and began to cast about for reliable aides to take to New York with him. He fussed

---

[7] Keller and Boldt: "Franklin's on His Own," p. 131.

[8] Howe to Roosevelt, quoted in Stiles: *Howe,* p. 293; Howe to Joseph McGoldrick, February 18, 1935, PPF, 200A, FDRL.

with the details of the Good Neighbor League, planning booklets, buttons, and organization charts—even raising money from Baruch and others. And he toyed with a motion picture designed to tell the story of the United States Constitution from a point of view friendly to the New Deal.

But there were moments when he could play the game no longer. Once when his aide tried to encourage him about the coming New York trip, Louis suddenly turned sober and said quietly: "No, I will not be there. Franklin is on his own now." [9]

By late January 1936 Louis was merely holding on, often in a coma, sometimes irrational, yet still struggling. Then on April 18, 1936, while Franklin Roosevelt sat with the newsmen at the Gridiron Dinner and Eleanor entertained the "Widows," Louis slipped quietly away from a world that had mixed much sadness with its pleasures and had given him one supreme satisfaction.

Louis would have been appalled and pleased with Franklin's last token to his "great, little" friend—the State Funeral in the East Room of the White House, the flags at half-mast, the solemn funeral train pulling up the East Coast to Fall River. The President of the United States and his sons stood bareheaded on the snow-covered Borden plot while Louis was gently carried from the hearse which Jere had driven from the station. Then came the dignified, comforting words of the Episcopal service. His much-loved son and Grace and Mary and Eleanor listened, frozen in the iron reserve with which their family training had taught them to meet crisis.

Time and history would deal harshly with Louis Howe. He had none of the sense of order and importance that would inspire him to make a record for posterity. It would be almost by accident that the dim outlines of his early career would come to light. There would be a few momentary memorials: a mountain in Antarctica, named by Dick Byrd "Mount Louis McHenry Howe" and soon forgotten by the mapmakers; [1] the C.C.C. boys' "Louis McHenry Howe Boulevard," soon to be rechristened by a

[9] Keller and Boldt: "Franklin's on His Own," p. 47.

[1] Richard E. Byrd to Roosevelt, November 16, 1940, September 9, 1944, PPF, Byrd File, FDRL.

forgetful city administration. Somewhere there would be a boy growing up, fondly named Howe by his father, who had been one of Louis's orderlies. There would be pleasant memoirs, gratefully recorded by Eleanor Roosevelt and Lela Stiles. If the President had had his way there would have been a stone on Louis's grave saying: "Devoted friend, advisor and associate of the President." [2] But in this intimate matter Grace Howe chose a subtler reminder of the old partnership, one that only the deeply interested would note. For the stone that stands beneath the spreading copper beech in Fall River is an exact, but smaller, replica of the one enshrined in the Rose Garden at Hyde Park.

Louis had left one monument that could never be erased. No one would ever write about the twentieth century without mentioning Franklin Delano Roosevelt. No one would ever be able to write about Roosevelt without mentioning Louis McHenry Howe.

[2] Quoted in *Personal Letters, 1928–1945,* p. 1406.

29

The Greatness of
a Little Man

*He hated sham and cowardice, but he
had a great pity for the weak and helpless. . . .*

(Eleanor Roosevelt, *1936*) [1]

LOUIS HOWE died at a major turning point in his old friend's
career. The first New Deal was on the verge of merging into the
second. Businessmen had become hostile to the man who had
sought their aid and promised their rescue in 1932. Hopes for a
balanced budget were even now giving way to more and more
spending. "Balanced Government" was even now appearing a
mere dream to be shattered by the new political alignment
which sought strength from labor, the consumer, the farmer,
and the minorities and singled out businessmen as targets for
attack. After the massive 1936 victory, a newly inspired Roose-

[1] Eleanor Roosevelt: Statement on the Death of Louis Howe, April 18,
1936, Copy in Personal Papers.

velt would try two of the most explosive gambits of his career: the attempt to "purge" the Democratic Party of its conservatives; the attempt to "purge" the Supreme Court of its monopoly of final decision.

It was all but inevitable that friends and foes alike would look fondly back on Louis Howe and pontificate that if Howe had only been around the new extremes would have been avoided, the mistakes prevented. Even as Howe's influence began to slip late in 1934, the careful Arthur Krock had suggested that "certain of the blunders and immature actions that have produced confusion and made the President's great task more difficult . . ." might stem from Howe's inability to get around and see people face to face.[2] Moley has insisted that Roosevelt's basic shift to the left in politics was a repudiation of Howe's fundamental strategy which emphasized a balanced appeal to agriculture and business. Ickes mourned during July 1936 the loss of the only man who could talk with Roosevelt straight and "hang on like a pup to a root until he got results."[3] One reporter claimed: "With Howe's passing from the front-line trenches, Roosevelt has lost both drive and direction."[4] Another said as early as 1935: "Roosevelt had better get his political brains out from under that oxygen tent."[5] Eleanor Roosevelt herself remained convinced that Louis might have helped her husband avoid such monumental failures as the "purge."

All of this was speculation. Yet what evidence there is hints at a quite different guess. Louis might very well have welcomed Roosevelt's move to the left. His own writing in 1934 indicates the kind of shift Roosevelt eventually made. Louis's anger at the Liberty League was monumental; his own sniping at plutocracy came in increasing tempo throughout 1934. He showed signs early that year of a renewed sensitivity to organized labor; he talked increasingly of the social-reform aspect of the New Deal, and he did nothing to hold it back. In any case, it is sheer non-

[2] *The New York Times*, December 6, 1934.
[3] Ickes: *Diary, 1933–1936*, p. 640.
[4] Paul W. Ward: "Roosevelt Keeps His Vow," *The Nation*, CXLI (September 25, 1935), p. 349.
[5] Quoted in Stiles: *Howe*, p. 288.

sense to presume that even Louis Howe could have restrained the fundamental economic and social problems to which Roosevelt had to respond, or that he would have done anything different than Farley and Roosevelt did in the face of the deepening business reaction. Louis would have loved the neatly relevant story which Roosevelt told of the frock-coated banker who had been rescued from the river in 1932 and four years later was berating his rescuer for losing his silk hat.

And no one can presume to guess just how effective this little man would have been as the personalities and problems of the New Deal became more and more complex. Given his perpetual pessimism, he might have cut his boss back to size on the "purge"; he might have avoided the 1940 crisis with Jim Farley. Or given his intense hatred of all those whose ambitions led them to "double-cross" his beloved boss, he might have been more vindictive than Roosevelt himself with Walter George, Millard Tydings, and even Jim Farley. Whatever the punches, Louis would have rolled with them. He had always insisted on being practical. In any case, there would have been limits to his influence. There always had been.

Louis had always carefully shaped his role to his talents, carefully truncated his operations to suit the things he could manage. He was an able political handyman, a generally successful juggler of personalities, a useful brake on an administration caught up in the reckless enthusiasm of its own action. He could protest tartly against sloppy administration, waste, and ruthless ambition. He gave the White House an intimate, relentless watch on public opinion which might otherwise have been slighted in the heady intoxication of ideas and work. But much of the New Deal he did not understand. Worse yet, he didn't care to understand it. His instincts were conservative; the real forces that moved him were the beat of public opinion and his own firm compassion for human beings in need. He thought of individuals, not masses. He could never face hardship with statistical analysis. He distrusted the glib, knowledgeable professors, the dreamers. He understood the simple, direct professionals like Ed Flynn, the tough old southern and western Congressmen. He could deal with Frances Perkins's sweet but experienced dedication, with Ickes's bluster and pride, with Morgenthau's sensitive, uncomplicated loyalty, but he could only sneer in the presence of Frankfurter's cocky young idea men. He was no architect of the New Deal. His own brief sallies into direct administration were often unsuccessful.

The real gauge of his influence remained hidden. He was, as a newsman once said, the "most private" of the President's private secretaries. He talked with Roosevelt daily; no one knew what they said. On a given matter he might have immense impact—or none at all. It depended upon whether he was interested, whether the President listened. His contemporaries were confused about him. An Ickes, a Hull, or a Hopkins never quite knew whether Louis spoke for himself or for the President. Louis made the most of this. When he retired to the beach in the summer of 1934 and Roosevelt left for an ocean cruise, Howe gladly let the local newsmen believe that the nation's business was being carried on from his front porch on Horseneck Beach. In fact, he was never "acting President"; few final decisions can be traced to his desk. But Eleanor Roosevelt, who respected him deeply, Ray Moley, who resented him, Rosenman, whose own career was deeply shadowed by Howe's suspicion, Ed Flynn, Frances Perkins, Jim Farley—all agreed that he had immense influence with Roosevelt. His major service was relentless criticism. He was the "no" man from whom the boss could never quite escape.

Yet even in this role he might not have continued much longer. As the first months of the New Deal faded away, Louis's grasp of the hectic maelstrom slipped badly. It was too much for any one man; he suffered the same kind of insulation that plagued Roosevelt himself. Operating on the telephone, he could no longer judge personalities as shrewdly as he once had. Illness separated him from Roosevelt for days at a time. And the President bristled more frequently at Louis's cynical critique. Jay Franklin noted with some aptness that Louis was like an "aging 'first wife' " in a harem.[6] Donald Richberg more accurately suggested that Howe and Roosevelt were like father and

[6] [Jay Franklin]: *New Dealers,* p. 221.

son. Roosevelt had a deep respect for Howe, but became a little irritated at the continued parental guidance. "I'm going to talk this over with Louis," the President once said. "He has forty ideas a day and sometimes a few good ones."[7] Then again, he would note wickedly that he was happy to arrive home only a half hour before a Fireside Chat. Otherwise, he said, he would have to argue the whole thing over with Howe, and he liked the speech as it was.

Louis probably suspected all of this. He was certainly only half joking when he had told his boss on election night: "Well, I guess I've worked myself out of a job."[8] But he was relentless. When he failed personally, he would plant his ideas with others, hoping to squeeze his boss gently in a ring of advice. Eleanor Roosevelt was one of his favorite agents. The fact that he must sometimes use her suggested the weakening of his influence during the White House days. It suggested also that he himself sometimes forgot his role as private critic and dangerously joined the mob of special pleaders who surrounded the oval study.

Yet his major strength remained to the end what it had always been, his steady presence, his integrity and loyalty, his willingness to do anything for Roosevelt, their deep personal friendship. Howe was Roosevelt's one complete refuge from the job he insisted was the loneliest in the world. Only with Louis could the President let his guard down completely.

Perhaps it was Eleanor Roosevelt who had the last word when she emphasized his personal qualities rather than his political influence. "There were few people," she wrote, "for whom he really cared, but those who had the privilege of calling him their friend knew that he could always be counted upon, and there never was a more gentle, kindly spirit. . . ."[9] Many times in the years to come she would gently remark that above all Louis loved power. The power had come to him from a nearly unique lifetime of struggle. He did not make Roosevelt

[7] Donald Richberg: *My Hero* (New York: G. P. Putnam's Sons; 1954), p. 295.

[8] Edwin C. Hill, in the *Boston American*, May 31, 1933.

[9] Ibid.

President, but, as Henry Morgenthau has noted, it would have been a much harder road to the White House without him. He could never be Number One man. Yet he had the wit and the soul to be one of the most remarkable Number Two men in the history of the modern world.

Bibliographical Essay

MATERIALS about Franklin D. Roosevelt are mountainous in volume, yet often disappointingly meager on the significant matters. Roosevelt kept every scrap of paper; but many of the great decisions were matured in personal discussions which were never recorded. The frustration shared by all Roosevelt scholars becomes particularly acute when dealing with Louis McHenry Howe. Howe and Roosevelt were together much of the time for 23 years. They seldom wrote to each other except when they were separated by business trips or vacation jaunts. Even when Louis was in New York and Franklin in Albany they preferred the telephone or Louis's weekly trips to the Executive Mansion to the more time-consuming business of writing. Besides, Howe had a distinct aversion to putting things on the record. And when Louis did write a letter, he seldom dated it; when he received one, he seldom filed it. Thus there are large periods of time which cannot be documented from Howe's correspondence. Fortunately, Louis's secretaries kept careful files, and his wife, Grace Hartley Howe, preserved a great many letters covering particularly Louis's life before he met Franklin Roosevelt.

This study is based principally upon the various collections of Louis Howe Papers and upon the monumental groups of papers in the Franklin D. Roosevelt Library at Hyde Park, New York. The largest and most significant collection of Howe Papers is contained in Group XXXVI in the Roosevelt Library. It includes all of the material which accumulated in Howe's files during his years as an aide to

F.D.R., plus some items later added by his wife. There is, of course, a great deal of Howe material in the Roosevelt papers running parallel to these files, particularly in Group IX (State Senatorship); Group X (Assistant Secretary of the Navy); Group XI (1920–8); Group XIV (Roosevelt's family, business, and personal papers); Group XV (1920 Campaign); Group XVI (1924 Campaign); Group XVII (1928 Campaign); and Group XXVII (Papers of the Democratic National Committee). Group XVIII (Official Files of the Governor) and Group XII (Personal Papers of the Governor) document the period between 1928 and 1932 but contain very little Howe material. Group XIII (White House Papers) is an enormous body of letters and documents arranged in four somewhat overlapping files. The President's Personal File (PPF) has been thoroughly researched for this study. The President's Official File (OF) and the President's Secretary's File (PSF) have been used selectively. I have not searched the Alphabetical File (AF) which contains masses of letters from the general public.

This study utilizes for the first time a second major group of Howe papers, discovered in Mrs. Howe's home after her death. Indicated in my footnotes as "Personal Papers," they are owned jointly by Howe's children, Mary Howe Baker and Hartley Edward Howe. These papers are described more fully in the comment on Part I (below). They include not only a great many Howe family papers and letters but also a number of hitherto unavailable letters from Eleanor Roosevelt to Grace Howe and from F.D.R. to Louis.

Also used for the first time is a third important collection of Howe letters in the Papers of Thomas Mott Osborne of Auburn, New York. These include personal letters between Howe and Osborne and a large number of political reports filed by Howe during his years as political aide to the Auburn Mayor. But the Osborne Papers have immense value in themselves, and I found the political correspondence between 1905 and 1928 extremely useful in documenting the story of upstate New York Democratic politics during the progressive period. These papers are owned by Osborne's heirs, and I consulted them in the office of the Auburn *Citizen-Advertiser* through the courtesy of the late Charles D. Osborne.

To supplement the manuscript collections, one must certainly consult Elliott Roosevelt (ed.): *F.D.R.: His Personal Letters*, 4 vols. (New York: Duell, Sloan and Pearce; 1947–50), which contains many personal letters not available in the Roosevelt Library. Samuel Rosenman (ed.): *The Public Papers and Addresses of Franklin D.*

Roosevelt, 5 vols. (New York: Random House; 1938), contains many of the significant Roosevelt speeches, but some of them are incomplete. Another valuable source for Roosevelt speeches and formal papers is *The Public Papers of Governor Franklin D. Roosevelt 1929–1932*, 4 vols. (Albany: J. B. Lyon Co.; 1930–9). This contains many items during the gubernatorial period which are not in Rosenman, and it differs from Rosenman occasionally on the specific phrasing. Donald Scott Carmichael (ed.): *F.D.R., Columnist: the Uncollected Columns of Franklin D. Roosevelt* (Chicago: Pellegrini and Cudahy; 1947), makes available Roosevelt's newspaper columns, the source for what little we know of his ideas on certain matters. Carroll Kilpatrick (ed.): *Roosevelt and Daniels: a Friendship in Politics* (Chapel Hill: University of North Carolina Press; 1952), contains the two friends' letters to each other. Edgar B. Nixon (ed.): *Franklin D. Roosevelt and Conservation, 1911–1945*, 2 vols. (Hyde Park: Franklin D. Roosevelt Library; 1957), brings together the significant material in the Roosevelt papers on this particular topic. The election statistics are available in Edgar E. Robinson: *The Presidential Vote, 1896–1932* (Stanford: Stanford University Press; 1934) and *They Voted for Roosevelt* (Stanford: Stanford University Press; 1947). New York State election statistics are available in the various annual volumes of the *New York Legislative Record and Index*.

Personal memoirs abound, and many of them fill what would otherwise be serious gaps in our knowledge. For Howe, the most valuable is Lela Stiles: *The Man Behind Roosevelt: the Story of Louis McHenry Howe* (Cleveland and New York: World Publishing Company; 1954). Miss Stiles was one of Howe's secretaries from the 1928 campaign on, and her book provides much specific information and many insights into her boss. It is most useful for the matters she personally observed.

Of the many memoirs about Roosevelt and his entourage I have found the following most valuable in their documentation of Howe's activities and their revelation of the peculiar Howe-Roosevelt relationship. Eleanor Roosevelt's books, though gentle and restrained, are useful for the pre-White House period particularly: *This Is My Story* (New York: Harper and Brothers; 1937); *This I Remember* (New York: Harper and Brothers; 1949); and *The Autobiography of Eleanor Roosevelt* (New York: Harper and Brothers; 1961). Frances Perkins: *The Roosevelt I Knew* (New York: The Viking Press; 1946), helps to correct the portrait of the young F.D.R. and provides some unique glimpses of Roosevelt and Howe in the White House. Josephus

Daniels: *The Wilson Era, Years of Peace—1910–1917* and *Years of Peace and After, 1917–1923* (Chapel Hill: University of North Carolina Press; 1944, 1946), give a romantic view of the wartime Roosevelt and Howe, distinctly colored by a respect for Roosevelt's later prominence. Jonathan Daniels: *The End of Innocence* (Philadelphia: J. B. Lippincott; 1954), written partly from his father's Diaries and partly from his own memories, brings out some of the elder Daniels's impatience with Roosevelt and Howe and some of Jonathan's bitterness about them. His portrait of Howe is sketched in acid. James A. Farley: *Behind the Ballots: the Personal History of a Politician* (New York: Harcourt, Brace and Co.; 1938), contains sympathetic sketches of Howe, reflecting Farley's immense admiration and close friendship for the little man. Raymond Moley: *After Seven Years* (New York: Harper and Brothers; 1939), was written with some of the bitterness of a disenchanted Roosevelt aide. Yet there is considerable restraint in it, and hence considerable value, for Moley adds much detail to both the story of the first New Deal and the story of Roosevelt and Howe. Moley's later *27 Masters of Politics in a Personal Perspective* (New York: Newsweek–Funk and Wagnalls; 1949), contains thought-provoking sketches of Howe and Roosevelt as well as of many of their contemporaries. Harold Ickes: *The Secret Diary of Harold L. Ickes: the First Thousand Days, 1932–1936* (New York: Simon and Schuster; 1953), makes available much valuable material on Howe's activities in the White House. Grace Tully's little memoir: *F.D.R., My Boss* (New York: Charles Scribner's Sons, 1949), tells many stories about life with Roosevelt and Howe in the White House particularly. Samuel Rosenman: *Working with Roosevelt* (New York: Harper and Brothers; 1952), is valuable for an understanding of Howe's relationships with the growing Roosevelt staff after 1928. Brief but useful commentaries upon Howe's role will be found in the following, among others: Cordell Hull: *The Memoirs of Cordell Hull*, 2 vols. (New York: The Macmillan Co.; 1948); Edward J. Flynn: *You're the Boss* (New York: The Viking Press; 1947); Charles Michelson: *The Ghost Talks* (New York: G. P. Putnam's Sons; 1944); John Morton Blum: *From the Morgenthau Diaries: Years of Crisis, 1928–1938* (Boston: Houghton Mifflin Co.; 1959); Robert Sherwood: *Roosevelt and Hopkins: An Intimate History* (New York: Harper and Brothers; 1948); [Jay Franklin]: *The New Dealers* (New York: Literary Guild; 1934); and Louis B. Wehle: *Hidden Threads of History: Wilson through Roosevelt* (New York: The Macmillan Co.; 1953). Elliott Roosevelt:

"The Most Unforgettable Character I've Met," *Reader's Digest*, LXII (February 1953), pp. 26–30, is a valuable, although brief, appreciation of Howe.

The secondary sources on Roosevelt, Howe, and their era have been growing at an astounding rate in the ten years since research began on this volume. I shall make no attempt to list all of them. This would merely create a mammoth list—impressive, perhaps, but of limited use. The most stimulating and accurate single volume on F.D.R. is James MacGregor Burns: *Roosevelt: the Lion and the Fox* (New York: Harcourt, Brace and Co.; 1956). Burns deals centrally with Roosevelt the politician. His bibliography and his description of the Roosevelt papers are the most useful available. For a balanced portrait of Roosevelt, the many-sided man, the classic source promises to be the multi-volume *Franklin D. Roosevelt*, by Frank Freidel. Freidel has published to date three monumentally researched and carefully written volumes: *The Apprenticeship, The Ordeal*, and *The Triumph* (Boston: Little, Brown and Co.; 1952, 1954, 1956). A classic of another cast is Arthur M. Schlesinger, Jr.: *The Age of Roosevelt*. Again, three volumes have now been published: *The Crisis of the Old Order, 1919–1933, The Coming of the New Deal*, and *The Politics of Upheaval* (Boston: Houghton Mifflin Co.; 1957, 1959, 1960). Schlesinger has a sympathetic point of view and a unique ability to catch the image of an age with great economy and discipline of style. He sweeps broadly across the whole period; this is a biography of an era, not a man, but in the process he adds much new specific information and a stimulating series of interpretations. Rexford G. Tugwell: *The Democratic Roosevelt* (Garden City: Doubleday and Co.; 1957) is a major contribution to the Roosevelt literature, adding to the material both from research and from Tugwell's personal memoirs, yet it bears the marks of a participant's own special involvement in the great action described. Valuable also is Tugwell's little series of essays: *The Art of Politics: As Practiced by Three Great Americans, Franklin Delano Roosevelt, Luis Muñoz Marin and Fiorello H. La Guardia* (Garden City: Doubleday and Co.; 1958). John Gunther: *Roosevelt in Retrospect: a Profile in History* (New York: Harper and Brothers; 1950), makes Roosevelt come alive. His analysis of the Roosevelt and Howe relationship is useful. Although the book suffers from some of the flamboyance of the journalistic approach, it is substantially accurate in detail, immensely stimulating in generalization. Thomas H. Greer: *What Roosevelt Thought: The Social and Political Ideas of Frank-*

lin D. Roosevelt (East Lansing: Michigan State University Press; 1958), is scholarly and analytical. Bernard Bellush: *Franklin D. Roosevelt as Governor of New York* (New York: Columbia University Press; 1955) is a careful and substantial study, and indispensable for the period 1928–33. Daniel R. Fusfeld: *The Economic Thought of Franklin D. Roosevelt and the Origins of the New Deal* (New York: Columbia University Press; 1956), is thorough, accurate, and stimulating. Harold Gosnell: *Champion Campaigner: Franklin D. Roosevelt* (New York: The Macmillan Co.; 1952), adds little that is new, but it has great value in bringing together the relevant materials for an understanding of Roosevelt's campaigning skills. Edgar E. Robinson: *The Roosevelt Leadership, 1933–1945* (Philadelphia: J. B. Lippincott Co.; 1955), is a scholarly but highly critical appraisal, measuring Roosevelt by the standards set by Herbert Hoover. John T. Flynn: *Country Squire in the White House* (Garden City: Doubleday, Doran and Co.; 1940) and *The Roosevelt Myth* (Chicago: Devin-Adair Co.; 1948), are hostile, broadly overgeneralized, but stimulating to thought. Warren G. Harris: *Herbert Hoover and the Great Depression* (New York: Oxford University Press; 1959), provides an important corrective at many points to the emphasis and interpretation of the Roosevelt-centered books.

Old, but still extremely useful, are three books by Ernest K. Lindley. *Franklin D. Roosevelt: a Career in Progressive Democracy* (Indianapolis: The Bobbs-Merrill Co.; 1931), is a model for campaign biographers; sound in fact, restrained in statement, it is friendly but still believable after 30 years, and it is still the basic source for many Roosevelt items. Lindley: *The Roosevelt Revolution: First Phase* (New York: The Viking Press; 1933), and *Half-Way with Roosevelt* (New York: The Viking Press; 1936), are more journalistic but remain useful sources for much information about the dynamics of Washington life. Earle Looker: *This Man Roosevelt* (New York: Brewer, Warren and Putnam; 1932), is more clearly of the campaign-biography genre, but Looker provides some inside views of the Roosevelt household which can be found nowhere else.

Little has been written about Louis Howe specifically, aside from Lela Stiles's book. Louis W. Koenig: *The Invisible Presidency* (New York: Holt, Rinehart and Winston; 1960), deals interestingly and usefully with the role of the Presidential assistants over the years, but it does not focus particularly on Howe.

Often the past can be read more clearly from photographs than from print. The picture files at the Roosevelt Library are an extremely valuable aid to scholars. The small collection of Howe photographs has been supplemented with copies of his family's snapshots, but many others remain in the family's possession. Among the most interesting published photographs of the Roosevelt group are those in Stefan Lorant: *F.D.R.: a Pictorial Biography* (New York: Simon and Schuster; 1950), and Richard Harrity and Ralph G. Martin: *The Human Side of F.D.R.* (New York: Duell, Sloan and Pearce; 1960).

My understanding of both Roosevelt and Howe has been generally and immensely enhanced by talks with Eleanor Roosevelt, Mary Howe Baker, Hartley E. Howe, and many others mentioned below. Among the valuable interviews recorded by George Palmer of the National Park Service and preserved in the Roosevelt Library, the most useful for this book have been those with John Mack, Thomas Leonard, and Grant Dickinson. The Oral History Project at Columbia University is a unique repository of information and opinion which would have been lost to history, had the University not undertaken this massive program of recorded interviews. I have gleaned substantial information from the reminiscences recorded there of R. S. Binkerd, Henry Bruere, George F. Chandler, William Wilson Cumberland, William Adams Delano, Roy S. Durstine, Edward J. Flynn, James W. Gerard, Florence Jarray Harriman, Arthur Krock, Langdon P. Marvin, Jackson E. Reynolds, and George S. Van Schaick. I am grateful for permission to consult these.

I • THE WINDS OF FATE (Chapters 1–6)

Among the many articles on Louis Howe which helped to shape the stereotype of him, the most important are: Jerome Beatty: "Here's Howe," *American Magazine*, CXV (March 1933), pp. 17–19, 69, 70, 72; W. E. Berchtold: "Press Agents of the New Deal," *New Outlook*, CLXIV (July 1934), p. 25; "Colonel Howe, Presidential Pilot," *Review of Reviews*, LXXXVII (February 1933), p. 50; "Diogenes": "News and Comment from the National Capital," *Literary Digest*, CXVII (March 17, 1934), p. 12; "President-Maker," *Commonweal*, XXIV (May 1, 1936), pp. 17–18; "The Roosevelt Kitchen Cabinet," *Literary Digest*, CXIV (December 17, 1932), pp. 19–20; A. D. H. Smith: "Roosevelt's Pilots—Colonel House and Colonel Howe," *Scribner's*, CXIII (January 1933), pp. 1–7; "White House Boss in the President's Absence," *Newsweek*, I (June 24, 1933), pp. 17–18. Also Dexter Teed: "Roosevelt—and Howe," *New York World Tele-*

gram, August 26, 1933; *The New York Times*, July 3, 10, 1932; and "Howe," *The New Yorker*, VIII (April 23, 1932), p. 13. The discussion of Louis Howe's early career with Osborne and of the Democratic League is based upon the Osborne Papers and the Howe Personal Papers. Also useful are the William T. Doty and the Chester C. Platt Papers in the Regional History Collection of Cornell University. Political reporting early in the century was both thorough and extensive. The files of the Albany *Knickerbocker-Press* and *Times-Union*, the New York *Herald*, *The Times*, and *Tribune* fill many of the gaps left by the manuscript collections. For all periods of Roosevelt's career, the extensive scrapbooks and clipping files in the Roosevelt Library are a great aid. Particularly valuable for the State politics before 1910 are Merlo J. Pusey: *Charles Evans Hughes*, 2 vols. (New York: The Macmillan Co.; 1951); George E. Mowry: *Theodore Roosevelt and the Progressive Movement* (Madison: University of Wisconsin Press; 1946); and Harold F. Gosnell: *Boss Platt and His New York Machine: a Study of the Political Leadership of Thomas C. Platt, Theodore Roosevelt, and Others* (Chicago: University of Chicago Press; 1924). Essential to an understanding of the relationships among the older New York State Democrats are Allan Nevins: *Grover Cleveland: a Study in Courage* (New York: Dodd, Mead and Co.; 1944), and Mark D. Hirsch: *William C. Whitney* (New York: Dodd, Mead and Co.; 1948). Rudolph W. Chamberlain: *There Is No Truce: a Life of Thomas Mott Osborne* (New York: The Macmillan Co.; 1935) is a balanced study, useful particularly for the Democratic League and the politics of the Wilson era. Henry F. Pringle: *Theodore Roosevelt: a Biography* (New York: Harcourt, Brace and Co.; 1931), is still a reliable guide to much of T.R.'s activities in State politics. Elting E. Morison and John M. Blum (eds.): *The Letters of Theodore Roosevelt*, 8 vols. (Cambridge: Harvard University Press; 1951–4), adds some new light. Henry F. Holthusen: *James W. Wadsworth, Jr.* (New York: G. P. Putnam's Sons; 1926), gives the conservative Republican point of view.

For Franklin Roosevelt's early life, the most important source is Elliott Roosevelt (ed.): *Personal Letters, Early Years*. There is much of value in Sara Delano Roosevelt's: *My Boy Franklin* (New York: Ray Long and Richard R. Smith; 1933). Group XIV, FDRL, contains a great many mementos of Franklin's boyhood, including school records.

The most extensive secondary treatments of the period covered in this section are Freidel: *The Apprenticeship*, and Alfred B. Rollins,

Jr.: "The Political Education of Franklin D. Roosevelt: His Career
in New York State Politics, 1910–1928" (Dissertation, Harvard University; 1953). Gunther, Tugwell, Fusfeld, Lindley, and Schlesinger:
Crisis of the Old Order, all have useful and extensive material.

Roosevelt's first campaign is thoroughly documented in the local
newspapers: the Poughkeepsie *News-Press, Eagle, Daily Eagle,
Enterprise,* and *Courier.* Palmer's recorded interviews with John
Mack, Thomas Leonard, and Grant Dickinson add interesting details
and are available in FDRL. My own interview with Morgan Hoyt
was most helpful. Hoyt has also written his memories of this period
in "Roosevelt Enters Politics," *The Franklin D. Roosevelt Collector,* I
(May 1949), pp. 3–9, and in letters to Roosevelt, January 27,
February 3, 1938, PSF, FDRL. Important new material is in L. J.
Magenis to Roosevelt, August 10, 1928, and Henry Neach to Roose-
velt, October 20, 1928, in Group XVII, FDRL. John K. Sague:
"Reminiscences" (manuscript in the possession of Mrs. John H.
Miller, Poughkeepsie), adds some new notes.

On Roosevelt's legislative career, the basic source is Group IX,
FDRL, which contains 35 boxes of correspondence between Roosevelt and his constituents. Some letters documenting his legislative interests are in the early files of Group X. One of the most important
sources for the Sheehan fight is Edmund R. Terry: "The Insurgents
at Albany," *Independent,* LXXI (September 7, 1911), pp. 534–40.
Terry was one of the Insurgents, and his description helps place
Roosevelt's role in the Insurgency in a more nearly accurate perspective. The Osborne Papers provide much information on the relationships between the Insurgents and their backers outside the
Legislature. Interviews with Frances Perkins, Charles D. Osborne,
Charles C. Burlingham, Constance Parsons Hare, John Godfrey
Saxe, and William O. Dapping added greatly to my understanding
of the young Roosevelt, the Insurgency, and the politics of the period, as have the helpful letters of Ashley T. Cole, a friend of Sheehan. Cole has also provided a scrapbook which he kept for Sheehan
and which includes some news items not available elsewhere. One
interesting letter in the Howe Personal Papers (William F. Sheehan
to Willard Marakle, April 5, 1911), describes Sheehan's own feeling
that he had been made the victim of a fight between the Governor,
John Dix, and Tammany's boss, Charles F. Murphy.

Any study of Roosevelt's legislative activities is inhibited by the
fact that the New York State Legislature keeps no record of its debates. But newspaper reporters created a reasonably complete record

for the period of Roosevelt's Senatorship. The printed copies of the Bills are another useful source; they have made possible a number of detailed corrections in the widely accepted picture of Roosevelt's early career. Useful guides to the bills on which Roosevelt voted and which he sponsored have been prepared by the New York State Legislative Reference Library and are available in the Roosevelt Library. In addition, see *Personal Letters, 1905–1928*. Current periodical literature provides much information regarding public opinion on the issues F.D.R. faced. Among the dissertations, A. Blair Knapp: "The Water-Power Problem in New York State" (Unpublished thesis, Syracuse University; 1928), is particularly useful. For a more thorough discussion of various aspects of Roosevelt's legislative career, see Alfred B. Rollins, Jr.: "Young F.D.R. as the Farmer's Friend," *New York History*, XLIII (April 1962) pp. 186–98; "Young Franklin Roosevelt and the Moral Crusaders," *New York History*, XXXVII (January 1956), pp. 3–16; "Franklin Roosevelt's Introduction to Labor," *Labor History*, III (Winter 1962), pp. 3–18.

The Osborne Papers, which contain Louis Howe's personal reports, Group IX, and the early files of Group X, FDRL, provide much information about the Empire State Democracy and the Wilson movement in New York State. There are a few items in the Howe Personal Papers. The Papers of Edward M. House, and particularly his Diary, are essential for the study of New York politics during this period. They must be used with great care, since House stated everything with an air of authority, but he was often limited by both inadequate information and strong bias. I am grateful to Yale University for permission to use these extensive files, which include correspondence with many significant figures in State and national politics. John K. Sague's "Reminiscences" help with some items as does George Haven Putnam: *Memories of a Publisher, 1865–1915* (New York: G. P. Putnam's Sons; 1915). Arthur Link: *Wilson: the Road to the White House* (Princeton: Princeton University Press; 1947), is the definitive study of Wilson's campaign for the nomination.

Roosevelt's and Howe's local campaign is documented in *Personal Letters, 1905–1928*, in Group IX, FDRL, and in the Howe Personal Papers which contain Louis's checkbooks and some letters, as well as helpful snapshots.

Louis Howe's early life had been practically a closed book until his personal papers were found recently in Fall River, Massachusetts. Most of what had been known about it had come from his own carefully guarded comments to reporters or from two newspaper articles, one in Indianapolis, the other in Saratoga, at the time of his death. The Howe Personal Papers is a large but heterogeneous collection of odds and ends. Fire and hurricane have wreaked havoc with many of the items which might have been useful, and much of what remains is in extremely fragile condition. But there is much of importance: an extensive correspondence between Grace and Louis Howe, as well as many letters from other members of the family; a great deal of material on Louis's newspaper career; mementos of the early days in Saratoga; several examples of his sketches, poems, and the illustrated booklets of funny verse he made for Roosevelt; and a large body of letters and family papers dealing with his parents' life in Indianapolis. Many of the letters are highly personal. I have been allowed to read them all, but much of the material must remain under restrictions for some time. The collection is particularly valuable for the period before 1928. Taken together with the Osborne Papers, it provides extensive evidence of Louis's early political and journalistic careers. Its coverage for the later period is extremely sketchy, aside from the political correspondence of Grace Hartley Howe.

Louis's West Indian trip is documented in a surprisingly thorough manner by the detailed Diary of Asenath Borden, which was kindly shown to me by her daughter, the late Margaret Delano of Adamsville, Rhode Island. Most of Louis's early signed articles may be found in Group XXXVI, FDRL, or in the Howe Personal Papers. One which has been previously overlooked is "Saratoga Springs," *New England Magazine,* n.s. XXXII (June 1905), pp. 471–86. Louis's report to the Saratoga Springs Commission may be found in truncated form in George Foster Peabody, Frank H. Godfrey, and Benjamin F. Tracey: *Report of the Commissioners of the State Reservation at Saratoga Springs, 1911* (Albany: J. B. Lyon Co.; 1911).

Mary Howe Baker spent many days sharing her reminiscences with me. She and I went back to Saratoga together to visit some of the Howe landmarks. There is no substitute for observation at Saratoga, or at Hyde Park or Horseneck Beach. The Howes' early homes, churches, and schools are still standing. Many of the hotels are gone, but the Adelphi and the Worden still suggest the style and elegance of the great days. Canfield's Casino is a Museum, and the race track features mammoth parking lots, but one can still spot Louis's old print shop, and find hints of the old affluence—marble walks on sections of Phila Street, the great homes along Union Avenue, the Trask

estate with its fabulous rose gardens. The City Historian's files in
the Saratoga Springs Public Library and the Saratoga County Historical Museum preserve many valuable mementos of the great days.

There are few remnants of the Howes' printing business, and only
a handful of copies of the Saratoga *Sun* in the years in which they
controlled it: June 28, 1883 (Library of Congress); December 8,
1893, and February 22, 1900, and a clipping from February 15,
1900 (Howe Personal Papers). But the extensive files of the *Saratogian* in that newspaper's present office suggest the nature of Saratoga
journalism when the Howes worked in it. Evelyn Barrett Britten
and Frank Sullivan told me much of Louis Howe's early work. Elizabeth Gorman helped me relive Louis's career as an actor and director.
John Corey and John Slade helped with other items. And Mary Baker
kindly showed me many of the items of furniture and furnishings
which had once been in their Saratoga home.

II • A TEAM IN THE MAKING (Chapters 7–10)

Materials on the upstate Democrats' contacts with Wilson are to be
found in the Osborne Papers, Group IX, FDRL, and in the "Reminiscences" of John Sague. The chief sources for Roosevelt's and Howe's
career in the Wilson administration are Group X and Group XXXVI,
FDRL; the Howe Personal Papers; and *Personal Letters, 1905–1928.*
Particularly important for the politics are the 43 boxes of patronage
papers in Group X. The Edward M. House Papers provide much detailed information on the crosscurrents of politics in New York, as
well as extensive documentation of House's own maneuvering. John
Blum: *Joe Tumulty and the Wilson Era* (Boston: Houghton Mifflin
Co.; 1951), is essential as are Arthur Link: *Wilson: the Road to the
White House; Wilson: the New Freedom;* and *Wilson: the Struggle
for Neutrality, 1914–1915* (Princeton: Princeton University Press;
1947, 1956, 1960). Ray Stannard Baker: *Woodrow Wilson: Life
and Letters,* 8 vols. (Garden City: Doubleday, Page and Co.; 1927–
39), provides some useful information. Essential among the memoirs
are James Kerney: *The Political Education of Woodrow Wilson*
(New York: The Century Co.; 1926); Eleanor Wilson McAdoo: *The
Woodrow Wilsons* (New York: The Macmillan Co.; 1937); William
Gibbs McAdoo: *Crowded Years* (Boston: Houghton Mifflin Co.;
1931); Daniel C. Roper: *Fifty Years of Public Life* (Durham, N.C.:
Duke University Press; 1941); Joseph P. Tumulty: *Woodrow Wilson
As I Knew Him* (Garden City: Doubleday, Page and Co.; 1921);

and William F. McCombs: *Making Woodrow Wilson President* (New York: Fairview Publishing Co.; 1921). Jacob A. Friedman: *The Impeachment of Governor William O. Sulzer* (New York: Columbia University Press; 1939), is an able and scholarly survey of State politics generally in the spring of 1913. The several collections of Sulzer manuscripts throughout the State are virtually useless.

For more elaborate discussion of Roosevelt's politics, see Rollins: "Political Education," and Freidel: *The Apprenticeship*. Current files of *Outlook, Independent, Harper's Weekly, Century Magazine, World's Work, Nation*, and *Literary Digest* are particularly useful for exploring public opinion on the politics of the Wilson era. Burns: *Roosevelt* has a stimulating discussion of Roosevelt's political tactics. Freidel: *The Apprenticeship* is particularly valuable for Roosevelt's official activities in naval matters and for its interpretation of Howe's role in these affairs. It benefits from careful use of the naval papers in the National Archives. Josephus Daniels: *Wilson Era* and Jonathan Daniels: *The End of Innocence* add much material on the working of the Navy Department not available elsewhere. Donald W. Mitchell: *History of the Modern American Navy from 1833 through Pearl Harbor* (New York: Alfred A. Knopf; 1946), is a sound, basic survey. An important study of one aspect of Roosevelt's work is Gerald D. Nash: "F.D.R. and the World War I Origins of Early New Deal Labor Policy," *Labor History*, I (Winter 1960), pp. 39–52.

III • THE TIME OF TESTING (Chapters 11–14)

Roosevelt's immediate postwar speeches and the increasing tensions between Congress and the Navy Department are discussed largely on the basis of newspaper sources, but there are significant materials in Group X and Group XXXVI, FDRL, and there are a few items in the Howe Personal Papers. There are 25 boxes of correspondence from the 1920 campaign headquarters in Group XV, FDRL, but the story of Roosevelt's nomination must be drawn from the memoirs of those present, and particularly from James M. Cox: *Journey through My Years* (New York: Simon and Schuster; 1946); from George Palmer's interview with John Mack, FDRL; and from Congressman Timothy Ansberry's interviews with reporters in the *New York Herald, New York Sun*, and *Albany Times-Union*, July 12, 1920. Roosevelt's campaign was thoroughly covered by the newspapers, and *The New York Times* is particularly useful. Rollins: "Political Education," Burns: *Roosevelt*, and Gosnell: *Champion*

Campaigner, all have extensive discussions. Freidel: *The Ordeal* is the most thorough and useful single volume for the period 1920–8.

The discussion of the Howe family during Washington years is based upon the Howe Personal Papers and upon interviews with Mary Baker Howe and Hartley E. Howe. The story of Roosevelt's family life in the same years has been told extensively in Eleanor Roosevelt: *This I Remember* and *This Is My Story*, and in *Personal Letters, 1905–1928*. The most revealing letters about Howe's illness are in the Halstead File of Group XII, FDRL. The source for my statements about Howe's business plans is the correspondence in the Howe Personal Papers. Howe's own family and friends are in sharp disagreement about what his plans were in the spring of 1921. Papers dealing with Roosevelt's business, philanthropic, and personal interests are in Group XIV, FDRL. But very personal items, such as financial records and tax reports, are not available. It is impossible to estimate Roosevelt's financial situation exactly, but "Roosevelt's Fortune," *Fortune Magazine*, VI (October 1932), pp. 40–4, 105, gives what is probably still a reasonably reliable picture. There are a few letters on business matters in Group XXXVI, FDRL.

Freidel: *The Ordeal* is excellent on Roosevelt's illness and recovery. More detailed is Jean Gould: *A Good Fight; the Story of F.D.R.'s Conquest of Polio* (New York: Dodd, Mead and Co.; 1960). Mrs. Charles Hamlin tells about some of F.D.R.'s treatments at Marion, Massachusetts in her manuscript: "Some Memories of Franklin D. Roosevelt," FDRL, and in "F.D.R.'s Recovery from Polio Given Impetus at Marion," *Boston Sunday Globe*, July 25, 1945. There are a few letters in Howe Personal Papers which place Louis's activities at Campobello in more nearly precise perspective. Eleanor Roosevelt describes what happened in *This Is My Story*. Dore Schary: *Sunrise at Campobello* (New York: Random House; 1958) is drama, not history. Without being precise in every detail, it achieves a substantial accuracy in the larger picture which is almost breathtaking, although Louis Howe is made to seem much more of a mere clown than he really was.

Papers in Group XIV, FDRL, are extensive enough to sketch a clear picture of most of Roosevelt's business activities in the 1920's. But Howe's work with the Crime Commission must be pieced together largely from newspaper sources and from odds and ends of items in Groups XIV and XXXVI, FDRL, and in the Howe Personal Papers. Moley: *After Seven Years* comments upon Howe's interest in crime prevention. Both Moley and Hartley Howe have helped me with this aspect of the story.

Turnley Walker: *Roosevelt and the Warm Springs Story* (New York: A. A. Wyn; 1953), is helpful on Roosevelt's interests in this second home. There is some significant correspondence on Warm Springs in Groups XIV and XXXVI, FDRL. James Roosevelt and Sidney Shallett: *Affectionately, F.D.R.: a Son's Story of a Lonely Man* (New York: Harcourt, Brace and Co.; 1959) is a mine of family stories and personal incidents which lend color and understanding to this whole period of Roosevelt's life. The question whether illness affected Roosevelt's thinking is discussed variously in Frances Perkins: *The Roosevelt I Knew,* and in John Gunther: *Roosevelt in Retrospect,* among others. No question is so sharply disputed among those who knew Roosevelt. *Personal Letters, 1905–1928,* offers many insights on Roosevelt's attitudes and personality, and is particularly useful at this point for its reprinting of his Diaries of the houseboat trips. Marked auction catalogues (FDRL) indicate Roosevelt's collecting interests and Howe's role as agent for him.

Political materials for Roosevelt's career in the twenties are largely in Groups XI, XVI, XVII, but there are many significant items scattered through Group XXXVI and the alphabetical files of Group XIV, FDRL. There are a few items in Howe Personal Papers. The replies to Roosevelt's Circular Letter of 1924 have been analyzed in Paul L. Fint, Jr.: "Self-Criticism in the Democratic Party, 1924–1926" (Master's thesis, Georgetown University; 1951). Carmichael: *F.D.R., Columnist* contains Roosevelt's views on many issues otherwise unrecorded. For the 1924 Convention, see William G. McAdoo: *Crowded Years* (Boston: Houghton Mifflin Co.; 1931); Alfred E. Smith: *Up to Now, an Autobiography* (New York: The Viking Press; 1929); and Joseph M. Proskauer: *A Segment of My Times* (New York: Farrar, Straus; 1950). John W. Davis helped me to understand the attitudes of some party leaders toward Roosevelt during the twenties. Freidel, Gosnell, Tugwell, and Rollins: "Political Education," all have extensive treatments of the politics of the twenties. Stiles: *Man Behind Roosevelt* describes Howe's activities from the vantage point of one who worked with him. Arthur Schlesinger, Jr.: *The Crisis of the Old Order* contains both a stimulating analysis of the forces and facets of the postwar years and a disciplined and rapidly moving narrative biography of the pre-gubernatorial Roosevelt. William E. Leuchtenberg: *The Perils of*

Prosperity, 1914–1932 (Chicago: University of Chicago Press; 1958), is a thorough and stimulating survey of the general problems of the twenties.

IV • APPRENTICESHIP FOR THE WHITE HOUSE
(Chapters 15–19)

The story of Roosevelt's nomination for Governor has been told from many points of view. Essential for a complete picture are the very full newspaper stories, particularly in *The New York Times;* Proskauer: *Segment of My Times;* Eleanor Roosevelt: *This Is My Story;* Edward J. Flynn: *You're the Boss* (New York: The Viking Press; 1947); Farley: *Behind the Ballots; Personal Letters, 1905–1928;* and Group XVII and Group XXXVI, FDRL. There is one letter from Howe to Grace Howe in Personal Papers which reveals strikingly Howe's discouragement over the nomination.

On the campaign itself, in addition to the sources above, one must consult Rosenman: *Working with Roosevelt,* which provides much detail on F.D.R.'s personal campaign and working techniques; Edmund A. Moore: *A Catholic Runs for President: the Campaign of 1928* (New York: Ronald Press Co.; 1956); and Stiles: *Man Behind Roosevelt.* Roy Peel and Thomas C. Donnelly: *The 1928 Campaign: an Analysis* (New York: Richard R. Smith; 1931), is a contemporary, but classic, analysis by political scientists. From the Republican point of view, see Herbert Hoover: *The Cabinet and the Presidency, 1920–1933* (New York: The Macmillan Co.; 1952), and Edgar E. Robinson: *Roosevelt Leadership.* Many of Roosevelt's speeches are in Samuel Rosenman (ed.): *Public Papers and Addresses,* vol. I. Newspaper accounts and the Speech File, FDRL, add records of other talks. Flynn and Farley have described the tension and uncertainty of the election night, and John Godfrey Saxe told me of the elaborate plans for checking the accuracy of the upstate vote. See also, for the nomination and the campaign generally, Rollins: "Political Education," Freidel, Burns, Gosnell, and Tugwell.

The basic papers for the Governorship are Group XII and Group XVIII, FDRL; *Personal Letters, 1928–1945; Public Papers of the Governor;* and Rosenman (ed.): *Public Papers and Addresses,* vol. I. Since Louis Howe's work in this period was largely divorced from the formal operations of the Governor's office, the bulk of the material on which he worked is in Group XXXVI, FDRL. Newspaper sources are helpful for the period of the twenties generally; the *Literary Di-*

gest and *Review of Reviews* provide running summaries of editorial opinion and public commentary on Roosevelt's activities.

The transitional period between the 1928 election and the inauguration is treated thoroughly in the memoirs, particularly: Rosenman: *Working with Roosevelt;* Perkins: *Roosevelt I Knew;* Flynn: *You're the Boss;* Blum: *From the Morgenthau Diaries;* Farley: *Behind the Ballots;* Tully: *F.D.R., My Boss;* and Eleanor Roosevelt: *This Is My Story.* These also treat Roosevelt's attitude toward Smith. F.D.R. himself later wrote a memo for the record describing the tension with Smith during the twenties: *Personal Letters, 1928–1945,* pp. 771–3. For Smith's own point of view, see Emily Smith Warner: *The Happy Warrior: a Biography of My Father, Alfred E. Smith* (Garden City: Doubleday and Co.; 1956). Louis Howe's post-election activities are described in Stiles: *Man Behind Roosevelt.*

Sound and thoroughly researched secondary sources for the Governorship in general are: Bernard Bellush: *Franklin D. Roosevelt as Governor of New York* (New York: Columbia University Press; 1955); the more extensive Bellush: "Apprenticeship for the Presidency: Franklin D. Roosevelt as Governor of New York" (Dissertation, Columbia University; 1950); and Freidel: *The Triumph.* Fusfeld: *Economic Thought of Franklin D. Roosevelt* is useful for an understanding of some of Roosevelt's policies. Warren Moscow: *Politics in the Empire State* (New York: Alfred A. Knopf; 1948), and Belle Zeller: *Pressure Politics in New York* (New York: Prentice-Hall; 1937), are useful on the dynamics of State politics. The Republican Party's activities in the twenties and early thirties in New York have not been studied carefully, and there is a great need for a scholarly treatment of the period which is not centered on Roosevelt and Lehman. Finla G. Crawford: "Recent Political Developments, 1915–1935," in A. C. Flick (ed.): *Modern Party Battles,* in *History of the State of New York,* VII (New York: Columbia University Press; 1935), provides a brief outline of developments. Jack Metzger: "Significant Aspects of New York State Administration under Governor Franklin D. Roosevelt, 1929–1932" (Thesis, University of Chicago; 1947), is helpful.

Particularly useful for the 1930 campaign are Farley, Flynn, Stiles, Rosenman, and Lindley. Copies of most of Roosevelt's speeches are in FDRL. Gosnell, Burns, and Freidel: *The Triumph,* all have good secondary accounts. Group XXXVI, FDRL is especially useful for this campaign. Among the many contemporary newsmen's appraisals of F.D.R., the most incisive and rewarding are: Robert

McManus: "Rise of a Roosevelt, a Portrait of the Governor of New York," *Outlook,* CLVI (November 5, 1930), pp. 374–6, 397–8; S. J. Woolf: "The Two Candidates for the Governorship," *The New York Times Magazine* (October 7, 1928); and Milton MacKaye: "The Governor," *The New Yorker,* VII (August 15, 1931), pp. 18–22, and VII (August 22, 1931), pp. 24–9.

V • FOR THE VICTORS: "TRIUMPH AND TRAGEDY"
(Chapters 20–29)

Basic for a study of the 1932 nomination and election campaigns are Group XII, Group XXXVI, and the massive Papers of the Democratic National Committee, Group XXVII, FDRL, which I have searched only selectively. The Papers of Mary W. Dewson, Group XXXVII, FDRL, include her own manuscript memoirs. There are extensive materials in the Howe Personal Papers on Massachusetts politics and especially the activities of Grace Howe, but there are only occasional items regarding Louis at this point. *Personal Letters, 1928–1945,* adds some material, particularly on the attitude of Governor Smith.

The various memoirs are particularly helpful in reconstructing the color and detail of the long campaigns. Farley: *Behind the Ballots;* Flynn: *You're the Boss;* Rosenman: *Working with Roosevelt;* and Moley: *After Seven Years* are particularly important. Moley is particularly useful for an understanding of the brain trust, and Tugwell: *The Democratic Roosevelt,* also throws much light on the work of Roosevelt's advisors. Stiles: *The Man Behind Roosevelt,* describes many of the lighter incidents at campaign headquarters as well the tense, dramatic days at Louis's Convention headquarters in the Congress Hotel. I am indebted to James A. Farley, Raymond E. Moley, and Henry Morgenthau, Jr., for sharing their memories of this period with me. Harriet Allen Kerr, who was an aide to Mary W. Dewson during the campaign, and Hartley Howe, who was at the Chicago Convention with his father, have also helped materially. Extremely useful is Earland I. Carlson: "Franklin D. Roosevelt's Fight for the Presidential Nomination, 1928–1932" (Dissertation, University of Illinois; 1955). On the incident of the nominating speech, see Moley, Rosenman, and Farley. Louis Howe's private reactions to the only partial adoption of his draft were never recorded. Bascom N. Timmons: *Garner of Texas, a Personal History*

(New York: Harper and Brothers; 1948), is important to an understanding of the Speaker's attitudes.

Many of the important campaign speeches are in Rosenman: *Public Papers and Addresses.* Moley is especially revealing in his discussion of the evolution of various Roosevelt speeches and of the strategy of the campaign in general. Michelson: *The Ghost Talks,* adds some items. The press coverage is a major source for this, as for other campaigns. Roy Peel and Thomas C. Donnelly: *The 1932 Campaign: an Analysis* (New York: Farrar and Rinehart; 1935) is unusually thorough and reliable for a study done so recently after the incident. On the campaign from the Republican point of view, see Herbert Hoover: *The Great Depression, 1929–1941* (New York: The Macmillan Co.; 1952).

Four of the many secondary accounts have proven particularly useful. Schlesinger: *Crisis of the Old Order,* provides a graphic, lively, scholarly, and friendly treatment. E. E. Robinson: *The Roosevelt Leadership,* is scholarly and highly critical. Freidel: *The Triumph,* is meticulous and balanced in his narrative of the great events. Burns: *Roosevelt,* has a fine analytical treatment which is part of a substantial, well-documented, interpretive study of the quality and character of the Roosevelt leadership.

Moley, Rosenman, and Tugwell, Group XXXVI of FDRL, and Howe Personal Papers are major sources for the interim period. *Personal Letters, 1928–1945,* has significant items, as does Group XII, FDRL. Hoover: *The Great Depression,* describes President Hoover's reactions to the deepening crisis and to Roosevelt's and Moley's conferences with him. Important to an understanding of the cabinet-making process are Farley: *Behind the Ballots;* Perkins: *The Roosevelt I Knew;* and Flynn: *You're the Boss.* Correspondence with Henry Wallace and interviews with Raymond Moley and Henry Morgenthau have been helpful at this point. Mary Baker recalled for me her memories of the inauguration festivities.

Schlesinger: *Crisis of the Old Order,* records vividly the tension of the burgeoning crisis and provides a sound and stimulating analysis of the background of the era. Also especially valuable for a grasp of the roots of the New Deal are Eric Goldman: *Rendezvous with Destiny* (New York: Alfred A. Knopf; 1952); Richard Hofstadter: *The American Political Tradition and the Men Who Made It* (New York: Alfred A. Knopf; 1948); and *The Age of Reform* (New York: Alfred A. Knopf; 1955). Particularly useful among Rexford G. Tugwell's many articles are: "The Experimental Roosevelt," *The Political Quarterly*, XXI (July–September 1950), pp. 239–70, and "Franklin D. Roosevelt on the Verge of the Presidency," *Antioch Review*, XVI (March 1956) pp. 46–79.

Research in the White House period remains a never-ending task. In addition to the four massive collections listed above, Group XIV continues to be significant mainly as an alphabetical repository of essentially personal correspondence. Even so, much of this material relates to politics in one way or another, and some of it refers to Louis Howe. The Howe Personal Papers contain a few items, but the most significant collection for revealing Louis's White House operations is Group XXXVI, FDRL.

Harold Ickes: *Secret Diary;* Perkins: *The Roosevelt I Knew;* and Moley: *After Seven Years* and *27 Masters* add significantly to the materials in the various manuscript collections in defining Howe's role in the White House. Also helpful in this respect are Michelson: *The Ghost Talks;* Blum: *From the Morgenthau Diaries;* Tully: *F.D.R., My Boss;* Rosenman: *Working with Roosevelt;* Hull: *Memoirs;* Donald Richberg: *My Hero* (New York: G. P. Putnam's Sons; 1954); Bernard Baruch: *Baruch: My Own Story* (New York: Henry Holt and Co.; 1957) and *Baruch: the Public Years* (New York: Holt, Rinehart and Winston; 1960); Margaret Coit: *Mr. Baruch* (Boston: Houghton Mifflin Co.; 1957); and Eleanor Roosevelt: *This Is My Story* and *This I Remember*. But the major source on Howe in the White House is Stiles: *The Man Behind Roosevelt*.

Moley shared with me his own story of the Inaugural Address; he believes that while they sat in the library at Hyde Park, Roosevelt personally rewrote Moley's draft in his own hand in order to avoid Louis Howe's wrath at the sight of another Moley speech. He is also convinced that it was Louis who later wrote into the draft the famous sentence about fear. Howe's own articles reveal much of the White House operations, and contemporary newspaper columns provide other odds and ends of information. Also especially helpful are Drew Pearson and Robert S. Allen: "How the President Works," *Harper's Magazine*, CLXXIII (June 1936), pp. 1–14; and S. J. Woolf: "As His Closest Friend Sees Roosevelt," *The New York Times Magazine* (November 27, 1932).

On the New Deal generally, the most thorough work to date is Schlesinger: *The Coming of the New Deal* and *Politics of Upheaval*. Basil Rauch: *The History of the New Deal, 1933–1938* (New York: The Creative Age Press; 1944), remains a sound basic outline. Brief scholarly treatments are provided by Dexter Perkins: *The New Age of Franklin Roosevelt, 1932–1945* (Chicago: University of Chicago Press; 1957) and by Denis W. Brogan: *The Era of Franklin D. Roosevelt: a Chronicle of the New Deal and Global War* (New Haven: Yale University Press; 1950). Broadus Mitchell: *Depression Decade, from New Era through New Deal, 1929–1941* (New York: Rinehart and Co.; 1947), is basic. Robinson: *Roosevelt Leadership,* is highly critical of Roosevelt. Alfred B. Rollins, Jr.: *Franklin D. Roosevelt and the Age of Action* (New York: Dell Publishing Co.; 1960), is an interpretive narrative and an anthology of primary and secondary materials. Tugwell: *The Democratic Roosevelt,* is particularly rewarding for the first New Deal, in which the author was closely involved.

On the first weeks of the New Deal and for the London Conference, see especially Moley: *After Seven Years.* For the latter, see also Hull: *Memoirs* and the brief but sound survey in Allan Nevins: *The New Deal and World Affairs: a Chronicle of International Affairs, 1933–1945* (New Haven: Yale University Press; 1950). For N.R.A. the best source is still Leverett S. Lyon *et, al.: The National Recovery Administration* (Washington: The Brookings Institution; 1935). Hugh Johnson: *The Blue Eagle from Egg to Earth* (Garden City: Doubleday, Doran and Co.; 1935) gives its first director's point of view in full color. On labor matters I have relied heavily on Milton Derber and Edwin Young (eds.): *Labor and the New Deal* (Madison: University of Wisconsin Press; 1957). And for the background of the Montevideo Conference I have used particularly: Samuel F. Bemis: *The Latin American Policy of the United States: an Historical Perspective* (New York: Harcourt, Brace and Co.; 1943); Dexter Perkins: *Hands Off* (Boston: Little, Brown and Co.; 1941); and Hull: *Memoirs.* Sumner Welles helped me to chart Roosevelt's personal commitment to the Good Neighbor policy before his Presidential election. Howe's own activities regarding the Conference are documented largely from Group XXXVI, FDRL.

Howe's involvement in the C.C.C. is thoroughly documented in Group XXXVI, FDRL. Edgar Nixon (ed.): *Franklin D. Roosevelt and Conservation,* contains much relevant material. The "mess-kit" incident is discussed in the newspapers. Frances Perkins's account of the development of C.C.C. is helpful. Howe Personal Papers contain Grace Howe's own mementos of her interest in the nearby C.C.C. camps, as well as of her extensive work in organizing the women's work of the F.E.R.A. in Massachusetts.

Group XXXVI, FDRL, contains extensive correspondence and materials on the Subsistence Home Projects. For various points of view, see Coit: *Mr. Baruch;* Eleanor Roosevelt: *This I Remember;* and Harold Ickes: *Secret Diary.* On Howe's continued interest in the crime crusade, Group XXXVI, FDRL, and Moley: *After Seven Years,* are useful. A hostile appraisal is William Seagle: "The American National Police: the Dangers of Federal Crime Control," *Harper's Magazine,* CLXIX (November 1934), pp. 751–61.

Copies of most of Howe's articles and scripts for his radio programs are in Group XXXVI, FDRL. The Howe Personal Papers contain some others, as well as two sound recordings of his radio programs and some candid snapshots taken by Luther Evans during Howe's lecture to Edward S. Corwin's American Government class at Princeton. There was much criticism of Howe's radio work—see Group XXXVI and PPF 324, FDRL. Moley, in 27 *Masters,* is highly critical of Howe's writing and speaking for money. For Howe's encouragement of Mrs. Roosevelt's writing and press conferences, see: Eleanor Roosevelt: *This I Remember;* and Ruby Black: *Eleanor Roosevelt: a Biography* (New York: Duell, Sloan and Pearce; 1940).

Among Howe's own articles in this period, the following are the most important: "The Winner," *Saturday Evening Post,* CCV (February 25, 1933), pp. 6–7, 48–9; "Behind the Scenes with the President," *American Magazine,* CXVII (March 1934), pp. 42–4; "The President's Mail-Bag," *American Magazine,* CXVII (July 1934), pp. 22–3, 118–20; "Women's Ways in Politics," *Woman's Home Companion,* LXII (July 1935), pp. 9–10; "Uncle Sam Starts After Crime," *Saturday Evening Post,* CCVI (July 29, 1933), pp. 5–6, 71–2; "Balanced Government the Next Step," *American Magazine,* CXV (June 1933), pp. 11–12, 84, 86; and "Life More Abundant," *Cosmopolitan,* CXXIV (April 1934), pp. 18, 19, 104–6.

Group XXXVI, FDRL, is the major source for Louis's interest in the 1934 election. Howe Personal Papers have much on Massachusetts politics and patronage. After 1934 the Howe Papers become extremely skimpy, reflecting Louis's increasing insulation from important affairs. But much of his activity can be pieced together from varied sources. Stiles: *Man Behind Roosevelt* is of great help, as are Farley: *Behind the Ballots;* Ickes: *Secret Diary;* and Eleanor Roosevelt: *This I Remember.* One of the most important sources is John Keller and Joe Boldt: "Franklin's on His Own Now—the Last Days of Louis McHenry Howe," *Saturday Evening Post,* CCXIII (October 12, 1940), pp. 42, 47, 131–2, 134, 136. Written by a man who acted as Howe's companion and aide in the Naval Hospital, it contains much information not available elsewhere. Newspaper articles are also helpful, particularly Bess Furman's interview with Howe for the Associated Press, a copy of which is in Group XXXVI, FDRL. Mary Howe Baker, Hartley Howe, Henry Morgenthau, and Frances Perkins have shared with me their memories of Howe's declining years. Ludger (Jere) Pacquette provided vivid details of Howe's life at Horseneck Beach as well as striking evidence of the intense admiration those closest to Howe had for him.

Louis Howe's medical records cannot be made available under existing government regulations. Judgments about the nature of his illness must be made from the widely ranging comments of friends and relatives. Howe Personal Papers contain photographs of Louis's funeral, extensive correspondence by old friends with Mrs. Howe, and records of the various funeral and memorial services.

General appraisals of Howe and his influence with Roosevelt have tended to be superficial and overgeneralized. Among the more stimulating are those in Rosenman: *Working with Roosevelt;* Farley: *Behind the Ballots;* Gunther: *Roosevelt in Retrospect;* and Eleanor Roosevelt: *This I Remember.* But Louis Howe can never be "wrapped up" neatly. The record is still riddled with tantalizing gaps. Those who knew him recall a fascinating variety of impressions. To his son, Louis always seemed a sensitive, idealistic, deeply humanitarian person, kindly and considerate of those around him. To Charles Osborne, whose father was Louis's first political employer, Howe appeared a scheming and objectionable person. Some of his political associates thought him crude. Eleanor Roosevelt remembered longest his passion for power. Lela Stiles re-creates him as a comic and lovable character. Marvin McIntyre called him "The Louse"—but he said it fondly. To F.D.R. he was always "Dear Old Louis." But on one thing they all agreed: Louis was fantastically and fanatically loyal to his "Franklin."

In dealing with a relationship like Howe's and Roosevelt's there is a constant temptation to wallow in pseudo-psychoanalysis. To do so with the evidence at hand is to flirt with glib clichés and glossy superficialities. Yet there is another danger. If one treats Howe and Roosevelt as disembodied spirits moving mysteriously through the world of public affairs without private lives, emotions, or personal concerns, one creates wooden images and false history. This book attempts a balance. In the complexities of Howe's character and of Roosevelt's there will always remain a fascinating field for the reader's speculation.

Index

A NOTE ABOUT THE AUTHOR

ALFRED BROOKS ROLLINS, JR., was born in 1921 in Presque Isle, Maine. He holds a B.A. and M.A. from Wesleyan University, and a Ph.D. from Harvard (1953). After serving in the Air Force during World War II, in which he was awarded the Distinguished Flying Cross, he joined the faculty of the State University College, New Paltz, New York, where he is now Professor of History. He is a member of Phi Beta Kappa and was awarded a Fellowship by the Fund for the Advancement of Education for 1951–2 and the State University Research Foundation Grant for the summers of 1958 and 1962. His articles have been published in *New York History*, the *Journal of General Education*, the *South Atlantic Quarterly*, and other periodicals. Mr. Rollins lives in New Paltz, New York, with his wife Ernestine and their three children.

A NOTE ON THE TYPE

THE TEXT of this book is set in CALEDONIA, a Lintoype face designed by W. A. Dwiggins (1880–1956), the man responsible for so much that is good in contemporary book design and typography. Caledonia belongs to the family of printing types called "modern face" by printers —a term used to mark the change in style of type-letters that occurred about 1800. Caledonia borders on the general design of Scotch Modern but is more freely drawn than that letter.

Composed, printed, and bound by
Kingsport Press, Inc., Kingsport, Tennessee.
Typography and binding design by
VINCENT TORRE